The Identity of the Constitutional Subject

The last fifty years has seen a worldwide trend toward constitutional democracy. But, can constitutionalism become truly global?

Relying on historical examples of successfully implanted constitutional regimes, ranging from the older experiences in the United States and France to the relatively recent ones in Germany, Spain and South Africa, Michel Rosenfeld sheds light on the range of conditions necessary for the emergence, continuity and adaptability of a viable constitutional identity – citizenship, nationalism, multiculturalism, and human rights being important elements.

The Identity of the Constitutional Subject is the first systematic analysis of the concept, drawing on philosophy, psychoanalysis, political theory and law from a comparative perspective to explore the relationship between the ideal of constitutionalism and the need to construct a common constitutional identity that is distinct from national, cultural, ethnic or religious identity.

The Identity of the Constitutional Subject will be of interest to students and scholars in law, legal and political philosophy, political science, multicultural studies, international relations and US politics.

Michel Rosenfeld is Justice Sydney L. Robins Professor of Human Rights, at the Benjamin N. Cardozo School of Law. Rosenfeld teaches and is widely published in the fields of American and comparative constitutional law and legal philosophy. His books include *Affirmative Action and Justice: A Philosophical and Constitutional Inquiry* (1991); *Just Interpretations: Law Between Ethics and Politics* (1998); and *Comparative Constitutionalism: Cases and Materials* (2003).

Discourses of Law

This successful and exciting series seeks to publish the most innovative scholarship at the intersection of law, philosophy and social theory. The books published in the series are distinctive by virtue of exploring the boundaries of legal thought. The work that this series seeks to promote is marked most strongly by the drive to open up new perspectives on the relation between law and other disciplines. The series has also been unique in its commitment to international and comparative perspectives upon an increasingly global legal order. Of particular interest in a contemporary context, the series has concentrated upon the introduction and translation of continental traditions of theory and law.

The original impetus for the series came from the paradoxical merger and confrontation of East and West. Globalization and the internationalization of the rule of law has had many dramatic and often unforeseen and ironic consequences. An understanding of differing legal cultures, particularly different patterns of legal thought, can contribute, often strongly and starkly, to an appreciation if not always a resolution of international legal disputes. The rule of law is tied to social and philosophical underpinnings that the series has sought to excoriate and illuminate.

Nietzsche and Legal Theory: Half-Written Laws
Edited by Peter Goodrich and Mariana Valverde

Law, Orientalism, and Postcolonialism: The Jurisdiction of the Lotus Eaters.
Piyel Haldar

Endowed: Regulating the Male Sexed Body
Michael Thomson

The Identity of the Constitutional Subject: Selfhood, Citizenship, Culture, and Community
Michel Rosenfeld

Forthcoming:

Novel Judgments: Legal Theory as Fiction
William Macneil

The Land is the Source of the Law: A Dialogic Encounter with Indigenous Jurisprudence
C.F. Black

Crime Scenes: Forensics and Aesthetics
Rebecca Scott Bray

Sex, Culpability and the Defence of Provocation
Danielle Tyson

The publisher gratefully acknowledges the support of the Jacob Burns Institute for Advanced Legal Studies of the Benjamin N. Cardozo School of Law to the series *Discourses of Law*.

The Identity of the Constitutional Subject

Selfhood, Citizenship, Culture, and Community

Michel Rosenfeld

Routledge
Taylor & Francis Group

LONDON AND NEW YORK

First published 2010
by Routledge
2 Park Square, Milton Park, Abingdon,
Oxon OX14 4RN

Simultaneously published in the USA and Canada
by Routledge
270 Madison Avenue, New York, NY 10016

Routledge is an imprint of the Taylor & Francis Group, an informa business

© 2010 Michel Rosenfeld

Typeset in Minion by
RefineCatch Limited, Bungay, Suffolk
Printed and bound in Great Britain by
CPI Antony Rowe, Chippenham, Wiltshire

British Library Cataloguing in Publication Data
A catalogue record for this book is available from the British Library

Library of Congress Cataloging-in-Publication Data
Rosenfeld, Michel, 1948–
   The identity of the constitutional subject : selfhood, citizenship, culture, and community /
   Michel Rosenfeld.
      p. cm.
   ISBN 978–0–415–94973–6—ISBN 978–0–415–94974–3
   1. Constitutional law—Social aspects.   2. Constitutional law—Psychological aspects.
   3. Constitutional law—Philosophy.   I. Title.
   K3165.R668 2010
   342—dc22   2009014424

ISBN10: 0–415–94973–4 (hbk)
ISBN13: 978–0–415–94973–6 (hbk)

ISBN10: 0–415–94974–2 (pbk)
ISBN13: 978–0–415–94974–3 (pbk)

ISBN10: 0–203–86898–6 (ebk)
ISBN13: 978–0–203–86898–0 (ebk)

For my children Maïa and Alexis

Contents

Dedication   vii
Acknowledgements   xiii

Introduction   1

PART ONE
Why Constitutional Identity and for Whom?   **15**

1   The Constitutional Subject: Singular, Plural or Universal?   17
    1.1   Who Is the Constitutional Subject?   18
    1.2   Constitutional Identity and the Dynamic Between
          Sameness and Selfhood   27

2   The Constitutional Subject and the Clash of Self and
    Other: On The Uses Of Negation, Metaphor and Metonymy   37
    2.1   The Constitutional Self and the Clash Between Self
          and Other   38
    2.2   Construction, Deconstruction and Reconstruction of
          Constitutional Identity   41
    2.3   The Constructive Tools of Constitutional Discourse:
          Negation, Metaphor and Metonymy   45
          2.3.1   Negation   46

	2.3.2	Metaphor	51
	2.3.3	Metonymy	53
2.4		Constitutional Discourse as Interplay Between Negation, Metaphor and Metonymy	58
2.5		The Constitutional Subject and the Potential Reconciliation of the Singular, the Plural and the Universal	65

PART TWO
Producing Constitutional Identity   **71**

3	Reinventing Tradition Through Constitutional Interpretation: The Case of Unenumerated Rights in the United States		73
3.1	Building and Differentiating Constitutional Identity		73
3.2	Setting American Unenumerated Rights Against Tradition		75
3.3	The Metaphoric and Metonymic Dimensions of Tradition		78
3.4	Reinventing Tradition Through Overdetermination: From the Sanctity of Marriage to the Dignity of Homosexual Sex		81
	3.4.1	Griswold and the Metonymic Path from Marriage to Contraception	82
	3.4.2	The Lockean Gloss on Griswold	90
	3.4.3	Eisenstadt and Molding the Tradition to Encompass Non-Marital Heterosexual Sex	96
	3.4.4	Roe and the Challenge of Fitting Abortion within the Reinvented Tradition	99
	3.4.5	The Reinvented Tradition's Contradictory Approaches to Homosexual Sex	104
		3.4.5(i) Bowers: Drawing the Line at Homosexual Sodomy	105
		3.4.5(ii) Lawrence's Encompassing of Homosexual Sex within the Reinvented Tradition	110
3.5	The Reinvented Tradition and the Clash Between Liberalism and Illiberalism		116
3.6	The Reinvented Tradition and Reliance on Foreign Legal Authorities		119
3.7	Concluding Remark: Overdetermination and Blending Tradition and Counter-tradition		123

4   Recasting and Reorienting Identity Through
    Constitution-Making: The Pivotal Case of Spain's
    1978 Constitution   127
    4.1   Constitution-making in Context   128
    4.2   The Place of Violence in Constitution Making   132
    4.3   The Extraordinary Case of Spain's Peacefully
          Pacted Constitution   134
          4.3.1   The King as Repository of National and
                  Constitutional Unity   142

PART THREE
Constitutional Identity as Bridge between Self and Other:
Binding Together Citizenship, History and Society   147

5   Constitutional Models: Shaping, Nurturing and Guiding
    the Constitutional Subject   149
    5.1   The German Constitutional Model   152
    5.2   The French Constitutional Model   156
    5.3   The American Constitutional Model   158
    5.4   The British Constitutional Model   163
    5.5   The Spanish Model   169
    5.6   The European Transnational Constitutional Model   172
    5.7   The Post-Colonial Constitutional Model   179

6   Models Of Constitution Making   185
    6.1   The Revolution-Based Model   188
    6.2   The Invisible British Model   191
    6.3   The War-Based Model   194
    6.4   The Pacted Transition Model   197
    6.5   The Transnational Model   201
    6.6   The Internationally Grounded Model   206
    6.7   Constitutional Amendment, Revision and Reform   209

7   The Constitutional Subject and Clashing Visions of
    Citizenship: Can We Be Beyond What We are Not?   211
    7.1   The Theoretical Foundations of Modern Citizenship:
          Universal Equality within a Particular Nation   213
          7.1.1   Historical Nexus Between Equal Citizenship and
                  the Nation-State   215

      7.1.2 Social Contract Theory and Modern Equal
           Citizenship   217
  7.2 The Functional Dimension of Citizenship   221
  7.3 The Identitarian Dimension of Citizenship and the
      Evolution from the Mono-Ethnic to the Multi-Ethnic Polity   223
      7.3.1 The Feminist Case for Differentiated Citizenship   225
      7.3.2 National Minorities and the Problematization of
           Differentiated Citizenship   227
  7.4 Global Migration and the Decoupling of the
      Functional and the Identitarian Dimensions of Citizenship   233
  7.5 Transnational Citizenship and Recasting the Dynamic
      between Function and Identity   235
      7.5.1 The Case of EU Citizenship   236
      7.5.2 The Changing Dynamic between EU and
           Member-State Citizenship   239
      7.5.3 Transnational Citizenship Beyond the EU?   241

8 Can The Constitutional Subject Go Global? Imagining a
  Convergence of the Universal, the Particular and the Singular   243
  8.1 Constitutional Reordering in an Era of Globalization
      and Privatization   245
  8.2 The Nexus between Human Rights and
      Constitutional Rights   251
  8.3 Constitutional Patriotism as Transnational
      Constitutional Identity?   258
      8.3.1 Constitutional Patriotism in Historical
           Perspective   259
      8.3.2 Constitutional Patriotism in a Layered and a
           Segmented Transnational Legal Order?   261
  8.4 Concluding Remarks: Reaching for the Transnational
      Constitutional Subject by Reconciling the Universal and the
      Singular Through the Plural   269

Notes   281

Bibliography   309

Index   319

Acknowledgements

This book is the culmination of a long process of gestation and concentration on constitutional identity and the constitutional subject which started nearly two decades ago. Many of the ideas developed in the book are the product of discussions and exchanges with numerous colleagues and students at the Cardozo School of Law and at various other institutions throughout the world. The number of individuals who have influenced my thinking, helped me refine my analysis, and stirred me away from errors is far too great for me to attempt to list here. I will therefore only single out my two fellow co-editors of the series *Discourses of Law*, Peter Goodrich and Arthur Jacobson for their great support and encouragement as well as for their insightful and useful comments and criticism on my manuscript. They have certainly helped me strengthen it significantly, but are, of course, in no way responsible for any remaining errors. I wish to thank, in addition, two of my research assistants at Cardozo, Elena Cohen and Benjamin Ledsham, for their outstanding work in connection with various phases of this book project.

I have also been fortunate to benefit from great personal support throughout the course of this book project. My wife, Susan Thaler, has provided all the encouragement and caring that anyone could wish for, and has helped me live through the ups and downs that a project such as this inevitably entails thanks, in part, to her keen and acute sense of proportion and to her disarming sense of humor. My children, Maïa and Alexis, who became of age as politically engaged citizens during the course of this project, have been a constant source of joy, pride and intellectual stimulation.

Introduction

For now well over a half a century, there has been a worldwide trend towards constitutional democracy. Moreover, the appeal of constitutionalism has reached beyond the nation-state and has become transnational if not yet fully global. At the same time, and particularly since the fall of the Berlin wall in 1989, internal strife and fragmentation within ethnically, religiously, linguistically, or culturally diverse polities, such as the former Yugoslavia, have underscored the fragility of constitutional democracy in heterogeneous and pluralistic settings.

On the one hand, the world political community appears embarked in a sometimes bumpy, but eventually inexorable journey towards globalization. Indeed, at least from a functional as opposed to a formal standpoint, the United Nations (UN) Charter, its covenants on Civil and Political Rights (ICCPR) and on Economic, Social and Cultural Rights (ICESCR), as well as various international conventions meant to be worldwide in scope, such as the Convention to Eliminate Discrimination Against Women (CEDAW) or the Convention on the Elimination of All Forms of Racial Discrimination, can be regarded plausibly as building blocks – albeit partial and fragmentary ones – in the construction of a global constitutional order. Furthermore, even if the prospects of fully-fledged global constitutionalism remain speculative, those of transnational constitutionalism, as the case of the European Union (EU) illustrates, seem farther along. Not only have the governments of the EU's then 25

1

member-states approved a fully-fledged formal constitution for the Union in 2004 (although that particular text never became effective due to its rejection by French and Dutch voters in referenda held respectively in May and June of 2005).[1] But also, for several decades now the EU has functioned in a systematic and harmonious way under a *de facto* constitution emerging primarily from a series of treaties binding EU member-states together and from the jurisprudence of the EU's European Court of Justice (ECJ) (Rosenfeld 2006).

On the other hand, standing against this transnational and potentially global expansion of constitutionalism, there is another tendency that threatens to fragment, derail, and perhaps ultimately undermine the consolidation or maintenance of stable constitutional order both within and beyond the nation-state. This latter tendency is driven by what may be broadly termed 'identity politics' – i.e., the group-based politics of a collectivity bound together by a shared ethnic, religious, cultural, or linguistic heritage, which is to a significant degree conceived as fundamentally at odds with that of other relevant groups within the polity. Thus, for example, Quebec as a distinct francophone culture within predominantly anglophone Canada rejected acceptance of the 1982 Canadian Constitution.[2] Also, certain ultra-Orthodox Jews in Israel have argued against adoption of a constitution for their country, on the grounds that the Torah is 'a more than fundamental law' (Jacobsohn 1993:102). In a less comprehensive vein, but along similar lines, religious fundamentalists have refused to abide by judicial decisions that set boundaries between the realm of the state and that of organized religion. In the United States (U.S.), such fundamentalists have flouted Supreme Court decisions prohibiting prayer in public state schools.[3] And, even in Germany, where the Constitutional Court has enjoyed extraordinary power and legitimacy, Catholic Bavaria rebelled against that Court's decision that displaying crucifixions in public schools classrooms was unconstitutional.[4]

These stances against the constitution or its interpretation differ among one another in very important ways. Quebec separatists are not against modern constitutionalism as it has evolved from its eighteenth century Enlightenment origins in Paris and Philadelphia. Indeed, were Quebec to secede from Canada, most separatists would undoubtedly insist on constitutional democracy for their newly sovereign nation-state. And so would, most likely, Basque and Catalan separatists in Spain. What these separatists object to is not constitutionalism *per se*, but constitutionalism on the scale of the multi-ethnic nation-state from which they aspire to secede.

In contrast, the religious fundamentalist,[5] whether he seeks to impose government rule according to the Christian Gospel, the Torah, or the

Koran, essentially rejects Enlightenment-based constitutionalism and the democratic politics associated with it. For the religious fundamentalist, constitutionalism has to yield to religion: either completely, as would be the case in a state ruled by Jewish Halacha or Islamic Sharia; or, in part, whenever constitutional rule came in conflict with religious precepts. Consistent with this, certain Christian fundamentalists may have nothing against American federalism, but may feel fully justified in using illegal means to frustrate the exercise of constitutionally protected abortion rights.[6]

To the two questions briefly addressed thus far – 1) *whether* or not to adhere to constitutionalism (e.g., constitutional democracy versus theocracy); and 2) assuming adhesion, *who* should be bound under a given constitutional order – must be added at least two more. These are 3), *what* should the constitution enshrine or encompass? And, 4) *how* can or should that which the constitution prescribes be legitimated or imposed in good conscience on those meant to come within its purview?

Disagreement concerning these last two questions is as rampant as is that relating to the two preceding ones. Regarding *what* ought to be enshrined in a constitution, there seems to be substantial agreement at the highest levels of abstraction. Constitutionalism – i.e., constitutional rule and order as an ideal – requires, in the broadest terms, imposing limitations on the powers of government, adherence to the rule of law, and affording protection to fundamental rights (Rosenfeld 1994:3). Once one focuses more concretely on this question, however, vexing issues and controversies appear endless. Indeed, there is no agreement over which limitations on the powers of government are best, or how extensive they ought to be. Are presidential systems preferable to parliamentary ones? Is federalism superior to unitary rule? Should the judiciary have the last word on all allocation of governmental powers and protection of fundamental rights issues? Furthermore, there are different conceptions of the rule of law: some are substantive, others primarily procedural. Also, the German *Rechtsstaat* differs from the French *État de droit* and the Anglo-American rule of law (Rosenfeld 2001). Finally, there is no consensus over which rights are fundamental, or which rights ought to be constitutionalized. For example, should social and economic rights be constitutionalized as they are in South Africa and many European constitutions (Nolette 2003)? Or, is it better to relegate such rights to the infra-constitutional realm shaped by majoritarian politics, as is the case in the United States?[7] Moreover, even where there is widespread consensus that a particular right, such as freedom of speech, ought to be constitutionally guaranteed, the nature and scope of such protection can vary greatly from one constitutional setting to another (Schauer 1994). Thus, for instance, flag burning and Holocaust denial are protected speech in the United States, but punishable crimes in other constitutional democracies, which guarantee free speech rights (Rosenfeld 2003).

There is also no agreement regarding the fourth question, namely *how* the bindingness of the prevailing constitution and of the order it prescribes ought to be justified. To a significant degree, constitutional norms constrain democracy, whether it be through forced endurance of the free speech rights of a reviled minority or through frustration of the political agenda of widely popular elected officials based on the constitutional interpretations of a handful of unelected judges seemingly exempt from all democratic accountability. In other words, the enforcement of unpopular constitutional rights and the entrusting of divisive and controversial constitutional issues to judges raise serious countermajoritarian difficulties (Bork 1990:146), and, on some conceptions of democracy at least, are downright anti-democratic. Beyond that, even a polity's constitutional prescriptions for democratic government, such as the delimination of the powers of parliament, choices between unicameralism and bicameralism, the division of powers between local, regional, and national government, the demarcation of electoral districts, etc., may be of contested legitimacy. It may well be democratic, for example, to entrust national majorities with the formulation of policies that will primarily impact on the life of localities, but this may quite plausibly alienate a large proportion of local residents and strike them as being unfair and unjustified.

Of the four questions mentioned above, only the latter three will be considered as both problematic and crucial for purposes of understanding contemporary constitutionalism and the recent worldwide trend toward constitutionalization. This is not to imply that the first question, which boils down to whether to embrace constitutional government or theocracy[8] is not problematic or crucial. It is instead to specify from the outset adherence to the premise that constitutional rule and commitment to constitutionalism are preferable to promotion of theocracy. This premise is not expected of course, to ever become acceptable to those committed to theocracy on religious grounds. Indeed, whether theocracy or constitutionalism would ultimately prove to be better for humankind is at bottom a metaphysical question that is not susceptible of any verifiable answer. Leaving metaphysics aside, however, a strong case can be made for the implantation of constitutionalism in all polities that are pluralistic – i.e., polities in which the inhabitants do not all share the same conception of the good (Rosenfeld 1998:70). Thus, in a polity in which there are competing religious conceptions of the good side by side with several non-religious ones, it seems preferable to try to accommodate the existing plurality stemming from these diverse conceptions within a framework of constitutional rule than to subordinate non-conforming conceptions to the dictates (or to one particular interpretation of the dictates) of a single religion. Moreover, arguably at least, wherever there is religious diversity either within the same religion – as when fundamentalist adherents disagree with their non-fundamentalist counterparts – or among different religions, constitutionalism is more likely to be conducive to extensive freedom of religion than theocracy.

Even in the face of unanimous agreement that constitutionalism is best for contemporary pluralistic polities, the questions raised above concerning the *who*, the *what* and the *how* of constitutionalism remain crucial and problematic for purposes of understanding and assessing constitutionalism and current constitutional developments. Many different often contradictory answers have been propounded for each of these three questions. Some have approached the *who* from the standpoint of conceptions of citizenship based on ethnicity or blood-based relationships (Schmitt 1996); others, have conceived of citizenship in terms of history or geography (Smith 1997). More recently, there have been proposals to detach citizenship from the confines of the nation-state and to link it directly to commitment to the very ideals of constitutionalism. This has prompted advocacy for transnational, if not global, citizenship predicated on the notion of 'constitutional patriotism' (Habermas 1996:118).

There have also been many competing answers to the question of *what* ought to be constitutionalized. Some have argued that the *meaning* of the question varies from one context to the next, and that the acceptable answers are context – specific and hence non-comparable (Montesquieu 1749). Others maintain that the question is the same for all, but that plausible answers are context-specific and not susceptible of transplantation from one actual constitutional setting to another (Glendon 1992:535). Finally, there are those who propose that, in the last analysis, both the question and the answer ought to be essentially the same for all those who are committed to constitutional rule and constitutionalism (Beatty 1995).

A comparable diversity of views is apparent when it comes to answers to the question of *how* a prevailing constitutional regime may be persuasively justified. The various answers involved can be roughly classified into three distinct categories: First, justifications based on history or tradition; second, justifications based on actual or hypothetical consent; and, third, justifications based on normative precepts that are either conceived as being universally valid or as being valid for all those affected by the particular constitutional regime sought to be justified. Moreover, when viewed closely, actual answers to this question often combine elements of these different categories. For example, originalism, a justification for constitutional limitations on majoritarian policies that is prevalent in the United States, provides a historical justification to the extent that it looks to the U.S. Constitution's framers and their intent to determine the legitimacy of constitutional constraints (Rosenfeld 2004:656). Moreover, at least some versions of originalism which predicate constitutional legitimation on the ratification of the U.S. Constitution by the citizens in various state conventions rely, in part, on a consent based justification (Meese 1987). Finally, to the extent that originalism is defended on account of the framers extraordinary vision and virtue or of their embrace of universally valid principles, it relies on a normative justification (Nelson 2003:547–48). On the other hand, legitimations of constitutionalism that combine Rousseauian and Kantian arguments, such as Rawls's defense of 'constitutional essentials' under the prescriptions of 'justice as fairness' (Rawls 1971:111–14), or Habermas's elaboration of constitutional patriotism as the product of universilizable norms that ought to garner consensus among all good faith members of all relevant polities (Habermas 1996:491–515), are predicated on both consent-based and normative precept-based justifications.

Taken generally and considered in their totality, the various approaches to the *who, what* and *how* questions can be divided into two overriding classes: those that cast an universalist imprint on constitutionalism and constitutional order; and those that conceive of constitutionalism and constitutions in particularistic terms. From a purely universalistic perspective, the *who*, citizenship, should encompass humanity as a whole, and in as much as a given actual constitution limits citizenship to discrete groups, this would amount to a mere contingency. Similarly, for universalists, the *what* would in essence be the same for all. In terms of constitutional essentials at least, all constitutions should aspire to a uniform sets of prescriptions. Finally, as for the *how*, the universalist would advance normative precept-based justifications equally valid for all constitutions regardless of their actual setting.[9]

From a thoroughly particularistic perspective, on the other hand, each constitution would be tied inextricably to a unique set of circumstances. The *who* would be a distinct group bound together by a common history, language, ethnic origin, etc., and citizenship would be confined to those who shared the particular characteristics that endowed the relevant collectivity with its singular identity. The *what* would also be unique and the particularity of the content of every given constitution would either be expressed by the concrete provisions it contained or by the particular meaning or interpretation given to provisions which on the surface resembled comparable provisions in other constitutions. Thus, as mentioned above, Holocaust denial is protected speech in the United States, but is criminally punishable in many other countries, such as Germany.[10] This is notwithstanding that both countries have comparable broadly phrased free speech provisions in their respective constitutions that do not, on their face, give any hint on how to treat Holocaust denial.[11] Nevertheless, within a particularist perspective the difference between the countries respecting Holocaust denial would be understood in terms of the strong contrast between their respective historical experiences. Finally, particularlists would regard the *how* in relation to the actual people involved and would ground legitimation in history, myth or some combination of the two. Moreover, to the extent that particularistic legitimation might have recourse to normative precept-based justifications, these would be tailored to the values of the actual people involved rather than striving to be universalist in nature. For example, a particularist could appeal to the American people's special devotion to liberty or to post-World War II Germany's unique commitment to human dignity as an overriding constitutional value.[12]

A large number of the most controverted issues surrounding contemporary constitutionalism and constitutional rule appear to be the product of an ongoing clash between a universalist vision and a particularlist one. Or perhaps, more precisely, of a clash between universalist tendencies and predilections and particularist ones, as few would argue that all constitutions are essentially the same or that each one of them is so singular that it shares nothing in common with any of the others. Accordingly, universalists and particularists would agree that there are similarities and differences among most constitutions, but the universalist would insist that the similarities clearly outweigh the differences in both number and importance whereas the particularist would emphasize the exact opposite.

Among the most salient issues framed by the clash between universalism and particularism are: whether it is possible to establish a working transnational or global constitution; whether constitutional norms or practices can be exported from one constitutional democracy and imported into another; whether international norms or foreign constitutional jurisprudence should ever be considered authoritative or relevant to the interpretation or application of a domestic constitution; whether human rights and constitutionally protected fundamental rights are essentially substantively equivalent; whether successful constitutions can be implanted in multi-ethnic states; and even whether the comparative study of constitutionalism can be fruitful in the same way as comparative analysis in the area of private law might be – e.g., there seems to be great similarity concerning the uses of contract by businesses across all advanced industrialized democracies in contrast to what a committed particularist would regard as each country's largely *sui generis* constitutional predicament.

A quick glance at any of these issues well illustrates how prominent a role the clash between universalism and particularism seems to play in framing problems and in delimiting the range of plausible solutions for them. Take, for example, the heated recent debate in the United States over the propriety of referring to foreign judicial decisions in adjucating American constitutional cases. This debate has flared both within the Supreme Court (Scalia and Breyer 2005:521) and beyond (Drobnig & Van Erp 1999). In several controversial areas of constitutional law, such as the death penalty,[13] the rights of homosexuals,[14] the rights to assisted suicide,[15] and the exercise of national powers in a way that is at once efficient and least intrusive on local autonomy,[16] the justices on the U.S. Supreme Court have bitterly divided over the relevance or weight to be accorded foreign constitutional standards or judicial decisions regarding the very issues which they are about to decide.

Justice Scalia, the most eloquent opponent of reference to foreign authorities, has sounded a clearly particularist tone emphasizing the historical uniqueness of the U.S. Constitution and the specific national identity of the American people. Thus, in a federalism case, Justice Scalia brushed off Justice Breyer's pragmatic argument which drew on the actual experience of other federal democracies, such as contemporary Germany. In so doing, Justice Scalia stressed that the framers of the US Constitution had explicitly refused to adopt a European model of federalism two centuries earlier.[17] Furthermore, in his vehement opposition against his court's consideration of foreign sources or authorities in death penalty or homosexual rights cases, Justice Scalia has repeatedly asserted that only the moral sensibilities and conscience of the American people could be of any relevance and that therefore the morals of Western Europe or even of the whole rest of the world were utterly without consequence for purposes of US Constitutional adjudication.[18]

US justices who draw on foreign materials, on the other hand, embrace an universalist approach or at least one that draws away from particularism and comes closer to universalism. Thus, Justice Breyer's pragmatic reference to European federalism referred to above evinces a functionalist approach that implies that apportionment of governmental powers issues transcend various particularisms. Similarly, Justice Kennedy's references to foreign sources of authority in death penalty cases seem based on universalist principles,[19] whereas those to Western European sources in the context of the rights of homosexuals appear based on an aspiration to universalism or at least on a rejection of nation-state based particularism.[20]

It may seem from the preceding discussion that when it comes to constitutional ordering the conflict between universalism and particularism is an inevitable and insoluble one. It may also appear that actual constitutional orderings are bound to fall somewhere within the spectrum that lies between particularism and universalism, with all the consequences that that would entail for the issues briefly addressed thus far. This picture becomes misleading, however, once the actual dynamic between particularism and universalism in the context of constitutionalism and constitutional ordering is properly understood. This book will explore the dynamic in question, and indicate how it results in a veritable dialectic in as much as committed aspiration to constitutionalism and establishment and maintenance of a viable constitutional order involve ongoing and constantly evolving struggles for recognition. These struggles, moreover, engage selves and others that seek to vindicate or reconcile identities and differences.

For example, who are to be included as citizens? Only those who like ourselves worship to the same God? Or, in addition, others who embrace different religions? Also, on which identities should one draw to render a given constitutional ordering concrete enough to become viable? An identity derived from a common history? A common ideology? Or, merely a common sharing of a contiguous geographic space? Furthermore, whatever the answers to these questions may be at a particular moment in time for a historically situated group, it is unlikely that that answer will remain satisfactory with the passage of time. Thus, if a constitutional pact were concluded with outsiders to better cope with an external threat that is equally menacing for the two groups involved, then the former other would become part of the same constitutional self. And the former self and other would join as one self to oppose the threatening external other. Internally, however, there may well be new issues regarding identities and differences among the two groups who joined together to better cope with the external other. Resolution of one conflict would hence lead to emergence of new, different, conflicts inserted in a dialectical dynamic requiring reordering relevant identities and differences to render them compatible with succeeding perspectives.

Imagine thus two polities, each with its own state religion, that merge into a single constitutional entity to better cope with an aggressive neighboring polity bent on destroying religious diversity within and beyond its borders. In that case, the newly formed constitutional entity might well be prone to an internal conflict among proponents of the two religions which must now coexist side by side, and that would call for some reordering of identities and differences in ways that might accommodate both religions within the new polity. The two formerly separate religious communities might each have lived in a polity with an official state religion and with a symbiotic union between state and religion. Upon the merger of the two communities into a single constitutional entity, however, maintaining the previous model without privileging one or the other religion involved would most likely prove impossible. That, in turn, should prompt the two religious communities bent on maintaining their unity in the face of their common enemy to evolve towards a different constitutional model characterized by a less exclusive relationship between the state and any particular religion. That would presumably solve or greatly diffuse the initial conflict, but would also most likely give rise to new tensions. Thus, if the two religions' needs and aspirations were markedly different, the new commonly adopted constitutional order might well have a disparate impact on the two religious communities, leading to new conflicts calling for further adaptation of the existing constitutional framework. More generally, every constitutional transformation or adaptation is likely to engender new conflicts calling for further changes, resulting in an ongoing dialectical process leading to a successive reordering of competing identities and clashing differences aimed at preserving the integrity and viability of the prevailing constitutional order.

The principal aim of this book is to explore and critically assess the most salient issues surrounding the three key questions raised above: To *whom* should the constitution be addressed? *What* should the constitution provide? And, *how* can the constitution be justified? The forthcoming analysis will spell out the dialectical process briefly evoked above and be grounded on the following two related basic general propositions. First, constitutions rest on a paradox inasmuch as they must at once be alienated from, and congruent with, the very identities that make them workable and coherent. And second, all constitutions depend on elaboration of a constitutional identity that is distinct from national identity and from all other relevant pre-constitutional and extra-constitutional identities. Moreover, these two propositions are related in that constitutional identity emerges from the confrontation of the very paradox on which its corresponding constitution rests.

Both of these propositions will be extensively elaborated and evaluated throughout the book, but a few preliminary observations are in order to anchor the analysis that follows. Constitutions rest on a paradox because the 'we' who gives itself a constitution must project beyond itself and even agree to become bound against (part of) what previously made it into a self. Whether it is by repudiating an *ancien régime* or by entering into a federation to transcend tensions or pathological tendencies among the political communities about to become federated entities in a larger political union, the formation of a new constitutional order requires repudiation of what once was and embrace of something that is as yet alien to one's core identity. Thus, when two warring communities decide to form a federation rather than mutually destroy one another, the federal entity they create seems most likely to succeed if it transcends and negates (i.e., it is neither one nor the other of) its two components parts.

Furthermore, to the extent that the 'we' that gives itself a constitution must per force adopt measures of self-restraint and self-constraint, it is called upon to protect against some of its most pronounced tendencies. A polity with a long history of discrimination and oppression of ethnic minorities, for instance, would be most in need of strong constitutional anti-discrimination rights. Along similar lines, when the former socialist states evolved into constitutional democracies in the early 1990's, they presumably needed constitutions that gave prominence to private property rights and that deemphasized social and economic rights (Sunstein 1994:398). Consistent with this, many of the constitutions adopted by the former socialist countries contain much more extensive protections of private property rights and of a free market economy than does the U.S. Constitution.[21] This difference is explained by the contrast between the former socialist countries' dependence on state control of the economy and the U.S.'s strong ideological commitment to capitalism and to private property rights.

At the same time that a constitution must be set (at least in part) against the constituent group's identity, it must not veer so far off from that identity as to become non-viable and hence incapable of genuine implementation. For example, if the structure of government prescribed by a given constitution is so alien to those ruled by that constitution that they cannot make use of it for purposes of giving expression to their political will, then the prevailing constitutional order will in all likelihood fail to endure. Similarly, if certain rights protected by the separation between religion and the state go so much against the core identity of the polity[22] that they remain largely unobserved and unenforceable, then they are more likely to contribute to undermining rather than reinforcing the prevailing constitutional order.

As already noted, the need for elaboration of a constitutional identity arises from the need to cope with the just described paradox on which all constitutions rest. Constitutional identity is distinguished from national identity, but both originate in the late eighteenth century and both are identities constructed and projected by 'imagined communities' (Anderson 1991). As Anderson emphasizes, unlike the family or the tribe which form concrete groupings, the nation links together strangers who are bound together into an imagined community that came to replace 'the divinely-ordained, hierarchical dynastic realm' whose legitimacy was undermined by the Enlightenment and the French Revolution (*Id.*:7). Modern constitutionalism and the constitutional identity associated with it are also products of the Enlightenment. They were launched by the eighteenth century American and French revolutions and by the respective constitutions to which these gave rise. The two imagined communities, the national and the constitutional, differ though they may overlap and though they may comprise the same exact membership or closely intertwined ones. Constitutional identity is constructed in part against national identity and in part consistent with it. More generally, constitutional identity must constantly remain in dynamic tension with other relevant identities. Moreover, because constitutional identity must remain distinct from national identity, there is no *prima facie* reason against the eventual success of transnational and even global constitutionalism. Indeed, whether modern constitutionalism can adapt successfully beyond the mold of the nation-state in which it was first enshrined depends ultimately on the implications of its dialectical adaptations, which will be traced in the pages that follow.

This book is divided into three parts. Part I is entitled 'Why Constitutional Identity and for Whom?', and consist of two chapters. Chapter 1, 'The Constitutional Subject: Singular, Plural or Universal?' places the question of the constitutional subject and the concept of a distinct constitutional identity in its historical, ideological and theoretical context. The very notion of a constitutional subject is ambiguous. Is it the maker of the constitution? Those for whom the constitution is made? The subject-matter covered or to be covered by the constitution? All of the above? Moreover, how is the constitutional subject related to the ideal of modern constitutionalism traceable to the Enlightenment? Or to the making and working of actual constitutions launched in the modern era? Whoever is the constitutional subject implies a constitutional identity in the two distinct senses of the term: identity as sameness and identity as selfhood. Finally, is the identity in question singular, plural or universal? Or else, it is some configuration or combination involving all three? Chapter 2, 'The Constitutional Subject and the Clash of Self and Other: On the Uses of Negation, Metaphor and Metonymy' situates the constitutional subject in terms of the struggle between the self and the other and considers the interpretive tools that seem most suitable for purposes of delimiting constitutional identity.

Part II is entitled 'Producing Constitutional Identity' and it comprises two chapters, each providing a detailed account and analysis of a salient and particularly relevant example of production of a constitutional identity. Chapter 3, 'Reinventing Tradition Through Constitutional Interpretation: The Case of Unenumerated Rights in the United States' traces how through judicial interpretation the U.S. Supreme Court elaborated a 'tradition' that differs from America's historical tradition, and that carves out elements of a constitutional identity allowing for the determination and legitimation of unnumerated constitutional rights. Chapter 4, 'Recasting and Reorienting Identity Through Constitution-Making: The Pivotal Case of Spain's 1978 Constitution', examines how giving birth to a constitution requires carving out an identity that is distinct from pre-constitutional and extra-constitutional identities. The case of the 1978 post-Franco Spanish Constitution is especially instructive, moreover, for at least two important reasons: it is the first major example of a pacted constitution, a form of peaceful constitution-making that became prevalent in the last quarter of the twentieth century; and, the Spanish 1978 constituents looked not only within, but also beyond their borders – namely to the European Community (the predecessor to the EU) which they aspired to join – to fashion a new constitution for their country, thus allowing for a first glimpse into the possibility of evolving towards a transnational constitutional identity.

Part III, entitled 'Constitutional Identity as Bridge Between Self and Other: Binding Together Citizenship, History and Society' comprises four chapters. Chapter 5, 'Constitutional Models: Shaping, Nurturing and Guiding the Constitutional Subject', and Chapter 6, 'Models of Constitution-Making' focus on how constitutions are made and structured and on how that shapes the constitutional subject and constitutional identity. To be sure, the birth of every constitution is a unique historical event, and so is the structuring of every constitution and its relationship to its socio-political environment. Nevertheless, constitutions can be usefully grouped together in terms of fit with different models of constitution-making and of constitutional structuring and functioning. For example, constitutions made after a violent revolution are likely to differ in important ways from peacefully pacted constitutions. Similarly, constitutions are likely to produce different kinds of identity depending on whether they lay greater stress on the *demos* or the *ethnos*.

Chapter 7, 'The Constitutional Subject and Competing Visions of Citizenship: Can We Be Beyond What We Are Not?', tackles the question of citizenship from the standpoint of the dialectic between the constitutional subject and its constitutional identity that emerged in the course of the preceding analysis, as well as in terms of the interplay between the universal and the particular and of the tension between the functional and identitarian dimensions of contemporary citizenship. Is citizenship ultimately bound to the nation-state? Can it meaningfully become transnational or global? Must citizenship be based on exclusion or can it be extended to those whom it has traditionally excluded?

This book concludes with Chapter 8, entitled 'Can the Constitutional Subject Go Global? Imagining a Convergence of the Universal, the Particular, the Singular and the Plural'. Modern constitutionalism and the kind of constitutional identity that goes hand in hand with it arose in the context of culturally homogeneous nation-states. To extend such constitutionalism to the multicultural nation-state or to transnational or global polities poses daunting problems. Some of those stem from the apparent impossibility of reconciling the singular, the plural, and the universal. The dialectical approach used throughout the book, makes it possible, however, to recombine the singular, the plural and the universal in dynamic ways that open the door to new visions of the constitutional subject. These new visions are explored through analysis of the emerging constitutional order, the relationship between human and constitutional rights and a critique of the concept of patriotism. These new visions, moreover, allow us to imagine how far the constitutional subject might move towards reconciling the singular, the plural and the universal without foregoing any of them.

PART ONE

Why Constitutional Identity and for Whom?

The Constitutional Subject: Singular, Plural or Universal?

'Je pense ou je ne suis pas, donc je suis où je ne pense pas'[1]

Both the constitutional subject and its identity are elusive and problematic as uncontroverted foundations and guideposts are hard to come by in modern constitutional regimes. Ever since the French and American revolutions of the late eighteenth century, constitutions are conceived as fundamental charters that a 'people' give to, and impose on, themselves. This is a sharp contrast to the most important historical antecedents of modern constitutions, such as the Magna Carta which was a negotiated pact between The English King and the leaders of his country's nobility (Amann 2000:834). As already noted, both the nation-state and modern constitutions originated in the Enlightenment, and not by mere coincidence. In both cases collapse of vertically structured hierarchical orders conceived as divinely ordained made room for reorganization along a new horizontally structured order. Indeed, the Enlightenment, as encapsulated in the French Revolution's slogan of 'liberty, equality, and fraternity,' demanded emancipation from feudal hierarchical constraints, abolition of the privileges of nobility and clergy in favor of equality for all, and supplanting dependence on patriarchy and obedience to a fatherly king with relationships modeled on fraternal bonding[2] and cemented by solidarity among equals.

Within the feudal order, society is held together by personal relationships of fealty and loyalty, thus making hierarchies among persons more

important than living together in a contiguous geographical space. Popula-
tions and territories could shift from one sovereign to another as the
consequence of a royal wedding (Anderson 1991:20). Moreover, the
legitimacy of feudal hierarchies derived from divinity, and hence had no
need for the accord or acquiescence of the monarch's subjects (*Id.*:19).

The modern nation-state, in contrast, needs a legally demarcated
territory within which it can exercise its sovereignty (*Id.*). Furthermore, it
is by and large the population within such a territory that constitutes the
citizenry of the corresponding nation-state. Unlike in a feudal monarchy,
the legitimacy of a nation-state's exercise of sovereign powers depends on
the acceptance or acquiescence of its citizens. In short, both the territorial
sovereignty of the nation-state and the union formed by those within the
space it encompasses converge in complementary horizontal relationships.
A modern constitutional order may not be strictly necessitated by the
order of the nation-state,[3] but it naturally goes hand in hand with it. It is
telling, from this standpoint, that modern constitutions are often depicted
as the products of a social contract among those who find themselves within
the confines of an independent territorial-based sovereign (Rosenfeld
1998a:1897). The nation-state is a contiguous space that brings those that
populate it together, and they, as free and equal, organize themselves into
a mutually binding voluntary association through elaboration and implementation of a constitutional pact.

Given the size and scope of even the smallest among nation-states,
national identity must necessarily be forged among strangers, people who
inhabit the same territorial unit, but who cannot come to know most of
their fellow inhabitants personally (Anderson 1991:6). Similarly, the constitutional order that binds together a nation-state represents a pact or
some other mutually acceptable enforceable fundamental charter that unifies a collectivity of strangers. Moreover, for a collectivity of strangers to
cohere into a nation it must become an 'imagined community' that weaves
together elements of history, culture, myth, etc., into a coherent narrative
(*Id.*:204–206). Analogously, the collectivity of strangers that become
encompassed within the same constitutional order must also construct an
'imagined community'. That latter community produces a constitutional
identity that though related to, must remain distinct from, its corresponding national identity.

1.1 Who Is the Constitutional Subject?

The very notion of the constitutional subject is ambiguous. It is not clear
whether the notion refers to the makers of the constitution, those subjected

to it, or its subject-matter. Moreover, even if one were to settle on one of these three possibilities that would hardly provide an adequate handle over the identity of the constitutional subject. Are the makers of the constitution those who have actually drafted it? Or, those in whose name it has been drafted? Or even, some but not all of the latter? On the other hand, who are those who are legitimately subjected to the constitution? Those within the actual reach of the newly minted powers derived from the constitution? Those who actually, or ought to, accept the new constitutional order? Citizens of the nation-state or other political unit that has adopted the constitution? Finally, what is the subject matter of the constitution? That which the constitutional text states? Its evolving interpretations throughout its history (the 'living' constitution as opposed to the constitution frozen at the time of its drafting)? The constitution's prescriptions only to the extent that they are compatible with the normative ideals of modern constitutionalism?

One can begin to sort out these different questions by appealing to the idea of the constitution as the product of a social contract. For Kant it is only through a social contract that a 'completely lawful constitution and commonwealth can ... be established'. (Kant 1970:79). Moreover, as conceived by Kant, the social contract in question does not refer to an actual historical event, but instead symbolizes 'an *idea* of reason, which nonetheless has undoubted practical reality ...' (*Id.*) (emphasis in original). In its Kantian conception, therefore, the social contract that endows the constitution with legitimacy is a counterfactual.[4] In other words, if a constitution can be viewed (or reconstructed) as the product of a social contract, then it can be legitimated and considered compatible with the dictates of modern constitutionalism. Conversely, a constitution that cannot be so reconstructed would be illegitimate. In the latter case, however, highlighting why the deficient constitution in question fails to measure up to the counterfactual should reveal the transformations, amendments, or revisions which it would need for purposes of reaching an acceptable level of approximation to the ideal of constitutionalism.

Used thus as a heuristic devise, the social contract counterfactual not only facilitates assessment of the legitimacy of constitutions, but also opens the way to fruitful exploration of the constitutional subject and of its identity. A social contract like an ordinary legal contract is entered into by two or more parties and divides its temporal universe into three distinct units: a pre-contractual period; the moment of entering into the contract; and the period earmarked for performance under the contract.[5] To the extent that the analogy between the social contract and the constitution holds, therefore, one should be able not only to distinguish between these three temporal units but also to identify *who* agreed to enter into a particular constitutional pact, *what* the contractors involved agreed to, and what rights and duties are to apportioned among those bound by the constitution which has been pacted for.

There is an apparent disanalogy between the social contract and an ordinary legal contract that looms large in the context of the constitutional subject. A social contract, and especially a constitutional pact, seemingly emerges as the product of a single people united in interest – and hence the 'contract' between the various individuals who belong to the same people seems reducible to a mere formality – whereas a legal contract necessarily involves two or more parties who come to it with a plurality of interests. On the one hand, there is a people with a common purpose, or, to use the words of the preamble to the U.S. Constitution, a 'We the People' seeking to form a 'more perfect union'. In a typical sales contract, on the other hand, buyer and seller are distinct parties with (at least somewhat) antagonistic interests who aim, not for union, but for compromise. The buyer seeks to pay as little as possible for what the seller is offering for sale whereas the latter seeks to charge as much as possible for it. In the end, after vigorous bargaining, the buyer will agree to pay more than initially desired but just less than what would have caused him or her to walk away from contracting; conversely, the seller will settle for less than initially hoped for, but a bit more than what would have prompted a refusal to sell. Accordingly, the seeming disanalogy between the two types of contract apparently boils down to the following. The constitutional pact presumably involves a single and singular subject ('We The People' is *a* people but also *the* American people) with a singular purpose, or, in Rousseau's social contractarian parlance, a people united in its commitment to a commonly shared 'general will' (Rousseau 1762:II,1). In this context, moreover, the constitutional 'pact' consists of little more than an expression of adhesion to the general will by all the individuals who make up the people, thus making this 'pact' of 'the people' essentially a pact with oneself, and only derivatively a pact among the multitude of individual parties who collectively add up to the 'people'.[6] In contrast, the legal contract necessarily depends on willing interaction among plural subjects who (taken together) seek to realize plural interests.

Upon closer scrutiny, however, the apparent disanalogy discussed above must be significantly qualified. First, when viewed more closely, the social contract and all constitutional pacts must ultimately rest on some kind and some level of plurality. In classical social contract theory, what prompts the would-be contractors to seek a common agreement is the clash of interests which produces insecurity and danger in the state of nature (Hobbes 1651:Ch. XIII). Similarly, constitutional pacts are concluded in the context of some clash among a plurality of actors within the precincts of the relevant pre-constitutional political order. This is perhaps most obvious in cases of actually pacted constitutional transitions such as those of Spain in 1978 or of Poland and Hungary after the 1989 fall of communism in Eastern Europe (Linz & Stephan 1996), but is also the case for constitutions made after a revolution, such as the eighteenth century French and American constitutions.[7]

Constitutions and constitutionalism only make sense under conditions of pluralism. A purely homogeneous society marching forward in unison would not require a constitution, and it would make little sense for such a society to enter into any pact with itself. Just as there would be no need for legal contracts absent all divergences in interests, so too a social contract or constitutional pact would seem entirely superfluous unless there were some differences in interests among the would-be contractors. Even an ethnically, culturally, religiously and ideologically homogeneous society can be sufficiently individualistically pluralistic[8] to call for a polity subjected to constitutional rule. Furthermore, contemporary constitutional democracies are typically both communally pluralistic (e.g., multi-ethnic, multi-religious, multicultural, multi-lingual) and individualistically pluralistic (e.g., individuals differ on conceptions of individual self-realization and self-fulfillment and on what is needed to optimize chances of success). Such democracies, therefore, revolve around a multiplicity of identities and differences in constant dynamic interaction resulting in a diverse array of selves (individual as well as collective) demarcated through a constant process of inclusion and exclusion. It is these selves relating to one another as self to other, yearning to preserve their identity, to achieve security, and to pave the way to harmony, that seem poised to greatly benefit by entry into a constitutional pact.

A constitutional pact is meant to be among strangers who can hurt as well as help one another. In the Hobbesian state of nature, individuals are a constant threat to one another, and they all live in conditions of fear and insecurity (Hobbes 1651:Ch. XIII). By concluding a social contract and leaving the state of nature for civil society, however, these same individuals can mutually assist one another to achieve security and ordered liberty (*Id.*:Ch. XVII). The social contract, moreover, consists of two separate agreements: the contract of association, whereby the strangers who associate as fellow contractors forgo the rule of force of the state of nature in favor the mutual cooperation of civil society; and the contract of government, whereby the social contractors settle on the ruler or form of government needed to lead the polity designed to safeguard the destiny of their newly minted civil society (Rosenfeld 1985:865).[9]

The constitutional pact also comprises these two separate agreements, though in many cases it would be more accurate to speak of a contract of *re*-association rather than of association. Indeed, constitution-making does not typically take place in a state of nature. The French a*ncient régime*, the American colonies, Franco's Spain and Communist Poland all incorporated elements of political association even if they were not voluntary ones. Where there is a violent break with the pre-constitutional socio-political order, and constitutional-making appears as creation *ex-nihilo*, the pre-constitutional status quo may come close to being the functional equivalent of the state of nature. But even then, as we shall see below,[10] the pre-constitutional past does not simply vanish, as does the state of nature in social contractarian narratives.

In a typical legal contract for the sale of goods among two strangers, buyer and seller relate to one another as self to other with divergent but coinciding interests. Once a bargain is struck and a contract made, however, performance of the terms of the contract provide the buyer and the seller with a (limited) joint intersubjective interest.[11] Analogously, out of the plural interests of those who agree to enter into a constitutional pact must be carved out a set of jointly held intersubjective interests which will allow for smooth performance of the common constitutional project. Just as the buyer and seller in an ordinary legal contract, constitutional contractors relate to one another as self to other prior to their contract and outside their joint contractual undertaking – i.e., in the case of constitutional contractors in their extra-constitutional and infra-constitutional dealings. Unlike the parties to a sales contract, whose intersubjective project is both superficial and of short duration, the constitutional contractors' joint intersubjective project casts them as a distinct (collective) self that is set against a corresponding other made up of those who do not share in the same constitutional project. The latter other, moreover, may be internal or external: internal to the extent that it is made up of domestic opponents to the constitution; and, external to the extent that it encompasses those who are neither constitutional contractors nor meant to be subjected to the constitution pacted by these particular contractors.

To recapitulate: these are the main insights concerning the constitutional subject gleaned thus far through the prism of the social contract counterfactual. First, the constitutional subject must be plural, either individualistically or communally pluralistic, and, in most cases, it is likely to be both. Second, at the same time, the constitutional people must be singular, a 'people' giving itself a (particular) constitution that lifts it out of its past without severing all ties to it and that binds it together to confront its future. Moreover, that the constitutional subject must be at once singular and plural is not contradictory as the singularity and plurality involved are not merely ascriptive, but rather relational. The singular and the plural must coexist in dynamic tension and their constant confrontation is bound to remain fruitful so long as it produces and shapes a constitutional identity that can (at least in part) fill the gap between them. Third, the constitutional subject in both its singularity and in its plurality carves out a project – much like the joint intersubjective common project of ordinary contractors, but much longer and deeper than the latter. That project concerns, to use Rawls's term, the 'basic structure' of the polity involved (Rawls 1971:9) and is distinguishable from infra-and extra-constitutional projects. Just as a social contract may carve out an area of self-governance to allow for greater freedom and security in the pursuit of private interests, so too can a constitutional pact leave ample room for fruitful extra-constitutional social and political interaction. Accordingly, the constitutional subject is distinguishable from other key subjects that profoundly influence the destiny of the polity, such as the nation as subject, or communal, regional, cultural, religious, and possibly many other subjects. Even if the very same people made up both the nation and the constitutional subject, the identity of the one would be different from that of the other, and as such, the two subjects would remain distinct owing to their different identities. Indeed, as history has often proven, abolishing constitutional democracy does not necessarily lead to destruction of the nation or of national identity. Thus, even the utter devastation wrought by Hitler's Third Reich on the German people did not extinguish the German nation, which has since rebounded vigorously and become endowed with a vibrant constitutional culture.[12]

Before indicating more specifically how the social contract counterfactual sheds light on the nature of the constitutional subject, it is necessary to briefly consider a key difference between the social contract as a hypothetical one in Kant's conception[13] – later adapted by Rawls into a hypothetical social contract concluded behind a 'veil of ignorance' (Rawls 1971:11–12) – and an ordinary *actual* (legal) contract between two or more parties. To a large extent, since the Enlightenment the validity of a legal contract is based on the *fact* of agreement rather than on the particular terms agreed to (Rosenfeld 1985:825). This is in contrast to the Kantian and Rawlsian social contract counterfactuals in which it is the *reasonableness* of the terms agreed to that legitimate what the social contract prescribes. The reason for basing legitimation of an ordinary contract on the fact of agreement is the premise that the equal and autonomous

individuals who choose to contract are the best judges of their own interests and of the (contractual) obligations, they ought to assume in furtherance of their self-interest. Furthermore, this contrast between ordinary and
social contract is quite important for it is not the same to argue that a
person ought to live by her contractual obligations because they are
reasonable than to argue that she should be bound by them because she
agreed to that.

The distinction between legitimacy based on reasonableness and that
based on actual agreement is crucial from the standpoint of the constitutional pact which is typically legitimated, in part, in reference to an
actual agreement and, in part, in terms of a hypothetical (social) contract.
To the extent that the validity of a constitution is predicated on its ratification, its legitimacy derives from the actual acquiescence of its ratifiers.
Thus, those who claim that the American Constitution ought to be interpreted in accordance with the intent of its ratifiers (ten Broeck 1939)
ascribe crucial weight to the latter's agreement to accept the constitution
submitted for their approval and to their understanding of what they
agreed to. Along similar lines, the failure in 2005 by the French and Dutch
voters to ratify the proposed Treaty-Constitution for the EU which had
been approved by the governments of all then twenty five EU member-
states in 2004 doomed the particular constitution involved.[14] In both cases,
the validity of the constitution depended on the fact of agreement, and in
the American case where such agreement did take place, the intent of the
ratifiers circumscribes what was agreed to much like the intent of the
parties does in an ordinary legal contract (Dorf 1997).

The analogy between ratification of a constitution and actual agreement
to the terms of a legal contract is, however, a limited one. Unlike a legal
contract to which all parties must actually agree, ratification of a constitution in a convention or in a referendum is never unanimous. Even if such
ratification must be by a qualified majority of two thirds or three quarters,
a sizeable number of persons who actually failed or refused to ratify the
constitution would end up being nevertheless bound by it. For those who
refuse to ratify an actually adopted constitution as well as for those who
belong to generations that are subsequent to that of the ratifiers, therefore,
the fact that others agreed to the imposed constitution does not provide
legitimacy for it. Nonetheless, this does not foreclose acceptance and recognition of the legitimacy of the imposed constitution on the Kantian and
Rawlsian social contractarian grounds that a rational self-interested person
living in the socio-political context in which the imposed constitution
operates ought to find adherence to the constitution in question to be
consistent with the dictates of reason.[15]

As historically grounded charters that require transgenerational legitimation, constitutions must be justifiable both in terms of an actual agreement, or of a widely accepted myth of actual agreement, and of an appeal to reason mediated through a Kantian or Rawlsian social contractarian counterfactual. What this means, however, is that neither the fact (or myth) of agreement alone nor appeal to the social contractarian counterfactual alone can legitimate a living constitution.[16] Moreover, in many cases, reliance on the latter does not complement reliance on former, but is in tension, if not in downright contradiction, with it. Thus, for example, the 1776 U.S. Declaration of Independence, which lay the foundation for American constitutionalism, proclaimed consistent with the basic tenets of the Enlightenment, that 'all men are created equal'. The 1787 Constitution, however, condoned and in important ways enshrined slavery, even if it did so without mentioning the institution explicitly.[17] Accordingly, prior to the adoption of the Thirteenth Amendment to the U.S. Constitution in 1865 which prohibits slavery, justification of the U.S. Constitution based on the *fact* of ratification could not be squared with justification on the basis of the terms of that constitution being consistent with a social contractarian counterfactual. Indeed, nothing could be more contrary to Kantian or Rawlsian social contractarianism than slavery.

In the case of the 1787, U.S. Constitution the contradiction was so sharp and fundamental that no reconciliation between history and (constitutional) reason was possible. It took a civil war and a new historical constitutional grounding launched by the abolition of slavery to overcome the insoluble impasse that plagued the 1787 U.S. Constitution (Richards 1994). In less extreme cases, however, the tension between historical and normative justification of a constitution can be managed through the production of narratives that project avenues of reconciliation between the two without ever succeeding in filling the gap between them. In other words, except where contradictions are too stark, one can always endeavor to better align a constitution steeped in its own history with the ideal of constitutionalism – understood as that which reason through deployment of the social contract counterfactual would prescribe for the basic structure of society and for its constitutional essentials (Rawls 1993:139–140) – without ever achieving full alignment.

In as much as constitutional history and constitutionalism pull in different or even opposite directions, the tension between them is a dynamic one that sets off a constant interplay between the two. The constitutional subject, in turn, defines, and is defined by, this dynamic. Within the ambit of the interplay in question, moreover, the constitutional subject is at once the maker of the constitution, those for whom the constitution is made, and the one who endows the constitution with its meaning – in the sense of projecting itself into the text (written or unwritten) of the constitution to specify its meaning as well as in the sense of living and spreading that meaning in its constant further specifications.

To preserve its coherence, at some level the constitutional subject must be imaginable as a single self. At other levels, of course, the constitutional subject is made up of different, often mutually antagonistic, selves. As we have already seen, there is the historical constitutional self versus the constitutional self derived from the social contract counterfactual. Also, to the extent that constitutions are inextricably tied to pluralism, the historical constitutional self must be made-up of several different selves that must in some way cohere sufficiently to legitimate the historical constitution. Similarly, those legitimately bound by the constitution must at once aspire to cohere into a single constitutional subject and acknowledge that they are made up of a multitude of distinct selves that are likely to disagree on how, or to what extent, they ought to be bound by the constitution even if they agree on who shall be bound by it. Finally, a similar division between a single self and a multiplicity of them emerges with respect to the subject that endows meaning to the constitution and that is at the same time shaped by that meaning. Out of the many interpretations of the constitution that are proposed or derived, interpretive harmony or authoritativeness must be constantly strived for.

What allows the multiple selves that partake in the ongoing process of carving out sufficient bonds of unity to sustain the constitutional subject as a single self is the elaboration of a commonly shared constitutional identity. The process involved is both a dynamic and a dialectical one – in that it requires confronting contradictions that must be sought to be overcome, but that once overcome would be bound to give rise to new contradictions which would in turn call for resolution, etc. In addition, that process necessarily remains forever unfinished, if for no other reason, because an existing identity, even if fully stable, would have to be adjusted to account for the presently unknown and to a large extent unknowable needs and aspirations of yet unborn generations. Furthermore, the strived for, yet always incomplete, unity of the constitutional subject depends on sufficient harmonization of the three different poles of identity that correspond respectively to the three distinct facets of the constitutional subject that were identified above: the subject as constitution-maker or as *pouvoir constituant;* the subject as the collectivity that is bound by the constitution; and the subject as interpreter, elaborator and custodian of the constitution. To this, we must add that each of the above mentioned poles of identity is itself dynamic and complex. For example, the subject as constitution-maker must be constructed from a combination of historical fact (the constitution was drafted and ratified or imposed by actual people in a particular historical setting), historical myth (a narrative of unity in the context of an actual historical event steeped in varying but inevitable instances of disagreement, conflict, controversy, etc., and resulting in an acceptance that even if fully voluntary was far from unanimous), and normative counterfactual (for the legitimacy of the constitution to endure, it must be more than merely historically grounded).

To distil threads of unity out of this complex, diverse, if not downright dissonant, constantly evolving, multiple, fractious, and fragile constitutional subject is the daunting challenge that confronts constitutional identity. In view of the sheer magnitude of the task reserved for constitutional identity, it should not be surprising that, as we shall now see, its chief tool turns out to be negation – the constitutional subject must largely be defined in terms of what it is *not* – and that it manifests itself primarily as a *lack* – constitutional identity, at least initially, emerges more as what it is not (e.g., national or religious identity) than as something that it is firmly and distinctly in its own right.

1.2 Constitutional Identity and the Dynamic Between Sameness and Selfhood

Self-identity can either connote sameness or selfhood (Ricoeur 1990). I can recognize myself either because I look the same as I did yesterday or because in spite of all the changes which I have experienced since childhood – I no longer look the same, think the same, feel the same, etc. – I have endured as a single self that is distinct from all other selves. Or, in other words, I have remained myself as against all others.

Analogously, constitutional identity can be constructed on the basis of sameness or of selfhood, or more precisely, based on dynamic interaction between projections of sameness and images of selfhood. Moreover, the interaction in question may at times evoke complementarity and at other times contradiction. For example, for more than two hundred years, the text of the U.S. Constitution has remained the same, except for the addition of twenty seven amendments. Interpretations of provisions contained within the original 1787 text have, however, evolved through the years. To the extent that these interpretations can be cast in organic terms as part of a process of adaptation and growth, they can be understood as constructing and preserving identity in the sense of selfhood. Furthermore, the combination of interpretive selfhood and textual sameness can be viewed as complementary for purposes of elaborating a distinct constitutional identity. Or, conversely, in as much as constitutional interpretations depart from textualism or valorize certain plausible meanings of the text at the expense of others, textual sameness may stand in contrast to, and seemingly contradict, the evolving sense of selfhood fashioned by evolving trends in constitutional interpretation.

This contrast regarding the relationship between sameness and selfhood as complementary and as contradictory can be illustrated by reference to the U.S. Constitution's Commerce Clause (U.S. Const. Art. I, Sec. 8, cl. 3). That clause grants the national government the power to regulate commerce 'among the several states,' and has been pivotal in the evolution of American federalism over the past two centuries. Indeed, the relative powers of the federal government *vis à vis* that of the states has fluctuated over the years, and has to a large extent depended on judicial line drawing between interstate and intrastate commerce. In the early nineteenth century, interstate commerce was limited to trade, bartering, and commercial navigation across state boundaries.[18] By the 1940's, in contrast, the cultivation of a small amount of wheat by an individual on his own farm was held to be subject to federal regulation on the ground that the cumulative effect of like activities by all those similarly situated in the several states would have a substantial effect on the national market for wheat.[19]

Both the relevant constitutional text and the categorical distinction between interstate and intrastate commerce remained the same between the early nineteenth and the mid-twentieth century. The scope of the federal power, however, changed dramatically during that period, from limited and confined during the early nineteenth century to nearly all pervasive by the middle of the twentieth. On one plausible interpretation, the meaning of the Commerce Clause has remained the same, but its 'extension' (i.e., that to which it refers) has changed as from the 1820's to the 1940's as the country's economy evolved from the beginnings of industrialization to advanced capitalism organized on a national scale. This evolution, moreover, can be analogized to the one that marks an individual person's passage from adolescence to mature adulthood, thus casting the Commerce Clause and its judicial elaboration as projecting an identity where sameness and selfhood emerge as complementary. On another plausible interpretation, however, textual sameness and organic evolution regarding the Commerce Clause stand in direct contradiction to one another as 'commerce among the states' does not seem to encompass purely local activity involving no crossing of state lines even when that occurs in the context of a fully integrated nationalized economy.[20]

Both in terms of sameness and of selfhood, identity depends on negation as well as on identification. For example, two persons may be the same as a consequence of identical defining traits, such as would have been the case for two Caucasians entitled to the privilege accorded to members of the 'white race' in apartheid South Africa. Or, they may be the same because they do *not* share a particular trait as in the case of non-whites in apartheid South Africa. Thus, those of Indian descent were not the 'same' as African blacks except in their being 'non-white' which equally relegated them to the status of second-class citizens.[21] Similarly, selfhood can also be understood in terms of identification and negation. I can capt myself as the same singular self by reviewing my life history and interpreting all the relevant sequences of experiences it contains as being *mine*. Or, I can realize that I am a self unto myself as a result of constantly feeling other than all others. In other words, I am myself because I am not any of the others. Furthermore, in any complex socio-political setting, identities are bound to be formed concurrently through a dynamic interplay between identification and negation. Thus, fellow Frenchmen identify with one another as fellow French-speakers, but also as non Swiss-or-Belgian-French-speakers and as non-Americans, non-Germans, etc.

Constitutional identity is also elaborated through a complex dynamic process aimed at integrating successive instances of negation and identification into coherent and mutually consistent narratives of sameness and selfhood. Moreover, the sameness involved is that of the constitution and of constitutional identity, which is determined to an important degree through and ever ongoing succession of negations of other identities all while incorporating elements of the latter. Constitutional identity is not national identity, and would cease having an identity of its own if it could simply be folded into the latter. By the same token, however, a nation-state's constitution could hardly produce an identity of its own without incorporating some features derived from national identity as will be more fully explored below.[22] In other words, an imagined constitutional community must constantly strive to differentiate itself from its corresponding imagined national community without severing its links to the latter to the point that the two cannot be imagined from a more comprehensive vantage point as markers of some overall sameness and corresponding selfhood which would bind a people to its nation as well as to its constitution.

Similarly, in as much as constitutional identity is constructed along an axis of selfhood, this also entails a concurrent process of identification and negation. The identity of the constitutional subject must be distilled through identification or projection of sufficient threads of continuity amid ceaseless change in order to create a sustainable image of selfhood. At the same time, this positive image must be constantly supplemented and boosted through negation of other selves, both within and without the relevant polity. Thus, the constitutional self must produce an identity that allows for casting it as other than other selves within the polity, such as the national self and those of other groupings that imagine themselves along an axis of selfhood. The constitutional self must also produce an identity in opposition to – and hence by negating – constitutional others both within the polity (e.g., against discarded former constitutions) and beyond the boundaries of the polity against other constitutional selves with different identities or with identities from which the prevailing constitution within the polity must be differentiated (e.g., an other polity's constitution with substantial similarities in constitutional text and structure having to be differentiated to render one's own constitution uniquely suited to the particularities of one's own polity).

The intricate interplay between sameness and selfhood and between negation and identification becomes vividly apparent in the context of the contrast between amending the constitution and constitution-making. Amending the constitution involves changing it without threatening its overall unity or identity. Constitution-making, on the other hand, does require creating a new unity and identity which, in turn, depends on repudiation of preceding constitutional identities and of other pre-constitutional and extra-constitutional ones. At the level of the formal constitution, constitution-making is clearly distinct from amending the constitution. The former issues from a constituent power (*pouvoir constituant*) whereas the latter proceeds in accordance with the prescriptions spelled out in the amendment provision(s) of a prevailing constitution. At the level of the *material* constitution – i.e., of the constitution as a 'living' or 'evolving' one, not confined to an official constitutional text, but supplementing the latter with a set of congruent constitutional interpretations and constitutional practices[23] – in contrast, the boundaries between making and amending the constitution and between constituent power and constituted power (*pouvoir constitué*) are frequently blurred and sometimes impossible to discern.

The tensions between the constitution's two faceted identity as sameness as a selfhood emerges particularly vividly in relation to constitutional amendments. Some constitutions explicitly restrict the scope of legitimate amendments;[24] others do not.[25] Moreover, some constitutions are much more rigid than others, making for great disparities regarding the ease with which constitutional amendments can be adapted.[26] In light of these wide ranging differences, can there be any cogent way to determine at what point do constitutional amendments threaten to destroy constitutional identity?

There are, of course, clear cases of amendments that do not threaten constitutional identity as well as of amendments that do. The Twenty Sixth Amendment to the U.S. Constitution adopted in 1971, which lowers the voting age to eighteen, is an example of the former. It would be absurd to claim that the U.S. Constitution's identity in terms of selfhood could be even minimally threatened as a consequence of this amendment.[27] On the other hand, whereas the U.S. Constitution is not, strictly speaking, exactly the same before and after adoption of the Twenty Sixth Amendment, the change involved hardly leaves a perceptible trace on the Constitution's identity-as-sameness.

At the other end of the spectrum, in the early 1990's, Hungary used the amendment process to effectuate a complete overhaul of its constitution, transforming it from a socialist one to one that protects private property and a market economy. Actually, since 1989 every section of the Hungarian Constitution has been changed, except for that section which specifies that Budapest is the capital of Hungary.[28] This radical course has certainly severed virtually all links of identity between the pre- 1989 version of the same constitution and its post – 1989 version. In this case, the amendment process has been used to negate the identity of the pre-1989 Constitution while preserving its formal shell.

A less extreme but more problematic case is that of the Civil War amendments in the United States. Did the transition from the constitutional acknowledgement of the legality of slavery to its explicit constitutional ban undermine or bolster American constitutional identity? Some argue that the Civil War amendments negate the constitutional identity that prevailed prior to that conflict (Marshall 1987:15). Others regard these amendments as continuing and perfecting the constitutional project launched by the American Revolution (Richards 1994). In the latter case, the Civil War amendments seem compatible with continuation of the Constitution's identity as selfhood, and as contributing to the maturation of the constitutional self involved.

In contrast to constitutional amendments which may be as prone to bolstering as to eroding constitutional identity, it might seem that constitution-making necessarily negates past constitutional identities to launch new ones. That impression, however, does not hold up to analysis as reveals comparison between the 1787 U.S. Constitution, which continues to endure and the fifteen constitutions that France has had since the 1789 Revolution (Bell 1992:1). Arguably, from a functional and material standpoint the United States has had many different constitutions and constitutional identities in the past two centuries. In addition to the break after the Civil War which led to a fundamentally transformed constitutional order, there were several others. These include: the New Deal Constitution (Ackerman 1991) involving a massive shift of power over the economy going from the states to the federal government; the civil rights constitution launched by the Supreme Court's unanimous rejection of the legitimacy of government required racial segregation in its landmark 1954 *Brown* v. *Board* decision; and plausibly, in some not too distant future a national security constitution informed by the exigencies of the struggle against global terrorism. All of these constitutions have a different identity, and it seems virtually impossible to weave together a continuous narrative of selfhood cutting across the different cultures involved. In other words, the passage from slavery to emancipation, from apartheid to racial integration, or from little state regulation of the economy to massive federal regulation of it involves more disjunctions and breaks than advisable in terms of securing the survival of any single constitutional identity dependent on a distinct sense of selfhood.

On the other hand, France's fifteen constitutions certainly have distinct identities from a formal standpoint. From a material perspective, however, there are very significant similarities and continuities that cut across the various succeeding constitutions. Thus, for example, France's current 1958 Constitution incorporates part of its immediate predecessor, the 1946 Constitution, and has been interpreted as incorporating the 1789 Declaration of the Rights of Man and the Citizen (Bell 1992:66–67). Are these similarities and continuities sufficient to promote an overall French constitutional identity in spite of major differences, such as the passage from a purely parliamentary system pursuant to the 1946 Constitution to a semi-presidential system under the 1958 Constitution? (Rosenfeld 2004) Conversely, in the case of the U.S., are the continuities grounded in the unity of the constitution and the basic sameness of its text[29] strong enough to withstand the profound constitutional upheavals that marked the passage from slavery, to apartheid and then to racial integration or the transformation from constitutionally backed *laissez-faire*[30] to the constitutionally sanctioned administrative welfare-state that became nearly all encompassing during the New Deal?[31]

Whether France can find sufficient unity and continuity to bind together its numerous successive constitutions into a single constitutional identity; or whether the U.S. Constitution's apparent unity and continuity can sustain the same constitutional identity in spite of the constitutional upheavals triggered by the Civil War the New Deal, and Civil Rights movement of 1960's; depends on willingness and ability to weave together a meaningful and integrated constitutional narrative. This, in turn, requires elaborating a delicate balance between negation and identification and exploring the possible convergence of paths of negation and paths of identification at an appropriate level of abstraction.

How constitutional identity may be actually constructed, reconstructed and deconstructed (in the sense of being elaborated, in part, through use of negation to separate itself from other, closely associated, constructs) will be extensively explored, by examining several actual examples, in the chapters that follow. Suffice it for now to emphasize that the process of confronting negation against identification and of striving for harmonization at appropriate levels of abstraction as well as the products emanating from such process are equally engaged in a dynamic and dialectic. In other words, not only is constitutional identity produced rather than given but also *once* produced and *as* produced it is still likely to be dynamic and conflictual rather than merely settled and static.

This dynamism is well illustrated by the uniquely American contentious debate over originalism (Dorsen, et al. 2003:189–194). American judges and legal scholars are sharply divided over whether constitutional interpretation should conform exclusively to the original intent of the Constitution's framers. Originalists insist on adhering to original intent or to original meaning – i.e., the meaning which the Constitution had for the generation of the framers (*Id.*:189). Non-originalists, on the other hand, insist that the Constitution should not be frozen in time, but adapted to meet the evolving needs of succeeding generations (Grey 1975). Consistent with this debate, American constitutional identity is neither originalist nor non-originalist, but it is marked by the dispute over originalism. This means that American constitutional jurisprudence differs from those prevalent in other polities, even if the latter rely on arguments that are analogous respectively to those of American originalists and non-originalists. For example, German constitutional interpretation relies on historical arguments that are akin to those of American originalists, and on teleological arguments that are comparable to those of American non-originalists (Dorsen et al:155). Unlike arguments from the framers' intent, German historical arguments are not accorded priority (*Id.*), and they are not considered to be antagonistic to teleological arguments. To American confrontation must be contrasted German harmonization and, hence, the major difference between the two jurisprudences concerns not the elements which they respectively incorporate, but the very different dynamic relationship among these elements within each of these two constitutional orders.

The dynamic that animates the pursuit of constitutional identity can thus lead to blurring the line between constitution-making and amending the constitution, to causing splits between their formal and material expressions, and to fostering ongoing opposition within entrenched clusters of identity, as the American debate over originalism evinces. The dynamic in question, therefore, casts constitutional identity as inherently fragile. Upon close inspection, moreover, the constitutional subject itself appears equally embroiled in a series of oppositional dynamics that threaten its stability or even, at times, the underpinnings of its self-identity. Indeed, in all three of its dimensions (as the *who*, the *for whom* and the *what* that links the *who* to the *whom*) the constitutional subject seems bound to remain incomplete, embattled and ever susceptible to further definition and redefinition.

Take for example, 'We The People,' which looms as the constitutional subject in the United States. In the abstract, 'We The People' seems to be all encompassing in its seemingly full embrace of both constitution makers and all those to whom the Constitution applies. 'We The People' merges together constitution makers and those subject to the Constitution, as well as the governors and the governed, much the same as Jean Jacques Rousseau's social contract is supposed to generate unity out of multiplicity, through adherence to the general will.[32] Moreover, if 'We The People' both formulate the Constitution and willingly submit to its dictates, the subject matter covered by the Constitution would be inherently legitimate as that which the constitutional authors have freely chosen to impose on themselves, and have voluntarily chosen to embrace in their capacity as citizens of a constitutional democracy.[33] In short, by focusing on 'We The People' in the abstract, and by regarding it as an encompassing unity comprising constitution makers and citizens subject to the Constitution, it seems possible to overcome the vexing difficulties raised by the who and what of the constitutional subject.

When approached from a more concrete vantage point, however, the unity of 'We The People' becomes shattered. For one thing, the authors of the 1787 American Constitution, a group of propertied white men (Beard 1935:73–149, 149–51; Simon 1985:1498 & n. 44), were in no way representative of all those who would be subjected to their constitutional prescriptions.[34] For another, when placed in its proper historic setting, 'We The People,' far from expressing a genuine unity, actually embodies a stark contradiction. The meaning of 'We The People' in the Preamble to the 1787 Constitution cannot be grasped without reference to the proposition that 'all men are created equal,' which is enshrined in the 1776 American Declaration of Independence.[35] Based on the fundamental creed that all 'men' – meaning all 'human beings' – are created equal, moreover, 'We The People' should have referred to, at least, all adults permanently residing in the United States in 1787. To the extent that the 1787 Constitution condones slavery,[36] however, 'We The People' cannot be fairly said to include the African American slaves then living in the United States. Accordingly, the 'We The People' of 1787 is inconsistent with 'all men are created equal.' Moreover, the exclusion of African Americans from 'We The People,' negates the possibility of any genuine identity between the authors of the 1787 Constitution – taken in the broadest possible sense as including anyone who may have reasonably been prompted to voluntarily acquiesce to the terms of that Constitution – and all those who were subjected to the weight of its prescriptions. Indeed, neither history nor logic justifies inclusion of African Americans in 'We The People,' as it existed prior to the American Civil War.[37]

There is also another important sense in which the 'We the People' in 1787 is radically different from its contemporary counterpart. The U.S. is a country of immigration, and its people the product of successive waves of immigration from all corners of the world that came to its shores throughout its entire history. Accordingly, the 1787 'We the People' is in most respects not yet a people and certainly not *the* people that populates American shores today. Unlike the contemporary French people who, for the most part, can trace their ancestry to the population of the French kingdom that preceded the French Revolution, most contemporary Americans have no actual ancestors who lived in the thirteen colonies that became independent upon the success of the American Revolution. Consistent with this, as will be discussed below,[38] in the American context it is much less that a people gave itself a constitution than that a constitution provided a focal point to waves of immigrants coming from different places at different times, thus allowing them eventually to cohere into a distinct people coexisting within a single nation-state.

To the *who* as subject of the American 'We the People' that is both partial and not yet formed must hence be added a for *whom* that is both largely not yet in place and that is constantly changing. Furthermore, the *what* that links the two – as the projection of the constitution-makers into the constitution so as to make it acceptable to those meant to be legitimately subjected to it – has also been prone to change and instability in the course of American constitutional history. As already pointed out, the meaning of the American Constitution does not appear to be the same before and after the Civil War or before and after the New Deal. And this is not only because of the adoption of new formal or informal amendments, but also because in time the changes led to new readings of original constitutional text not directly targeted by the new amendments.[39]

These initial observations concerning the constitutional subject and its identity along the dual axes of sameness and selfhood reveal that it is mush easier to determine what they are not than what they actually are. In other words, it is easier to grasp relationships along the axis of sameness in terms of not being the other. Given this, it seems best to conceive the constitutional subject in its logical and ontological foundation as an absence rather than a presence, or, above all, as a *lack*. Put differently, the very question of the constitutional subject is prompted because we find a lack in the place where we seek an ultimate source of legitimacy and authority for the constitutional order. Furthermore, as strongly suggested by the analysis thus far, the constitutional subject must be considered as a lack or an absence in at least two different senses: First, the absence of the constitutional subject does not negate its indispensability, thus necessitating its reconstruction; and, second, the constitutional subject always involves a lack because it is inherently incomplete, and hence always open to a necessary but impossible quest for completion. Because it starts as a lack, the constitutional subject is in constant need of construction, reconstruction and deconstruction as already noted. It is caught between constantly having to invent and reinvent itself as other than the other and yet at the same time as sustaining through recombination of discarded elements a minimum of positive identification (both along the axes of sameness and selfhood) lest it disintegrate into nothingness.

The conception of the identity of the constitutional subject as originating in a lack or absence bears strong affinities to certain philosophical (Hegel 1979) and psychoanalytical (Freud 1961; Lacan 1966) theories of the subject. Taken together, these theories posit that construction and reconstruction of identity occurs in the context of a struggle between self and other, and that the subject's quest for a meaningful identity depends on successful combined uses of three interpretive tools: negation, metaphor and metonymy.

CHAPTER 2

The Constitutional Subject and the Clash of Self and Other: On the Uses of Negation, Metaphor and Metonymy

One of the key insights of Hegelian philosophy (Hegel 1979:109–19) and of psychoanalytic theory (Freud 1961:13–14) is that the subject is defined not in relation to its objects, but in terms of its interaction with other subjects. From this perspective, the subject desires objects, but none of these fulfill its quest for satiation. In relation to its objects, the subject defines itself purely negatively as being other and as exceeding all the objects of its desire (Hegel 1979:104–11). Frustrated by the failure of its quest for identity and fulfillment through the appropriation of objects, the subject realizes that its aims are most likely to be achieved through recognition by other subjects.

In the Hegelian account, however, the shift toward other subjects does not immediately lead to mutual recognition as equals. Instead, as symbolized by Hegel's celebrated account of the struggle between the Lord and the Bondsman in the *Phenomenology* (*Id.*:111–19), the first encounter between subjects leads to a struggle for domination. Self and other suffering from a lack of distinct identity want their interlocutor to provide them with a positive one by recognizing them as worthy of honor and respect. As the self wants the other to recognize him, he fears that the other will only do so for purposes of domination. Thus, the struggle for recognition quickly turns into a struggle for domination, and it is only after a series of dialectical reversals that mutual recognition as equals can be established.

Similarly, in the psychoanalytic account, the failure of the child to merge into the object of her desire causes her to experience herself as a lack. To acquire an identity as a subject, the child must relate to others through the symbolic order of language. That proves, however, alienating, as the rules of language are imposed on the child from the 'outside', and as even her name, by which she first acquires a positive identity, is imposed on her by the other, namely her father (Lacan 1966:298–300, 655, 839–40). It is therefore only by reappropriating (at least in part) the language of the other for one's own purposes, that the subject will be able to establish an identity of her own.

2.1 The Constitutional Self and the Clash Between Self and Other

The question of the subject arises out of the need to confront the other. So long as human interaction is not perceived as involving a cleavage between self and other, neither the existence nor the place of the subject is likely to raise any significant problems. (Freud 1961:13–14). From the perspective of modern constitutionalism, moreover, the premodern political order could avoid dwelling upon the opposition between self and other, to the extent that it could hold together a unified vision shaped by commonly shared and mutually supporting religious, ethical, political, and legal norms.[1] Modern constitutionalism, on the other hand, cannot avoid the confrontation between self and other as a consequence of its inherent pluralism. On one level, the pluralist constitutional self encounters as the other the tradition that held together the premodern sociopolitical order. This other can be referred to as the 'external other.' On another level, constitutional pluralism requires that a group constituting a collective self recognize similarly positioned groups as other selves, and/or that each individual self treat the remaining individuals as other selves. In contrast to the external other, this latter other dwelling within the constitutional polity can be called the 'internal other.'[2]

Upon first impression, the constitutional subject may seem fundamentally different from its philosophical and psychoanalytic counterparts. Particularly, if it emerges in the aftermath of a revolution, the constitutional subject – at least in its initial stage – may seem in control, having smashed the antirevolutionary other, and not yet having to confront directly the other of future generations. As the holder of constituent power, the constitutional subject appears to be in a position to impose its will, or in Ulrich Preuss's words, to 'create a political world *ex nihilo*' (Preuss 1994:143). Hence, far from emerging as a lack or as alienated, the constitutional subject seemingly undertakes to fashion a new political order in its own image, from a position of absolute mastery, perched high above the smoldering remnants of traditions laid to waste by the revolution.

Upon more exacting scrutiny, however, the constitutional subject's quasi-divine appearance begins to unravel. This is not only because as the generation of constitution makers recedes further into the past, we become increasingly the prisoners of our constitutional heritage. Indeed, even if we focus exclusively on the generation of successful revolutionaries who have become constitution makers, in the realm of human affairs there is ultimately no such thing as creation *ex nihilo.*(*Id.*) Not even the radical rupture of violent revolution makes for complete differentiation between pre-revolutionary and post-revolutionary political orders. In many cases, pre-revolutionary traditions are not completely eradicated, but transformed and selectively incorporated into the new order fashioned by the constitutional subject.[3] To a significant degree, therefore, the past sought to be countered determines the content of constitutional provisions elaborated by revolutionary constitution makers.[4]

Not only the past, but also the present and the future, are bound to constrain revolutionary constitution makers. This belies the notion that a genuine constitutional self may impose its will by eliminating or disregarding the other. Unrestrained imposition of revolutionary will leads not to constitutionalism, but to the reign of terror. As demonstrated by the experience of the French Revolution, untempered revolutionary zeal merely succeeds in replacing a repressive tradition, which disregards the other, with an equally rigid and repressive order predicated on exclusion rather than inclusion. (Le Bon 1913:18, 168–70).

Inasmuch as constitutionalism is wedded to pluralism, it must take the other into proper account, which means that constitution makers must forge an identity that transcends the bounds of their own subjectivity. Accordingly, from the standpoint of the constitution makers, the identity of the constitutional subject emerges as a lack produced by the distance that separates their own self-image from that of the pluralist constitutional polity. Constitution making, moreover, can be regarded as an attempt to make up for this lack, by reaching to the other to forge a common identity rooted in a shared constitutional text. But, because neither the language of the self nor that of the other is suited to express their common vision, the emerging constitutional discourse must inevitably enter the scene sounding like a foreign language, thus alienating all those who must learn how to use it.

More specifically, as already mentioned, modern constitutionalism requires limited government, adherence to the rule of law, and protection of fundamental rights. Consistent with this, victorious revolutionaries who undertake the role of constitution makers must stake their claim to occupying the place of the legitimate constitutional subject by renouncing a significant amount of power, submitting to the prescriptions of law, and refraining from impinging on the fundamental interests of others. There are, of course, many different ways in which constitution makers may seek to fulfill the conditions for emergence of a legitimate constitutional subject, but they all involve alienation of power and a construction of self-identity dependent on the will and self-image of the other. To take but one example concerning modern constitutionalism's requirement of limited government, it is instructive to compare the distinct approaches employed in the eighteenth century by American and French constitution makers, respectively. In the U.S., limited government was sought to be achieved through a division of powers between the federal and state governments, and between the three branches of the federal government.[5] Underlying this stress on the division of powers is the conviction that, even in a democracy, unchecked political power tends toward abuse, which can be prevented through the institution of a system based on 'checks and balances.'[6] Thus, from the standpoint of the American constitution makers, opting for limitations on powers pursuant to a scheme of 'checks and balances' meant a renunciation and alienation of much of the power generated as a consequence of the triumph of the American Revolution. From the perspective of the definition of the self-identity of the American polity framed by the Constitution, on the other hand, the division of powers makes the identity of the whole dependent on clashes between the identities of the various parts. For example, federalism must mediate between a national identity shaped by federal interests and various state identities.[7] Accordingly, neither the national identity nor that of the states can prevail as the self-identity that encompasses the polity as a whole. Instead, both national identity and state identities must struggle and, in important respects, yield to one another in the course of striving towards a coherent self-identity of the constitutionally structured polity as a whole.

In contrast to the American Constitution, the French Constitution of 1793 vests supremacy on the national legislative branch,[8] thus promoting the idea that democratic values are best instituted through undivided state powers. This idea, moreover, is grounded on the notion that limited government is best achieved through democracy based on universal and rational values informed by a Rousseauian conception of the general will (Rousseau 1762:II, 2,3). Notwithstanding that the self-identity of the French constitutional government originates in unity rather than in division, however, it ultimately requires no less alienation and deference to the other than does its American counterpart. Indeed, below the surface, the unity fostered by the general will dissolves into a series of oppositions in which the conflict between self and other is displaced but not overcome. In Rousseau's conception, the general will is neither the will of the individual, nor even that of the majority. Instead, as Rousseau sees it, the general will is the sum of the differences between all the individual wills, or the 'agreement of all interests' which 'is produced by opposition to that of each.' (*Id.*). In sum, whereas in the United States the construction of constitutional self-identity through limited government must account for divisions among various factions, in France the unity of self-identity may be served through the general will, but only at the price of allowing the other into the inner precincts of the self. Thus, under the strain of the general will, the individual must split into two oppositional figures: that of the publicly spirited citizen, and that of the privately motivated *bourgeois*.[9]

Based on the lack and alienation that emerge out of the self's encounter with the other, the constitutional subject finds itself in a position that requires it to forge its identity through the medium of a constitutional discourse, embedded in a common language, that binds together the multi-faceted constitutional self with its multiple others. This constitutional discourse, moreover, must build upon a constitutional text[10] which must be placed in its proper context, taking into account relevant normative and factual constraints. As text is dependent on context, and as the context is open-ended and subject to transformation over time, the constitutional subject must resort to constitutional discourse to invent and reinvent its identity. In other words, motivated by the urge to overcome its lack and its inherent incompleteness, the constitutional subject must avail itself of the tools of constitutional discourse to construct a coherent narrative in which it can locate a plausible self-identity.

2.2 Construction, Deconstruction and Reconstruction of Constitutional Identity

Once it is admitted that the constitutional subject can only acquire an identity in the intersubjective realm circumscribed by constitutional discourse, it should become apparent that personifying the constitutional subject ought to be avoided. Neither the constitution makers, nor the interpreters of the constitution, nor those who are subject to its prescriptions, are properly speaking the constitutional subject. They all form part of the constitutional subject and belong to it, but the constitutional subject as such can only be grasped through expressions of its self-identity in an intersubjective discourse linking all the human actors who were, are, and will be brought together by the same set of constitutional norms. The full expression of constitutional self-identity is only conceivable through an imaginary exercise involving an extreme compression of all times, and a simultaneous grasp of all possible interpretive variations, combined with an ability to distill it all into an authoritative and coherent narrative. Short of that, however, constitutional self-identity can only be articulated piece-meal by a partial subject who must construct it from disparate fragments that need to be projected into an uncertain past and future. Moreover, for such construction to escape being perceived as merely arbitrary, as already alluded to, it must be supplemented by deconstruction and reconstruction. As we will see, the construction affords but a glimpse of constitutional identity, and the function of deconstruction and reconstruction is to trans-form that glimpse into a determinate image.

To understand the relationship between construction, deconstruction, and reconstruction one must bear in mind that constitutional self-identity revolves around the antinomies between fact and norm, and between real and ideal. The antinomy between fact and norm manifests itself through the juxtaposition of constitutional norms, and sociopolitical and historical facts, as well as, through the conflict between an actual existing constitution and the normative requirements of constitutionalism. In terms of the rela-tionship between constitutional norm and historical fact, application of the same constitutional norm may lead to different outcomes, depending on the relevant historical facts. Thus, for example, because of different experi-ences with Nazism at home, similar freedom of expression norms are respectively interpreted as protecting pro-Nazi speech in the United States, but not in Germany (Rosenfeld 2003:1537–1538, 1550–1551). Also, differ-ent factual conditions may in certain circumstances change the meaning of the same constitutional norm. For example, a constitutional right to sub-sistence may well amount to a legal guaranty in an industrially advanced society, but can be no more than an aspirational hope in an under-developed country with widespread starvation (Dorsen, et al. 2003: 1219).

The conflict between actual constitutions and constitutionalism as embodying certain normative prescriptions is in a sense a clash between the fact of a particular constitution and the norms that prescribe what constitutional democracy ought to be. This conflict, however, can also be viewed as a clash between different norms, namely between those norms promoted by an actual constitution and inconsistent norms inherent in constitutionalism. Dealing with such inconsistencies, as we shall see, is one of the important tasks that might be best handled by reconstruction.

The antinomy between the real and the ideal figures prominently in the determination of the self-identity of the constitutional subject as a consequence of the limitations and deficiencies inherent in the actual empirical and historically determinate position of that subject. The reality of the constitutional subject, as riddled by lack and incompleteness, is too impoverished to generate a viable self-identity capable of furnishing a coherent grounding for the constitutional order. Thus, for example, from the limited and fragmented perspective of the single constitutional judge, who at best has a partial and incomplete access to the empirical reality of the constitution makers and but the faintest insight into the reality of future generations, it seems all but impossible to develop a coherent picture of constitutional self-identity based exclusively on historically accessible and empirically verifiable data. Because of this inherent poverty of the real, it is necessary to have recourse to the ideal to frame an adequate conception of constitutional self-identity. Indeed, inasmuch as we cannot see from our own limited historical vantage point, the constitutional self of which we are a part, we must strive to imagine it. To establish a viable constitutional self-identity, the real must be supplemented by the ideal. Consistent with this, construction and reconstruction are meant to erect bridges linking the real to the ideal, and facts to counterfactuals. However, because the ideal not only supplements the real but also contradicts it, construction, deconstruction and reconstruction, while necessary, are dangerous tools which must be properly used and adequately legitimated.

Construction, deconstruction and reconstruction to deal with antinomies between fact and norm, and between the real and the ideal, have a long and venerable lineage that includes reconstructive theories ranging from Hobbes to Habermas (Rosenfeld 1995). Moreover, reconstructive theory has been creatively applied in legal and constitutional interpretation by Ronald Dworkin (Dworkin 1986). Since an infinite variety of ideals are imaginable, however, the key to properly assessing the worth of a particular reconstructive theory lies in determining the logic and persuasiveness with which that theory matches the real and the ideal, or facts and the counterfactual imagination.[11]

Construction and reconstruction (based in part on deconstruction) represent two distinct moments in the ongoing quest to obtain a better grasp of the evolving and incomplete self-identity of the constitutional subject. Constitutional decision making always arises under conditions that preclude full determinacy, and makes construction necessary. In fact, constitutional decision making involves construction to the extent that constitutional issues always require making choices between two or more plausible alternatives. Thus, for example, the 1973 decision by the United States Supreme Court in *Roe* v. *Wade*,[12] recognizing for the first time a constitutional right to abortion, certainly involved creative judicial construction. Indeed, neither the text of the Constitution nor previously articulated Supreme Court jurisprudence could fairly be taken to compel or preclude the decision reached by the Court. Moreover, the act of judicial construction that resulted in the holding in *Roe* had an unmistakable and significant impact on the constitutional identity of the United States. On the one hand, given the nature of the religious, moral, and political debate concerning abortion, recognition of a constitutional right to abortion projects a noticeably different image of American constitutional identity than that which would have emerged had the Supreme Court refused to recognize such a right. On the other hand, given the bitter controversy that followed the *Roe* decision[13] and the vigorous efforts over the years to have the *Roe* decision overturned,[14] it is hardly an exaggeration to claim that it provoked a crisis in the constitutional identity of Americans.

Although *Roe* is exceptional because of the magnitude of its impact on American constitutional identity, all significant constitutional decisions have some impact on constitutional identity and hence call for justification. Deconstruction and reconstruction afford the means to tackle the task of justification and makes possible cogent vindication or condemnation of the constructs associated with constitutional decision making. In other words, constitutional interpretation and elaboration introduce new elements that have a bearing on the makeup of constitutional identities. The task of reconstruction is to harmonize these new elements with previous existing ones; or, to the extent that the new elements disrupt relationships established among previously existing elements, to break up and recombine all the elements involved into an intelligible and cogent picture. Such harmonization or recombination, however, cannot be achieved exclusively on the basis of the fragmentary reality which it confronts, and thus calls for the exercise of our counterfactual imagination.

It seems advisable to submit reconstruction, as it relates to the discovery of the identity of the constitutional subject, to the normative constraints inherent in constitutionalism. Indeed, all these constraints – namely, commitment to limited government, adherence to the rule of law, and protection of fundamental rights – promote mutual recognition between self and other, and maintain self and other on a footing of equal dignity. Moreover, by submitting to these constraints, reconstruction naturally lends itself to the task of evaluating the legitimacy of actual constitutional norms.

In addition to requiring compliance with the constraints of constitutionalism, counterfactual reconstruction should be subjected to a condition of logical plausibility, to be assessed in terms of the prevailing circumstances. This latter condition mandates a contextually grounded reconstruction adapted to the actual tensions and contradictions found within prevailing social and political relations. At each stage of its historical development, the constitutional subject encounters certain contradictions that motivate it to seek coherence through use of counterfactual imagination. Accordingly, reconstruction seems most useful if it points to a plausible resolution of prevailing contradictions by elaborating a counterfactual picture that does not exceed the horizon of possibilities delimited by existing material conditions. In sum, from the standpoint of the identity of the constitutional subject, the legitimacy of reconstruction depends on adherence to the norms embodied in constitutionalism, coupled with respect for the limits imposed by the relevant horizon of possibilities.

2.3 The Constructive Tools of Constitutional Discourse: Negation, Metaphor and Metonymy

Constitutional discourse must articulate a self-identity by means of a counterfactual narrative that takes into account both the applicable constitutional text and the normative constraints flowing from constitutionalism. Such a narrative, moreover, must strive to bridge the gap that splits the constitutional subject into self and other, while, at the same time, furnishing sustenance to the constitutional subject by endowing it with a distinct identity. From the standpoint of those who seek to vindicate the constitutional status quo, constitutional discourse must bridge the gap between the actual constitution and the precepts of constitutionalism, and forge sufficient common grounds between self and other to lend the requisite support for the constitutional subject to maintain a distinct identity. From the standpoint of those who appeal to the counterfactual imagination to launch a critique of existing constitutional arrangements, on the other hand, constitutional discourse must expose mere semblances of harmony between the constitution and constitutionalism, and pierce through constitutional identities that oppress or unduly constrain self or other. Whether constitutional discourse is used to justify or to criticize existing constitutional arrangements, however, it operates mainly by means of the same essential tools: negation, metaphor, and metonymy.

Negation, metaphor, and metonymy combine to select, discard, and organize pertinent elements with a view to producing a constitutional discourse in, and through which, the constitutional subject can ground its identity. Negation is crucial to the extent that the constitutional subject can only emerge as distinct, through exclusion and renunciation. Metaphor or condensation, on the other hand, which proceeds by stressing similarities at the expense of differences, plays a key unifying role, in producing partial identities around which constitutional identity can revolve.[15] Finally, metonymy or displacement, with its emphasis on contiguity and context, is essential to guard against the constitutional subject fixating on identities that remain so condensed and abstract as to gloss over the differences which must be taken into consideration if constitutional identity is genuinely to encompass both self and other. An accurate picture of how constitutional discourse can shape the identity of the constitutional subject through the work of negation, metaphor, and metonymy, depends on a proper account of the interaction between the three. Indeed, it is through such interaction that constitutional discourse acquires determinate meaning. But before examining how negation, metaphor, and metonymy interact, it is necessary to look at each of them individually to get a better handle on their respective roles in shaping constitutional discourse.

2.3.1 Negation

The role of negation in the process of establishing the identity of the constitutional subject is multifaceted, intricate, and complex. It involves, among other things, rejection, repudiation, repression, exclusion, and renunciation. These functions, moreover, may intertwine in various ways and simultaneously operate at different levels of reality. In view of this rich diversity, I can only briefly outline some of the most general aspects of the essential contribution of negation to the definition of constitutional self-identity.

The path towards the establishment of the identity of the constitutional subject can be reconstructed as a three stage process. In the first stage, the constitutional subject's identity can be conceived as pure negation because the constitutional subject acquires a distinct identity by negating that it is (the same as) the preconstitutional subject, or a mere product of existing cultural, historical, ethnic, or religious identities. In other words, the constitutional subject first enters the scene, by cutting loose from all those already constituted subjects found within the relevant spaciotemporal framework. Moreover, the constitutional subject arrives at this purely negative identity through: repudiation of the (pre-revolutionary) past; rejection of traditional identities; repression of the urge to embrace a dominant, positive identity to the detriment of the plurality of (nonconstitutional) identities sought to be protected by constitutionalism; exclusion of any militantly antipluralistic tendency that would defeat constitutionalism; and, renunciation of dreams of hegemony by those in a position to shape the destiny of the constitutional subject.

As pure negativity, the constitutional subject experiences itself as a lack, and consequently strives to fill the void within itself, by developing a positive identity. The search for a positive identity marks, moreover, the second stage in the logical development of the constitutional subject. But such positive identity only proves possible if recourse is had to the very identities discarded in the first stage of the constitutional subject's formation. Indeed, the objectives of constitutionalism cannot be pursued in a vacuum; they require establishing a viable institutional apparatus that must, of necessity, draw upon the history, traditions, and cultural patrimony of the relevant polity.

Recourse to identities discarded during the first stage does not signify, however, a return to the realm of the preconstitutional. Consistent with Hegelian logic, the dialectical transition from one stage to the next involves a process of 'Aufhebung' or sublation, whereby what emerges in the first stage is at once preserved and transcended within the perspective of the second stage.[16] Applied to the constitutional subject, this means that the second stage is marked by a selective incorporation of discarded identities rather than by any wholesale return to preconstitutional identities. In other words, the traditions incorporated into the constitutional subject during the second stage are not pursued for their own sake. Instead, these traditions are only invoked inasmuch as they are capable of serving the interests of constitutionalism.

The logic that underlies the development of the constitutional subject is analogous to that which informs the implantation of pluralism as a comprehensive conception of the good.[17] Accordingly, a brief glance into the first two logical moments of pluralism will serve to provide a more vivid illustration of the constitutional subject's transition between stage one and stage two. In the broadest terms, pluralism seeks to promote the greatest possible diversity of conceptions of the good as a means to maximize human dignity and autonomy.[18] Consistent with this, pluralism's first moment must be a negative one, whereby it denies all competing conceptions of the good (except that of pluralism), exclusivity, or predominance. Thus, for example, pluralism must combat intolerant religions claiming a monopoly on the truth. Carried to its logical extreme, however, pluralism's first moment leads to self-destruction. Indeed, if all conceptions of the good are thoroughly countered, the very diversity sought by pluralism would become meaningless. To avoid self-destruction, pluralism must therefore supplement its negative moment with a positive one, whereby excluded conceptions of the good are readmitted into the pluralist universe. But the readmitted conceptions cannot occupy the same position that they had prior to their expulsion. For example, religions are only readmitted on the condition that they pose no threat to other religions or to nonreligious conceptions of the good. And one plausible way of accomplishing this would be by relegating readmitted religions to the private sphere.[19]

Analogously, as partial preconstitutional identities become incorporated into the constitutional subject during its second stage of logical development, they combine in novel ways and come to occupy different positions from those they held in the preconstitutional era. Imagine, for example, that a polity divided into several different regions along ethnic and religious lines decides to become a constitutional democracy, and opts for a federal system of government. Under such a federal system, moreover, imagine that each ethnically and religiously homogeneous region were to be accorded equal representation in the upper chamber of the national legislature, but that representation in the lower chamber were exclusively a function of the size of the population, with the consequence that more numerous ethnic groups would be likely to achieve greater representation than their less numerous counterparts. Finally, assume that the constitution in this new federal democracy divides the sovereign powers of the state between the national legislature and the respective legislatures of the various constituent states, based on a desire to institute a system of 'checks and balances.' Under these circumstances, the identity forged by the new federal democracy would be neither that projected by the national legislature, nor that put forth by the various state legislatures. Instead, the identity of the new federal democracy would seem bound to be grounded in the opposition between state and national legislatures. Furthermore, existing ethnic and religious identities would certainly figure in the identity of the new federal democracy, but they would do so in a significantly transformed way. Thus, points of convergence would more likely be stressed than points of divergence; some differences would probably be left out altogether through the implementation of 'gag rules'(Holmes 1988: 19–58); and some particular ethnic and religious identities would inevitably figure more prominently than others, either because of their spread over greater numbers, or for other reasons.

In the process of incorporating the partial identities that enable it to project a positive image, the constitutional subject is bound to become alienated. Because of its initial lack of positive identity, the constitutional subject is forced to turn outward to other identities. But as the process of incorporating the latter unfolds, the constitutional subject becomes prey to outside influences that appear to be beyond its control. Thus, the very necessity of acquiring a positive identity leads the constitutional subject to a confrontation between survival and loss of subjectivity. Pursuant to the dictates of dialectical logic, therefore, the constitutional subject must negate its subjectivity to maintain an identity.

The culmination of the dialectical evolution of the constitutional sub-ject is brought about by yet another reversal of perspective made possible by the work of negation. In this case, it is the negation of the negation – or, in other words, the negation of the proposition that the pursuit of identity entails the loss of subjectivity – which allows the constitutional subject to reach a vantage point from which it can perceive its unfolding positive identity as being ultimately shaped by its own will, rather than by outside forces beyond its control. Specifically, the negation of the negation has completed its work when the constitutional subject realizes that, although the raw materials that figure in its positive identity originate in the outside objective world, their selection, combination, organization, and deploy-ment into a coherent whole is the product of its own work, of its own efforts to strive towards a distinct identity. Here again, the analogy to pluralism is instructive. As will be remembered, pluralism must rein-corporate in its positive moment conceptions of the good that it excluded in its negative moment. But which such conceptions of the good are to be thus reincorporated, and to what extent, is determined by the normative criteria imposed by pluralism, thus making it clear that pluralism's toler-ance of diverse conceptions of the good results from an active rather than passive stance. Likewise, the constitutional subject's construction of its positive identity cannot be completed without subjecting the raw material originating outside the constitutional sphere to the normative constraints prescribed by constitutionalism.

Negation is not only a crucial tool in the constitutional subject's pursuit of the ideal defined by constitutionalism, but also in its endeavors to nego-tiate the space that separates the actual constitution from the normative universe of constitutionalism. To the extent that an actual constitution – either because of its textual provisions or its interpretive or implemental practices – falls short of the fundamental prescriptions of constitutional-ism, negation is bound to figure as an essential tool at the levels of con-struction, deconstruction and at that of reconstruction. A particularly good example of this is provided by the contradictions that surround the United States Constitution of 1787. As already mentioned, the 'We The People' of the 1787 Constitution's Preamble, who are, at least nomin-ally, the relevant constitutional subject at the birth of the American Consti-tution, must be linked to the 'all men are created equal' of the 1776 Declaration of Independence. But by condoning slavery, the 1787 Consti-tution became mired in a glaring contradiction in relation both to its own historical and ideological premises, and to the fundamental prescriptions of constitutionalism. The use of negation thus became important to cope with these contradictions. On the one hand, by not importing 'all men are created equal' into the constitutional text, those standing behind 'We The People' could conceal the contradiction without eliminating either of its terms. Equality was recognized as an essential pillar of the entire constitutional project, but precisely because of its absence from the four corners of the constitutional text, it could be consistently rejected as an operative constitutional norm.

On the other hand, when it came to reconstruction to bridge the gap between the 1787 Constitution and constitutionalism, simply denying constitutional and legal force to the premises embodied in the Declaration of Independence, would not do. Indeed, purely textual solutions are inherently insufficient to deal with contradictions between constitution and constitutionalism. What is needed, instead, is some reconciliation at the level of concepts. Slavery is antithetical to the concept of equality embedded in constitutionalism. This notwithstanding, reconciliation was still possible through the use of negation. And, the tragic and shameful solution – but nonetheless a solution – consisted in treating African-Americans as being less than fully human. In other words, by negating that African Americans deserved to be treated as full-fledged human beings, slavery in America could somehow be reconciled with the precepts of constitutionalism. To be sure, this reconciliation would prove extremely precarious and it would produce monstrous results. This is perhaps best illustrated in the Supreme Court's infamous decision in *Dred Scott*,[20] which provides one of the most glaring examples of how, through reconstruction based on negation, slavery and constitutionalism could be presented as compatible. Dred Scott dealt with the constitutionality of a federal law that provided for the emancipation of slaves upon being brought into federal territory by their owners. Dred Scott was thus emancipated, but upon his subsequent return to the state where he had been a slave, his former owner reclaimed ownership over him. The question before the Supreme Court was whether the federal statute providing for emancipation was unconstitutional as a violation of the slave owner's constitutionally protected property rights.[21]

The Court held that the federal statute providing for emancipation was indeed unconstitutional as violative of the legitimate property rights of the (former) slave owner, a decision that would have been patently incoherent but for the negation of full membership into the human race for African Americans.[22] Had the Supreme Court treated Dred Scott as a full human being, considering him property would have been preposterous. And even if the Court had acknowledged that the Constitution condoned slavery in the states that made it legal, it could still have held, without doing violence to the constitutional text or to accepted canons of interpretation, that once on federal territory Dred Scott had acquired full citizenship, and accordingly, his liberty Due Process rights had to prevail over any property rights that his former owner might have possessed. But if the Supreme Court had decided for Dred Scott, it would have officially acknowledged a glaring contradiction between the Constitution and constitutionalism. By deciding as it did, the Court upheld the facade that linked the Constitution and constitutionalism, but it did so at the high price of accelerating the country's plunge into bloody civil war. Finally, whereas negation made possible the albeit precarious and ephemeral reconciliation between the Constitution and constitutionalism during the time of slavery, it also made possible the condemnation of the 1787 Constitution as inconsistent with the fundamental precepts of constitutionalism. For all those who share the belief that 'all men are created equal' admits of no exceptions, condoning slavery negates the very possibility of satisfying the requirements of constitutionalism.

2.3.2 Metaphor

If negation is crucial inasmuch as identity can only be conceived in terms of what one is not, metaphor is essential to the interplay between identity and difference that sustains the constitutional subject's quest for a positive self-identity. As a tool designed to establish similarities and equivalences, metaphor provides the discursive underpinning for the pole of identity in the dialectic between identity – in the sense of sameness or of selfhood – and difference – in the sense of dissimilarity or of otherness. Through a process of combination and substitution, metaphor ferrets out similarities and equivalences to forge links of identity.

Metaphor is the discursive equivalent of Freud's concept of condensation. According to Freud, condensation is a psychic process whereby similarities are drawn together and emphasized, at the expense of differences. In the context of dream formation, for example, the image of a single face can serve as a representation of several different persons, by means of the work of condensation, which consists of drawing a composite picture that emphasizes common facial features and disregards or cancels out divergent ones (Freud 1965:327–28). Moreover, by combining and organizing complex and multifaceted elements in terms of similarities, condensation makes possible, or sharpens, our grasp of where genuine identities might be found. Condensation, however, can also perform a function of substitution, whereby an objectionable picture can be replaced by a composite substitute made up of similar but not identical features. For example, imagine that a single face made up of a composite of similar facial features belonging to different persons symbolizes in a dream those persons to whom the dreamer is sexually attracted. Suppose further, that sexual attraction to one of the symbolically represented persons could not be consciously acknowledged, because it would violate a fundamental taboo. Under these circumstances, condensation serves to conceal the forbidden attraction by substituting the actual features of the person who is the object of such attraction with similar features, which are close enough to permit an unconscious link, yet removed enough to protect the dreamer from becoming conscious of his or her forbidden desire. In short, through substitution along a series of similar, though not identical, features, condensation opens a channel of expression for repressed material. As we shall see, moreover, the availability of an analogous channel of expression for the constitutional subject is important. It allows for both substitutions of identities incompatible with the constitutional order, and for criticism of identities associated with the constitutional subject as mere stand-ins for identities that ought to be banished.

Through his concept of metaphor, Lacan systematizes Freud's notion of condensation in the context of linguistic theory (Wilden 1968:246). Building on Roman Jakobson's linguistic theory, (*Id*.:244) Lacan conceives of the metaphoric function as establishing relationships of similarity (*Id*). Meaning, moreover, is generated through interaction between the metaphoric function and the metonymic function.[23] Metaphor contributes to the production of meaning by cementing relationships of similarity in reference to a code, or, in other words, by linking signs along a paradigmatic axis.[24]

The metaphorical function plays an essential role both in legal rhetoric and in constitutional discourse. Legal argumentation relies prominently on establishing analogies and similarities, as vividly exemplified by common law adjudication based on precedent. Let us assume, for example, that there is judicial precedent to the effect that the owner of a house is liable for injuries suffered there by a person hired to do work in the house. Consistent with this, an attorney representing a house guest suing the owner for injuries suffered there would seek to analogize the two situations, by emphasizing the similarities and downplaying the differences.

In the realm of constitutional discourse, on the other hand, metaphor not only operates at the level of rhetoric, but also contributes in setting the cardinal reference points of the constitutional order. Beginning with 'all men,' in the sense of all humans, 'are created equal,' underlying the postulate of equality on which modern constitutionalism rests,[25] there are a large number of fundamental constitutional constructs that rely heavily on metaphorical processes. Thus, 'all men are created equal' certainly emphasizes similarities at the expense of differences, and, on close inspection, may ultimately depend more on substitution than on combination. Indeed, it is not so much the fact that all human beings share certain characteristics in common, but rather the counterfactual proposition that all human beings are equal as moral agents, that forms the backbone of the normative universe associated with constitutionalism (Rosenfeld 1991:20–21).

Metaphor also figures in the famous American dictum that 'the Constitution is colorblind.'[26] Concentrating on the metaphoric qualities of this dictum[27] reveals that it results from emphasis on the similarities between the races – that is, those things which they share in common in spite of their racial differences – coupled with disregard for racial differences, and for that which must be deemed to arise as a consequence of these differences. In other words, through combination and substitution, the metaphor of colorblindness brackets off racial differences and differences associated with race. This metaphor, moreover, legitimates constitutional doctrine that prohibits legal classifications based on race, and promotes a constitutional identity that rises above the divisiveness of racial politics. From a normative standpoint, constitutional doctrine backed by the metaphor of colorblindness has the virtue of prohibiting the use of racial differences as a means to legally disadvantage oppressed racial minorities. By the same token, however, such legal doctrine can also inhibit the march towards racial justice. For example, if strictly applied, legal doctrine based on the principle of colorblindness would prohibit any race-conscious remedy as a means to integrate racially segregated public schools.[28]

The range of the metaphoric function within the realm of constitutional discourse extends beyond equality rights. Indeed, as will be discussed below other rights, such as privacy rights, also depend to a significant extent on the deployment of relationships of similarity.

2.3.3 Metonymy

In contrast to metaphor's pursuit of similarities in relation to a code, metonymy promotes relations of contiguity within a context. (Wilden 1968:245–46). The metaphoric process tends to be acontextual, whereas the metonymic process represents the opposite tendency. Drawing again on Jakobson's linguistic theory, Lacan conceives of metonymy as the discursive embodiment of Freud's notion of displacement. (*Id.*:244). According to Freud, displacement makes expression of repressed thoughts possible by redirecting them in all of their emotive intensity toward a target that bears a relationship of contiguity to the would-be target rendered inaccessible by repression.(Freud 1965:209–10). Thus, for example, if one's unconscious hatred of an uncle who uses a cane cannot find conscious expression because of repression, such hatred may be displaced toward canes, resulting in a conscious aversion to canes.

Elaborating on Freud's notion of displacement, Lacan envisages metonymy as symbolizing the flight of desire from object to object, as frustration stemming from the need to repress the original object of desire leads to the unsatisfactory pursuit of contiguous objects which might approximate, without ever matching, the original object. Thus, for Lacan, the metonymy of desire points to a lack of being, or to self-perception as a lack. (Wilden 1968:242).

As a meaning-endowing device, metonymy proceeds by establishing contextual relations along a syntagmatic axis (Jakobson 1968:70). Thus, to metaphor's paradigmatic axis which can be regarded as a vertical axis, corresponds metonymy's syntagmatic axis which can be viewed as horizontal (Wilden 1968:246). Or to put it in another way, the opposition between metaphor and metonymy corresponds to the contrast between synchrony ('the axis of simultaneities') and diachrony ('the axis of successivities'). (*Id.*)

The metonymic function, like its metaphoric counterpart, also plays an important role in legal rhetoric and in constitutional discourse. At the most profound level, Lacan's notion of the metonymy of desire is reflected in the constitutional subject's above mentioned grasp of its identity as a lack. Inasmuch as the constitutional subject's search for identity is analogous to the metonymy of desire, the constitutional subject cannot fully overcome the experience of itself as (at least in part) a lack. Indeed, the metonymy of desire is ultimately animated by the desire of desire[29] which can only be sustained so long as there remain objects of desire.[30] Similarly, the constitutional subject could only fully overcome its lack if it became fully determined. Accordingly, the constitutional subject's lack is ultimately the unfulfilled desire for exhaustive determination. Such exhaustive determination, however, could only be realized as a consequence of full contextualization – that is, a synthesis of all past, present, and future instantiations of the place of the constitutional subject within the constitutional order. And that is, of course, impossible; not only because the future cannot be fully prophesied, but also because the past cannot be fully remembered.

In legal rhetoric, the metonymic function plays as important a role as the metaphoric function against which it is pitted. In the context of adversary proceedings, arguments stressing similarities are bound to be countered by arguments emphasizing differences. Legal arguments based on metonymy evoke differences by contextualizing, relying on relations of proximity to carve out a picture that reveals as many concrete details as possible. In common law jurisdictions, metonymic legal argument militates against the extension of precedent by contextualizing the relevant situations to the point that differences appear to far outweigh similarities. The rhetorical strategy of metonymic legal argument is to demonstrate that proposed analogies are besides the point. And taken to its logical extreme, metonymic legal argument would systematically undermine reliance on precedents, since upon being exhaustively contextualized every situation is ultimately unique.

The metonymic function also plays an important role in constitutional discourse since it figures in constitutional constructs, and contributes to the definition of constitutional rights and constitutional identity. The metonymic function pulls in the opposite direction of its metaphoric counterpart. At the level of constitutional arguments, metonymy leads to greater contextualization just as metaphor points to similarities. Moreover, as in metaphor, metonymy may be used to foster extension as well as constriction of constitutional rights, depending on the circumstances. Thus, for example, through metonymic contextualization, it becomes possible to surmount the colorblind hurdle in the pursuit of racial justice.[31] Against Whites who seek to disadvantage African Americans because of their race, the colorblind principle remains a barrier. But such a barrier need not be made into an impediment against redressing the lingering injuries stemming from racism.[32] Once the difference between healing the wounds of racism and further aggravating them is firmly in mind, rigid adherence to the principle of colorblindness seems both unnecessary and undesirable.

The metonymic function's contribution to the delimitation of constitutional rights becomes manifest in the implementation of such rights. In the abstract, everyone should enjoy the same equality or freedom-of-religion rights. In practice, however, such rights cannot be equally enjoyed unless they are properly tailored to the diverse needs and circumstances confronting their intended beneficiaries. To the extent that equality requires proportionality rather than mere similarity of treatment, it is necessary to contextualize and to take certain differences into account. Thus, for example, equality for women arguably involves more than being treated the same as men. Similarly, freedom to exercise one's religion requires contextualization since generally applicable laws may not have the same impact on different religious practices. A Sunday-closing law, for instance, is likely to be burdensome on sabbatarians inasmuch as it would force them to close their businesses for two days, whereas their competitors could close on only one day without violating their religious convictions.[33]

The metonymic process also contributes to the definition of the identity of the constitutional subject. Inasmuch as constitutionalism implies pluralism and heterogeneity, constitutional identity cannot be reduced to a mere relationship of similarity. Because constitutional identity must bridge a gap between self and other, it must incorporate differences through contextualization to avert subordination of some to others within the same constitutional regime. For example, in a multicultural or religiously pluralistic society, it is most unlikely that a positive identity that is neutral as between all cultural or religious groups could ever be achieved.[34] Accordingly, taking certain differences into account may lead to a more satisfactory constitutional identity than simply glossing over them.

Metonymic influence on constitutional identity may on some occasions involve more than mere contextualization and amount to downright displacement. When a partial identity is too powerful to be successfully suppressed, yet too divisive to be openly and fully acknowledged, its impact may be masked through a focus upon contiguous partial identities. The American constitutional experience with the relation between the state and religion – or at least a plausible interpretation of that experience – provides an example of metonymic displacement as a means to bridge the gap between constitutional identity and the forces animating constitutional practice. From a cursory look at the Religion Clauses of the First Amendment,[35] it would appear that the state should maintain a completely neutral stance towards religion. On the one hand, the state should do nothing to promote religion; on the other, it should do nothing that would interfere with its citizens' freedom to practice the religion of their choice.[36] Accordingly, whereas Americans may be by and large a religious people,[37] their constitutional identity would appear to be one of neutrality, fairness, and equanimity towards religion. Based on a consideration of relevant practices and the Supreme Court's jurisprudence regarding the Religion Clauses, however, it is certainly a plausible conclusion that American constitutional identity is at bottom predicated on endorsement of a particular religion – or more precisely, a particular brand of religion – to the detriment of other religions.

Although the Supreme Court's Religion Clauses jurisprudence has been subject to fluctuations (Felsen 1989) overall and when taken in conjunction with prevalent institutional practices, it is arguably best understood as an endorsement of a moderate mainstream, mainly Christian, brand of religion. This endorsement, moreover, militates against, on the one hand, atheism, and on the other, more fundamentalist brands of Christianity; as well as against other religions removed altogether from the Judeo-Christian tradition, such as Native American religions. (Fort 1993).

The most ubiquitous and powerful metaphor, in the Religion Clauses, is that of the 'wall of separation' between church and state.[38] And the most controverted public debate concerning the Religion Clauses is whether this 'wall' should guarantee complete separation between church and state, or whether it should be lowered to permit state aid to religion so long as the state refrains from officially endorsing any particular religion. (Tribe 1988:1166–68). This debate, however, conceals the dominant constitutional identity that emerges from institutional practices and Supreme Court opinions on the Religion Clauses.

The official endorsement of mainstream religion is effectuated through several different practices and discursive processes, among which metonymy plays a limited but crucial role. Official endorsement of God against atheists is prevalent in institutional practices, such as, the recitation of prayers by official chaplains at the opening of a legislative session;[39] or the printing of 'In God We Trust' on official paper and coin currency; or the statement by a Supreme Court Justice, in the course of an Establishment Clause opinion, endorsing belief in a 'Supreme Being'.[40] At the doctrinal level, the Supreme Court has upheld a congressional statute exempting from combat, conscientious objectors opposed to 'war in any form' because of their 'religious training and belief' – 'belief' being defined as a 'belief in a relation to a Supreme Being involving duties superior from those arising from any human relation, but [not including] essentially political, sociological, or philosophical views or a merely personal moral code.'[41] Taken together, these developments unmistakably point to a constitutional identity that is not neutral on questions of religion, but rather biased in favor of broad theistic views, at least as against atheistic or agnostic views.

The constitutional bias in favor of mainstream religion to the detriment of other religious practices emerges, on the other hand, from the Supreme Court's Free Exercise Clause jurisprudence. This bias is reflected in the Court's general tendency to refuse exemptions from generally applicable laws for practices such as polygamy[42] or ritual use of peyote,[43] which are repugnant to mainstream religion or to the mores of the majority. Finally, both the bias against atheists and that against nonmainstream religion underlie modern Supreme Court Establishment Clause jurisprudence, most notably the 1984 decision in *Lynch* v. *Donnely*.[44] In *Lynch*, the Court upheld a city's Christmas display that included a crèche, located at the heart of the shopping district, as not violative of the Establishment Clause. To reach this result, the Court had to overcome two doctrinal hurdles: it had to find that there was a secular purpose to the display of the creche, and it had to conclude that the display did not amount to an official endorsement of religion by the city.[45] Since the creche depicts the nativity scene, which is of profound religious significance to Christians but not to those who adhere to other faiths, such as Judaism, the hurdles confronting the Court's five-four majority seemed rather formidable. Nevertheless, through a combination of negation and metonymic displacement, the Court managed to decide that public display of the crèche amounted to neither a lack of secular purpose nor an official endorsement of (a particular) religion. As against atheists and advocates of rigid separation between church and state, Justices in the majority argued that display of the crèche did not endorse any particular religion any more than generally accepted practices, such as printing 'In God We Trust' on coins.[46] As against both non-Christians and Christians for whom the crèche evokes strong religious convictions, the Court's majority trivialized the crèche, by stressing its display in the context of commercial and other national secular traditions now associated with the Christmas holiday.[47]

From the perspective of atheists or rigorous separationists, *Lynch* is an impermissible endorsement of religion. From the perspective of a profoundly committed Christian, on the other hand, *Lynch* represents a trivialization of religion and an ultimate surrender to secularism.[48] By nurturing the antagonism between these two entrenched positions, the Court's majority in *Lynch* manages to promote mainstream religion through a double displacement that may appear to be an effort to appease both sets of antagonists. Indeed, mainstream religion is contiguous to both separationists, on one side, and to those who are profoundly religious, on the other. Accordingly, both the holding in *Lynch* and the American constitutional approach to the relation between state and religion can be metonymically portrayed as carving a nonreligiously motivated, and predominantly neutral, middle course between ardent secularists and profoundly committed adherents to religion. At bottom, however, *Lynch* promotes a particular brand of religion which is neither neutral, nor heterogeneous. Consistent with this, metonymic displacement enables a constitutional identity shaped by mainstream religion to remain hidden behind a mask of fairness and neutrality toward religion(s).[49]

2.4 Constitutional Discourse as Interplay Between Negation, Metaphor and Metonymy

The preceding discussion of negation, metaphor, and metonymy reveals the complexity of the discursive processes associated with the reconstructive search for constitutional identity. This complexity is compounded when one considers the ways in which negation, metaphor, and metonymy operate while they interact. Indeed, such interaction not only modifies and delimits the ways in which these three discursive devices combine to project images of constitutional identity; it also shapes the elements slated to become building blocks in the (re)construction of constitutional identity. To illustrate this, we need only briefly return to the double displacement whereby an image of constitutional identity as it relates to religion is structured in *Lynch*.[50] This double displacement can only succeed in fostering state endorsement of mainstream religion as benevolent neutrality towards religion, if the crèche can plausibly be depicted as sufficiently detached from its origins in a purely religious context to stand for something other than a transparent endorsement of Christian religion. Consistent with this, the majority in *Lynch* used both metaphoric and metonymic arguments to establish that the crèche at stake in that case was, at least in part, severed from purely religious concerns. Through metaphoric analogy, display of the crèche was equated to exhibiting paintings depicting a religious subject matter as part of the collection of a state-owned museum.[51] Through metonymic focus on contiguity and context, on the other hand, the location of the creche next to less, or nonreligious, Christmas symbols in the context of the dominant commercial pursuits associated with shopping centers, was meant to suggest that the principal motivation for the display of the crèche was commercial rather than religious.[52] As this example indicates, interaction between negation, metaphor, and metonymy occurs at many different levels resulting in multiple combinations and intersections, which would have to be successfully integrated to present an exhaustive account of the reconstructive formation, evolution, and dissolution of constitutional identities.

It would take us too far a field to attempt any comprehensive account of the intricate ways in which negation, metaphor, and metonymy actually combine in the course of the reconstructions of constitutional identity. Instead, I will concentrate on the most salient aspects of the interaction between the three above mentioned devices in relation to the determination of constitutional identity as a whole, without special regard to how the individual elements involved are themselves derived. From such an overall standpoint, negation – particularly through determination, repression, and renunciation – assumes the principal role in carving out the identity of the constitutional subject, with metaphor and metonymy fulfilling the important task of providing content to the respective roles of identity and difference. Indeed, negation delimits the constitutional subject by mediating between identity and difference. But only through the work of metaphor and metonymy can identity and difference acquire determinate forms. In other words, only metaphor and metonymy will reveal which identity – or, more precisely, identities – and which difference – or differences – ought to be mediated through negation to yield a plausible reconstruction of a suitable constitutional subject.

The function of metaphor and metonymy in delimiting constitutional identity must be understood in terms of the previously discussed overall role played by negation in the definition of the constitutional subject. By upsetting the status quo and uprooting settled meanings, negation creates a vacuum which must be filled through the pursuit of equivalent meanings along the paradigmatic axis, and contiguous meanings along the syntagmatic axis. The replacement of uprooted meanings, moreover, requires a concurrent journey along both these axes, as all meanings hinge on relations of similarity as well as on relations of contiguity. Thus, constitutional meaning and identity depend on establishing coordinates along the syntagmatic and paradigmatic axes. In order to understand how reconstruction of the constitutional subject's identity works, therefore, it is necessary to take a closer look at the relationship between metaphor and metonymy, and, in particular, at how interaction between the two results in securing determinate coordinates along the paradigmatic and syntagmatic axes.

As already mentioned, metaphor functions by setting relations with reference to a code, whereas metonymy does the same with reference to a context. Neither metaphor, standing alone, nor metonymy, completely cut loose from any code can generate any coherent meaning. In other words, for meaning to be produced, the semantic path made up of metaphoric relations must intersect with its counterpart built on metonymic relations. Indeed, journeying along the metaphoric path can be analogized to attempting to ascertain the meaning by exclusive reference to a dictionary. Assuming no reference whatsoever to any context, reliance on the dictionary proves completely circular. Each term would have to be defined by other terms, with the original term sought to be defined eventually figuring in the definition, thus referring back to itself. On the other hand, should the syntagmatic relations along the metonymic path be considered completely separately from any paradigmatic relations, it would also be impossible to generate any coherent meaning as each term within a sequence would lead to the next term within the same sequence, without ever acquiring an identity of its own.[53] It would be as if one became familiar with a set sequence of words in a completely foreign language. After a while, upon reading the first word in the sequence, one would be able to recite the rest of the sequence in its proper order, but without thereby being in any better position to understand the meaning of the sequence.

Notwithstanding that meaning requires reference to both the metaphoric and the metonymic paths, particular utterances may rely on a preponderance of either metaphoric or metonymic relations (Jakobson 1973:61). Depending on differences in personality, culture, and style, metaphoric or metonymic processes may gain the upper hand.[54] Moreover, as already mentioned, in the realm of legal argumentation, tilts towards metaphoric or metonymic processes are to an important degree determined by stakes in the legal outcomes; with those wishing to extend application of an existing legal norm relying on metaphor, while those seeking to contain the spread of such norm, appealing to metonymy.

At the more global level of the formation and evolution of constitutional identities, metaphoric processes are intertwined with metonymic ones in an ongoing dialectic. At the highest level of abstraction, this dialectic confronts the challenge of projecting an identity lending support to the perception that the same constitution endures through the generations, stretching back to that of the constitution makers. At the more concrete level of particular constitutional rights, moreover, this dialectic strives to promote equilibrium between the pole of identity and the contrary pole of difference. This is perhaps best illustrated by reference to constitutional rights to equality.

Viewed from a formal standpoint, constitutional equality requires properly accounting for relevant identities and relevant differences.[55] Consistent with this, ideal constitutional equality would fully account for, and optimally integrate, all relevant identities and differences. Practically, however, the relevance of identities and differences will be contested. Moreover, this problem is compounded to the extent that identities and differences are not simply given, but rather constructed (Cain 1991). Finally, given the logic of the dialectic between identity and difference, both identity and difference can be invoked, depending on the circumstances, either to make equality rights more inclusive or more exclusive. For example, against the background of African American slavery, stress on the metaphoric process that leads to an identity beyond race seems bound to result in a more inclusive conception of constitutional equality.[56] By contrast, in a polity divided into a majority and a minority linguistic group, identity in disregard of linguistic differences practically resulting in advantages for members of the linguistic majority, would lead to a relatively more exclusive conception of constitutional equality.[57] On the other hand, it is obvious that stress on the metonymic process to highlight differences can serve the purposes of restricting the scope of constitutional equality. Thus, differences relating to gender have been used to deny women equality.[58] Less obvious, perhaps, is that emphasis on differences can also go hand in hand with efforts to expand the scope of equality rights. As examples, one can mention equal catering to the different needs of men and women, or of diverse linguistic groups.

In general, the evolution of equality rights can be reconstructed as comprising three different stages. The first of these is marked by a strong emphasis on the correlation between inequality and difference. Moreover, such correlation may be projected back into a preconstitutional past – such as pre-revolutionary feudalism – or derived metonymically in contrast to a purely formal equation of equality to identity.[59] The second stage is dominated by the correlation between identity and equality, and is reached through heavy reliance on metaphoric processes. The evolution from the first to the second stage is marked by the passage from race-based subordination to colorblindness, and from the tutelage of women to equality between the sexes regardless of gender differences. Finally, the third stage is marked by a more encompassing and finely tuned equality that accounts for differences without exploiting them to institute patterns of domination or subordination. Typical of this third stage would be equality based on the slogan, 'to each according to his or her (different) needs.' Thus, for instance, a woman's constitutional right to have an abortion could be justified as a third stage equality right. Based on a second stage conception of equality, men and women should have the same control over their body. But further contextualization, through a metonymic chain of thoughts, leads to the conclusion that for a woman's control over her body to be comparable to a man's over his, requires awarding her certain different rights, including the right to abortion.

Passage through contextualization from second stage equality as identity, to third stage equality as difference depends for its success on simultaneous preservation and transcendence of certain key identities, consistent with Hegel's concept of *Aufhebung*.[60] Accordingly, the metonymic process leading to equality as difference can move away from the metaphoric identity that locks in second stage equality, but only so far as it does not altogether lose, sight of that identity; or, put in another way, so long as it does not stray from the sphere of influence circumscribed by the identity in question. In short, equality as difference hinges on mutual influence of determinate forms of metaphoric identity and metonymic difference. Once the delicate balance between those determinate forms pulling in opposing directions is upset, however, the movement from identity to difference seems more likely to regress towards first stage equality where difference is paired with inequality, rather than to advance towards third stage equality as difference.[61] Thus, whereas the interplay between metaphor and metonymy plays an essential role in the progression through the three stages of equality, every step must be measured to balance metaphor and metonymy so as to avoid the twin dangers of overly restrictive identity and insufficiently constrained difference.

Granted that developments along the metaphoric path must be correlated to those along the metonymic path, the question remains how trajectories along both these paths can be reined in so as to single out identities and differences best suited to reconcile the self and other within the constitutional subject. In other words, all the terms susceptible of substitution along the metaphoric path have the same exchange value, and the question is, what makes some of these terms have greater use value than others? For their part, all terms along the metonymic path relate to one another in terms of contiguity, and the question becomes, what determines the location of meaning-endowing pauses which render metonymic sequences intelligible? Or, put somewhat differently, what accounts for the punctuation which endows sequences of contiguous terms with determinate meaning?

The selection of particular identities and differences to figure in a given project of constitutional reconstruction is a function of the confluence of structural constraints imposed by the constitutional order, and of the sociocultural heritage of the relevant polity. These structural constraints account for the establishment of a plausible constitutional identity depending on the production of a meaningful narrative through negation, substitution (metaphor), and displacement (metonymy). The sociocultural heritage, on the other hand, furnishes the material which must be reshaped through negation, metaphor, and metonymy; in such a way as to promote both links to, and contrasts with, the preconstitutional and the extraconstitutional self.

To understand how negation, metaphor, and metonymy combine to reshape materials drawn from the sociocultural heritage of the polity into a constitutional identity, it is necessary to first briefly consider the role of constitutional law in a democratic legal order. Even in a democracy, law looms as an alienating intrusion of the other upon the self. Law is by and large experienced as coercive, and submission to its edicts can be likened to bowing to the constraints devised by the superego (Lacan 1966:130). Notwithstanding a law's democratic enactment, and one's support of such enactment, that law's application imposes external constraints on all those who come within its sweep.[62] Inasmuch as constitutional law is law, moreover, it is also constraining and alienating. Inasmuch, however, as constitutional law can be invoked to counter or set aside coercive democratically enacted laws, it also contributes to self-affirmation and to emancipation.[63]

In the last analysis, both the self whose self-affirmation and emancipation are promoted by constitutional law, and the other who pursues self-affirmation through majority backed legislation are meant to be included in the constitutional subject. Accordingly, besides being constraining qua law, the constitution is at once constraining and emancipatory: it constrains all those who come within its sweep as members of the legislating sovereign; and it contributes to the emancipation of the members of the very same group, to the extent that enacted laws further their pursuit or that constitutional law allows them to overcome unjust legal coercion. Consistent with this, moreover, negation, metaphor, and metonymy must combine to reshape materials issued from the sociocultural heritage of the relevant polity so as to construct a constitutional identity at once suited to the constraining and to the emancipatory role of constitutional law.

Remembering that from any given (partial) perspective at any given time and place, constitutional identity emerges predominantly as a lack; negation, metaphor, and metonymy must combine to deal with available materials with a view to overcoming that lack. The precise contours of any particular historically situated lack, depend, however, on the prevailing circumstances. For example, if the grip of a society's sociocultural heritage is too tight, no space may be left for a positive constitutional identity, with the consequence that the first step towards overcoming such lack (of space) would have to consist in negation of (at least part of) the omnipresent sociocultural heritage. If, on the contrary, repudiation of such heritage has been so thorough and systematic that the space for constitutional identity is more than adequate but completely barren, then overcoming the lack would require developing new materials or reincorporating previously discarded ones. But such reincorporation could not be made wholesale, for that would undermine rather than further the quest to overcome the lack within the constitutional subject. Hence, reincorporation may be viewed as a process involving the return of the repressed, (Freud 1970:104), and calling for the deployment of metaphor and metonymy. More precisely, for its return to be successful, the repressed must become sufficiently transformed to endow the constitutional subject with elements of a positive identity, by establishing connections between discarded past materials and new materials through a series of substitutions and displacements.

As constitutional identity must promote reconciliation or equilibrium between self and other; identity and difference; constraint and emancipation; sociocultural heritage and sociocultural renewal or reinvention; the most privileged points along the metaphoric and the metonymic paths are likely to be those best suited – in terms of the particular circumstances involved – to advance most, if not all, of these objectives. Thus, it is over-determination as understood in Freudian theory, (Freud 1965:341–43,

517–18), which lays down the landmarks along the metaphoric and the metonymic paths in constitutional identity. According to Freud, a particular dream-image or symptom is likely to be the product of a confluence of different causes. Freud gives the example of a woman prone to hysterical vomiting, a symptom that provided an (albeit unconscious) expressive outlet to contradictory wishes (*Id*.:609). One of this woman's wishes was to become impregnated as often as possible by as many men as possible; the other, was the punitive counter wish to be so unattractive that no man would have any desire for her. Vomiting, moreover, came to symbolize both these contradictory wishes through substitution and displacement. Along the metaphoric path, vomiting became a substitute for unattractiveness; along the metonymic path, on the other hand, vomiting displaced pregnancy (with which it is closely associated through morning sickness). Vomiting could thus stand out as a hinge linking together the two contradictory wishes along both the metaphoric and metonymic paths. Given its metaphoric and metonymic coordinates, vomiting provided these contradictory wishes with an expressive outlet that remained inaccessible to the woman's consciousness. In short, the confluence of all these factors overdetermined vomiting as a suitable symbolic vehicle for the expression of the woman's contradictory unconscious desires.

A similar process of overdetermination plays a key role in shaping constitutional meaning and in delimiting the key features of the constitutional subject. This process will be extensively examined through close analysis of the salient example provided by the 'reinvention' of tradition in the context of the privacy rights jurisprudence of the U.S. Supreme Court in Chapter 3. But before I turn to overdetermination, I will conclude this chapter by an initial inquiry into the *possibility* of reconciling the singular, the plural and the universal in relation to the constitutional subject and to its identity in light of what the preceding analysis has revealed about them. Whether any *actual* such reconciliation has been achieved or is likely to be achieved within the horizon of plausible constitutional arrangements, on the other hand, is a question that will be postponed till the last chapter, after having more fully fleshed out the constitutional subject and its identity.

2.5 The Constitutional Subject and the Potential Reconciliation of the Singular, the Plural and the Universal

It should by now be clear that the constitutional subject must be both singular and plural. 'We The American People,' We The French People' and 'We The People of India' are all distinct and singular peoples. And this remains true even if each of these 'peoplehoods' is imagined much like each nation as an imagined community or like each constitutional order as an (albeit different kind of) imagined community. Moreover, the singularity of the imagined collectivity that coalesces into the particular people that gives itself a constitution is equally in play whether a distinct fully formed people – such as the German or the Spanish people after World War Two – gives itself a constitution or whether a 'people' for the most part yet to be formed – like the American people of 1787 – gives itself a constitution that will in turn help it imagine itself and unify itself as a people.[64]

The constitutional subject is also plural at least in the sense that within the particular 'We The People' involved, there must be, as we have seen, a plurality of individual regarding interests. In as much as the constitutional subject can be construed or reconstructed as the product of a contract of association, the parties to that contract are bound to have diverse and even antagonistic individual interests. Moreover, in many cases the constitutional subject must emerge in group-regarding pluralist settings. For example, the Swiss polity is made up of a population divided into four distinct linguistic groups, German, French, Italian and Romanch and two principal religious groups, Catholics and Protestants. There are also further group-based subdivisions such as that between French-speaking Protestants living in the Canton of Geneva and the French-speaking Catholics of the Canton of Fribourg. Similarly, in Canada, there are important group-regarding pluralities such as those between Anglophones and Francophones and those between aboriginal people and non-aboriginal Canadians which are enshrined in the Canadian Constitution.[65]

Finally, whereas the constitutional subject is not itself (yet?) universal, its identity certainly appears to be in key respects. Indeed, the 1789 French Declaration of the Rights of Man and of the Citizen and the 1791 American Bill of Rights are couched in universal terms, addressed to human beings and to citizens in general rather than to members of a particular nation, ethnic group or locality. In the French case, it is the rights of 'Man' and not of 'Frenchmen' that are emphasized; in the American case, the freedom of speech and of religion, or the right against arbitrary expropriation of private property[66] of any person regardless of particular attributes or affiliations. Moreover, the 1776 American Declaration of Independence, which lays the foundation of American constitutionalism, states in its famous dictum that 'all men are created equal', not that all Americans or all Christians or all Anglo-Saxons are. More generally, there is a great amount of convergence and overlap regarding the content of Human Rights, the 1789 French Declaration, the 1791 American Bill of Rights, the 1966 UN

Covenant on Civil and Political Rights, the 1951-European Convention of Human Rights (ECHR) and numerous other transnational and national covenants or charters for the protection of fundamental rights and freedoms (Dorsen et al. 2003:2). This convergence towards the universal traces back to the Enlightenment and it is cemented by modern constitutionalism's embrace of the values and goals of the Enlightenment. Stripped to its essentials, the project of the Enlightenment can be said to consist in promoting universal adoption of the rule reason and in insuring protection of liberty and equality for all.

Moreover, from the perspective of the Enlightenment, the rule of reason is supposed to rise above all religious particularism and above all metaphysically grounded conceptions of the good. The Enlightenment's universalism is that of free and equal rights bearing abstract individuals who relate to one another and to their environment pursuant to the dictates of universal reason. And that universal reason has spanned the spectrum that extends from Kant's social contractors[67] to Rawls's hypothetical social contractors operating behind a 'veil of ignorance'.[68]

How the singular, the plural and the universal may actually converge to project a coherent constitutional identity will emerge in the course of the following analysis. And what the nature and scope of such convergence might entail, particularly in terms of the potential for harmonizing national, supra-national and global constitutional orders, will be explored in the last chapter. For now, suffice it to stress that the convergence in question is not likely to derive from laying side by side the singular, the plural and the universal, or by superimposing them one on top of the other. Instead, such convergence will most likely prove to be the product of overdetermination through dynamic interplay among intersecting multidimensional discourses traveling respectively along paths of negation, metaphor and metonymy.

One important axis of convergence is embodied in the already encountered metaphor of the constitution as a social contract that is legitimated both on account of the fact of agreement and on account that its terms conform to reason. Thus, for example, the American Constitution is the product of an actual historical agreement among the framers present at the 1787 Convention in Philadelphia and the ratifiers who partook in subsequent state ratifying conventions as well as of the dictates of reason. The framers and ratifiers symbolically stood for all Americans – though that required negation and suppression of women, African slaves, etc. At the same time, the spirit and actual provisions of the Constitution were deeply steeped in the Enlightenment and its commitment to universal reason. Moreover, the historical singularity and the ideological universality at stake were bound together in the construct (built upon negation, meta-phor and metonymy) of the American people as a new chosen people destined to spread freedom, rational government and democracy (as opposed to the arbitrariness of feudal tyranny) (Smith 1997:35–39).[69]

A different example of the dynamic and the dialectic between the singu-lar and the universal is provided by the French Revolution and the ensuing 1793 Constitution. From an ideological standpoint, the French Revolution and its devotion to reason and to 'liberty, equality and fraternity' comes closest to the ideal of Enlightenment universalism. Not only are the Revolu-tion, the 1789 Declaration and the Constitution embedded in an ideology that is universalist in its aspirations. But also, the third estate, who led the Revolution against the entrenched aristocracy and the clergy, stood as a metaphor for universal man pitted against feudal hierarchy and against the guardians of one religious truth among many who also doubled as the living embodiments of Religion as the negation of Enlightened Reason (Rousseau 1762).

For all its universalist discourse, ideology and aspirations, however, the French Revolution remained embedded in a singular historical and socio-political context. The French Revolution's discourse may be universal, but its language, is singular and unique as well as being one among many[70] (even if it doubled as Europe's *lingua franca* at the time). Furthermore, the aspirations of the French Revolution being universal in scope made it logically conceivable that it could become global in scope. From a practical standpoint however, implementation of the French Revolution's universal-ist agenda loomed impossible beyond the confines of a nation-state. Thus, the French Revolution availed itself of the centralized French state appar-atus consolidated under France's absolute monarch to deploy its consti-tutional project and its political agenda (Berkowitz, Pistor & Richard 2003:173). At the same time, whereas the message of the Revolution may have been addressed to all humanity, its effective reach was limited – by language, space, available institutional design and culture – to a single nation, the nation, which was in part, already formed, and whose full formation would be greatly accelerated by the Revolution's political project and by the foreign wars it provoked.

By a twist of dialectical fate, the third estate, which carried out the Revolution, and which was firmly universalistic in ideology came meto-nymically to embody French nationhood as a singular and distinct one among many. The assault launched by the Revolution against the French monarchy and French nobility promoted the latter to seek their counter-parts in neighboring European monarchies to come to their aid in their struggle against the revolutionaries (Kegley 1998). This led to foreign military interventions which thrust the third estate as defenders of France's national patrimony in order to salvage the implementation of their universalist ideology. In short, the political struggle engendered by the Revolution pitted a transnational allegiance cemented among those bent on safeguarding feudal privileges against a French Third Estate which became a proponent of universal values turned nationalist. Thus, for the French revolutionaries, the quest to impose universalism and the type of constitutional order that is prescribes required a concurrent turn to nationalism. Is that concurrence purely historically contingent or does it essentially circumscribe a French model of constitutionalism originating in the 1789 Revolution?

This question will be extensively explored in connection with the assessment of the viability of transnational constitutionalism in Chapter 8 below. The most immediate concern, however, is to supplement the preceding inquiry concerning the broad outlines of the dynamic that animates the constitutional subject and that channels its relationship to its identity with a closer look at some of the most salient particulars involved in constitutional identity production. Two individual examples with salient implications will be examined in some detail in Part Two of the book: the reinvention of tradition in the American jurisprudence on unenumerated fundamental constitutional rights; and, constitution-making in post-Franco Spain.

PART TWO

Producing Constitutional Identity

Reinventing Tradition Through Constitutional Interpretation: The Case of Unenumerated Rights in the United States

3.1 Building and Differentiating Constitutional Identity

The production of constitutional identity through over determination at the interstices of discursive paths forged by negation, metaphor and metonymy occurs both at the level of the constitutional subject as a whole and at that of its manifold particular instantiations. In both cases, the identity involved is elaborated both with and against the other relevant identities discussed above, such as national identity.[1] Moreover, not only can constitutional identity draw on other identities, but the latter can also rework materials found in the former. For example, devotion to what seems to be by far the most extensive freedom of speech rights found in any constitutional democracy is not only a salient feature of American constitutional identity. It is also one of America's foremost cultural symbols (Bollinger 1986:7), transcending its original constitutional confines (*Id.*:5). Devotion to the First Amendment, therefore, is a constitutive element of America's national identity over and above being in its broad protection of free speech a pillar of American constitutional identity. More generally, constitutional concerns and constitutional identity may bear a closer or a more distant relationship to political life and national identity, depending on the polity involved.[2]

Whether the relationship between constitutional and national identity is closer or more distant, it is always the product of a dialectical process involving both negation and incorporation. National and constitutional self are but two complementary dimensions of the overall self that is meant to provide unity and coherence to the polity in which it dwells. Depending on whether negation or incorporation *appears* to predominate, constitutional identity may *seem* more or less central in relation to national identity. But, appearances may sometimes be deceiving. It may well be that a constitutional order plays a key role in fashioning or sustaining a corresponding national identity, or vice versa, and that the interplay between negation and incorporation works in ways that conceal the import of the role in question.

All constitutional provisions, including those directly imported from foreign constitutions bear traces of extra-constitutional identities either in their articulation or in their application (Rosenfeld and Sajo 2006). These traces, moreover, are not always easy to disentangle from fragments of constitutional identity with which they become dynamically intertwined. For example, the Israeli Supreme Court has embraced American First Amendment doctrine to deal with racist speech, but has reached diametrically opposite results in its racist speech adjudications (Jacobsohn 1993:Ch. 6). Such speech is extensively protected under American constitutional jurisprudence[3] whereas it is pretty systematically banned under its Israeli counterpart (*Id.*). That difference, which seems puzzling at the levels of constitutional identity, is readily explained at the level of national identity. Indeed, the U.S. is individualistically pluralistic, tending to abstract the individual from the group, and it has experienced diffused intolerance spreading over a multiplicity of targeted groups, with the consequence that no single group has borne more than a fraction of the overall threat (*Id.*).[4] Israel, in contrast, is dominantly communally pluralistic, and it has traditionally experienced concentrated intolerance focused primarily on a single group, its Arab minority (*Id.*).

Given these national differences, the doctrinal convergence between the two countries is all the more puzzling in view of American exceptionalism in the constitutional treatment of racist speech. Unlike the U.S. most other democracies do not afford constitutional protection to racist speech (Rosenfeld 2003:1542–1554). Accordingly, it would appear that it would have been more natural for Israel to emulate Canadian, French or German free speech doctrine rather than American doctrine regarding racist speech. Nevertheless, upon closer analysis, Israel's embrace of American doctrine was by no means arbitrary. It was instead an attempt to overcome, or at least to cope with, the tension between concurrent democratic and anti-democratic tendencies and between inclusivist and exclusivist proclivities (Jacobsohn 1993:Ch. 6). In short, by importing American free speech doctrine but by interpreting it in a diametrically opposed way, Israel strived to project a constitutional identity that at the same time embraced tolerance and democracy, protected communal integrity, and negated without hope of effectively dislodging intolerant and antidemocratic tendencies firmly engrained in the national psyche.

To obtain a better grasp of how the various relevant identities interact and intertwine, it is helpful to focus on the elaboration of constitutional doctrine through judicial interpretation. Moreover, in this connection, the judicial treatment of unenumerated constitutional rights under the U.S. Constitution provides a particularly telling example of the work of overdeterminaiton at the interstices of discourses of negation, metaphor and metonymy. Unenumerated rights loom as the most unbound and open-ended. Yet, precisely because of this, they have the greatest need for anchoring and binding within the confines of constitutional identity and beyond. Indeed, whereas a sufficiently determinate enumerated right might be interpreted authoritatively, at least to a significant extent, against the grain of relevant extra-constitutional identities, that seems highly implausible in the case of unenumerated rights. Because they seem far less anchored in the constitutional firmament, unenumerated rights must forge links to realms that extend beyond that carved out by the constitution. In the case of American unenumerated rights, those links are to historical nationally grounded traditions. But as we shall see, these traditions end up being invented or reinvented rather than merely found in the annals of the nation's history and culture.

3.2 Setting American Unenumerated Rights Against Tradition

American unenumerated rights derive principally from two provisions within the Constitution. The first of these is the Ninth Amendment (1791) which provides that 'the enumeration in the Constitution of certain rights shall not be constructed to deny or disparage others retained by the people'. As part of the American Bill of Rights, the Ninth Amendment indicates that listing of a number of explicit rights within that Bill is not meant to exclude the constitutionalization of other rights. Moreover, by characterizing these latter unenumerated rights as being 'retained by the people', the Ninth Amendment suggests that they pre-exist the Bill of Rights and are hence grounded in tradition.[5]

The second provision of the U.S. Constitution that has been invoked in defense of unenumerated rights is the Due Process Clause of the Fourteenth Amendment (1868), which provides that no state shall 'deprive any person of life, liberty or property without due process of law'.[6] The Fourteenth Amendment is a much less obvious source of unenumerated rights than is the Ninth Amendment. As we shall see, on some interpretations, the Due Process Clause merely furnishes procedural guarantees and as such does not afford any justification for unenumerated rights. On other interpretations though, the Due Process Clause has substantive content and it does accordingly protect unenumerated rights.

The extensive use of tradition in American Due Process jurisprudence provides a good example of the role of overdetermination in shaping constitutional meaning. Viewed from a broad perspective, tradition's role in relation to Due Process emerges with the aid of overdetermination, as a particularly well-suited semantic vehicle to bind together various symbolic strands extracted respectively through negation, metaphor, and metonymy. As will be demonstrated below, tradition can at once serve to make negation determinate, and to frame suitable coordinates along the metaphoric and metonymic axes.

As already mentioned, tradition is important in all modern constitutional settings, as it is bound to figure prominently in the crucial relationship between the preconstitutional and the constitutional self.[7] Moreover, whereas no constitutional regime can completely do away with tradition, one can distinguish generally between two different approaches: engrafting a set of constitutional norms on an ongoing tradition; or, replacing the order framed by tradition with a new order defined by the constitution. Although, as we shall see below, the U.S. Constitution did not attempt a complete break with preexisting tradition,[8] it certainly provides a clear example of the second of these approaches. Indeed, in the U.S., the Constitution forms a centerpiece of national identity rather than a mere adjunct to it (Jacobsohn 1993:9,109). This is not surprising, since as a nation built upon successive waves of immigration, the U.S. encompasses a wide diversity of national and ethnic traditions, none of which are representative of the polity as a whole. Thus, whereas it is not difficult to visualize French or German identity without reference to their respective constitutions, the same would not apply to the U.S.

To the extent that the U.S. Constitution is set against tradition – or, in other words, is the tradition – it needs to reincorporate rejected traditions in developing a positive identity. Thus, whereas negation of tradition is constitutive of not only American constitutional identity, but also of American national identity; the negation of this negation – in the form of reintegration of elements of the rejected tradition – likewise forms an integral part of the (re)construction of the identity of the constitutional subject. Moreover, the negation of tradition, and the negation of this negation represent two distinct, successive, logical moments within a scheme of dialectical deconstruction and reconstruction. But, it does not follow from this that the two cannot operate simultaneously within the time frame delimited by a particular constitutional practice. Actually, at least in some cases, the two must operate simultaneously, which requires that coherent constitutional meaning be extracted from contradictory drives. This, in turn, is made possible by distancing the tradition to be reincorporated from the discarded tradition through substitution and displacement.

What is particularly remarkable about the American Due Process jurisprudence as it pertains to liberty rights is that tradition itself has come to occupy, through overdetermination, the place of both countertraditional constitutional negation, and neotraditional negation of the negation. Constitutional liberty rights are fundamentally countertraditional, inasmuch as claims to liberty in a democratic polity amount to assertions of entitlement to deviate from majority backed norms and values. Thus, for example, in a democracy, freedom of speech is much less necessary to protect the views of the majority than the views that the majority rejects as unworthy or repugnant. Constitutional liberty, however, cannot be unlimited for that would undermine the very notion of constitutional order. Accordingly, constitutional liberty is necessarily subject to certain constraints, and these constraints are of primarily two kinds: structural constraints inherent in constitutionalism and the constitutional order,[9] and constraints derived from the sociocultural heritage of the polity.[10]

Due Process liberty rights are particularly open-ended since they are stated in such broad and general terms as to leave ample room for diverse, and even contradictory, interpretations. Thus, Due Process liberty has been interpreted variously as being procedural rather than substantive;[11] as encompassing substantive economic liberty rights;[12] and, as encompassing substantive personal liberty rights relating, among others, to marriage, procreation, and intimate associations.[13] Consistent with this, the identity of liberty rights under the Due Process Clause can be said, quite literally, to amount to a lack only susceptible of determinate content through reconstruction.[14]

To illustrate how tradition factors into dealing with the lack circumscribed by the Due Process Clause, let us take a closer look at reconstructions of liberty rights as substantive, in relationships of intimate association. In *Griswold* v. *Connecticut*,[15] the Supreme Court invoked tradition to uphold liberty and privacy rights within the marital relationship in the face of a state's prohibition against the use of contraceptives. Viewed closely, however, the invocation of tradition to strike down a prohibition against contraceptives as unconstitutional is quite problematic. On the one hand, the very constitutionalization of liberty and privacy interests is to an important degree countertraditional. Indeed, even if these interests were actually protected in the preconstitutional polity, their constitutionalization transported them onto a whole new plane. Prior to constitutionalization, these interests were prey to religious traditions, historically rooted mores, the will of political majorities, or the edicts of a monarch. After constitutionalization, in contrast, these interests become severed from all these dependencies thus standing in opposition to their roots in tradition. In short, even if they can be traced back to tradition, but for the negation of such tradition, the liberty and privacy interests in question could not acquire a meaningful constitutional dimension.

On the other hand, the neotraditional aspect of the liberty and privacy interests vindicated in *Griswold* is also quite problematic. The specific liberty and privacy interest recognized as constitutionally protected in *Griswold* is the right of a married couple to use contraceptives. But, this is not a traditionally protected interest. Indeed, whereas respect for the 'sanctity' of marriage was well within America's tradition, martial use of contraceptives was not (Johnson 2006:1619). Accordingly, it would undoubtedly shock a vast majority of America's preconstitutional ancestors who were deeply steeped in the Judeo-Christian tradition to learn that uninhibited use of contraceptives, even if only within the marital relationship, should be considered as an integral part of that tradition.

Tradition does occupy a central position in the constitutional jurisprudence articulated in *Griswold*, but it is by no means a simple or straightforward one. In its projection towards the past, *Griswold*, in fact negates (by constitutionalizing) a tradition that was; in its projection towards the future – that is, a future at least from the vantage point of the constitution-making generation – by contrast, Griswold makes into a tradition something that was not. Moreover, to understand how tradition can come to symbolize simultaneously both the uprooting of established traditions and the invention of new ones, it is necessary to take a closer look at the workings of metaphor and metonymy in the Supreme Court's Due Process liberty jurisprudence.

3.3 The Metaphoric and Metonymic Dimensions of Tradition

The metaphoric and metonymic connotations of tradition become evident in the debate over the appropriate level of abstraction at which a tradition may be appropriated to sustain the constitutionalization of a particular liberty interest. This debate sharply divided the justices in *Michael H. v. Gerald D.*[16] In that case, a genetic father demanded visitation rights to see his child notwithstanding a state statute that established a conclusive presumption that a child born to a woman living with her husband is a child of the marriage. In a closely divided decision, the Supreme Court refused to recognize a constitutional right to visitation for genetic fathers under the circumstances of the case. Writing for a plurality, Justice Scalia declared that a relevant tradition had to be taken at 'the most specific level,'[17] and since he could find no tradition affording out-of-wedlock fathers visitation rights to see their illegitimate children, recognizing a constitutionally protected liberty right under the circumstances was unwarranted.[18]

Justice Brennan, however, took sharp issue with Justice Scalia's approach, noting that it deprived the notion of tradition of any independent constitutional meaning. Indeed, in Justice Brennan's view, the only traditions that would be vindicated under Justice Scalia's criterion would be those already protected by legislative majorities, for which constitutional protection would be merely redundant.[19] Instead, Justice Brennan indicated that the relevant interest involved in the case was 'that of a parent and child in their relationship with each other';[20] thus, construing the 'tradition' at a relatively high level of abstraction, which made his proposed constitutionalization of the liberty interest involved far from superfluous. In direct response to Justice Scalia, moreover, Justice Brennan argued that:

> the plurality ignores the kind of society in which our Constitution exists. We are not an assimilative, homogeneous society, but a facilitative pluralistic one . . . Even if we can agree . . . that 'family' and 'parenthood' are part of the good life, it is absurd to assume that we can agree on the content of those terms and destructive to pretend that we do. In a community such as ours, 'liberty' must include the freedom not to conform.[21]

Embedded, therefore, in Justice Brennan's abstract notion of tradition, is the 'tradition' not to conform to tradition; or in other words, countertradition as a constitutional (as opposed to a preconstitutional) 'tradition.'

Justice Scalia's approach is predominantly metonymic, whereas Justice Brennan's is above all metaphoric. Indeed, Justice Scalia contextualizes the disputed liberty interest, and by refusing to draw more general and more abstract inferences from the invoked tradition, he exalts context and contiguity at the expense of parallels and similarities. Overemphasis along the metonymic path, however, not only makes the constitutionalization of tradition ultimately pointless, but also eventually undermines the very concept of tradition. In the quest for utmost specificity, every occurrence would be given such an exhaustive specification, that no two contiguous occurrences could ever emerge as continuous, thus undermining the very basis upon which the possibility of building any tradition rests. Or, to put it somewhat differently, if all the differences, no matter how minute, between two occurrences had to be unearthed, it would become increasingly difficult to perceive any similarity between them. And without threads of similarity, there can be no tradition.

Engaging a tradition at higher levels of abstraction, as does Justice Brennan, on the other hand, requires extracting similarities that transcend the particular contexts in which they are inscribed. What ties together the traditional conception of the family unit, according to which the father exercises control over his children born in wedlock, and the genetic father and his child in *Michael H.*, is the relation of parent to child shorn of all its specific contextual determinations. By traveling along the metaphoric path, one can seek to distill the essence of a tradition, and thus adapt that tradition to changing circumstances. This process of metaphoric distillation requires decontextualization, and hence ascent to higher levels of abstraction. But as decontextualization becomes more radical, and hence as abstraction reaches the highest levels, metaphoric substitution becomes increasingly unconstrained. As a consequence of this, the metaphoric condensation that reveals the 'essence' of a tradition is so removed from any solid contextual moorings as to become arbitrary. Thus, what is the essence of the tradition involved in *Michael H.*? Is it the protection of the integrity of the family unit? Or, is it the protection of the relationship between parent and child (even beyond the bounds of the traditional family unit)? For those who would opt for the latter, the former could be characterized as a substitute that was appropriate for a time, unlike our own, when paternity could not be established with sufficient scientific probability to avoid uncertainty and disputes concerning who was the real father of a child born to a married woman who had had an affair with a putative genetic father.[22] On the other hand, for proponents of the position that integrity of the family unit as such constitutes the essence of the relevant tradition, extending parental rights beyond the bounds of that unit cannot count as an acceptable substitute. To reach that conclusion, moreover, these latter proponents must disregard – that is, abstract from – the current proliferation of intimate association arrangements that go beyond the bounds of the historically recognized family unit. Thus, by taking different journeys through the metaphoric path, one can distill different essences from the same tradition, but none of these seems any more compelling than any other.

Ultimately, elevating a tradition to the highest possible levels of abstraction is as destructive of tradition as is reducing it to its utmost specificity.

Indeed, unconstrained substitution or distillation makes it possible to extract such a broad array of competing meanings from the same tradition as to reduce such tradition to an empty placeholder to be filled in according to the predilections of its current proponents. Consistent with this, traditions cannot be either exhaustively contextualized or thoroughly abstracted, but must operate at some intermediate level at which contextual factors constrain the process of distilling and adapting the essence of a particular tradition, without blurring the distinction between what is enduring (and hence context-transcending) and what is context-specific about that tradition. In short, the very notion of tradition requires the selection of suited coordinates along both the metaphoric and the metonymic axes.

3.4 Reinventing Tradition Through Overdetermination: From the Sanctity of Marriage to the Dignity of Homosexual Sex

To fully appreciate how the reinvention of tradition through over-determination along the paths of negation, metaphor and metonymy has endowed the American jurisprudence on unenumerated rights with determinate content, it is necessary briefly to retrace the path carved out by *Griswold* and its progeny. As already noted, the tradition constitutionalized in *Griswold* is the sanctity of marriage. That tradition, in turn, has been invoked first to afford constitutional protection to use of contraceptives by married couples (*Griswold*) and later by heterosexual non-married individuals (*Eisenstadt* v. *Baird*);[23] next to afford constitutional protection to the right to obtain an abortion (*Roe* v. *Wade*);[24] and finally, successively to deny constitutional protection to homosexual sex among consenting adults (*Bowers* v. *Hardwick*)[25] and then, in a reversal, to grant such protection (*Lawrence* v. *Texas*).[26]

On the surface, it seems totally incongruous that the sanctity of marriage, a tradition deeply steeped in Judeo-Christian values, should provide the source of legitimation for constitutional rights to contraception, non-martial sex, abortion and homosexual sex. Further analysis reveals however, that the tradition given constitutional dimension is a reinvented one that incorporates (previously deconstructed) elements of preconstitutional traditions and that integrates these elements into its logic. Consistent with this, moreover, *Griswold* and its progeny can be harmonized into a coherent narrative that casts them as the products of a single dynamic and evolving tradition.

3.4.1 Griswold and the Metonymic Path from Marriage to Contraception

In *Griswold* itself, the key move is a metonymic one: contraception by a displacement comes to symbolize the sanctity and privacy of the marital bond of spouses sharing intimate moments sheltered within their own home. Furthermore, what is perhaps the Court's most stinging argument against the legitimacy of state regulation of marital use of contraceptives is also stated in metonymic terms:

> Would we allow the police to search the sacred precincts of marital bedrooms for telltale signs of the use of contraceptives? The very idea is repulsive to the notions of privacy surrounding the marriage relationship.[27]

A police search of the marital bedroom is indeed more repulsive than a prohibition against the use of contraceptives, thus rendering the metonymic displacement from prohibition to enforcement particularly effective from a rhetorical standpoint.

This double metonymic move from marriage to contraception and from the latter to violation of intimate privacy in search for evidence of illicit use of contraceptives is supplemented by a metaphoric argument built upon the image of privacy under threat due to police intrusion. In the very next sentence following the passage cited above, the Court states, referring to marriage, that 'we deal with a right of privacy older than the Constitution and the Bill of Rights'.[28] Thus, privacy as freedom from police intrusion in one's home and privacy within marriage to decide whether to procreate coalesce into a more abstract right projected into the past that preceded the 1791 Bill of Rights and the 1787 Constitution – in short a pre-constitutional past bereft of any *constitutional* rights.[29]

Not only is the tradition that legitimates the right to marital privacy derived through the conjunction of negation, metaphor and metonymy, but so is the right to privacy itself. There being no explicit textual basis for that right in the U.S. Constitution, the Court in *Griswold* sought to enshrine it by means of three distinct, but related, interpretive approaches respectively detailed in the majority and concurring opinions. The majority opinion emphasizes that many of the rights explicitly protected by the Bill of Rights contained elements of privacy or constitutionalized particular forms of privacy. Thus, the First Amendment which protects freedom of conscience and freedom of association and the Fifth Amendment right against self-incrimination contain elements of privacy. Furthermore, the Third Amendment, which protects against the quartering of soldiers in private homes during times of peace, and the Fourth Amendment, which protects against unreasonable government searches and seizures, affords constitutional protection to some kinds of privacy within a person's home. Based on this, moreover, the Court's majority infers that a general right to privacy emerges at the penumbra of the rights that encompass elements, or specific kinds, of privacy.[30]

The move from a right to its penumbra clearly occurs along a metonymic path. The alignment of privacy in general and of elements and specific kinds of privacy, on the other hand, unfolds alongside a metaphorical path. As encompassed within a penumbra, the general right to privacy is contiguous to the particular instantiations explicitly constitutionalized in the Bill of Rights. At the same time, the general right of privacy has in essence something crucial in common with the particular instances of privacy explicitly protected by the Bill of Rights. And what links general privacy and particular privacy is a metaphoric bond that allows for common identification at a certain level of abstraction.

The concurring opinion by Justice Goldberg, for its part, relies heavily on the Ninth Amendment in order to justify the right to privacy.[31] As we have seen, the Ninth Amendment provides that the rights explicitly mentioned in the Bill of Rights are not exclusive and that they are not intended to 'deny or disparage' other rights 'retained by the people'. This raises two important questions: Which are these other rights? And how does one find that out?

Justice Goldberg's answers are essentially that the right to marital privacy is so deeply engrained in American society that to exclude it would render the Ninth Amendment meaningless;[32] and that the basis for that last conclusion is not judicial subjectivism, but reliance on whether marital privacy is so rooted in the 'traditions and [collective] conscience' of the American people as to be 'ranked as fundamental'.[33] Justice Goldberg does indeed answer this latter query in the affirmative, and treats the answer in question as being self-evident. Accordingly, Goldberg's justification for the constitutional enshrinement of the unenumerated right of marital privacy seems entirely circular.

Beneath the surface, however, many contradictions and paradoxes surround the rooting of a right to privacy in the Ninth Amendment. First, viewed on the whole, bringing together enumerated and unenumerated rights in the Bill of Rights seems paradoxical in one of two ways. Either both enumerated and unenumerated rights are deeply steeped in the country's pre-constitutional (and most likely extra-constitutional) conscience and tradition, and then it is not clear what accounts for the division into enumerated and unenumerated. Or, only the unenumerated rights are deeply rooted in the country's pre-constitutional tradition, but then why lump together rights that are not pre-constitutionally grounded with those that are.

The first of these two hypotheses is logically plausible, but inconsistent with history. Logically, all rights may have been similarly pre-constitutionally grounded, with several possible explanations for the enumeration of some, but not of others. One explanation is that it is simply impossible to be exhaustive and that the enumerated rights are illustrative of the entire set of rights meant to be included. Another explanation is that the enumerated rights are those thought to be most vulnerable to government violation or abuse absent explicit reference.

From a historical standpoint, however, at least some of the enumerated rights cannot be realistically grounded in pre-constitutional tradition regardless of which plausible historical period is used as the frame of reference for purposes of ascertaining the relevant pre-constitutional traditions. Indeed, whether one focuses on 1776 to 1791, from American independence to adoption of the Bill of Rights, or on the preceding colonial era, or even on English history going back to precolonial days, at least some of the enumerated rights in the Bill of Rights cannot be historically derived from any relevant pre-constitutional tradition. One such right is that guaranteed by the Establishment Clause of the First Amendment against the imposition of an official state religion. Because some state constitutions in the United States provided for an official state religion much as England had long had (Albert 2006), the Establishment Clause clearly looms as counter-traditional. More generally, whereas some right to marital privacy may be readily traced back to pre-colonial England, many rights enumerated in the Bill of Rights, such as freedom of speech and freedom of the press rights, cannot. Indeed, it is precisely against British restraints on speech and the press, and to differentiate the newly independent nation from its former colonial master, that First Amendment rights were constitutionally enshrined (Van Alstyne 2002).

Consistent with the preceding analysis, it appears that the conjunction of enumerated and unenumerated rights in the context of the American Bill of Rights lumps together traditional and counter-traditional rights. This implies that the constitutional order was constructed in part through negation of tradition, and in part through incorporation if it. Or, in other words, that constitutional construction involved at the same time a selective rejection of the pre-constitutional past, and a selective incorporation in an almost completely unmediated form – the only palpably mediation being the Ninth Amendment's 'lifting' the preconstitutional tradition of marital privacy from the totality of such traditions and placing it side by side with the counter-traditional rights created by the Bill of Rights.

Furthermore, whereas as viewed shortly after adoption of the Bill of Rights the Ninth Amendment emerges as catalyst for the blending of pre-constitutional tradition and constitutional counter-tradition, by 1965 when *Griswold* was decided, enumerated rights such as those protected by the First Amendment had become, as we have seen, part of tradition. They formed part not only of America's constitutional identity, but also if its national identity.[34]

One may think that what was a fortuitous, or even an incongruous, amalgamation of tradition and countertradition in 1791 had become an unproblematic blending of traditions by 1965. This is in some sense true in as much as the American constitutional order and the nation's identity remain closely linked. There is constitutionalization of the (pre- or extra-constitutional) national (e.g., marital privacy) and nationalization of the constitutional (e.g., the First Amendment) which work to bring together national traditions and constitutional ones. Accordingly, one may be lulled into believing that by 1965, and in terms of America's overall self-perception, national and constitutional identity converged around a set of widely shared overlapping traditions which were no longer clearly distinguishable in function of their respective origins.

That latter impression would be misleading, however, as should become obvious if one focuses on the fact that the unenumerated right of marital privacy recognized in *Griswold* ultimately stands metonymically for the right that was actually constitutionalized in that case, namely the right to use contraceptives within the marital relationship. At the very least, this indicates that the pre-constitutional tradition incorporated into an unenumerated constitutional right via the Ninth Amendment is not a virtually unmediated one directly incorporated into the constitutional order. The tradition in question is, instead, an evolving one, one that grows out of its pre-constitutional origins rather than enduring nearly identical to it.

One may object that what is essential in *Griswold*, and in particular in Justice Goldberg's concurring opinion, is the recognition of marital privacy as an unenumerated constitutional right. On that view, the right to contraceptives figures merely as being incident to marital privacy, and as such, is only important in *Griswold* as an a means for underscoring the constitutional status of marital privacy.

This last objection may appear sound if *Griswold* is taken in isolation, but becomes inapposite as soon as *Griswold* is projected back into its relevant past and forward into its relevant future. Regarding the past, as already noted, it is highly improbable that the Judeo-Christian pre-constitutional tradition of marital privacy did encompass a right to artificial contraceptives.[35] From the standpoint of *Griswold's* future, on the other hand, marital privacy seems more incident to the right to contraceptives than vice versa. Indeed, in 1972 with *Griswold* as a precedent, the Court recognized in *Eisenstadt* a constitutionally protected individual right to the use of contraceptives in the context of non-marital heterosexual sex. Furthermore, in *Roe* v. *Wade* decided a year after *Eisenstadt*, *Griswold* was put to use as a precedent to support recognition of a right to abortion, in a case brought by a non-married pregnant woman seeking the invalidation of laws criminalizing abortion.[36] In this context abortion derives metonymically from contraception, either as a means to the same end after conception has occurred, or as that which stands next to contraception in a line that extends from sexual abstinence to giving birth in relation to the decision of whether or not to procreate. Moreover, *Roe* v. *Wade* may be in line with *Griswold* and *Eisentadt* in relation to the private decision of whether or not procreate, but it clearly parts company with those two precedents when it comes to the intimacy of spatial privacy. As mentioned above, the majority in *Griswold* refers to the sanctity of the marital bedroom.[37] In contrast, as emphasized by (then) Justice Rehnquist in his dissent in *Roe*, an abortion performed by a physician in a hospital lacks the spatial intimacy and exclusivity of the marital bedroom.[38]

Projecting *Griswold* further into future beyond *Roe*, one comes upon the two cases that dealt with whether homosexual sex among consenting adults is constitutionally protected. In *Bowers* v. *Hardwick*,[39] the Court held 5–4 that it was not, and seventeen years later in *Lawrence* v. *Texas*,[40] the Court reversed itself in a 6–3 decision. What is remarkable about these two decisions, for our immediate purposes, is that besides reaching diametrically opposed conclusions as to what the tradition enshrined in *Griswold* implies in the context of homosexual sex, they stretch the tradition in question beyond marriage or procreation. Indeed, although *Lawrence* was decided against an intense legal and political struggle over same sex marriage – and may conceivably one day count as a precedent for recognition of a constitutional right to same sex marriage[41] – neither it nor *Bowers* focuses on the question of same-sex marriage in connection with their evaluation of constitutional status of homosexual sex.[42]

The metonymical chain that links *Griswold* to *Eisenstadt* and to *Roe* does not therefore extend to *Bowers* or *Lawrence*. What does bind all these cases together, however, is the expression of a shared identity along a metaphorical axis. Indeed, all these cases involve different manifestations of a right to be free from state interference in relation to intimate sexual association among consenting adults. This is obviously true of *Griswold*, *Eisenstadt*, *Bowers* and *Lawrence*, which all concern sexual relationships.

But this is also true, though less obviously so, of *Roe*, which involves dealing with the aftermath of a sexual relationship and thus with the consequences of intimate sexual association.

To complete the picture of *Griswold* thus far elaborated by reference to the Court's majority opinion and to Justice Goldberg's concurring opinion, it is necessary briefly to consider Justice Harlan's concurring opinion. Justice Harlan bases his support for the constitutional right of a married couple to use contraceptives not on any provision of the Bill of Rights but exclusively on the Due Process Clause of the Fourteenth Amendment. Ascribing a substantive content to that clause, Justice Harlan found that prohibiting the use of contraceptives by married couples violates 'basic values implicit in the concept of ordered liberty'.[43] In Justice Harlan's view, moreover, due process liberty requires striking a balance between the liberty of the individual and the demands of organized society. That balance, according to Justice Harlan,

> is the balance stuck by this country having regard to what history teaches are the traditions from which it developed as well as the traditions from which it broke. That tradition is a living thing.[44]

Justice Harlan goes on to specify that what is most fundamental to the tradition of liberty in the English speaking world is the privacy of the home, and 'the home derives its preeminence as the seat of family life'. Finally, marital privacy is at the very core of family life.[45]

In spite of his reliance on the liberty of the individual and the privacy of the home, Justice Harlan goes at great pains to explain that due process liberty does not forbid criminalizing adultery, homosexuality, fornication or incest regardless of how privately or deeply within the precincts of a person's home they are practiced.[46] Viewed from the standpoint of *Lawrence*, which has become an integral part of *Griswold's* progeny, Justice Harlan's statement about homosexuality seems incongruous, inconsistent and hard to reconcile with the relevant tradition as reinterpreted in *Lawrence*.

There are points of convergence in the respective concurring opinions of Justices Goldberg and Harlan, as well as points of divergence. They both envision the right to marital privacy as an unenumerated one based on tradition. They differ, however, as to the source of that right, Justice Goldberg finding it in the Ninth Amendment, Justice Harlan, in the Fourteenth. This latter difference is not merely technical. The Ninth Amendment explicitly refers to unenumerated rights whereas the Due Process Clause of the Fourteenth Amendment does not.

As already mentioned, endowing the Due Process Clause with substantive content is highly controversial.[47] At the very least some plausible link must be drawn between the procedural implications of the Clause – 'liberty' shall not be 'deprive[d]' 'without due process of law' – and the conclusion that the Clause *must* be given some substantive content – that no matter what 'process' is accorded, there is some subset of liberties of which no person can be deprived.

There is also an apparent divergence between the two justices' conception of tradition as it relates to the unenumerated right of marital privacy. For Justice Goldberg as discussed above the tradition invoked seems to be the pre-constitutional (and extra-constitutional) tradition that played a fundamental role prior to the adoption of the Bill of Rights.[48] For Justice Harlan, in contrast, the relevant tradition is, in part, the same pre-constitutional tradition invoked by Justice Goldberg – the former does indeed speak of the traditions of the 'English-speaking world'.[49] But at the same time, Justice Harlan refers to the 'traditions' from which the United States 'broke' as well as to those 'from which it developed', and adds that 'tradition' is a living thing. In other words, from the standpoint of the Due Process Clause, as Justice Hardan sees it, pre-constitutional tradition must be blended with constitutional counter-tradition to yield the 'living' tradition that undergrids unenumerated 'liberty' rights. If Justice Goldberg's conception of the relevant tradition seems more logically coherent, Justice Harlan's seems more historically plausible.

Just as the majority's and Justice Goldberg's opinion rely on negation, metaphor and metonymy to derive the right to privacy enshrined in *Griswold*, so does Justice Harlan's opinion. Indeed, recourse to a 'living' tradition requires negation of (part of) pre-constitutional tradition as well as metaphorical weaving together strings of traditional elements that change over time. Furthermore, to ground the Due Process liberty at stake in *Griswold*, Justice Harlan moves metonymically from the liberty to do as one pleases within one's home, to the centrality of family life within the home, and to the privileged position of the marital relationship within the ambit of family life. Justice Harlan does also rely on one final metonymic link between marital privacy and the use of contraceptives by the married couple, but does so with seeming reluctance. The relationship of contiguity between the home, the family, and the married couple is one that is strongly held together by the pre-and extra-constitutional traditions of English-speaking peoples. On the other hand, the next relationship of contiguity along the metonymical axis between the married couple and contraceptives is not so clearly steeped in the same tradition. It may be perhaps safely integrated at the interstices of the tradition and counter-tradition that molds Due Process liberty, but it also opens the door to further travel along the metonymical axis, leading through close relationships of contiguity to adultery, homosexuality and incest. Justice Harlan is all too aware of this, and he hence seeks to slam the door on these further metonymic moves while treating the inclusion of contraceptives as borderline and the metonymic progression from the married couple to contraceptives as the last admissible one, and that barely so.[50]

To recapitulate all three of the *Griswold* opinions examined above make use of a combination of negation, metaphor and metonymy, and the two concurring opinions do so to a large extent to delimit a relevant tradition. All three opinions, moreover, lead to paradoxes and contradictions. Their use of negation seems at times arbitrary and the levels of abstraction reached through their metaphorical reasoning as well as the degrees of contiguity validated by their metonymic processes of interpretation seem underdetermined. In other words, one may well sense that the result in *Griswold* is constitutionally sound – in the sense of comporting with the basic tenets of constitutionalism – but that the series of metaphoric and metonymic arguments that are supposed to lend support to that result only do so partially.

Specifically, the most glaring shortcomings of the three opinions start with the majority opinion's extraction of a general right to privacy encompassing marital privacy from particular rights constitutionalizing limited concrete privacy interests. Thus, the interest in not being forced to testify against oneself protected by the Fifth Amendment or the interest against quartering soldiers in private homes during times of peace, may or may not imply a general a more general broadly encompassing right of privacy. The majority opinion, however, does not provide sufficient support for lifting the general right from its more limited particular counterparts. Justice Goldberg's opinion, in turn, cannot reconcile the logic and the history of the tradition that he relies on. Finally, Justice Harlan fails to draw a cogent and systematic enough distinction between relevant traditions and relevant counter-traditions to dispel the impression that his endorsement of a right to contraceptives while at the same time condoning punishment for homosexuality is ultimately arbitrary.

These deficiencies can be overcome, and reinvented tradition refashioned, to transform the above-mentioned inconsistencies and underdeterminations into a convergent and overdetermined justification for the rights vindicated in *Griswold*. The two principal sources of support for purposes of arriving at such justification, moreover, are Lockean liberalism and natural rights theory, on the one hand, and the trend towards greater individualism and a more permissive society that gripped the United States in the 1960's, on the other. Both of these sources are extra-constitutional and Lockean philosophy is also pre-constitutional. Furthermore, though there are philosophical traditions, and though many of these can be linked to particular countries or cultures – e.g., Descartes to France or Rawls to the United States – a philosophy's appeal is supposed to be based on the persuasiveness of the theses it propounds and on the arguments it garners in the latter's support rather than on that philosophy's place in a polity's tradition. Finally, though there are conceivable links between Lockean liberalism and 1960's style permissiveness, the latter cannot be directly derived from the former. The links in question, therefore, require a reinterpretation and a readaptation of Locke's own views.

3.4.2 The Lockean Gloss on Griswold

The extent of the influence of Locke's ideas on the framers of the 1787 American Constitution, the 1791 Bill of Rights and the 1868 Fourteenth Amendment is a matter of dispute (Farber and Sherry 2005:5–6, 8, 368) but it is incontrovertible that it was considerable (*Id*). For present purposes, suffice it to focus on Locke's theory of inalienable natural rights and on his liberal individualism. Both of these are grounded on his broad conception of property, which encompasses not only lands, goods and other possessions, but also an individual's life, liberty, human capacities and the fruits of his labor (Locke 1690:Paras. 27, 87 and 173). For Locke, the individual is prior to organized society and is essentially autonomous and capable of being self-sufficient, provided he can enjoy his inalienable natural right to broadly conceived property (*Id.*:Paras. 6, 44, 123; MacPherson 1975:131). Moreover, Locke believes that the individual can enjoy this natural right in the state of nature 'yet the enjoyment of it is very uncertain, and constantly exposed to the invasion of others' (Locke 1690:Para. 123). This prompts individuals to enter into a social contract and to associate into a civil society, but, as Locke specifies, the government established to surmount the shortcomings of the state of nature 'has no end but the preservation of property' (*Id.*:Para. 94). In other words, for Locke, civil society and government have no legitimate object other than maintaining the necessary conditions for the individual to be secure in the enjoyment of his natural rights and in the pursuit of self-interest. Moreover, within this vision, the role of government is essentially negative: it does not positively assist the individual in the latter's pursuits; it merely seeks to prevent interference with the individual's enjoyment of his natural rights and with his pursuit of self-interest.

A purely Lockean government would not have to be constrained by a bill of rights, for it would be clear that it could not legitimately interfere with its citizens' natural rights. However, neither at the federal nor at the state level, was the constitutional order in the United States ever purely Lockean (Farber and Sherry 2005:14–15; Diggins 1984:16). And to the extent that it is legitimate for government to promote communal objectives, there seems to be no guarantee against abridgement of natural rights.

Although overall the constitutional order prevalent in the United States in 1787 was far from purely Lockean, the federal structure it engineered confined the national government to the exercise of 'limited and enumerated powers'. Accordingly, as conceived in 1787, the federal government came much closer to the Lockean ideal than did that of the states. This buttressed the view, held by many, that there was no need for a *federal* bill of rights, and the claim that adoption of such bill would be counterproductive in as much as any listing of rights within it was bound to leave out others, including natural rights. In short, explicit listing of certain natural rights in a bill of rights could be interpreted as requiring exclusion from constitutional protection of others.

In arguing in favor of amending the Constitution in order to include a bill of rights before the First Congress of the United States on June 8, 1789, James Madison acknowledged that several among his respected interlocutors considered such a bill 'dangerous' for the very reasons listed above (Cogan 1999:807). Nevertheless, Madison argued that a bill of rights would be far from superfluous. Indeed, although the limited constitutional powers of the federal government did not trample on natural rights, there were nevertheless certain dangers of abuse. Madison was most concerned about two such dangers: the tyranny of the majority, and the potential for misuse by Congress of the broad discretionary powers which the 'Necessary and Proper' Clause granted it for purposes of carrying out its constitutionally circumscribed legislative mandate (*Id.*:808–809).[51] The Bill of Rights constitutionalized certain natural rights, such as freedom of speech, freedom of religion,[52] and freedom from expropriation of private property,[53] as well as certain rights which had no place in a Lockean state of nature, such as the right to trial by jury.[54] In addition, as already seen, the Bill of Rights, through the Ninth Amendment, specifies that its enumeration of certain rights is not meant to 'disparage' or deny' others 'retained by the people.' And, at least in Madison's conception, the unenumerated rights in question were essentially natural rights (Cogan 1999:810).[55]

The proponents of the post-Civil War amendments to the U. S. Constitution, which included the prohibition of slavery,[56] and the Fourteenth Amendment with its Due Process Clause, were also influenced by Locke (Farber and Sherry 2005:368). Of particular importance, in this respect, was Locke's labor theory of property according to which 'God gave the world to men in common' (Locke 1690:Para 34), but a man by having 'mixed his labour' with part of nature, such as a parcel of land, makes it his property (Id.:Para 27). As Locke further specifies, 'labour being the unquestionable property of the Labourer, no man but he can have a right to what that is once joyned to . . .'(Id.).[57] Locke's labor theory of property rests on the premise that human beings are inherently equal and there can be no legitimate place in any polity for slavery.[58] The same premises underly the impetus behind the post-Civil War Amendments. These were chiefly concerned with providing a constitutional imprint on the abolition of slavery and of the injustices associated with it.[59]

Two principal consequences emerged consistent with Locke's labor theory of property and with the fact that the Fourteenth Amendment imposed on the governments of the states restraints against impinging on individual rights much as the Bill of Rights had over seventy years earlier on the federal government.[60] First, the labor theory of property would soon come to occupy a prominent place in the Lockean natural rights deemed constitutionalized by the Fourteenth Amendment Due Process Clause. Thus, in its 1905 Lockner decision, the U. S. Supreme Court held that a New York state law limiting the hours of employment of bakery workers violated Due Process property and freedom of contract liberty rights.[61] And second, over time, the natural rights applicable against the federal government through the Bill of Rights became gradually constitutionalized as against impingements by the states. This occurred primarily as a result of the US Supreme Court's virtually total incorporation of all provisions of the Bill of Rights, including the Ninth Amendment, into the Fourteenth.[62] Moreover, the incorporation in question was complemented by the derivation of traditionally grounded pre-constitutional rights, such as marital privacy, from the concept of liberty constitutionalized by the Fourteenth Amendment Due Process Clause as exemplified by Justice Harlan's Opinion in Griswold. And taken together, this incorporation and derivation expanded the realm of constitutional prohibition against infringement of Lockean based rights from that of the federal government to that of all government. In short, in the course of its history, the Fourteenth Amendment has made all government action within the American polity subject to constraints imposed by constitutional rights grounded in the natural rights tradition.

Based on the preceding analysis of the influence of Locke on the conception and design of the Bill of Rights and the Fourteenth Amendment, it is now possible to shed further light on the three opinions in Griswold considered above.[63] As we have seen, the three opinions involved rely on interpretive means that make use of a combination of negation, metaphor and metonymy. What appears paradoxical and contradictory with respect to all three opinions, and in particular with the uses of tradition made by the two concurring opinions, was their respective uses of the three axes involved and of the possible intersections along them. In other words, it did not seem clear why negation was limited to certain particulars and assimilation or absorption to certain others; why reasoning along metaphorical paths stopped upon reaching this rather than that level of abstraction; or why its counterpart along metonymic paths stopped upon reaching a particular degree of contiguity rather than a more proximate or remote one.

Reference to Lockean liberalism and natural right tradition can go a long way in clarifying the seeming paradoxes and contradictions noted above and in providing justification for the particular uses made of the various paths of interpretation used to garner support for the decision in *Griswold*. In interpretive terms, the Lockean gloss avails means to impose cogent punctuation upon the semantic flows traveling along the distinct yet intersecting paths carved out respectively by negation, metaphor and metonymy. Specifically, by adding a reference to Locke, one can go a long way in solving the particular difficulty raised by the majority opinion in *Griswold*, namely the seeming arbitrariness involved in deriving a general right of privacy from the discrete elements thereof found in particular provisions of the Bill of Rights.[64] Indeed, within a Lockean perspective, a general right of privacy is part and parcel of the broadly encompassing natural right to property over oneself and over the space and possessions that one has acquired. This right which existed in the state of nature could not be legitimately infringed by a consensual government. In contrast, the discrete elements of privacy constitutionalized in some provisions of the Bill of Rights – such as the prohibitions against quartering soldiers in private homes in times of peace or against unreasonable searches or seizures or against soliciting self-incriminating testimony – all relate to legitimate positive functions of a liberal Lockean government, namely the maintenance of a military force to protect against foreign enemies and the provision of a system of justice to better secure natural rights. Accordingly, far from excluding natural rights to which it does not explicitly refer, the Bill of Rights specifies that even when government legitimately exercises positive powers granted to it pursuant to the social contract, it must as far as possible avoid limiting the full scope of natural rights. Under this Lockean interpretation, the general right to privacy is not ultimately derived from those parts of it that are explicitly enshrined in the Bill of Rights. Quite on the contrary, the specification of the latter would make little sense in the absence of the former.

Reference to Locke also goes someway in resolving the apparent contradiction between logics and history noted in relation to Justice Goldberg's
concurring opinion in *Griswold*.[65] Indeed, given Locke's influence on the
relevant constitutionally enshrined norms, the proper tradition associated
with the unenumerated rights invoked by the Ninth Amendment is not
pre-constitutional historical tradition as such. Instead, it is Lockean philosophical tradition – a particular historically grounded systematic
philosophical approach originating in England which both draws on, and
counters, pre-existing English tradition. As we shall see below, the logic
involved in Justice Goldberg's reasoning does not exactly mesh with
Locke's own actual philosophical conclusions but it approximates the historical philosophical tradition originating in Locke much more than the
actual practical everyday historical tradition prevalent in America in the
late eighteenth century or the mid-nineteenth.

A similar argument applies to Justice Harlan's concurring opinion to
the extent that the latter draws on a reinvented tradition that relies more
heavily on Lockean antecedents than on the everyday traditions of the
English – speaking peoples. Indeed, the libertarian tradition issuing from
Locke lends support to liberty and privacy within the marital relationship
regardless of whether the English or the Americans of the eighteenth
century felt that such privacy encompassed the free use of contraceptives.
More problematic, from a Lockean perspective, however, is Justice Harlan's
drawing the line at homosexuality or incest. From the standpoint of a
Lockean logic, thus drawing the line would be unjustified unless homosexuality and incest were deemed unnatural, in which case they could not
be included within any natural right. From the standpoint of Locke's own
views on marriage, on the other hand, there seems to be scant support for
the claim that marital privacy encompasses the freedom to use contraceptives (Locke 1690:Para 78).[66]

More generally for all the support that the decision in *Griswold* can draw
from the Lockean tradition, building the tradition that weighs so heavily in
Griswold on Locke poses two major problems. The first is that part of the
tradition built on Lockean natural rights, namely that which had been
constitutionalized in *Lochner* and which enshrined property and freedom
of contract rights, had long been repudiated by the time *Griswold* was
decided.[67] Locke's conception of natural rights encompassed both economic and personal liberties. How then could the Lockean tradition relied
upon in *Griswold* highlight the latter while reaffirming the repudiation of
the former?

The second problem is that whatever Locke's logic many imply,
Locke's own view was that marriage was for procreation and child rearing

(*Id.*:77–83).[68] That being the case, how could Locke be at the source of a tradition that supposedly justified affording constitutional protection to the use of contraceptives by married couples?

These problems cannot be simply overcome by placing the logic implicit in Locke's philosophy over and above Locke's actual views regarding natural rights, marriage and procreation. Indeed, Lockean logic alone cannot justify Justice Harlan drawing the line between use of contraceptives and homosexuality where he did. Nor can that logic reconcile the repudiation of *Lochner* with the legitimation of *Griswold*. To be reconciled with the result in *Griswold*, the Lockean tradition must be, in part, rechannelled to account for the repudiation of economic and social libertarianism during the New Deal. And it must be extended, through further development of the implications of its logic in order to mesh with the permissive trend that bolstered liberal individualism in the area of personal choice and expression during the 1960's.

Arguably, the abandonment of economic libertarianism both in policy and in constitutional law[69] does not signify a repudiation of Lockean tradition, but only a modification or limitation requiring some rechannelling. As already noted, for Locke the purpose of government is to help secure the individual's ability to exercise his or her natural rights and to pursue self-interest. A pre-condition to such exercise and pursuit is the attainment of an adequate level of individual material welfare. Economic libertarianism assumes that with support provided by property and contract rights, the individual can achieve self-sufficiency. What the Great Depression caused a vast majority of Americans to believe in the 1930's, however, was that to maintain the minimum level of welfare to enable individuals to exercise their rights and pursue self-interest required government interventionism in the economy. Lockean economic libertarianism was therefore no longer a viable option, but that did not require abandoning Lockean natural rights or the pursuit of self-interest in areas of personal choice.

On the other hand, the permissive trend unleashed in 1960's demanded greater freedom regarding individual choice and individual expression, including tolerance for greater variety in lifestyles and for greater freedom to conduct intimate relationships without societal or governmental interference. These demands fit within the logic if not the actual positions of Locke. Locke's philosophy was revolutionary in relation to the prevailing moral and political order of seventeenth century England. His insistence on the equality of all human beings and on the extensive natural rights of each ran squarely counter to the basic tenets prevalent within the realm. At the same time, the full theoretical implications of Locke's philosophy remained partially concealed behind some of his particular

pronouncements. As we have seen, Locke's statement that a man has property over what his servant has produced seems to contradict his labor
theory of property and his views of marriage as dedicated to childbear-
ing and childrearing are potentially in conflict with individual autonomy
within the private sphere.

The *logic* behind Locke's philosophy is perhaps best captured by John
Stuart Mill's distinction between self-regarding and other-regarding acts
(Mill 1859:73–74). According to Mill's liberal philosophy, society can only
legitimately regulate an individual's conduct if the latter is not purely self-
regarding. This is consistent with Locke's libertarian and natural rights
based theory. The individual should be free to exercise his or her rights and
pursue self-interest so long as that does not infringe upon any other individual's equal rights. And, from that it follows logically that it should be
up to the married couple, as against the rest of society, to decide whether
or not to procreate, and whether or not to use contraceptives in that
connection.

The Lockean tradition as rechannelled and extended consistent with the
above observations conjoined with the interpretive use of negation, metaphor, and metonymy noted above overdetermine the actual result reached
in *Griswold*. The process that lends to the overdetermined result in question
involves absorbing, discarding, reworking and reinventing tradition, or
more precisely, multiple traditions. This process also revolves around a
complex interplay between constitutional identity, and other relevant identities within the polity, sometimes accentuating convergences and sometimes divergences. Before considering this in greater detail and before
attempting to address the broader implications of the preceding analysis of
the uses of tradition, however, it is first necessary briefly to examine whether
and how *Griswold's* progeny might fit within the interpretive framework
articulated thus far.

3.4.3 Eisenstadt and Molding the Tradition to Encompass Non-Marital Heterosexual Sex

Eisenstadt, which seven years after *Griswold* extended the constitutional
right to use contraceptives to non-married individuals, was decided on
equality grounds rather than on any of the grounds invoked to justify the
result in *Griswold*. From a purely technical standpoint, *Eisenstadt* is an
Equal Protection decision, not a Due Process or a Ninth Amendment one.
Placed in its broader jurisprudential context, however, *Eisenstadt* is a clear
extension of *Griswold*. *Einsenstadt* at once expands the privacy right recognized in *Griswold* and sheds further light on the amalgam of tradition and
counter-tradition constitutionally enshrined in *Griswold*.

The Massachusetts law invalidated in *Einsenstadt* came afoul the Equal Protection Clause because instead of drawing a straightforward line between use of contraceptives within and without marriage, it prohibited some uses by non-married people, but not others. Whereas married couples under the law in question were entitled to free use of contraceptives, non-married individuals were allowed to use contraceptives for health purposes, but not for prevention of conception purposes.[70] The Court considered that drawing the line between these two purposes was arbitrary and hence did not provide legitimate grounds for different treatment of married and non-married individuals in violation of Equal Protection.[71]

What accounts for Massachusetts's distinction between promotion of health and prevention of pregnancy in relation to non-marital sex is the clash between tradition and a rapidly growing trend running directly counter to that tradition. The tradition in question was concerned with preserving 'purity and 'chastity' to bolster marriage and the 'sanctity of the home'.[72] Consistent with that, the Massachusetts's legislation at issue in *Einsenstadt* aimed to 'discourage premarital sexual intercourse'.[73] On the other hand, social mores during the 1960's and 1970's in Massachusetts and throughout most of the United States were rapidly changing and premarital sex became widespread, openly acknowledged and increasingly accepted. To account for that, the Massachusetts Legislature sought to address the health concerns linked to the new permissive age while holding on as much as possible to traditional morals concerning sex and marriage. This, in turn, lead to drawing what the U.S. Supreme Court would characterize as an 'arbitrary' distinction between married and non-married persons with respect to the right to use contraceptives.

Massachusetts and to a large extent the country as a whole were struggling to reconcile old traditions and new realities in the realm of sexual mores. This struggle, moreover, became part and parcel of the fabric of American national identity in the 1960's and 1970's, giving new expression to the country's perennial tension between communal ordering based on morals derived from religion and Lockean individualism. Had the Court in *Eisenstadt* merely struck down the law before it on equal protection grounds, it would have had but a minimal imprint on the interplay between national and constitutional identity. However, though not strictly necessary to justify its decision, the Court was intent on linking *Eisenstadt* to *Griswold* stating in its decision's most oft cited passage

> It is true that in *Griswold* the right of privacy . . . inhered in the marital relationship. Yet the marital couple is not an independent entity with a mind and a heart of its own, but an association of

two individuals each with a separate intellectual and emotional makeup. If the right of privacy means anything it is the right of the *individual*, married or single, to be free from unwarranted governmental intrusion into matters so fundamentally affecting a person as the decision whether to bear or beget a child.[74]

By thus linking *Eisenstadt* to *Griswold*, the Court takes what is a clash between tradition and counter-tradition in the nation's (then) present day life and reinterprets it as an element that fits within the constitutional tradition elaborated in *Griswold*. From the standpoint of constitutional identity, therefore, there is a continuous 'tradition' that originates in the judeo-Christian notion of the sanctity of marriage, which predates America's founding fathers but was largely embraced by them, that continues and is further specified in *Griswold*, and that culminates (as of 1972) in *Eisenstadt*.

Seen most narrowly, this 'tradition' that becomes integrated into American constitutional identity does clash with the contemporary national division, culture wars and struggle opposing traditional to more permissive lifestyles. Viewed more broadly, however, the interplay between national and constitutional identity as it stood in 1972 was much more complex and nuanced as similar tensions between individualism and communal values had generated similar dynamics in both of these spheres of identity. Moreover, several different factors must be taken into account to get a proper sense of the overall dynamic between a particular national identity and its corresponding constitutional identity. For example, it is the very purpose of a constitution's bill of rights to bolster individual-regarding interests and concerns, but that need not set a polity's individual-regarding values and communal values on a collision course. Viewed from a constitutional perspective, individual concerns may loom larger than they are when viewed overall. That may not be because of any serious conflict but rather because whatever issues may be raised, no matter how peripheral or few and far between, would mostly emerge in the constitutional sphere. Be that as it may, that is not the case in *Griswold* and *Eisentadt* to the extent that the 'tradition' elaborated in those cases is not merely one side of a multifaceted tradition, but instead a construct that negates both the nation's traditions and its (then) divisive conflict over lifestyle values.

From an interpretive standpoint, *Eisenstadt* is joined to *Griswold* through overlapping metaphoric and metonymic links. On the metaphorical axis, marriage is the equivalent to the free association of two individuals for purposes (in the relevant context of these cases) of engaging in intimate sexual relationships involving deciding whether or not to bear and beget children. Along the metonymic axis, on the other hand, the individual is a necessary part of the married couple, and just as contraception is a part of marital intimacy, it is also part of intimacy among any two individuals who convene for sex just as a married couple does. In short, by combining an analogy between any couple having sex and a married couple doing the same; and a double displacement from marriage to contraception relating to marital sex and from the (married) couple to the individual within such a couple; the Court weaves together an actual historical tradition, its extension along Lockean lines (consistent with Locke's logic, but contrary to his actual views), and what seems to stand clearly counter to actual historical tradition to the extent that widespread practice and acceptance of non-marital sex may eventually weaken or undermine traditional marriage.

Consistent with these observations, *Eisenstadt* not only redefines or, more precisely, reinvents the original historical tradition from which it derives, but it also recasts the tradition that emerges in *Griswold*. Indeed, as seen most clearly in the context of Justice Harlan's concurring opinion, standing alone *Griswold* appears to merely extend traditional marital rights by adding to them recourse to modern artificial contraception. *Eisenstadt*, on the other hand, seems to stand respect for traditional marriage on its head as it provides constitutional shield for practicing non-marital sex without deterrence relating to concern about unwanted procreation. This notwithstanding, *Eisenstadt* does not merely reject tradition, but it reinvents it. It negates and deconstructs the historical tradition – as did up to a point *Griswold* – but it does not simply discard it. Instead, it takes certain threads within it and weaves them into a continuous narrative that takes us from an eighteenth century conception of the sanctity of marriage to the permissive views of the 1960's and 1970's through deployment of Lockean logic and strategic exploitation of available metaphoric and metonymic semantic paths.

3.4.4 Roe and the Challenge of Fitting Abortion within the Reinvented Tradition

As mentioned above, *Roe v. Wade* decided a year after *Eisenstadt* does not fit together with the latter or with *Griswold* in terms of the protection of the spatial privacy generally associated with intimate sexual relations.[75] Roe, however, does mesh with its two precedents in terms of decisional privacy, and does also follow metonymically, as already pointed out, as far as the decision to bear or to beget a child is implicated.[76] Before proceeding to examine how the Court managed to fit *Roe* within the reinvented tradition launched in *Griswold*, two general points about *Roe* must be underscored. First, the Court's decision in *Roe* exacerbated the sharp divisions over abortion within the polity rather than smoothing them over.[77] And second, the presence of the fetus in the context of abortion raises serious doubts about the plausibility of the argument that abortion, like the sexual relationships involved in *Griswold* and *Einsestadt*, involves a Lockean-Millian type of purely self-regarding conduct.

Roe as reaffirmed by *Casey* in 1992[78] has formed part of American constitutional jurisprudence and of American constitutional identity for more than thirty five years, but, as the continuing abortion wars attest to, there is no widespread agreement on the subject within the polity. This is in sharp contrast to the widespread acceptance of the constitutional right to privacy as elaborated in *Griswold* and *Eisenstadt*.[79] Although the constitutional jurisprudence emerging from *Griswold* was soundly criticized by leading constitutional scholars (Ely 1973), the constitutional right to privacy itself became widely accepted as the law at stake in *Griswold* was rarely enforced being a mere remnant of bygone social mores (Encarnación 2005:162). In relation to *Griswold* and *Eisenstadt* therefore, constitutional jurisprudence and constitutional identity adjusted to better conform with widely shared mores and beliefs that had become sufficiently distinct to inform national identity. In relation to *Roe*, on the other hand, the Court's new constitutional jurisprudence on abortion appears to have directly intensified the division over the issue within the polity, thus opening a new gap between constitutional and national identity.

To the extent that unenumerated rights seem inherently more contestable than enumerated ones, *Roe* casts a shadow on the emerging strand of constitutional identity originating in *Griswold*.[80] Indeed, regardless of constitutional objections that may be raised against *Griswold* or *Einsestadt*, the decisions in these two cases seem strongly supported by their conformity with widely and rapidly emerging social mores. And that, in turn, allows for a broad based acceptance of the relevant reinvented tradition. In other words, because of America's particular concern regarding tradition from the standpoint of its constitutional identity – as attested by its unique focus on originalism in sharp contrast to most other constitutional democracies (Dorsen, et al 2003:194) – the fact that *Griswold* conformed to then prevailing national mores went a long way in making it acceptable to recast non-traditional mores as issuing out of a (reinvented) tradition tracing back to the founding fathers. National identity thus reinforced constitutional identity and vice versa. *Roe*, however, by seeking to insert within the same reinvented tradition a highly divisive position did exactly the opposite. It cast doubt on the reinvented tradition, thus undermining rather than reinforcing the endeavor to reconcile the constitutional past with the constitutional present. Accordingly, *Roe* both raised questions regarding the integrity of the evolving constitutional identity of which it became a part and it opened a new wedge between the country's constitutional identity and its national identity. Moreover, had a right to abortion been explicitly provided for in the American Constitution, the latter wedge may well have been very similar, but it would have been inconceivable that the stability or integrity of the country's constitutional identity would have been similarly threatened.

The second general point concerning *Roe* is that the presence of the fetus sets abortion apart from the particulars surrounding marital and non-marital sex at stake in *Roe's* precedents. Cutting to the core, if the fetus is a person, then the disanalogy between *Roe* and its precedents would seem to far outweigh any analogy between them. Abortion like contraception may relate to a decision on whether to bear or beget a child, but if the fetus is a person or a life, then abortion unlike contraception cannot be plausibly viewed as being purely self-regarding. And accordingly, *Roe* would not be properly inserted in the Lockean-Millian tradition embraced by *Griswold* and constitutionally in play at least as far back as *Lochner*. To overcome this difficulty and to make it plausible for a right to abortion to become integrated into the tradition emerging from *Griswold* and *Eisenstadt*, therefore, it would seem necessary to commit to the proposition that a fetus is neither a life nor a person. As we shall see the Court in *Roe* sought to fit a right to abortion within the reinvented tradition articulated in *Griswold* and *Eisenstadt*. In so doing, the Court did address the question of when life begins, but it did not provide any answer to it.

Specifically, *Roe* is linked along a metaphorical path to *Griswold* and *Eisenstadt* in that all three cases relate to the right to decide whether to bear or to beget a child. *Roe* is also linked to these two other cases along a metonymic path in that abortion is aimed at the same objective after conception as contraception is before conception. However, unlike contraception which is linked metonymically to tradition in *Griswold* and *Einsenstadt*, as a mere adjunct to martial and to individual sexual intimacy, abortion in *Roe* is principally considered on its own terms for purposes of determining whether it fits within the relevant tradition. In other words, whereas neither *Griswold* nor *Eisenstadt* dealt with how contraception had fared in the relevant tradition, Roe devoted great attention to how abortion had.[81]

The Court in *Roe* considers a plurality of Western traditions regarding abortion going all the way back to biblical and Greek and Roman times. Two features that emerge from that comparison are particularly salient. First, toleration of abortion in the first part of the pregnancy before 'quickening' has fluctuated over the centuries, with a sharp turn in the

United States towards almost complete criminalization, except to save the life of the mother, starting in the mid-nineteenth century, and continuing for the most part up until the decision in *Roe*.[82] Second, except perhaps to some extent during the Greek and Roman periods,[83] in those periods in which there was greater toleration for it, abortion was not treated as a right, but rather as a lesser crime.[84] Accordingly, to fit abortion within the tradition relied upon to legitimate the unenumerated right to privacy, the Court in *Roe* not only had to reinvent tradition, but also had to negate the most recent prevailing tradition to revive traditions that had been discarded for over a century. Moreover, to project abortion as a right in the discarded traditions that it has just reinstated, the Court focuses on the *difference* between abortion as a capital crime and abortion as a lesser or non-truly prosecuted crime. Thus, by shifting attention from the fact that even in the most tolerant periods of the Christian era abortion was by and large still a crime to the difference in the severity with which it was treated in the most lenient periods, the Court conveys the impression that it was almost treated as a right.

The revival of discarded traditions combined with the displacement from the fact of criminality to the gap between a capital crime and a lesser one is not purely arbitrary. Indeed, to the extent that criminalization of abortion was predicated on religion, a husband's rights over his wife and over their offspring, the state's interest in controlling sexual mores, or other such grounds, it clearly seems to run afoul the Lockean-Millian principle constitutionally enshrined in *Griswold*. Furthermore, though the previous discarded tradition did not support a *right* to abortion, it was more tolerant of it than the then prevailing tradition. Therefore, reliance on this older discarded tradition could serve at once as a bridge to a stance that is more compatible with the Lockean-Millian principle and to refer back to tradition consistent with the *Griswold*-based requirement that unenumerated rights be grounded in tradition.

The Court in *Roe* also strives to do the best it can with the thorny problem posed by the fetus and the vexing question of when life begins. From the standpoint of reconciling the right to abortion with the Lockean-Millian principle, the best would be for life to commence at birth and for the fetus not to have any of the attributes of personhood. The Court in *Roe*, however, refused to take a stance on when life begins, pointing out that neither medicine nor philosophy nor theology have achieved any consensus on the subject.[85] Had the Court stopped there, that combined with its refusal to deem the fetus a person for constitutional purposes[86] would have provided adequate grounding for the right to abortion to become subsumed under the Lockean-Millian principle. But the Court did not stop there. It held that the fetus was potential life, and that when it became 'viable' – i.e., when it could survive outside its mother's womb – the state had a compelling interest to prohibit most abortions.[87] Furthermore, the Court also held that the state can restrict the right to abortion in order to protect the health of the mother.[88]

In as much as the fetus is viewed as a potential life, abortion looms as an other-regarding act. On the other hand, if the state can legitimately interfere with an adult woman's informed choice to have an abortion, then, even in the context of determining whether to bear or beget a child, the state is empowered to act out of paternalistic concerns inconsistent with the Lockean-Millian principle.

In spite of this, the Court in *Roe* managed to carve out a constitutional right to abortion that, at least during the first trimester of pregnancy, is, in the end, compatible with the Lockean-Millian principle.[89] This is achieved primarily through two interpretative moves that have the effect of neutralizing the other-regarding and paternalistic considerations referred to by the Court. With respect to the fetus as a potential life, the Court draws the line at viability, specifying that after viability the state has a compelling interest in protecting the fetus against its mother's wish to abort (absent a threat to her life or health). From the standpoint of logic, there seems to be a continuum without significant break that encompasses the fetus as 'potential life' from conception to birth. As far as 'potential life' is concerned, therefore, viability ought not to be a particularly relevant marker, and other-regarding considerations ought to remain equal throughout the pregnancy. On the other hand, emphasis on viability makes sense from the standpoint of drawing a line concerning life or personhood. A fetus that could live outside its mother's womb presumably has sufficiently in common with a new born to justify using viability as a credible marker for distinguishing purely self-regarding from other-regarding abortions. Consistent with this, moreover, the combination of the Court's concentration on potential life and on viability acts as a displaced substitute for the Court's *de facto* substantive conclusion that viability is the point at which a life or person other than the mother comes into play in the context of abortion. And ultimately, it is this latter conclusion that justifies characterizing pre-viability abortion as self-regarding, thus making it consistent with the Lockean-Millian principle.

A second interpretive move also stirs the Court in *Roe* towards conformity with the Lockean-Millian principle notwithstanding recognizing the legitimacy of paternalistic legislation. The Court stresses that precedents establish that the constitutional right to privacy does not comprise an 'unlimited right to do with one's body as one pleases'.[90] Legislation to

promote the health of the mother is a constitutionally permissible limitation on that right, but the Court in *Roe* nevertheless deems paternalistic
anti-abortion legislation illegitimate with respect to the first trimester of
pregnancy based on the medical fact that a first trimester abortion poses a
lesser threat to the mother's health than carrying her pregnancy to term.[91]
In other words, though paternalistic legislation to promote health is legitimate, there is no credible such paternalistic justification for interfering
with first trimester abortion.

What the preceding analysis reveals is that the Court in *Roe* embarked on
a elaborate interpretive journey to forge a narrow path that allowed it to cast
the right to abortion – albeit one that is far from unlimited – within the
ambit of the Lockean-Millian liberty-privacy rights constitutionally
enshrined in *Griswold*. That the path in question is overdetermined to
further the (constitutional) identity emerging from *Griswold* and *Eisenstadt* becomes plain upon comparing *Roe* to the nearly contemporaneous
German constitutional decision on abortion.[92] The German Constitutional
Court's 1975 decision actually recognized a right to abortion that is for
practical purposes largely equivalent to its American counterpart articulated in *Roe*. The justification given by the German Court for such a right,
however, was markedly different from that offered by the U.S. Supreme
Court. Whereas the latter starts from the liberty-privacy right of the mother
which prevails subject to protection of the potential for life of the viable
fetus and of the health of the mother, the German Court starts by asserting
the constitutional paramouncy of the right to life. The latter derives from a
German post World War Two national and constitutional identity built
upon a swift repudiation of the Nazis' utter disrespect for human life. Starting from the protection of life, moreover, the German Court arrives at its
decision through a balancing of the requirement to protect prenatal life
against the mother's physical and mental health needs. It is therefore not
the privacy right of the mother, but the state's concern for her well being
that is principally in play in the German abortion jurisprudence. What this
means, for our purposes, is that commitment to the Lockean-Millian principle is not required to justify a right to abortion. That the American right
emerging in *Roe* ends up relying so heavily on that principle, therefore, is
the product of a deeply entrenched constitutional identity that is clearly set
apart from its contemporary German counterpart.

3.4.5 The Reinvented Tradition's Contradictory Approaches to Homosexual Sex

Though the two US Supreme Court decisions seventeen years apart on
whether the right to privacy should encompass a right to homosexual

sodomy among consenting adults, *Bowers* v. *Hardwick* in 1986 and *Lawrence* v. *Texas* in 2003, reach diametrically opposite results, they share a common framework and make use of the same interpretive tools. Both decisions revolve around a clash between a tilt towards the metaphorical axis and a countervailing tilt towards the metonymical axis. They also underscore the question of the limit which is inevitably problematized in connection with the deployment of the Lockean-Millian principle. Taken together these two decisions provide a vivid illustration of the practical struggle between liberalism and illiberalism that the question of the limit it is bound to unleash. Finally, both decisions make use of materials imported from outside the borders of the United States for purposes of reinventing tradition. The respective postures taken by *Bowers* and *Lawrence* with respect to these materials differ, however, as do the respective debates generated by their use. Besides pointing to how the reinvention of tradition is overdetermined, the differences concerning recourse to foreign materials afford a valuable glimpse into a novel and contentious issue imperceptible in *Bowers* but prominent in *Lawrence*. That issue concerns the propriety of importing foreign, transnational or international norms or traditions for purposes of reconstructing one's national constitutional order and identity in general, and of the reinvention of one's tradition, in particular.

Whether the Lockean right to privacy should extend to homosexual sodomy, or whether the line should be drawn at homosexual sex as argued by Justice Harlan in his concurring opinion in *Griswold*,[93] depends ultimately on the view that one has of such sex. If one views homosexual sex as analogous to heterosexual sex and heterosexual and homosexual sodomy as normal practices to be left entirely to the discretion of the adults involved, then homosexual sodomy should be protected just as heterosexual non-marital sex was in *Einsenstadt*. On the other hand, if one regards homosexual sodomy as deviate or unnatural, as hindering rather than furthering wholesome self-realization and self-fulfillment, then the line should be drawn as Justice Harlan suggested. As we shall now see, given the prevailing divergences over homosexual sex, proponents of the first view seem best served by emphasis on metaphorical links whereas proponents of the second view seem to do best by concentrating on metonymic contextualization.

3.4.5(i) Bowers: Drawing the Line at Homosexual Sodomy

The recourse to both the metaphorical and the metonymic lines of argumentation suggested above was already fully put in play in the *Bowers* decision. As noted before in that case, by a 5-4 majority, the Court upheld the constitutionality of a statute that criminalized homosexual sodomy.

The Court's majority and concurring opinions relied heavily on metonymic contextualization. The dissent, in contrast, relied for the most part
on metaphorical reasoning to reach the levels of abstraction at which the
analogies between homosexual and heterosexual sex become most obvious
and most pervasive.

The Court's refusal in *Bowers* to extend privacy protection to homosexual sex is buttressed by a two pronged recourse to metonymic contextualization. The first of these is procedural; the second, substantive.
On the surface, the *Bowers* majority's decision is simple to understand.
A review of historical tradition spanning from Judeo-Christian mores to
English common law and to law throughout most of American history
clearly indicate that there was no tradition, much less a fundamental tradition grounded in notions of fairness, justice and ordered liberty, of
treating homosexual sex as a fundamental right. Moreover, whereas contemporary mores had significantly evolved, homosexual sex was still much
less generally accepted by American society in 1986 than was non-marital
heterosexual sex (Kaiser Report 2000).

Below the surface, however, the challenge confronting the *Bowers*
majority was actually quite daunting. This was primarily due to two factors: the emerging constitutional identity regarding privacy framed by the
reinvented tradition issuing from *Griswold* and *Eisenstadt*; and the fact that
the challenged state of Georgia statute involved criminalized all sodomy,
heterosexual as well as homosexual, and provided for up to twenty year
prison sentences upon conviction.[94]

The Georgia statute at stake in *Bowers* was so sweeping that it actually
criminalized, among other widespread practices, oral sex within the confines of the marital relationship, a practice so commonly accepted in the
1980's America that it was routinely addressed in mainstream sex manuals
aimed at married couples (Comfort 1972). Had the *Bowers* majority
squarely dealt with the statute before it on its face, it would have had either
to declare it unconstitutional under *Griswold's* marital privacy right or to
repudiate *Griswold* and its progeny holding that there is no right to privacy
under the U.S. Constitution.

The latter alternative was unthinkable as utterly incompatible with the
constitutional identity emanating from *Griswold*, which had become firmly
entrenched in the two decades that followed that decision, and with the
nation's then prevailing mores. The former alternative however, would
have been entirely plausible. The Court could have invalidated the Georgia
law reasoning that state intrusion into the marital bedroom for proof
of sodomy was as unseemly as a similar intrusion for evidence of use of
contraceptives.

The court's majority in *Bowers* decided instead to make use of the challenged Georgia statute which generally prohibited all sodomy to establish that there was no constitutional impediment to criminalization of homosexual sex. To do so, the *Bowers* majority first had to give the Georgia statute before it a metonymically contextualized reading which would put it in a procedurally defensible position to focus exclusively on homosexual sodomy. Since the statute in question criminalized all sodomy, it was warranted to infer that the Georgia legislature deemed sodomy reprehensible and worthy of punishment. Nothing in the statute, however, suggested that homosexual sodomy was any worse than its heterosexual counterpart.

Accordingly, the only plausible justification for the Court's majority to confine itself to homosexual sodomy was that individuals who had engaged in same sex sodomy stood before it as parties in the case it was about to decide. Significantly a married couple had joined the homosexuals' challenge against the Georgia sodomy statute, but had been barred for technical reasons not relevant here from continuing as parties to the lawsuit by the trial court which entertained the challenge in the first instance.[95] In the latter couple's absence, the court's majority, by use of a metonymic shift that placed the entire focus on the homosexuals before it, transformed the issue from one concerning all sodomy to one concerning exclusively homosexual sodomy.

From a substantive standpoint, the Court's majority relied on a long standing moral and legal condemnation of homosexual sex to support its conclusion that such sex was not entitled to any constitutional protection. The most vivid invocation of traditional reprobation of homosexuality is found in Chief Justice Burger's concurring opinion. After referring to strong condemnation pursuant to Judeo-Christian morals and Roman law, the Chief Justice quotes from Blackstone's commentaries on English law written in the Eighteenth Century:

> Blackstone described 'the infamous crime against nature' as an offense of 'deeper malignity' than rape, a heinous act 'the very mention of which is a disgrace to human nature' and 'a crime not fit to be named'. W. Blackstone Commentaries 215.[96]

Besides being unnecessarily inflammatory in an age in which homosexual sex was not regarded as unnatural or pathological by health professionals,[97] the cited passage's direct appeal to centuries old English tradition seems to ignore the reinvented tradition issuing from *Griswold*. Indeed if the relevant tradition were the one embodied in the moral and legal mores of Biblical times and pre-1776 England, then neither contraceptives for married couples nor non-marital heterosexual sex would qualify for constitutional protection under the criteria adopted in *Griswold*.

The *Bowers* majority does seek to reconcile its conclusion with *Griswold* and its progeny, and it does so mainly through metonymic contextualization. *Griswold* itself had resorted to metonymy to shift the focus from the 'sanctity of marriage' to use of contraceptives within the ambit of marital sex. The majority in *Bowers* uses metonymy to travel in the opposite direction: *Griswold* gave explicit constitutional recognition to the sanctity of marriage which is starkly distinguishable from the practice of homosexual sodomy. No such convenient available interpretive path was available to the *Bowers* majority, however, for purposes of reconciling its decision with the holding in *Eisenstadt*. No plausible credible means seem at hand to subsume the latter case under the sanctity of marriage as such (as opposed to as one among many metaphorically linked ways to enable the individual to choose and fulfill aims of sexual intimacy). This is because *Eisenstadt* explicitly extends constitutional rights to sexual intimacy to non-married individuals. To distinguish *Bowers* from *Eisenstadt*, therefore requires recourse to metonymic contextualization along other lines. Through metonymic displacement, *Eisenstadt* can be portrayed as a case about heterosexual, that is 'normal', sex which the Constitution protects among consenting adults. In contrast, by concentrating on the long history of its moral reprobation and criminalization, the *Bowers* majority can portray homosexual sex as 'deviant' or 'abnormal' (in part by referring to sexual practices like oral or anal sex once considered as deviant for heterosexuals as for homosexuals, but by narrowing its focus to cover homosexuals exclusively), and thus as distinguishable from the kind of sex afforded constitutional protection in *Eisenstadt*.

The metonymic use of the dichotomy between 'normal' and 'abnormal' or 'natural' and 'unnatural' does open the way to lending support to the result in *Bowers* without squarely repudiating the reinvented tradition articulated in *Griswold* and *Eisenstadt*. Recourse to the particular use of metonymic contextualization in question, however, is not sufficient to reconcile *Bowers* with *Griswold* and its progeny. What would also be necessary would be to link the above metonymic dichotomy to that between 'natural' and 'unnatural' in the context of the Lockean-Millian principle. But before further examining that latter possibility, it is first necessary to consider the reasoning and interpretive moves of the dissenting justices in *Bowers*. This is all the more important since the dissenting views in *Bowers* eventually became the views of the Court's majority in *Lawrence*.

The dissenting justices in *Bowers* did not dwell on the historic treatment of homosexuality in various cultures throughout history. Instead, they primarily focused on similarities between homosexuals and heterosexuals and through metaphorical thinking managed to depict them as being essentially alike. In the words of Justice Stevens,

> From the standpoint of the individual, the homosexual and the heterosexual have the same interest in deciding how he will live his own life, and more narrowly, how he will conduct himself in his personal and voluntary associations with his companions. State intrusion into the private conduct of either is equally burdensome.[98]

Consistent with this metaphorical reasoning, Justice Stevens reconciles consensual homosexual sex with the reinvented tradition issuing from *Griswold* by stressing that what binds these cases together is protection of 'the American heritage of freedom' which 'makes certain state intrusions on the citizen's right to decide how he will live his own life intolerable'.[99] Thus, by moving away from the particular sexual practices involved, and from the historical, cultural and religious mores concerning these practices, metaphorical reasoning leads to the abstract level where each individual is similar to every other individual, as possessing a need for intimate associations and as deserving privacy to freely pursue fulfillment of so fundamental a need. More generally, reaching higher levels of abstraction through alignment of similarities along a metaphorical interpretive path plays an important role in framing constitutional rights and in defining constitutional identity.

Ascending on a metaphoric path 'all the way up', however, seems as unwarranted as descending along a metonymic path 'all the way down'. Indeed, excessive abstraction would lead to the loss of all but formal identity much as excessive contextualization would lead nothing but irreducible differences. Regarding *Bowers*, if all we are left with is the freedom to choose intimate partners and practices conceived at the highest possible level of abstraction, then how could we distinguish between homosexual sex, incest, bestiality, voluntary sado-masochistic practices involving injury and considerable pain etc.?

In his dissenting opinion, Justice Blackmun addresses this last question as he draws the line between homosexuality and incest, among other practices, in relation to the divide between self-regarding and other-regarding practices. In Justice Blackburn's view, homosexual sex 'involves no real interferences with the rights of others, for the mere knowledge that other individuals do not adhere to one's value system cannot be a legally cognizable interest . . . '.[100] In contrast to the self regarding nature of homosexual sex, Justice Blackmun finds incest to be sufficiently other-regarding in as much as it is most often not truly consensual to warrant state prohibition.[101]

Consistent with Justice Blackmun's understanding of the relevant distinction between homosexual sex and incest one can find a stopping point at a particular level of abstraction along the metaphorical path traveled in search of a fit within the reinvented tradition issuing from *Griswold*. At the level of abstraction in question, it becomes possible to draw a line concerning what should be integrated within the reinvented tradition designed to set constitutional boundaries and to inform constitutional identity. Specifically, in this view travel along the metaphorical path is constrained by adherence to the Lockean – Millian divide between self-regarding and other – regarding practices.

Drawing the line at incest is certainly contestable as it is easy to imagine that at least certain kinds of incest, involving adult siblings as opposed to parent and child, could well be truly consensual and hence essentially similar to comparable sex among non-relatives. This issue will be further explored in the context of the discussion of the nexus between liberalism and illiberalism. Before turning to that discussion, however it is first necessary to consider briefly how the dynamic established in *Bowers* was further elaborated in *Lawrence*.

3.4.5(ii) *Lawrence's Encompassing of Homosexual Sex within the Reinvented Tradition*

In *Lawrence* the Court overruled *Bowers* and held in a 6-3 decision that the criminalization of homosexual sex among consenting adults was unconstitutional.[102] The *Lawrence* majority pretty much tracks the *Bowers* dissenters as the *Lawrence* dissenters do the *Bowers* majority. With this in mind, what follows will only address those aspects of *Lawrence* which have a significant bearing in the context of constitutional identity.

Justice Kennedy's majority opinion in *Lawrence* does not merely replicate the *Bowers* dissenting positions. It instead takes them further along the same metaphorical path while at the same time engaging in metonymic contextualization designed to undermine that put forth by the *Bowers* majority. On the metaphoric front, the *Bowers* dissenters equated homosexual and heterosexual sex as means for the individual to choose partners for sexual intimacy and to be free from government intrusion concerning the particular sexual practices engaged in with such partners. In *Lawrence*, Justice Kennedy takes this metaphoric link to a higher level of abstraction. He shifts the emphasis from sexual intimacy to 'personal bond[s] that are more enduring', the former being but one 'element', among many of the latter.[103] In Justice Kennedy's words,

> To say that the issue in *Bowers* was simply the right to engage in certain sexual conduct demeans the claim the individual put forward, just as it would demean a married couple were it to be said marriage is simply about the right to have sexual intercourse.[104]

On the metonymic front, Justice Kennedy aims to undo the *Bowers* majority's metonymic displacement from homosexual *sodomy* to *homosexual* sodomy, by traveling in the opposite direction. For the *Bowers* majority, homosexuality became predominant and sodomy secondary. Justice Kennedy seeks to reverse that relationship in *Lawrence* by recontextualizing sodomy, placing it in its proper historical legal setting. Because both English and nineteenth century American law equally criminalized heterosexual and homosexual sodomy, the focus on sodomy as an immoral and unnatural form of non procreative sex was essential whereas the focus on homosexuality was merely incidental.[105] Moreover, this shift of attention from the actor to the act allows Justice Kennedy to remark:

> The absence of legal prohibitions focusing on homosexual conduct may be explained in part by noting that according to some scholars the concept of the homosexual as a distinct category of person did not emerge until the late 19th century.[106]

In sum, by folding the sexual act into the more enduring multifaceted bonds that link an individual to a chosen partner and by a displacement from the homosexual actor to the act of sodomy (which was considered reprehensible in the past, but is now widely accepted at least in regards to heterosexuals), Justice Kennedy emerges as the defender of a seemingly unassailable position. Indeed, it seems absurd to allow the state to disrupt solid citizens in enduring and stable serious partnerships because in the privacy of their home they occasionally engage in a sexual act that most Americans consider natural and acceptable. Furthermore, in terms of the reinvented tradition issuing from *Griswold*, Justice Kennedy elevates 'the sanctity' of marriage into a higher level of abstraction and turns it into the 'sanctity' of enduring bonds among any two mutually committed individuals. On the other hand, he reconciles once proscribed sodomy with the reinvented tradition to the extent that this once reviled act has now become accepted as one among many perfectly natural acts through which two individuals can express their mutual affection. As one who thus expresses affection and as one capable of enduring bonds, the homosexual is thus no different than any other person.

One of the most controversial aspects of Justice Kennedy's opinion, and one that raises questions while opening new horizons in relation to America's evolving constitutional identity, is his reference to foreign law in addressing the constitutional issue before him. As noted above, Chief Justice Burger had referred to foreign law and morals in his concurring opinion in *Bowers*, focusing particularly on Judeo-Christian mores and Roman and English law.[107] In part, Justice Kennedy reference to foreign law in *Lawrence* is for purposes of demonstrating that Chief Justice Burger's sweeping conclusions were one-sided and misleading.[108] In part also, in what would prove much more controversial, Justice Kennedy seems to rely on foreign law as added authority – not in the sense of a binding precedent but in that of a better emerging tradition – for his invalidation of the Texas law before him as a violative of the American Constitution. In his own words,

> The right the petitioners seek in this case has been accepted as an integral part of human freedom in many other countries. There has been no showing that in this country the governmental inter-est in circumscribing personal choice is somehow more legitimate or urgent.[109]

By referring to European norms through specific citations to decisions of the ECtHR,[110] Justice Kennedy makes use of foreign authorities and norms in his elaboration of America's reinvented tradition. This has unleashed vehement reaction, which has included calls for Justice Kennedy's impeachment (Gerard 2005) and a proposed U.S. Senate reso-lution suggesting that U.S. judges not cite foreign law in constitutional adjudication.[111] These developments stand in sharp contrast to the virtu-ally complete lack of reaction to Chief Justice Chief Justice Burger's refer-ences to foreign authorities in *Bowers*. Why Justice Kennedy's reliance on foreign law has been considered by many as posing a threat to American constitutional identity whereas Chief Justice Burger's has not raises an important question that will be dealt with briefly below.

Another important issue relating to American constitutional and national identity lurks ominously in the background of *Lawrence*. Indeed, whether to recognize and legalize same-sex marriage was one of the most prominent issues on the American national scene at the time *Lawrence* was decided. The highest state court in Massachusetts had decided that that state's constitution mandated legalization of same-sex marriage[112] while many other states were conducting referenda for purposes of banning such legalization. At that time, moreover, approximately two thirds of the American people were against legalizing same-sex marriage, but were also opposed, by a large majority, to the criminalization of homosexual sex among consenting adults.[113] In short, a snapshot of American national identity at the time of *Lawrence* indicates broad tolerance of homosexual lifestyles, but firm opposition against same-sex marriage.

In its dynamic relationship to national identity, constitutional identity can pull ahead of it or lag behind it, but not by such a wide margin as to prompt widespread disregard or open defiance of the country's prevailing constitutional jurisprudence. This is all the more important in a country like the U.S. where constitutional identity is so closely intertwined with national identity. Constitutional identity cannot be automatically harmonized with national identity, however, as it has its own frame of reference and its own inner logic. Justice Kennedy's opinion in *Lawrence* provides a vivid illustration of this last point. From the standpoint of the level of abstraction at which homosexual sex becomes folded into the more enduring bonds that link together two individuals possibly for life, same-sex marriage seems as deserving of 'sanctity' as its heterosexual counterpart. In other words, in the reinvented tradition as conceptualized by Justice Kennedy in *Lawrence*, same-sex marriage ought to stand on the same footing as traditional marriage between a man and a woman – a point vehemently driven home in Justice Scalia's dissent. As the latter sees it,

> Today's opinion dismantles the structure of constitutional law that has permitted a distinction to be made between heterosexual and homosexual unions, insofar as formal recognition of marriage is concerned . . . This case 'does not involve' the issue of homosexual marriage only if one entertains the belief that principle and logic have nothing to do with the decisions of this Court.[114]

In contrast, Justice Kennedy's disavowal that his opinion opens the door to constitutional recognition of a right to same sex marriage seems rather feeble. He merely declares that *Lawrence*

> does not involve whether government must give formal recognition to any relationship that homosexual persons seek to enter.[115]

Justice Kennedy thus alludes to mere contingent fact to hide logic, and does so by indirection, never mentioning same-sex marriage directly, presumably hoping that the constitutional logic which he unleashed does not outpace too soon or too far the prevailing national mood.

Justice Scalia's dissent in *Lawrence* addresses two other important issues from the standpoint of reinvented tradition and of constitutional identity. The first of these issues concerns drawing the link between included and excluded practices under the reinvented tradition which had bedeviled the Court since Justice Harlan's concurring opinion in *Griswold*. The second issue relates to the controversy over incorporation of foreign mores or legal authorities within the reinvented tradition and within the precincts of American constitutional identity. With respect to the line-drawing issue, Justice Scalia's position is sharp and clear:

> State laws against bigamy, same-sex marriage, adult incest, prosti-
> tution, masturbation, adultery, fornication, bestiality and obscen-
> ity are . . . sustainable only in light of *Bowers'* validation of laws
> based on moral choices. Every single one of these laws is called
> into question by today's decision . . .[116]

In other words, Justice Scalia is of the view that the only cogent and relevant way to distinguish between permissible and impermissible intim-ate practices is by reference to substantive moral norms. This implies a rejection of the distinction between self-regarding and other-regarding acts so important in the Lockean-Millian tradition. It also seems to strike at the heart of the notion of a reinvented tradition. Indeed, consistent with Justice Scalia's conception, either the moral values of the majority should prevail which would mean leaving the issues at stake to ordinary lawmak-ing. Or, at most, moral values embodied in actual tradition and considered fundamental at the time of the founding, such as the sanctity of marriage in its eighteenth century formulation, ought to be elevated to the level of constitutional protection. Taken to its logical conclusion, Justice Scalia's constitutional vision would seem as far afield from contemporary views as would Justice Kennedy's. Tolerance among Americans in 2003 for crimin-alization of contraception or consensual non-marital heterosexual or homosexual sex among consenting adults would be in all likelihood no greater than tolerance for legalized same-sex marriage. In the end, Justice Scalia does not appear to offer a viable alternative to Justice Kennedy's, but his analysis underscores the need for a more convincing way of drawing the line between those intimate practices that deserve constitutional protection and those that do not.

On the issue of reliance on foreign mores or legal authorities, Justice Scalia is adamant. First, he asserts that the '*Bowers* majority opinion *never* relied on values we share with a wider civilization'.[117] Second, more generally, Justice Scalia maintains that

> The Court's discussion of . . . foreign views (ignoring, of course, the many countries that have retained criminal prohibitions on sodomy) is therefore meaningless dicta. Dangerous dicta, however, since this '*Court . . . should not impose foreign moods, fads, or fashions on Americans*'[118]

In other words, for Justice Scalia actual commonly shared traditions between Americans and others (mainly Europeans to the extent that Judeo-Christian mores and Roman and English law are involved) are irrelevant from a constitutional standpoint. Moreover, any reliance on foreign views for purposes of informing American constitutional norms or tradition is downright dangerous.

That Scalia is particularly afraid of foreign 'moods, fads or fashions' is quite remarkable as he uses these terms not only to characterize foreign sexual mores but also Europe's rejection for over a generation of the death penalty in general and the rejection by all countries in the world except the United States and Somalia of the death penalty for juveniles.[119] The contrast between Justice Scalia and Justice Kennedy on this issue could not be starker and it clearly frames the debate over whether and to what extent a national constitutional identity can incorporate foreign influences without compromising its efficacy or legitimacy.

Beyond the disagreement between Justices Kennedy and Scalia in *Lawrence* there is a serious philosophical question regarding viability of the Millian-distinction between self- regarding and other-regarding acts. There is also a serious question as to whether it is ever possible to draw a non-arbitrary or non-merely contingent line between sexual practices that ought to be protected under the reinvented tradition issuing from *Griswold* and those that ought not. As we shall now see, reference to the dialectic between liberalism and illiberalism provides at least a partial answer to this last question, but more importantly for our purposes, it also lends support to the conclusion that the decisions in *Griswold* and its progeny are overdetermined rather than ultimately based on purely contingent line drawing.

3.5 The Reinvented Tradition and the Clash Between Liberalism and Illiberalism

A close glance at the distinction between self- regarding and other-regarding acts reveals that it must be ultimately based on normative rather than factual grounds. To the extent that no individual can live in complete isolation, no act can be strictly speaking self-regarding. Whether it be suicide, getting regularly inebriated while alone, deciding to devote more time to work or leisure, etc., others are bound to be somewhat affected. This is all the more true in the case of a couple, married or not, deciding whether to beget or bear a child. Accordingly, in all such instances, the key question is not whether the act involved does not affect others, but whether it ought to be treated as being within the sole discretion of the actors engaged in that act. Thus, for example, in case the birthrate within a polity is too low or too high, decisions concerning begetting children matter very much to others. Nevertheless, for liberals who subscribe to the Lockean-Millian principle, it would be unthinkable to allow the state or society to prescribe or proscribe that a couple should procreate. Consistent with this view, although procreating is actually other-regarding, it must be treated as if it were self-regarding to safeguard the fundamental liberty and autonomy of the individuals concerned.

Once the distinction between what is properly self-regarding as opposed to other-regarding is understood as being normative, then it becomes difficult to devise a principled and convincing way to draw the requisite line. Why should use of cocaine or heroine or incest among consenting adult siblings be considered different for these purposes than the sexual practices afforded protection in *Eisenstadt* and *Lawrence*?

There seems to be no permanent or direct answer to this last question, but the inevitable line-drawing can be understood and justified, at least in part, in terms of the dialectic between liberalism and illiberalism. As noted above, there is a discrepancy between the logic of Locke's liberalism and many of the actual views he held, such as those concerning the relationship between master and servant.[120] This discrepancy is but an example of a more general dichotomy between liberalism as a comprehensive normative approach and the promotion of such approach in actual historical socio-political settings characterized by various levels and kinds of illiberalism. In other words, liberalism is at once an ideology and a means to combat particular configurations of entrenched illiberalism (Rosenfeld and Sajo 2006).

The twofold dimension of liberalism as a comprehensive ideology and as a wedge against particular forms of entrenched illiberalism plays out concurrently at the factual and the normative level. At the factual level, for any particular society at a specific moment in history, the struggle for greater individual liberty and autonomy is set against certain specific targets viewed as presenting the most important obstacles to the realization of liberal ideals. For example, in confronting feudalism or an authoritarian regime, the focus may be exclusively on the defeat of social hierarchy or of non-democratic rule, without regard to existing inequities based on gender or wealth. At some other place and time, the illiberal obstacle may be religious intolerance, but the liberal thrust limited removal of such intolerance for some individuals in connection with some religions – say, removal of all intolerance against Christians by building bridges among Catholics and Protestants without altering prevailing intolerance against Jews and Muslims. The reason for such limitations, moreover, maybe due to limited perceptions leading to restrictive conceptions of the *subject-class* that ought to enjoy greater liberalism (a we/they divide) or of the relevant *object-class* (some liberties seem more worthy than others; some restrictions on liberty more reasonable than others). Alternatively, such limitations may result from strategic or tactical reasons – e.g. if tolerance for all religions rather than only for Christian ones is sought, due to anticipated resistance no greater religious tolerance is likely to be achieved within the foreseeable future.

At the normative level, on the other hand, liberalism is characterized by placing the individual above the community. The individual should not be subordinated to the communal, but rather collective cooperation should foster the greatest possible liberty and autonomy to pave the way to individual self-fulfillment and self-realization. Liberalism, however, requires two important limitations on individual liberty and autonomy. The first is that one individual's liberty and autonomy not extend to allow for impingement on another individual's equal liberty and autonomy. The second is that freedom to pursue self-fulfillment and self-realization should only be accorded to the extent that an individual has the capacity to set and go after his or her goals coherently and responsibly. The child and the mentally handicapped may thus be significantly restricted as may those embarking on 'unnatural' or 'abnormal' pursuits.

Consistent with this latter limitation, there can be no neat separation between what should be left to individual choice and what ought to be entrusted to communal regulation. For example, if non-procreational sex were genuinely deemed 'abnormal' and destructive, then communal prohibition against it may be compatible with liberalism, though communal denial of all freedom to choose one's mate for procreational sex may not be. More generally, the inability to neatly disentangle what ought to be subject to communal norms and what ought to be left to individual freedom – which is largely due to the fluidity of line between 'normal' and 'abnormal', 'natural' and 'unnatural', etc. – is often highly contestable. This difficulty is also analogous and related to the impossibility to clearly differentiate between self-regarding and other-regarding acts.

The line between what is properly communal and what is legitimately individual is not only most frequently contestable, but it also shifts over time. For example, it is as consistent with the mores of the times that Justice Harlan excluded homosexual sex from the individual's constitutional freedom respecting intimate sexual relations in 1965, as it is that Justice Kennedy included it in 2003. Moreover, the contestations and line-shifting pressures involved produce a dialectic between liberalism and illiberalism at the normative level that complements and intertwines with that prevalent at the factual level.

At bottom, though liberalism often speaks as if the individual could stand apart from the communal, the individual is in the end always conditioned and limited by the communal. The struggle between liberalism and illiberalism is ultimately a struggle between claims for greater control for the individual and claims for a greater control by the community. In this struggle, liberal arguments are most often along the metaphorical axis, stressing expansion of the subject or object-class to be encompassed within the sphere of individual autonomy. For example, the liberal thrust may require expanding legitimate sexual autonomy to encompass homosexuals as well as heterosexuals, and sodomy as well as sexual practices that may result in procreation. In contrast, illiberal arguments aimed at preserving current levels of communal controls or at reverting to greater such controls are most likely to occur within the metonymic axis. For example, from an illiberal standpoint communal restrictions against homosexual sex may be justified in as much as such sex could be portrayed as deviating from the norm.

Consistent with the preceding remarks, the judicial line drawing among the range of practices considered in the cases spanning from *Griswold* to *Lawrence* can be explained, at least partially, in terms of the particulars of the struggle between liberalism and illiberalism at the time of the Court's decision. As already noted, the Court need not stand exactly where the public does, but it is hard to imagine that it could stand too far afield from mainstream views if it is to keep its reinvented tradition within the bounds of legitimacy. Furthermore, all other things being equal, to the extent that courts as constitutional adjudicators approach the divide between individual and communal control in the context vindicating individual rights, it stands to reason that they should lean on the side of the liberalism of the moment rather than on that of its illiberal counterpart. This last conclusion is borne out by the Court's decision in all cases discussed above, except *Bowers*. And *Bowers* could have easily gone the opposite way as Justice Powell, the crucial fifth vote for the majority, stated upon his retirement from the Court, four years after that decision, that he 'probably made a mistake' (Sullivan & Gunther 2004:601 n.2).

3.6 The Reinvented Tradition and Reliance on Foreign Legal Authorities

Before concluding, I will briefly address the question raised above of why reference to foreign law and mores by justices in the majority in *Bowers* did not cause an uproar like similar references by Justice Kennedy in *Lawrence* seventeen years later. This question is important not only in relation to a determination of the proper role of foreign and transnational influences in the particular case of defining the reinvented tradition in American unenumerated rights jurisprudence. It is also important, albeit in a more indirect way, with respect to the broader questions of the place of foreign and transnational influences on national constitutions and nation-state constitutional identities, and of the possibility or viability of transnational constitutionalism and of transnational constitutional identity. For now, the focus will be limited to the American context. The transnational context will be addressed in Chapter 8.

The reasons for the remarkable shift between 1986 and 2003 may well be manifold, but for our purposes, two of them stand out above all. The first is the global spread of constitutionalism and its effect on American constitutional identity; the second, the dramatic exacerbation of a long standing split regarding America's national identity. These two reasons are closely intertwined, moreover, because American constitutional identity figures so prominently in the country's national identity.

1989 marks a major turning point in the world-wide spread of constitutionalism much like two centuries earlier 1789 saw the dawn of modern constitutionalism with the entry into force of the American Constitution. After the 1989 fall of the Berlin Wall, constitutionalism promptly spread throughout the formerly communist polities in Europe (Ludwikowski 1996) followed by rapid expansion into other polities throughout the world, including South Africa, much of South America and many countries in other parts of the world (Hirschl 2004). This trend toward constitutional rule throughout the globe started after World War Two when Germany and Japan turned into constitutional democracies, but it enormously accelerated after 1989. Furthermore, this trend not only brought constitutional democracy to an ever increasing number of polities, but it also led to the proliferation of constitutional adjudication by courts extending to all corners of the world.

These developments had two salient consequences for American constitutionalism. They put an end to American constitutional hegemony and they yielded a rich and varied judicial constitutional jurisprudence available to be mined for various purposes involving either identification or differentiation between American and non-American approaches and results with respect to similar issues.

Concurrently with the spread of constitutionalism, and particularly after the U.S. became the only superpower upon the dissolution of the Soviet Union in the early 1990's, there was an intensification of the divide among the respective proponents of two opposed visions of America. The first of these is the exclusivist vision (Tushnet 2006:310–311). Under the exclusivist view, the United States is a country with a unique destiny, exemplary values and ideals, who serves as a model for the rest of the world. Under the universalist view, on the other hand, the United States is a diverse cosmopolitan nation which is as much influenced by trends and developments coming from abroad as the rest of the world is influenced by it. The exclusivist view fosters a national identity focused on divergences; the universalist view, one centered on convergences. Furthermore, the divide over these views became much more contentious after George W. Bush became president, reaching its peak in 2003, the year *Lawrence* was decided, because of the rift over going to war in Iraq between the United States and many of its traditional European allies such as France and Germany.[121]

In their current incarnation, the exclusivist view is mainly held by political conservatives; the universalist, by progressives (*Id*). Moreover, for the exclusivists the U.S. Constitution must remain purely American and free from foreign influence or contamination (Conversation between Scalia and Breyer 2005:521, 525).[122] For the universalists, in contrast, there is a convergence of norms and values, at least among advanced constitutional democracies, which makes constitutional cross-fertilization attractive and often useful (*Id*.:528–529). The split between these two constitutional visions is sharp and seemingly irreconcilable and reveals how closely related a particular conception of national identity may be to its corresponding conception of constitutional identity.

It is understandable that the above rift be particularly acute in the context of spelling out the reinvented tradition associated with unenumerated rights. Indeed, that task requires reprocessing elements of national identity – core elements at that – for purposes of elaborating key aspects of constitutional identity. The convergence of political ideology, conceptions of national identity, constitutional philosophy, and inferences from the dramatic historical changes since 1989, goes a long way in explaining the differences concerning references to foreign authorities between *Bowers* and *Lawrence* as well as those within *Lawrence*. Largely because of this convergence, moreover, these differences are overdetermined.

What most obviously accounts for the different impact of references to foreign authorities in *Bowers* and *Lawrence* is the change in historical circumstances and its effects on American self-perception. *Bowers* was decided before the end of the cold war and before the explosion and proliferation (at least within sight of the American legal and judicial community) of foreign constitutional adjudication. At the times of *Bowers*, it was the U.S. versus the Soviet Union, with Western Europe largely on the side of the former. At the times of *Lawrence*, the United States stood as the lone superpower at odds with much of Europe over, among other things, Iraq. In addition, in *Bowers* foreign authorities were relied upon by justices whose constitutional conclusions were most compatible with conservative politics whereas in *Lawrence* it was the opposite, the majority judicial position going hand in hand with progressive politics. This is important in as much as progressives, tending to be universalists, are much less likely to object to the use of foreign references as such. Finally, and this is greatly magnified in relation to reinvented tradition, *Bowers* refers mainly to ancient and historically distant foreign sources that emphasize religious morality at least as much as law. *Lawrence*, on the other hand, relies primarily on the contemporary jurisprudence of the ECtHR. Accordingly, *Bowers* can be viewed as asserting that America's deepest traditions have roots in religious moral and legal values that it shares with the broad Judeo-Christian vision as it emerged throughout the Western World. *Lawrence*, in contrast, can be portrayed as having bowed to foreign contemporary legal precedent. Moreover, although Justice Kennedy makes it clear that he regards European judicial decisions as evidence of the relevant tradition (above all to refute the *Bowers* Court's erroneous account of that tradition), to an exclusivist what *Lawrence* does may seem worse than simply following foreign precedent. It may be, in part, the functional equivalent of following foreign precedent, but it also uses the latter to define reinvented tradition. For that reason, for the exclusivist such use of foreign precedents not only subverts America's constitutional jurisprudence, but it also pollutes its self-perception at the level of national identity.

The clash between the majority and the dissent in *Lawrence* replicates the basic rift between *Lawrence* and *Bowers*, but it does so against an altered backdrop. The universalist, progressive majority looks to Europe to further elaborate the reinvented tradition issuing from *Griswold*, and relies on decisions of the ECtHR not as precedents, but as examples of successful progressive judicial resolutions of the very issue before the U.S. Supreme Court. The exclusivist conservative minority, on the other hand, rejects the example of Europe, and insists upon confining the relevant tradition to that already present in the U.S. at the time of the founding. Within this setting, what seems most puzzling is Justice Scalia's flat denial that *Bowers* relied on any foreign values, let alone foreign legal authorities, and his characterization of the European jurisprudence cited by the Court's majority as the product of 'moods', 'fads', and 'fashions'.[123] Indeed, even from a most exclusivist standpoint, American exceptionalism does not call for rejection of the Judeo-Christian heritage, but on the contrary, for its adoption and its perfection (Smith 1997). By the same token, it would seem sufficient for an exclusivist to reject European, or for that matter any other, jurisprudence on the conviction that it can neither be authoritative nor become part of any relevant tradition upon which it would be legitimate to rely on respecting unenumerated rights cases.

The above puzzle can be solved, however, if one considers that European jurisprudence stands for what is most enlightened and most advanced in modern constitutionalism, and what therefore ought to be ideally embraced by all constitutional democracies. This last conclusion is consistent with the universalist position and implicit in Justice Kennedy's majority opinion.[124] As against this universalist position, it is not enough for an exclusivist simply to reject foreign authorities because they are foreign. What is needed instead, and Justice Scalia does exactly that, is both to challenge the uniqueness and exemplarity of the European jurisprudence and to trivialize its importance and aspirations to universality. This Justice Scalia seeks to accomplish by reminding us that many non-European countries continue to criminalize homosexual sex,[125] and by belittling the potential attractiveness of the European jurisprudence by labeling it a 'fad' and a 'fashion'.

Exclusivists and universalists sketch out different conceptions of national identity and of constitutional identity, though in both cases the former is closely intertwined with the latter. This raises the question of whether it would be more accurate to speak in the plural of competing national and constitutional identities rather than in the singular. Moreover, if the answer were in the affirmative, then it would seem that at both the national level and the constitutional one a clash of identities would be more likely than the consolidation of a commonly shared identity.

Viewed more closely, what the controversy between exclusivists and universalists reveals is that both American national identity and constitutional identity are dynamic, conflictual and multifaceted. Exclusivists and universalists, however, are ultimately dialectically linked as they represent two distinct competing facets of America's self-perception as a country of destiny called upon to set and example for the rest of the world (Stephanson 1995). For the exclusivists, America can only accomplish this by strictly adhering to what makes it different. For the universalists, on the other hand, overemphasis on such differences led America to lag before the most advanced constitutional democracies in certain respects, thus requiring that it catch up to them before it can legitimately reassert its leadership role. Overall, exclusivists and universalists provide two different means to the same end, but in the course of aiming at that end, they each seem to reinvigorate the very obstacle that the other seeks to overcome. Hence, the vehemence among the two, and the significant contribution that the conflict among them makes to the contemporary delimitation of America's national and constitutional identity.

3.7 Concluding Remark: Overdetermination and Blending Tradition and Counter-tradition

Based on the preceding analysis, we are now in a position to grasp how reinvented tradition, through overdetermination, occupies a privileged place from which it can tie together the various disparate and even contradictory strands of the unenumerated rights as they emerge from *Griswold* to *Lawrence*. On the one hand, tradition binds together the countertradition embedded in constitutionalism with the neotradition required to fashion a positive constitutional identity. Precisely because the American Constitution supplants tradition rather than merely becoming engrafted on tradition, it has a strong need to fill the void left by its repudiation of tradition. This need, in turn, is met in part by symbolizing its countertraditional past as a tradition. Moreover, if this symbolization does not ring false, it is because overdetermination amalgamates two distinct semantic connotations: first, the Constitution is itself the tradition; and, second, whereas the Constitution is in significant measure countertraditional, it nevertheless does not filter out all preexisting traditions, and can thus appropriate for its own use those traditions that do not threaten its integrity. In Freudian terminology, tradition thus stands for both repression of tradition – by erasing tradition through the display of that which is counter-to-tradition as tradition – and for the return of the repressed – since the American Constitution is in fact so firmly countertraditional, the return of partial and watered-down practices, even if clothed in the trappings of tradition, fills a lack without undermining the original repression.

On the other hand, the neotradition is also linked to the countertradition and to preexisting (preconstitutional) traditions through overdetermination. In one sense, the neotradition – such as, for example, the use of contraceptives within the marital relationship – is no tradition at all. But that does not preclude tracing its pedigree in the countertradition of the Constitution, which has been resymbolized as a tradition in its own right. In another sense, however, the neotradition can be linked back to preexisting traditions through the establishment of suitable metaphoric and metonymic connections between the two. Thus, whereas it may be that the preexisting tradition justifies its latter day derivative – and while it may be important for legitimation purposes that such appearance be widely held true – in fact, it is the neotradition, which partly reincorporates the preexisting tradition, and which appropriates it as transformed for its own purposes. For example, it is freedom to use contraceptives, non-marital heterosexual and homosexual sex etc., which subsumes the 'sanctity' of marriage rather than the converse.

Determination of suitable coordinates along the metaphoric and metonymic axes for purposes of grounding a tradition to be incorporated into unenumerated liberty and privacy rights depends on several different factors. Specifically, these include, as we have seen convergences among historical, political, ideological, philosophical, and constitutional logic and coherence elements. More generally, to become successful, a reinvented tradition must satisfy four conditions. First, the tradition in question cannot undermine or threaten the countertradition that sustains the constitutional order. Second, this tradition cannot contravene or weaken structural constraints inherent in constitutionalism. Third, this tradition must be susceptible of plausible (after-the-fact) linkage to a preexisting (preconstitutional) tradition. And fourth, this tradition must be susceptible of wide acceptance as being authoritative among a sizeable majority within the polity. This is why, for example, *Griswold* seems on much more solid footing than *Roe* though in nearly every other respect they are similarly grounded. Consistent with this, moreover, the relevant question in constitutionalizing a tradition is not what level of abstraction is appropriate, but rather whether the contemplated tradition can fully meet the hurdles stemming from the four above mentioned conditions. And if a tradition can successfully meet these hurdles at a certain level of abstraction, then that level is the appropriate one.

Over determination both links preconstitutional tradition, the countertradition of the constitution and the neotradition necessary to construct a positive constitutional identity; and, insures that the uses of tradition to frame constitutional rights are both legitimate and appropriate.

Overdetermined tradition is thus not arbitrary, but that does not mean that it must become fixed for all time. Paradoxically, one of the chief virtues of tradition insofar as it frames unenumerated constitutional rights, is its open-endedness, malleability, and porousness. Indeed, the very process of overdetermination is sensitive to differences of time and place. Thus, what may satisfy the requirements derived from the four conditions listed above under one set of circumstances, may fail to do so under another. A tradition fit for one occasion may not be suited for the next, or at least it may not be suited if taken at the same level of abstraction. In sum, by condensing the process of blending together fragments of preconstitutional traditions, constitutional countertradition, and new elements in need of a pedigree relating back to tradition into special species of tradition, constitutional identity can evolve and reinvent itself without seemingly abdicating its rootedness in some plausible collective past.

CHAPTER 4

Recasting and Reorienting Identity Through Constitution-Making: The Pivotal Case of Spain's 1978 Constitution

As the preceding Chapter illustrates, the production and alteration of constitutional identity occurs at all levels of engagement of the constitutional subject. Constitutional interpretation as the case of the American jurisprudence concerning unenumerated rights demonstrates, weaves together narratives that cast constitutional identity as distinct yet inextricably interwoven with other key identities such as national identity. Constitutional interpretation operates most often at a micro-level elaborating and reworking constitutional identity for the most part implicitly and gradually. Constitution-making, on the other hand, operates at a macro-level; frequently follows the violent overthrow of the preceding socio-political and legal order as in the case of the eighteenth century American and French revolutions; and seems bound to carve out a distinct new identity that differs sharply from prevailing pre-constitutional and extra-constitutional identities.

In this Chapter, I examine how constitution-making contributes to defining a new constitutional identity by focusing on the making of the 1978 Spanish Constitution. That constitution elaborated on the heels of Franco's death, which ended more than three decades of authoritarian dictatorship, provides a particularly instructive example. This is for two principal reasons. First the 1978 Spanish Constitution is the first major example of a pacted constitution, one that was not preceded by some kind of violent break, which became a model for the peaceful making of many subsequent constitutions, such as those of the post-socialist countries in Eastern and Central Europe in the Early 1990's and of South Africa in the mid-1990's. And second, the constituents in post-Franco Spain did not only look inwardly to carve out a new constitutional identity. They also looked to the European Community (now the EU), which they hoped to eventually join, for norms which they could incorporate into their new constitution, thus affording an initial glimpse into the possibility of transnational constitutional identity.

4.1 Constitution-making in Context

Transitions from authoritarian regimes to constitutional democracies have traditionally involved violent breaks with the past. The American and the French eighteenth century transitions, which gave birth to modern constitutionalism, occurred in the wake of bloody revolutions (The Federalist 45, 1961:325) – though, strictly speaking, it would be more accurate to refer to the American Revolution as a war of liberation (Farber & Sherry 1990:9–13; Reid 1988). Similarly, the more recent transitions in Germany and Japan in the aftermath of World War II came after complete military defeat and surrender (Young 1980:393–416).

The link between violence and the establishment of constitutional democracy seems perfectly logical when considering that despots have not been prone to relinquish their powers willingly (*Id.*). Accordingly, the making of a democratic constitution appears to require a clear break from the grip of an authoritarian past (Elster 1994:57). As emphasized by a member of the constituent assembly during the French Revolution, '[a]narchy is a frightening but necessary transitional stage; the only moment in which a new order of things can be created.' (*Id.*:65).[1] Moreover, a period of anarchy may be necessary not only to rid the polity of its despot and of the latter's closest collaborators, but also to generate a shift in collective identity. Indeed, the successful implantation of a constitutional democracy seemingly depends both on disempowering despots and on undermining prevailing submissive mentalities and self-images nurtured to suit the *ancien régime.*

A striking example of this phenomenon is provided by the post-World War II Constitution (known as the 'Basic Law') of the Federal Republic of Germany which embraces the right to life as a fundamental constitutional value. In the words of the German Constitutional Court, 'the categorical inclusion of the inherently self-evident right to life in the Basic Law may be explained principally as a reaction to the "destruction of life unworthy to live" the "final solution," and the "liquidations" that the National Socialist regime carried out as governmental measures.' Various provisions of the Basic Law imply 'an affirmation of the fundamental value of human life and of a state concept which emphatically opposes the views of a political regime for which the individual life had little significance and which therefore practiced unlimited abuse in the name of the arrogated right over life and death of the citizen.'[2]

While breaking with the past looms as a necessary precondition to a successful implantation of constitutional democracy, such a break, particularly if violent, is problematic from the standpoint of the emergent constitutional order. For one thing, consistent and continuous adherence to the rule of law is an essential pillar of constitutional democracy, and violent breaks with the past sever the chain of legality, thus casting doubt on the legal legitimacy of the new constitutional order. Indeed, inasmuch as the constitutional framers must exceed the bounds of the pre-constitutional legal order to craft their new constitution, they cannot avoid what Jon Elster has termed 'constitutional bootstrapping' (Elster 1994:57), thus rooting allegiance to the rule of law in an act of legal transgression. Furthermore, to the extent that successful constitution-making depends on replacing an incompatible pre-constitutional identity with a more congenial collective self-image, the new constitutional framework could prove too destabilizing to allow the polity to rally sufficiently around the requisite common identity.[3] For example, the radical break with the past launched in the course of the French Revolution led to the reign of terror, paving the way for the restoration of despotic rule in the Napoleonic Empire instead of consolidating the transition to constitutional democracy. (Van Caenegem 1995:174–178). In contrast, the American Revolution's much more limited break with its colonial past, proved much more favorable to the successful implantation of constitutional democracy. In short, the success of a transition from authoritarianism to constitutional democracy seemingly depends, in part at least, on some kind of firm repudiation of the polity's pre-constitutional identity, though such repudiation is likely to lead to failure if it does away with too little or too much.

Inasmuch as history teaches that violence usually accompanies successful transition to constitutional democracy – though it remains unclear which violence and how much of it might be optimal for these purposes – Spain's peaceful transition from the Franco dictatorship to constitutional democracy in the mid-1970s and its ability to develop a vibrant constitutional culture in the subsequent three decades is truly remarkable.[4] Moreover, the Spanish case is all the more striking because it hardly qualifies as an anomaly. Instead, it marks a turning point towards peaceful

transitions to constitutional democracy which has reached global propor-
tions since the 1980s.[5] In the last two decades, there has been a veritable
global trend towards constitutional democracy and a majority of the
transitions involved – in Eastern and Central Europe, Latin America, and
South Africa – have been peaceful (Johansen 1993:39; Kim 1993:55).

This new trend towards peaceful transitions is puzzling because it raises
serious questions about the accepted wisdom that genuine transitions
to constitutional democracy require a violent tear in the political fabric
and a radical shift in the polity's conception of its own identity. Perhaps
the trend towards peaceful transition does not pose a challenge to the
accepted wisdom because the bulk of the recent transitions did not involve
constitutional revolutions, but rather constitutional restorations (Sajo
1994:335). If this latter view is warranted, then the Fascist and Socialist
authoritarian regimes in Spain and Eastern Europe respectively did not
erase the past, but merely suppressed it. Accordingly, upon the dissolution
of their authoritarian experiences, these countries would be able to reclaim
past identities and rebuild democracy upon once tried institutional
foundations.

On the other hand, if recent peaceful transitions do not really involve
restoration constitutions – and the cases of Spain, many East European
countries, and South Africa strongly suggest that they cannot[6] – then
reexamination of the conditions for successful constitution-making in the
context of transitions to democracy is clearly called for. With this in mind,
I will first briefly discuss some of the most salient features of traditional
constitution-making and its relation to identity building in the context of
transition to democracy, attempting to place the recent trend of peaceful
transitions in context, on the basis of observations derived from the
Spanish experience.

At a bare minimum, radical political transformation depends on two
essential factors: leadership that will shepherd the transition, and a move
away from old habits and obsolete self-images for purposes of evolution
towards a new collective self-identity suited to the emergent political and
institutional order. For example, the transformation of the Jewish people
from slavery in Egypt to free nationhood in Israel required, according to
the Bible, divine legislation disseminated through the leadership of Moses
and forty years in the desert to shed the vestiges of bondage (Exodus 3:1 to
4:17, 6:2 to 7:13). Moreover, modern constitution-making, as Ulrich K.
Preuss emphasizes, represents a secularized version of divine creation, and
legislation as the constituent power's constitution-making amounts to a
creation *ex nihilo* (Preuss 1994:143–144).The *pouvoir constituant* of the
constitution-makers must therefore be freed from any pre-constitutional

constraints, or in other words, constituent power must be unbound but binding (*Id.*:144). To be free from the bonds of the past, the constituent power cannot emerge except in the context of a revolution, but to constrain the polity, and particularly subsequent generations, it must put an end to the revolution by instituting the constitution it crafts (*Id.*:144–45). Constitution-making in the course of transition to democracy seems inextricably linked to revolution though the relationship may be inherently ambivalent (*Id.*:144). Accordingly, for constitution-making to be genuinely a creation *ex nihilo* it would seem necessary that it go hand in hand with some form of violence.

While it may not require forty years to shed pre-constitutional self-images and to embrace a suitable constitutional identity, adaptation to the new order requires significant changes in mentality, and those changes are unlikely to occur overnight. For example, the changes brought about by the French Revolution and the constitutional movement it launched had their origins in the philosophy of the Enlightenment. This movement developed over the course of several decades preceding the Revolution and did not become successfully implanted for a long time, possibly not until the advent of the Third Republic in the 1870s.[7] Similarly, constitutional identity in the United States was not consolidated until after the Civil War. Unlike the first French Constitution, the 1787 American Constitution has proved enduring,[8] yet the core of its constitutional identity – encapsulated in the phrase 'all men are created equal' included in the 1776 Declaration of Independence – could not be fully deployed until the abolition of slavery.[9]

Constitutional identity as distinct from both pre-constitutional and extra-constitutional identities must depart from tradition, but it cannot completely sever its links with the other identities or with all traditions if it is to fulfill its critical role in cementing the new constitutional order. For example, whereas the French Revolution brought about a radical shift from absolute monarchy to a constitutional parliamentary democracy, the French remained to an important extent united through their common nationhood. Or more precisely, the French nation endured through the tears and ruptures to the polity's social and political fabric caused by the Revolution, but its self-perception evolved. As conceived by Abbé Sieyès, the third estate not only became the legitimate representative of the nation, but it also emerged as its full embodiment (Sieyès 1789:58). In other words, what had been but a part – and the least powerful part – of what the old order came to stand for and to symbolize, became the image of the whole emergent constitutional order launched by the Revolution.

Many factors undoubtedly contribute to the shift away from a pre-revolutionary identity towards a self-image better suited to constitutional democracy. Moreover, the passage from a pre-revolutionary authoritarian polity to a post-revolutionary constitutional democracy may well require a profound transformation in collective identity, but not all changes would, strictly speaking, concern constitutional identity. For example, a rigid theocracy tightly run by an entrenched hierarchy of clerics would be clearly incompatible with the implantation of any workable version of contemporary constitutionalism. In that case, transition to constitutional democracy would require a loosening of the political grip of the clerics as well as a modification in the perceived bonds between religion and politics. Any change concerning the former would obviously inform constitutional identity, but the same would not necessarily be the case in connection with shifts in the latter. Indeed, a shift from an integrated vision of religion and politics to one that allows for reasonable daylight between the two would form an integral part of an emergent constitutional identity. In contrast, a more profound secularization among the people leading to a large scale weakening of the grip of religion in favor of culture significantly steeped in Enlightenment values might play an important role in making room for a constitutional culture, but would clearly involve the polity's social, political, and cultural identity, as well as its constitutional identity.

4.2 The Place of Violence in Constitution Making

Regarding the prominent place of violence in constitution-making, the level of it that might be required in the context of a successful transition to constitutional democracy may fluctuate significantly as a function of several distinct factors. For example, pre-constitutional identities may vary in intensity, or they may be kept in place through easier to dislodge external forces or through more deeply entrenched internal forces. From the standpoint of the relevant identities, and regardless of the actual material assets at the disposal of various relevant players, external forces, such as colonialist or foreign occupiers, would seem less likely to have a firm or lasting grip on the collective self-image of those under their tutelage than would internal forces who share in a common heritage though they may wield excessive powers. Accordingly, in cases where transition to constitutional democracy is impeded by foreign rule and where there does not lurk any potential divisive internal strife, unproblematic assumption of a workable constitutional identity and smooth transition may be entirely within reach upon emancipation from colonial power. Conversely, in cases where internal forces are deeply divided, such transition may remain elusive absent an interim period marked by considerable violence and account settling between proponents of a new order and defenders of traditional prerogatives.[10]

The *amount* of violence surrounding a transition to constitutional democracy is likely to depend on the degree of entrenchment of the forces that oppose change. On the other hand, the *need* for interim violence, between the fall of the old order and the emergence of the new, seems closely linked to the call for changes in self-perception conceived in the broadest terms. Specifically, the citizenry's perception of its polity's system of justice figures significantly in that citizenry's collective self-image. Moreover, transitions to constitutional democracy usually involve a switch in systems of justice that requires discrediting the old legal regime and the ways in which it purported to dispense justice. At the same time, such transitions must successfully institute and legitimize a new legal regime to foster adherence to newly adopted constitutional values and renewed respect for the rule of law. It is difficult to concurrently dismantle the old regime and build up the new one without violence. Especially when those oppressed by the old regime call for retribution, and those favored by it refuse to relinquish their privileges, an interim period for settling old accounts without sullying the new legal regime would seem desirable, if not indispensable.[11] In short, an interim period marked by some violence and account settling may significantly facilitate passage from obsolete criteria of justice to a new conception of justice that is congruent with the emergent self-image launched by the constitution-makers.

In more general terms, pre-constitutional identity must be transformed, or at least mediated, in order to allow for the possible emergence of a constitutional identity. Moreover, the process involved is likely to be complex and on occasion even seemingly contradictory. As one observer has pointed out, 'It is often said that constitutions, as a form of higher law, must be compatible with the culture and mores of those whom they regulate. In one sense, however, the opposite is true. . . . Constitutions should work against the particular nation's most threatening tendencies.' (Sunstein 1994:398).

In sum, constitution-making cannot be successful without achieving a degree of coordination capable of dealing with the series of complex problems littered through its path. Also, to the extent that constitution-making requires a clear break with the past, some measure of violence – though its nature and intensity may vary depending on the relevant circumstances – seems inevitable. Thus, transition from despotic rule to constitutional democracy depends on getting rid of the despot, forging a new identity for the polity, and furnishing an interim period for the settling of certain accounts without compromising the new system of justice about to be put in place.

4.3 The Extraordinary Case of Spain's Peacefully Pacted Constitution

To place Spain's peaceful transition to constitutional democracy in proper perspective, reference must be to the two predominant types of transition prevalent prior to the mid-1970s. These two types are, respectively, transition to constitutional democracy after a revolution, as in eighteenth century France and the United States; and transition imposed by the victors after total defeat and surrender of tyrannical belligerent regimes such as Nazi Germany and the Japanese Empire at the end of World War II.[12] Moreover, in the latter case, the success of the transition hinges on reconstruction of the defeated polity and on an embracing of the new constitutional order by the citizenry as was clearly the case in postwar Germany (Komers 1997). Furthermore, for constitutionalism and democracy to thrive in the last quarter of the twentieth century, there must have been room for fruitful interaction among what Juan Linz and Alfred Stepan have termed the 'five arenas of a consolidated democracy,' (Linz & Stepan 1996: 7) to wit:1) the existence of a 'free and lively civil society'; 2) the functioning of a 'relatively autonomous . . . political society';[13] 3) the implementation of the rule of law; 4) the organization of a state bureaucracy usable by democratic government for the implementation of policy; and 5) the presence of an 'institutionalized economic society.'[14]

Spain's transition to constitutional democracy is remarkable in several key respects. Above all, not only did the transition in question avoid violence, but it also managed to proceed from beginning to end without any break in legality. Furthermore, the transition that led to the making of the Spanish Constitution does not belong to either of the two types previously mentioned. Finally, the Spanish transition seems in many ways unique due to a confluence of historical circumstances unlikely to ever be reproduced (*Id.*:87–115), including significant achievements in four of the five above listed areas of consolidated democracy (*Id.*:112). Yet, as will be discussed below, in certain significant respects, the Spanish transition looms as the harbinger of a third type of transition, namely peaceful transition. Keeping this in mind, I will now turn to some key aspects of the Spanish transition with a view towards better grasping its contribution to our understanding of constitution-making and towards building a workable constitutional identity.[15]

Although Franco's thirty-six-year-authoritarian regime was preceded by democratic rule, the Spanish transition in no way amounted to a restoration. (Linz & Stepan 1996: 89). This is because it was neither possible to return to pre-Francoist democratic institutions nor to use existing institutions to lend necessary support to democratic rule. (*Id.*). Moreover, Franco's provision for the installation of a monarchy upon the end of his rule did not forge any workable links to the previously abolished Spanish Monarchy, notwithstanding any superficial indications to the contrary. While King Juan Carlos would play a key role in Spain's successful transition, at the moment he acceded to the throne he was neither the legitimate heir to the Spanish throne,[16] nor did he enjoy legitimacy among the partisans of democracy who saw him as a pawn of Franco's heirs, or among hard line Francoists, who sensed that he was not committed to their cause (Rubio Llorente 1988:243).

Ironically, the Spanish transition might well not have been peaceful were it not for the fact that both the political heirs of Franco and those who wished to institute a democracy proved too weak to take the country's destiny into their own hands. Indeed, the partisans of authoritarianism could not realistically expect to stay in office absent excessive repression due to external pressure from surrounding Western European polities (Linz & Stepan 1996:88). For their part, those who wanted to bring about democracy lacked sufficient strength to violently overthrow those still in power, particularly since the latter had the benefit of the loyalty of the Armed Forces (*Id.*). Thus, Spain's peaceful transition apparently grew out of the initial deadlock among the principal antagonists who stood on the political stage at Franco's death.

This initial deadlock may account for the lack of violence at the outset of Spain's transition, but it does not explain why the entire process remained peaceful. Although in retrospect, the Spanish transition may be portrayed as smooth and relatively straightforward, in reality it was fraught with difficulties and uncertainties and its success was by no means a foregone conclusion (*Id.*:89). Actually, it seems fair to conclude that the success of Spain's peaceful transition was due, at least in part, to a fortunate confluence of a series of events, to the outstanding leadership of certain individuals, and to certain other factors unlikely to be reproduced in other historical contexts (*Id.*).

Before further exploring the most salient factors that shaped the Spanish transition, a brief look at the time frame of that transition is warranted to help shed light on the essentials of the process involved. Indeed, depending on one's conception of what a successful transition requires, one may select among a series of significant dates as being best suited to mark the successful completion of the process of transition. Whereas there is consensus that the transition began with the death of Franco in November

1975, several different dates have been mentioned as marking the success-ful completion of the process (*Id.*:106–107) and the consolidation of Spain's constitutional democracy (*Id.*:108–109). Arguably, the success of the Spanish transition was assured as early as the fall of 1977, when, after the first democratic elections to Parliament, the process of government accountability to Parliament was formally established (*Id.*:106). At the other end of the spectrum, plausibly, success was not assured until Spain actually entered into what is today the EU in 1986 (*Id.*:113). In between these two dates, moreover, there are several others that loom as critical in relation to the success of the transition. These include: December 1978, when the new constitution was ratified in a nationwide referendum (*Id.*-106); October 1979, when the Basque and Catalan referenda on regional autonomy consistent with the constitution were held; February 1981, when a military coup failed, due in large measure to the King's courageous intervention in order to save democracy (*Id.*:109); and October 1982, when power peacefully transferred to the Socialist Party upon the latter's victory in Parliamentary elections (*Id.*:108).

Although the relative importance of each of the above listed dates may vary depending on one's conception of the transition, they all serve to demarcate key moments in the shaping of Spain's emerging new dem-ocracy and in the construction of its constitutional identity. The first of these dates, that of the death of Franco, has special significance not only because it clearly marks the beginning of the transition, but it also serves to set the Spanish transition, apart from both the two types of violent transi-tion that preceded it and from the peaceful transitions that followed it. Whereas the earlier transitions in France, Germany, or the United States involved putting a violent end to despotic rule; and whereas later peaceful transitions in Eastern and Central European countries like Poland and Hungary resulted from pacted arrangements worked out among weakened incumbent socialist regimes and their democratic opponents;[17] Franco's regime ultimately never ascended beyond one-man rule (Rubio Llorente 1988:239); and hence his death truly marked the end of a political era. Ironically, Franco was not indifferent when it came to his succession, and he did take measures to insure an orderly transition – such as providing for a king upon his death (*Id.*:242) – but those measures did not allow his would-be heirs to remain in power, and would prove eventually to be a key link in the successful transition to democracy due to the King's use of his considerable powers to that end.

Franco's regime has been characterized as a 'kingdom without a king' (*Id.*). Drawing from fascism as well as from tradition, Franco shaped the state according to three fundamental principles. First, 'subordination of the individual to the communal interests of the nation' (*Id.*:241); second, rejection of capitalism and Marxism in favor of a corporatist economy designed to harmonize the interests of business and labor (*Id.*); and third, 'concentration of political power in a charismatic leader' only answerable to 'God and History' (*Id.*). Moreover the collective identity designed to blend together with Franco's state was highlighted by an embrace of Catholicism as the state's religion, a rejection of liberalism and all else that smacked of relativism – including political parties – and an unbending commitment to the unity of Spain, resulting in complete intolerance of any aspiration towards regional autonomy – especially among the Basques or Catalans (*Id.*:240).

The above mentioned identity stands in sharp contrast to that forged in the wake of the Spanish transition to constitutional democracy. Not only has Spain become a typical Western constitutional parliamentary democracy, but it has also abandoned corporatism, collectivism and the close nexus between church and state, in favor of a pluralistic and secular political society that has institutionalized a large degree of regional auto-nomy within its new constitutional framework.[18] This raises the question of what accounts for these dramatic changes in identity between Francoist and post-Francoist Spain. Specifically, have these considerable changes really come about within the short period between Franco's death and the consolidation of the Spanish transition to constitutional democracy?[19] Furthermore, to what extent are these changes in Spain's social and political self-image attributable to the formation of a new constitutional identity in the course of that transition?

Upon closer examination, Spain's changes in identity were more gradual than they may first appear because they were prompted by a series of internal and external factors at work well before Franco's death. Although Franco's death marks the starting point of Spain's political transition to constitutional democracy, the conditions that lent support to the national identity forged by Franco began unraveling during the latter part of his regime due to a confluence of internal and external causes.

Franco never gave up authoritarian one-man rule, but his grip on power did not prevent Spain from embarking during the last twenty years of his regime on the path that would ultimately culminate in democracy. As already mentioned, at the time of Franco's death, Spain had already managed considerable achievements in four of the five arenas of consoli-dated democracy,[20] and was only seriously lacking in the development of a political society (Linz & Stepan 1996:113). In particular, by the mid-1970s Spain was a well-institutionalized economic society ranking tenth among all capitalist economies and having experienced the greatest growth rate throughout the world during the period 1961–1970 (*Id.*:112). Finally, Spain's working state bureaucracy, though run in an authoritarian way, was usable by a democratic government, (*Id.*:113) and the country had, 'a reasonably strong recent tradition of rule of law' (*Id.*).[21]

Whereas one might disagree on whether the cause of Spain's economic and cultural development in the years preceding Franco's death were primarily internal or external,[22] it seems clear that one key factor that played a major role in leading to a peaceful transition was squarely internal. That factor was the cultural reconstruction – over the course of the last two decades of Franco's regime – of the historical memory of the Civil War in a way that transformed what had been a deep tear within the very fabric of the Spanish polity into a building block on the path to democracy (Linz & Stepan, 1996:88 n.3). In other words, the severe wounds that Spain's bloody civil war inflicted on the nation's self-image had to be healed before it could forge ahead towards democracy. And this was accomplished through cultural reconstruction of the country's histori-cal identity so as to emphasize the commonalities among all Spaniards rather than the irreconcilable differences that led to fratricidal strife. Moreover, the importance of this shift in identity can hardly be over-emphasized. Indeed, the contrast between the Spanish shift in identity and the complete lack of meaningful change in the forty years that followed the 1940s civil wars between Serbs and Croats could not be more dramatic (*Id.*).

Several other factors, both internal and external, which became significant during Franco's lifetime, also helped pave the way towards democracy. First, the alliance between the Catholic Church and the regime, which, as we have seen above,[23] was an important ingredient in the collect-ive self-image promoted by Franco, began to change as the Spanish Church belatedly started to adapt to the program of modernization launched by Vatican II in 1965 (Rubio Llorente 1988:240).[24] In addition, as already mentioned,[25] Franco undertook to transform his personal rule into a last-ing institutional framework for government during the last years of his life. He appointed Carrero Blanco as prime minister, thus separating for the first time the function of head of government from that of head of state (Rubio Llorentz 1988:242). Soon afterwards, however, in December 1973, Carrero Blanco was assassinated by Basque terrorists (Linz & Stepan 1996:107).

Basque terrorism in general, and Carrero Blanco's assassination in par-ticular, had an important impact on the end of the Franco regime and on the onset of the transition. Basque terrorism destabilized the regime and the repressive measures adopted to combat against it led to further discrediting of Franco's rule abroad (*Id.*). Moreover, while the full implications of Carrero Blanco's assassination are still a matter of debate, it seems reasonable to assume that had Carrero Blanco been in office at Franco's death, the heirs of the regime would have been in a much better position to delay or greatly complicate the transition (*Id.*).

Although the Spanish transition was not itself violent, the preceding brief review reveals that it was surrounded by violence. At the time the transition was about to begin, violence, the threat of violence, and the memory of violence were all very much present. It seems quite plausible that the memory of the extreme violence of the civil war as culturally reconstructed in the years preceding the transition provided a great incentive to all parties involved in the transition to preserve the peace. Moreover, Basque terrorism would continue throughout the transition and thereafter, but would also become increasingly politically isolated (*Id.*). By all indications, Basque terrorism did not shape the transition but it remained ever present within the political landscape.

In the immediate aftermath of Franco's death, Arias Navarro, Carrero Blanco's successor, was confirmed as head of government by the King, and began weak attempts at reform (Rubio Llorente 1988:242). Because of great suspicion and mistrust among Francoists and their opponents – none of whom really trusted the King[26] – these attempts met with little success. Decisive action was needed, and the King apparently provided it as it is believed that he forced the resignation of Arias Navarro and had him replaced on July 1, 1976 by Adolfo Suarez, the man who would lead Spain to democratic elections and to the making of its new constitution (*Id.*).

The situation was precarious, but remarkably Suarez managed to launch the path towards a working democracy without ever exceeding the bounds of legality. The task was formidable as, to remain within the realm of legality, Suarez could only count on Francoist law and had to work together with the Cortes – the corporatist legislature created by Franco and whose membership comprised a significant number of his appointees (Linz & Stepan 1996:92). Insisting on the importance of adhering to the rule of law, and adroitly navigating in treacherous political waters, through appeals to the Cortes and through television addresses to the nation as a whole, Suarez managed to have the Cortes enact two crucial pieces of legislation in 1976. The first of these legalized political associations and paved the way for the establishment of full-fledged non-Francoist political parties. The second – which was even more remarkable, because in enacting it the Cortes were in effect voting themselves out of office – provided for political reform and called for free elections (*Id.*:95).

For his part, the King made full use of the powers awarded him by the dictatorship, but did so not in furtherance of authoritarianism but with a view toward breaking away from it. Aside from his role in the installation of Suarez as premier, the King took care to legitimize his position as rightful heir to the Spanish Monarchy by having his father renounce his succession rights (Rubio Llorente 1988:248). That important step had the symbolic effect of casting the Monarchy (which had been abolished in 1931) in the light of a restored government, thus bolstering the King's support among the military and a sizeable proportion of the political right (*Id.*). Furthermore, after the first elections which took place in June 1977, the King declared at the opening of the new Parliament in July 1977 that it was the Spanish people who were sovereign and that as a constitutional monarch he would take no role in fashioning a political program for Spain (*Id.*). From that moment on, the King rose above politics and became a symbol of national unity as the vexing and delicate process of constitution-making was about to commence.

In the meantime, Suarez proved a deft master of politics during the potentially explosive period that preceded the election. In particular, against very high odds, Suarez managed to legalize the Communist Party, thereby enabling the entire political spectrum to participate in the parliamentary elections (Linz & Stepan 1996:96–98). This in turn maximized the chances for the newly elected Parliament to become a genuine constituent assembly.

The June 1977 elections were carried out without significant problems and gave Suarez's centrist party the largest number of seats in the Parliament (Rubio Llorente 1988:247). The next largest number of seats went to the Socialists, while the Communists, Basques, and Catalans all managed to achieve significant representation (*Id.*). Accordingly, the Parliament had broad enough representation for most concerned to regard it as a legitimate constituent assembly (*Id.*).

Prior to launching in a full-fledged process of constitution-making, several key actions essential for purposes of facilitating the task ahead were undertaken by the Suarez government and by the Parliament. For our purposes, two such actions are worthy of mention. The first is the Amnesty Act of 1977 which was the culmination of a series of amnesties dating to the King's accession to the throne (*Id.*:249). These amnesties were designed to lift all sanctions going as far back as 1936 – the beginning of the civil war – imposed for politically motivated acts, including some of those perpetrated by ETA, the Basque organization responsible for many terrorist incidents (*Id.*). The purpose of the Amnesty Act was to eliminate restrictions on political activity imposed by Franco's dictatorship (*Id.*), and its broad scope was well suited to promote a break away from the past without emphasis on account settling.

The second action undertaken by the Suarez government was as bold as it was crucial to the success of the constitution-making process. Pressured by Basque and Catalan nationalists as well as by the Socialists and Communists who had become partisans of federalism, Suarez provisionally granted autonomous rule to Catalonia and the Basque region and to all other regions of Spain even though the latter were not particularly interested in such rule (*Id.*:250). Suarez's strategy was to accommodate the Basque and Catalan quest for autonomy while underplaying their uniqueness. Moreover, by redrawing the map of Spain into a number of autonomous regions through a series of decrees, Suarez hoped that the changes involved would be endorsed by the constituent Parliament which was in the process of crafting the new constitution (*Id.*).

The constitution-making process took place between September 1977 and October 1978, (*Id.*) and the constitution that emerged from it was approved by a nationwide referendum on December 6, 1978 (*Id.*:256). The story of this constitution-making has been amply told (Bonime-Blanc 1987) and it need not be repeated here. Suffice it, therefore, to very briefly summarize its outcome and mention some of the most important features that appear to have had a determinative impact on its success. The Spanish Constitution of 1978 opts, in stark contrast to the preceding dictatorship, for a federal or quasi-federal system headed by a constitutional monarch and comprised of a national bicameral parliament, as well as broadly and vaguely spelled out autonomous communities with certain enumerated powers (Rubio Llorente 1988:250, 262). Moreover, the constitution provides for a political life dominated by political parties and guarantees rights and liberties that are standard throughout Western Europe (*Id.*:250).

The determinative features that loom as crucial to the success of the Spanish constitution-making experience can, in turn, be encapsulated in the following three words: delegation, ambiguity, and consensus. Delegation of the initial drafting of the constitution to a group of lawyers and legal academics, who worked largely in secret, and made it possible to deal with divisive issues such as the aspirations to autonomy of Basques and Catalans without alienating a large segment of the population. Furthermore, the seven drafters of the constitution were representatives of the major parties, and each of them was responsible to his own party (*Id.*:251–252). The parties represented were Suarez's UDC; the Socialists and Communists; Popular Alliance, the principal rightist party; and the Catalan party, whose representative also took into account the Basque point of view (*Id.*).

These various parties did not see eye-to-eye on many important subjects. This would have made reaching the requisite agreement to craft a workable constitution highly unlikely had it not been for the successful strategic use of ambiguity. As a matter of fact, ambiguity not only played an important role in constitution-making proper but also in many of the steps that led to it. Thus, Suarez's 1976 political reform legislation that, as already mentioned, led to democratic elections which were a precondition to constitution-making,[27] was so ambiguous that it created great confusion among both Francoists and their opponents (Rubio Llorente 1988:244). Under the guise of being merely one more law added to an existing corpus of law regulating political activity, the political reform legislation in substance repealed prior law by endorsing the principle of popular sovereignty (*Id.*). Similarly, constitution-making and the constitutional text it produced were also rife with ambiguity. The most striking example of this is the constitution's simultaneous commitment to national unity and regional autonomy without clearly or sufficiently spelling out how these potentially contradictory objectives ought to be reconciled (*Id.*:263–264).

Both delegation and, more importantly, ambiguity made it possible for the constitution-making process to proceed by means of consensus rather than majority rule. Indeed, delegation to the seven drafters made it possible to reach agreements on many contentious issues which would have been most unlikely in the context of an open debate in Parliament (*Id.*:251). Furthermore, ambiguity allowed for compromise where consensus, strictly speaking – that is agreement for the same reason by all concerned – was impossible as in the case of distribution of powers among the central government and that of autonomous communities (*Id.*).

After the initial drafting by the group of seven, the constitution was debated and its text amended in Parliament (*Id.*:254–257). The drafters had managed by and large to lay down the essential framework. The Constitution was overwhelmingly approved by Parliament. Only a handful of extreme right and extreme left parliamentarians voted against it, while the Basques abstained (*Id.*:256). As already mentioned, the Constitution was approved by an overwhelming majority of the Spanish voters. Finally, this constitution, described by its drafters as 'a pact reached through consensus,' (*Id.*:257) was promulgated by the King at a joint session of the two houses of Parliament on December 27, 1978.

4.3.1 The King as Repository of National and Constitutional Unity

As already indicated, Spain's transition to constitutional democracy is properly characterized as a new type of transition – peaceful transition – and its principal features include: lack of violence concerning the process of transition in itself; lack of any convulsive break in legality; and presence of a common interest among those identified with the old regime and those committed to the institution of constitutional democracy to reach a negotiated agreement rather than resort to confrontation – a common interest undoubtedly buttressed by the inability of either side to impose its will by force. Moreover, this type of transition is undoubtedly greatly boosted by the presence of a rallying point capable of providing a signifi-cant measure of unity commonly shared by all relevant actors regardless of what otherwise divides them. In Spain, the unifying factor in question was provided by the King once it became broadly accepted that he had risen above politics.

Emergence of the King as a symbol of national unity was due to a series of intricate shifts in collective identity. These various shifts came from many different directions and were often initiated for inconsistent reasons, but they fortunately resulted in a convergence of views among proponents of otherwise antagonistic perspectives. As stressed above, upon his ascent to the throne, the King was not the legitimate heir to the Spanish Monarchy; and although given his throne by Franco, he was regarded as an unreliable heir by Francoists and as a mere pawn by proponents of democracy. Paradoxically, precisely because of his lack of identification with traditionalists[28] as well as with those who wished to shed tradition to pursue constitutional democracy, the new King had room to grow into a source of national unity and identity. In other words, the King could become a symbol of Spain's unity provided he acted in ways that gave him legitimacy in the eyes of both traditionalist and advocates of constitutional democracy.

The King succeeded remarkably in becoming different things to differ-ent people through his straightening of the Monarchy's legitimate line of succession by having his father renounce any aspirations to the throne and his rising above politics once the democratically elected Parliament was in place in July 1977. For Francoists, legitimation of the King's position on the throne afforded an opportunity to both fully reinstate Franco within tradition – for the King whom he had made his successor was now the legitimate heir to the Spanish throne – and to extend the horizon of Francoism beyond that of the man who embodied it during his lifetime. For non-Francoist conservatives, on the other hand, formal legitimation of the King's position could be construed as a symbol of restoration of Spain's historical traditions and used as a telling sign of hope that Spain's uncertain future would eventually be guided by the sound values that had held the nation together in the past.

For their part, the proponents of democracy could accept the King after becoming convinced that he would uphold democracy and lend support to its institutions, even if they were not particularly in favor of the Monarchy.

Moreover, proponents of democracy had an incentive to share in the vision of the King as a symbol of national unity inasmuch as this allowed virtually all Spaniards to remain within the fold of the new democracy notwithstanding preferences to the contrary. Also, for those who associated democracy with a significant level of regional autonomy, casting the King as a symbol of an indissoluble national unity had the virtue of countering the fear that devolutions of power from the nation to regions would imperil the very survival of the Spanish nation.

The position of the King as guarantor of national unity and as the rallying point for groups with otherwise antagonistic visions of the polity was greatly bolstered in the aftermath of the attempted military coup that led to the seizure of Parliament on February 23, 1981. Without a doubt, the King played a pivotal role in the quick resolution of the crisis as he spoke out for democracy and, donning his military uniform, issued an order to desist to the rebels (Linz & Stepan 1996:101). On the other hand, all partisans of democracy, even if foes of the Monarchy, had to admire the King's personal courage in intervening so decisively in the crisis. Indeed, as a consequence of the King led extremely negative reaction to the attempted coup, the self-image of Spain as a democracy became firmly consolidated to the exclusion of all rival visions (*Id.*:109). Thus for some, it may be the Monarchy as an institution and the King as its present embodiment that is the guarantor of national unity, while for others it is the King as a man rather than as a monarch who has earned that position. In any event, albeit for overlapping, rather than commonly shared reasons, the King became a focal point of the new constitutional identity that played an important part in the consolidation of Spain's new democracy.

The Spanish experience suggests the emergence of a new constitutional model. The chief characteristics of this new model revolve around a twofold transformation of the relationship between the nation and the state that is motivated, in part by external factors, and, in part, by internal ones. Moreover, the transformation in question consists of the reframing of the relationship between the nation and the state in terms of the broader perspective projected by political actors engaged in a common supra-national project, such as the European Community (now the EU) and of a movement toward a more subtle, nuanced, and complex relationship between nation and state, designed to include and accommodate national diversity without thereby threatening the integrity or viability of the nation as a whole. Furthermore, the internal and external factors that promote this transformation loom as more interdependent than independent, and although they may at times pull in opposite directions, they nonetheless combine to prompt the creation of a constitutional order designed to accommodate their respective demands in the best manner possible.

It is not always obvious which of the factors that had an influential role in the Spanish transition are properly characterized as external, and which as internal. What is important, however, is to recognize that the Spanish constitutional model is configured by an interplay of internal and external factors in ways that differ considerably from the way in which these factors figured in past cases of constitution making. To cite but one example, consider the importance of the nexus between Spain and the (now) EU for purposes of the constitutional order crafted in the course of the transition.[29] On the one hand, Spain arguably internalized the democratic values embodied by the (now) EU member states as part of the process of preparing for admission into the (now) EU, which was a natural step given Spain's cultural and economic position in the mid-1970s. On the other hand, it is arguable that Spain's evolution toward constitutional democracy was primarily internally generated, but it also called for forging external links in order to achieve consolidation, thus looking to the (now) EU as a means of reinforcing the emergent order rather than as a magnet for change.

Furthermore, it is also plausible that links to the (now) EU were essential (through a concurrent process of internalization and externalization) for purposes of mediating successfully between preservation of national unity and recognition of regional autonomy. Indeed, recourse to the supra-national space occupied by the (now) EU allows for a variety of possible three-way relationships capable of defusing the tensions created by power conflicts which can only be resolved in favor of either the nation as an indivisible entity or of the autonomous region as a separate entity.

To recapitulate: The constitutional model launched by Spain's constitution-making is shaped by the convergence of internal and external trends and it emerges out of negotiations among various political actors who pursue divergent objectives but are (or perceive themselves to be) too weak to impose their will on their antagonists. Within this model, the constitution is much more likely to be the product of consensus than majority politics.[30] Moreover, such a consensus-based constitution is likely to remain ambiguous in significant respects, and adherence to it notwithstanding strong disagreements concerning its ambiguous provisions – in the case of Spain, the provisions regarding regional autonomy – is likely to be buttressed both by fear of violence and by transnational aspirations. In short, the success of the Spanish model hinges on finding a viable equilibrium between internal compromises and external influence allowing for the spread of a distinct constitutional identity which provides a focal point of national unity while remaining open to transnational trends and solutions.

The peaceful type of transition that occurred in Spain and the kind of constitutional model to which it gave rise seem above all the products of an internal erosion of authoritarianism, concurrent with a gradual strengthening of democratically inspired opposition, coupled with increased influence or pressure coming from abroad. As noted in the outset, a large number of the transitions to constitutional democracy that took place after Spain's have been peaceful in kind. To what extent these transitions ought to be considered to be of the same kind as Spain's, and to what extent the constitutional orders which they have spawned ought to be deemed to fit within the Spanish constitutional Model, remain open questions that will be further examined in chapter 6.

In any event, if other transitions and the constitutional orders to which they give rise will ultimately prove to fall within the scope of the Spanish model, it will undoubtedly be because they found a workable equilibrium between internal compromise and successful adaptation to external influences, as well as reasonable accommodation of transnational aspirations without undermining their recently minted constitutional identities.

PART THREE

Constitutional Identity as
Bridge between Self and Other:
Binding Together Citizenship,
History and Society

CHAPTER **5**

Constitutional Models: Shaping, Nurturing and Guiding the Constitutional Subject

As illustrated by the Spanish example examined in the last chapter, the making of every constitution is a unique historical event, and so is the structuring of every constitution and its relationship to its socio-political environment. Nevertheless, constitution making and constitutional structuring and functioning can be usefully grouped in terms of fit with different salient models. For example, as noted in the last chapter, Spain's peacefully pacted constitution-making stands in sharp contrast to constitution-making on the heels of a violent revolution or in the aftermath of total military surrender to a foreign power. Similarly, Spain's multi-ethnic constitution, which is shaped in part by internalization of foreign norms operative within the EU, is clearly distinguishable from that of a unitary ethnically homogenous state that looks exclusively inwardly for purposes of selecting norms susceptible of becoming constitutionalized.

Delimiting different models of constitution-making is particularly useful in as much as it casts light on alternative ways of handling the relationship between pre-constitutional, constitutional, and extra-constitutional identities. Does constitution-making after a violent revolution, for example, tend to call for greater repression of *ancient régime* identities than would a pacted constitution? Moreover, it is also important to distinguish among distinct models of constitutional structuring and functioning. Each of these models casts the relationship between self and other in a different

149

light and consequently tends to carve out a constitutional subject that is distinguishable from those issuing from other models.

For example, an ethno-centric model built around a single ethnic group will tend to define the self in terms of belonging to the dominant ethnic group and the other in terms of membership in other ethnic groups. Such ethno-centric model, moreover would use belonging to the dominant ethnic group as the marker for differentiating the constitutionally relevant self from both the 'internal' and the 'external' other – that is, the 'other' within the constitutional polity as opposed to the 'other' found, or projected as being, outside that polity. Thus, the 'internal' other may include members of ethnic groups other than the dominant group and those who form part of identities defined by criteria unrelated to ethnicity.

In contrast, a constitutional model build around the *demos* rather than the *ethnos* will downplay, if not altogether eliminate, the constitutional relevance of ethnicity. Accordingly, within the model in question, the other, whether internal or external, will not be perceived or construed in reference to ethnic belonging.[1] On the other hand, whereas the mono-ethnic ethno-centric constitutional polity should have little trouble in establishing its legitimate boundaries, the same is by no means the case for a constitutional polity built on a *demos*-based model. This should become obvious from the following examination of the *demos*-centered French model.[2]

In more general terms, all complex contemporary constitutional democracies must confront a set of important common issues including: the relation between national and constitutional identity; internal pluralism, whether individual-based, group-based, or both; the relationship between the constitutional self and the external other; the conception and deployment of the constitutional subject; the relationship between the prevailing constitution and constitutionalism; and that between the latter and democracy. All plausible constitutional models must be able to cope with these issues, but what distinguishes one such model from the next is that each is prone to dealing differently with them. And because of that, each constitutional model is likely to process the crucial issues mentioned above in its own unique way and to yield a different ordering of the same basic ingredients.

I will now briefly describe the main constitutional models that have emerged to date, starting with those that originated in relation to polities that were (or imagined themselves to be) ethnically homogenous. I will next focus on models meant for the multi-ethnic polity, and then on models designed to accommodate the needs of transnational polities.

One can distinguish at this writing seven distinct constitutional models.

These are: the German, the French, the American, the British, the Spanish, the European and the post-colonial model. These models are prototypes constructed with reference to actual historical experiences. The first five refer to their country of origin. The sixth model, the European one, in contrast, refers to its transnational historical setting, the EU, and differs from the five preceding ones in that the actual constitutional experience to which it is linked is one that has arguably not yet borne fruit. As already noted, the European Treaty Constitution approved by all the then EU member states in 2004 has not seen the light of day due to its rejection in the French and Dutch referenda of 2005.[3] This notwithstanding, some have argued that the EU has been operating under a substantive as opposed to a formal constitution for numerous years (Moravcsik 2006), and others believe that the future adoption of an EU constitution is imperative (Habermas 20006). Finally, the seventh model, the post-colonial one, refers not to a single actual historical experience, but to a number of them in as much as newly independent former colonies have adopted constitutions that may differ significantly from one another but that nonetheless can be subsumed under the same overall model.

The seven constitutional models detailed below stand somewhere between the actual unique historical experiences from which they are extracted and the abstract ideal of constitutionalism. The latter's commitment to limited government, adherence to the rule of law and protection of fundamental rights calls for a polity suited for self-government, a functioning rule of law regime, and a working delimitation of a bundle of operable fundamental rights. The ideal of constitutionalism, however, does not specify which polity, which self-government for whom, which form of government or how it should be limited, the form or substance of a viable rule-of-law-regime, or the actual nature or scope of the requisite fundamental rights. On the other hand, as gleaned from the Spanish case in the last chapter, it is plain that every actual historical constitutional structuring and functioning must be particularly tailored to unique prevailing circumstances. Thus, the particular legacy of the Franco regime, the aspiration to peaceful harmony within Spain and to suitability for membership in the EU combined to yield a particular constitutional structuring that conferred a unique status to subnational ethnocentric geographical concentrated units such as the Basques and the Catalans.[4]

The seven constitutional models examined below can reach their optimal heuristic potential at a level of abstraction situated at the midpoint between constitutionalism in the abstract and the actual concrete historical experiences that are inextricably weaved into the particular constitution(s) or constitutional constructs on which a corresponding model is based.

Consistent with this, in some cases the constitutions of different polities may be grouped together as belonging to the same constitutional model. Thus, for example, a number of ethno-centric constitutions devised for a mono-ethnic nation-state may fit neatly within the German model which as we shall see, grants exclusive primacy to *ethnos.*

In other cases, a particular constitution may have affinities with two or more models without fitting neatly within any single one of these. This is well illustrated by the 1982 Canadian Constitution which at once bears certain affinities with the Spanish model and certain common elements with the British model. Canada's links to the Spanish model are predicated on the congruence between Quebec's relationship with the rest of Canada and that of the Basques or the Catalans with the rest of Spain as well as on Canada's and Spain's reliance on international or transnational norms to inform and shape their respective constitutionalization of fundamental rights. On the other hand, as a former British colony that did not break away violently as did the United States, Canada has internalized many particular instantiations of constitutionalism which figure prominently in the British model.[5]

Finally, the counterfactual dimension of the constitutional models at stake in this chapter is vividly underscored by the fact that the polity that generates a particular constitutional model may well subsequently significantly deviate or depart from that model. This is clearly the case of Germany which gave rise to the German model based on the priority and dominance of *ethnos,* but which after World War Two has configured and practiced a constitutionalism that departs in important ways from its ethnocentric predecessor (Kommers 1997:37–38; Schlink 1996:435). Indeed, as we shall see below, current German constitutionalism maintains key links to the original German model, but clearly departs from it through its overriding emphasis on human dignity,[6] federalism and 'militant democracy'.[7]

With these considerations and qualifications in mind, I now proceed to a brief account of the seven constitutional models identified above.

5.1 The German Constitutional Model

The central defining feature of the German constitutional model is the *ethnos* which stands in sharp contrast to the *demos,* its counterpart in the context of the French model. As Ulrich Preuss notes, 'Whereas in the French concept the nation is the entirety of the *demos,* in the German . . . concept the nation is a group defined in terms of ethnicity – the nation is *ethnos*' (Preuss 1994:150). In essence, therefore, the German model is built upon the concept of self-governance by and for a single homogenous ethnic group.

Based on its reliance on *ethnos*, the German model imagines the existence of indissoluble pre-political bonds cemented through a common language, culture, ethnicity, religion, etc., which enjoy absolute primacy (*Id.*:152). Consistent with this, the ethnic-based nation is conceived as indivisible, homogenous, and fully formed prior to the adoption of any constitution or to the advent of the state. Within this perspective, recourse to a constitution is necessary for purposes of enabling an already existing clearly delimited nation to give expression to its will and to fulfill its own unique destiny through the instrumentalities of a suitably structured full functioning state. In the German model, therefore, the state figures as a mere vehicle at the disposal of an already well-defined nation rather than as an indispensable instrument for nation-building purposes. Consistent with this, and as envisioned by the German model's foremost constitutional theorist, Karl Schmitt, democracy and constitutionalism must be reinterpreted in ethnicist terms (Schmitt 1928; Preuss 1994:153). According to Schmitt's ethnicist conception, democracy and the constitution must produce an institutional framework capable of affording political expression to the nation's unique culture and character both as opposed to those of other ethnic groups and as distinguished from the liberal-universalist aspirations originating in the American and French revolutions (Preuss 1994:153–155).

In the Schmittian vision, true democracy provides authentic expression to the unified pre-political identity of the ethnically defined people (*Id.*:155). To achieve this, it is necessary to counter pluralism and tolerance for any views or pursuits that might detract from implementation of a purely ethnocentric agenda. Furthermore, it follows from this – although it may at first glance seem paradoxical – that, as Ulrich Preuss puts it, 'democracy and dictatorship are not essentially antagonistic; rather dictatorship is a kind of democracy if the dictator successfully claims to incarnate the identity of the people' (*Id.*).

Schmitt's lack of concern for democracy is congruent with his conception of ethnic identity and ethnic destiny as transparent, unified, indissoluble, and hence as closed to any internal pluralism. A dictator committed to advancing the ethnic destiny of his nation would thus have the very same political agenda as a democratically elected government devoted to the same objective. Under these circumstances, moreover, the dictator may well be more efficient than a democratic government in as much as the latter is likely to involve inevitable strife among ambitious politicians even in the absence of any significant discord regarding the ultimate aims of policy.

In the context of Schmitt's conception of a fully formed pre-political ethnic identity, constitutional identity looms as essentially identical to national identity. More precisely, the context of the two identities is exactly the same, the only difference between them being one of perspective. National identity would then be what the ethnic group is and aspires to be; constitutional identity, what the ethnic group must do given what it is and what it aspires to be.

To the extent that the Schmittian vision equates ethno-centric dictatorship and ethno-centric democracy and that it collapses constitutional identity into national identity, any model derived from it would only qualify as a constitutional one in a purely formal sense. Moreover, such model would be completely incompatible with any genuine striving towards, or emulation of, the fundamental precepts of constitutionalism. The German ethno-centric constitutional model, however, need not be confined to any Schmittian straightjacket. Indeed, as we shall now see, Schmitt's extreme ethno-centric vision has been belied both by past history and by the history of post World War Two Germany.

Schmitt's ethnocentric model was set against the Weimar Constitution which embodied liberal ideals and values (*Id.*:153). Accordingly, notwithstanding any appearance to the contrary, basing constitutional identity on the German ethnos could not be achieved through simple incorporation of a fully formed national identity. Instead, the passage from Weimar to Nazi Germany required negation of the liberal constitutional identity associated with the Weimar Constitution and reconstruction consistent with ethnocentric images and values. Such reconstruction, moreover, could not simply rely on an existing all encompassing ethnocentric national identity. Even if German national identity has always been ethnocentric, it traditionally was not, nor did it have to be, as monolithic or as racist as it would become during the Nazi era. Consistent with this, to fully realize the Schmittian vision, it was equally necessary reconstruct national identity as it was to reconceive constitutional identity.

It is possible, however, to be an ethnocentric constitutionalist without having to embrace Schmittian intolerance and anti-pluralism. A constitutional model which adheres to the values of constitutionalism and democracy may be grounded on *ethnos*, provided the latter is given primacy without being treated as monolithic, hermetically closed, or absolute. Although contemporary German constitutionalism departs in significant respects from an ethnocentric model (Dorsen, et al. 2003:44–45), it still has many ethnocentric features, such as its conception of citizenship (Brubaker 1992). It is therefore quite possible to conceive of a non-Schmittian German constitutional model.

The main features of the German model as thus conceived would still be ethnocentric with the constitutional subject being clearly delimited by the nation's *ethnos*. This would mean that both those who articulate the constitution and those for whom the constitution is made are supposed to belong to the same *ethnos*. Moreover, the constitution is to promote the collective destiny and it ought to be interpreted consistent with the *ethos* of that *ethnos*. Constitutionalism and democracy would nonetheless be imperative within this conception of the German model inasmuch as ethnocentrism is (and ought to be) compatible with internal pluralism. Indeed just as great cultures and great religions are replete with nuances and complexities so can the *Volkgeist* of a great nation. If the destiny of the *ethnos* is to be discovered and deployed rather than merely mechanically followed, then subjecting plausible ranges of alternatives to constructive discussion would be clearly called for. Consequently, democracy would be highly preferable to dictatorship for purposes of articulating and carrying out policies best suited to advancing the destiny of the *ethnos*. Similarly, whereas the *ethnos* would circumscribe the constitutional self and sunder it from both the internal and the external other, differences within the bounds of genuine ethnic identification would be enriching rather than impoverishing or threatening. Accordingly, internal pluralism – that is, pluralism within the bounds of a complex and differentiated *ethnos* – should be encouraged and protected through adherence to constitutionalism. Finally, under these circumstances, even if national identity based on *ethnos* is imagined as pre-given and pre-political, constitutional identity would have to differ from it. At the very least, the ethnocentric constitutional identity in question would have to differ from its national identity counterpart as a consequence of its having to be recast through the prisms of constitutionalism and democracy.

Although the German model requires that constitutional identity negate and differentiate itself from national identity, because the two mostly remain within the confines of the same *ethnos*, the range of differentiation between the two is likely to be much narrower than that associated with other constitutional models. By the same token, internal pluralism within the *ethnos* as envisaged by the German model is also likely to be significantly narrower than would be compatible with other models. Within the German model, all acceptable internal pluralism would have to remain intra-group whereas other models may have room for fairly far reaching inter-group internal pluralism.

Under the German model, both citizenship and national boundaries are determined by the *ethnos*. More generally, the constitutional subject in terms of the who, the what, and the where, is determined by the *ethnos*.

Those who do not belong to the *ethnos* that glues the nation together are cast as the external other, whether or not they reside within the boundaries of the relevant ethno-centric polity.

Under the German model, the constitutional subject is ultimately prisoner to the *ethnos*, and it cannot be deployed beyond the bounds of that *ethnos*. The German model thus excludes a multinational and multicultural constitutionalism or constitutional subject. That means that those who do not belong to the national *ethnos* must simply remain outsiders, and that a constitutional subject not conceived in terms of *ethnos* cannot be a legitimate one. Finally, under the German model, both constitutionalism and democracy are limited to conform to the prevailing *ethnos*. Thus, for example, democracy would have to be constricted in scope so as to exclude *ex ante* all initiatives that might threaten the identity or deployment of the prevailing *ethnos*.

5.2 The French Constitutional Model

In contrast to the German model, in the French model, the nation is built upon the *demos* with the *ethnos* receding to the point of becoming almost invisible. Like the German model, the French conceives the constitutional polity on the scale of the nation-state. But whereas the German model is difficult to imagine beyond the confines of the nation-state given its inextricable grounding on *ethnos*, the French model's ties to the nation-state appear to be historically contingent. Indeed, the French model is grounded on democratic self-government for a polity of equal citizens bound together by a social contract. Consistent with this model, each citizen regardless of his or her ethnic origin, enjoys rights conceived as universal – significantly, as already noted, the 1789 Declaration refers to the rights of 'man' and 'citizen' rather than to those of 'Frenchmen' – and contributes to the democratic shaping of the polity's general will as conceived in Rousseau's political philosophy (Rousseau 1762:II.2).

The French model is thoroughly individualistic and leaves no room at the constitutional level for recognition or deployment of group or national identity. As expressed in the famous dictum of Clermont-Tonnerre in connection with the emancipation of the Jews during the French Revolution, 'Everything must be refused to the Jews as a nation and everything must be accorded to the Jews as individuals . . . they must be individual citizens . . . It would be repugnant to have groupings of non-citizens within the state, a nation within the nation'.[8] In other words, to be a citizen as opposed to a *bourgeois* or purely private person, in a nation-state based on a Rousseauan *demos* (Rousseau 1762:II, 2–3), the Jew – and for that matter every one else – must shed his particularity and embrace the ideal of reason, equality among abstract individuals – that is, citizens pulled away from their actual historical circumstances and their multiple links of identity. The Rousseauan citizen must also strive for universality – in the sense that reason, individuality, equality, citizenship, and the democratic polity are conceived as being the same (or at least potentially the same) for everyone everywhere (as opposed to being differentiated in function to linkage to different particular ethnic identities).

The French revolutionary Abbé Sieyès envisioned the nation as 'a body of associates living under common laws and *represented* by the same *legislative* assembly' (Sieyès 1789:58). Within this conception, the constitution is meant to enshrine a democratic nation united through equal citizenship with a political framework suited to give an effective voice to the people as a whole. While Sieyès fitted the constitutional order within the bounds of the nation-state, there seems to be no logical impediment for a *demos* constructed along the lines suggested by Sieyès or Rousseau to become implanted beyond the confines of the nation-state, or even eventually to thrive on the scale of the planet as a whole.

If the twin pillars of the French model are abstract equal citizenship and democratic self-rule; and if the eighteenth century reliance on the nation-state as the proper setting for constitutional rule is a mere historical contingency; then the French model seems to yield pure constitutional form. This is in contrast to the German model's tendency towards pure substance (that in the most extreme case may be no more than barely constitutionalized in that it arguably must only provide against that which runs counter to the nature or will of the polity's *ethnos*). Viewed more closely, however, the French model's ties to the nation-state loom as by no means contingent. In fact, what is ultimately most salient about the French model is that it implants an abstract universalist conception of democracy not only within the frame of the nation-state but within a particular concrete version of it. At the time of the Revolution, the French absolute monarchy had already firmly implanted a highly unified and centralized state and was well into building a single nation revolving around a common language, culture, and civilization (Preuss 1994:151–152). Nation-building was far from complete at that time, as, for example, only about half of the country's population spoke French (*Id.*:152). It would take time and ruthless and bloody action during the course of the Revolution, but in the end, French was imposed throughout the state's territory while regional languages were suppressed or demoted. In the end, the French nation became contiguous with the French state.

In the last analysis, the French model's universal idea of democracy and citizenship was made workable by being fitted to the scale of the nation-state – or more precisely, a particular type of nation-state that is highly centralized and unified. Based on a Rousseauian conception of republican-ism that allows for no mediating identities between that of the individual citizen committed to self-government and that the polity as an indivisible whole propelled by the general will produced in the course of the citizen-ry's cooperative engagement in self-government,[9] the French model pro-motes a constitutional identity that casts the constitution as predominantly political. The *demos* unifies the polity encapsulated within the nation state; democratic self-government conducted by the citizens of the republic pro-duces the general will; and institutionalized democracy pursuant to the constitution is supposed to secure the fundamental rights of the *bourgeois* or private person and those of the citizen.

The French model and the type of constitutional identity it frames were thus initially fitted to suit particular sets of circumstances prevalent in France. That does not mean, however, that the French model is not 'exportable' elsewhere. For example, French constitutional identity has depended on appropriating an existing language, French, imposing it throughout the territory of the nation-state to make possible political deliberation extending to all citizens within the democratic polity. What is important from the standpoint of the French model, though, is not the French language as such, but a common language, and that could as well be Spanish, English, Chinese, etc. Thus, at least in theory, any unified central-ized republic where all members of the polity speak the same language and where individualism trumps collective identities could adopt the French Model and adapt it to its own particular circumstances.

5.3 The American Constitutional Model

The American constitutional model is closer to the French than to the German. But whereas the French Model requires an existing nation – albeit one that needs further adaptation – the American Model does not. Indeed, the 'We the People' that stood behind the 1787 American Constitution were but an embryonic prefiguration of the America which was to be assembled gradually through multiple waves of immigration. For these highly diverse successive waves of immigrants to be able to cohere into '*E Pluribus Unum*', the motto inscribed on the Great Seal of the United States, it would be first necessary for them to become immersed in a 'melting pot' fueled by the norms and values enshrined in the U.S. Constitution. Consistent with this, in the American model, the constitution frames and provides a launching pad to the state and it precedes and anticipates the nation.

The 'We the People' that stood at the source of 1787 American Constitution was largely a construct projected into the future in two crucial respects. First, at the time of the making of the constitution, there were no American people in the sense that there was a French people or a German people at the corresponding juncture in the constitutional journeys of those countries. Indeed, at the American constitution-making moment, it was the peoples of the various American states, the Virginians, the New Yorkers, the Pennsylvanians, etc, whose confederation was rapidly losing its viability, who embraced the mantle of an undivided people prior to the creation of the state that would hold them together, and prior to the formation and consolidation of the American nation. To be sure, over time, 'We the People' certainly grew into the powerful symbol of a strong and united nation-state that saw itself as the beacon of constitutional democracy and that successfully projected that image all the way back to the constitution-making moment. But at the constitution-making moment itself, when it was inscribed into the Preamble of the American constitution, 'We the People' amounted to little more than an empty placeholder to cover-up glaring lacks of peoplehood, nationhood or statehood.

The second key respect, in which 'We the People' was a construct in 1787 concerns, more particularly the already alluded to matter of nationhood. Today's multi-ethnic, multi-religious, multi-cultural American nation – unquestionably one of the most diverse nations on the globe due to its being from its very beginning above all a country of immigrants – is certainly very different from the population that might have been plausibly projected into the future as a nation in 1787 America. Again, set against the kind of identity and continuity characteristic of the British, French or German people (at least till the end of World War Two), the American people looms as striking in its diversity and its discontinuity. Around 1787, the nascent American Union was predominantly populated by descendants of the British and by imported African slaves.[10] Since then, the American people and American nationhood have been build upon a series of immigration waves, which brought to American shores a very wide array of diverse ethnic, cultural, linguistic and religious groups. From the nineteenth century massive influx of impoverished Europeans, such as the Irish and the Southern Italians, and of non-Europeans such as the Chinese, to the more recent waves of immigration from Latin America, Asia, Russia, etc., the socio-political, cultural, linguistic and ethnic landscape in America has been in a permanent state of change requiring constant adjustment and accommodation.

In a large number of cases, particular groups of immigrants were initially treated as 'outsiders', subjected to massive discrimination, and in some cases became the focal point for calls for constitutional change. One such case concerns the large-scale Chinese immigration in the middle of the nineteenth century. Not only were Chinese immigrants at the time subjected to massive discrimination, but their presence in the United States prompted for the first time widespread demand for English to be designated as the country's official language (Rosenfeld:2000).

Over time, most immigrant groups have become assimilated into the American mainstream and transformed into veritable 'insiders'. Today, for example, Americans of Italian or Irish origin have been fully incorporated in the country's civic and political life in ways that their ancestors over a century ago could have hardly imagined. Moreover, the Constitution and American constitutional identity have served as great catalysts for these transformations.

How the Constitution and constitutional identity have played a major role in weaving together common elements and recasting the disparate strands of identity brought to American shores by successive groupings of immigrants from all corners of the world to forge a single people and a unified nation involves complex dynamic processes that cannot be examined in any detail here. What is crucial for present purposes and constitutes a key feature of the American constitutional model is the pivotal role that the Constitution and constitutional identity have had in transforming over time a diverse multi-ethnic and multicultural population made up of 'insiders' and of varying degrees of 'outsiders' into a veritable people and into a unified distinct nation that coheres into a vibrant polity.

The most salient example of the American Constitution's role as catalyst in the formation of peoplehood and nationhood is provided by the multi-faceted work dome by constitutional liberty, America's paramount right and most cherished value. As already noted, America's devotion to freedom of speech has transcended the bounds of the realm of constitutional ordering and has come to occupy a place of pride among the entrenched markers of national identity.[11] Constitutional liberty has also provided a rallying point for diverse groups of 'outsiders' landed on American shores, and paved the way to elaboration of a common ground for 'insiders' and 'outsiders'. Thus, the French Huguenots and the Irish Catholics, both subjected to religious persecution in their respective native European lands, and each adhering to a religion that had in Europe been the mortal enemy of the religion embraced by the other, could find common ground in America as the beneficiaries and, eventually, the defenders of religious liberty. The defense of religious liberty, moreover, should pave the way to greater religious tolerance, thus providing a means for once mutually exclusive religious communities to forge common bonds. And in so doing, not only is liberty used to mediate among religions, but also, at least in principle, liberty's mediation would seem eventually bound to alter the relationship of a religious community to its own religion. In other words, because of the pervasive moral authority of constitutional liberty, religious intolerance is cast in a most unflattering light. Accordingly, there is great pressure to smooth over the intolerant edges of one's religion, to conform it as much as possible to liberty, and consequently to 'Americanize' it. Furthermore, to the extent that they become 'Americanized', America's diverse religious communities share more in common with each other. And at the same time, as they become more imbued with the American passion for liberty, each of these religious communities presumably distances itself to a noticeable degree from its counterpart left behind in its country of origin.

Constitutional liberty not only provides a positive pole in the formation of a common national identity, but it also furnishes a negative pole that enables America's diverse population to discover common trends of identity in its opposition to external others cast as the enemies of liberty. Whether plausible or purely imaginary, and whether borne out of an ideological pursuit of liberty or as a screen for other pursuits such as the opening or preservation of markets, America has cast its external antagonists and adversaries from the British monarchy of the colonial days to the communists of the twentieth century and the Islamic fundamentalists of the twenty first as the 'enemies of liberty'.[12]

The powerful imprint of America's constitutional identity, in general, and of its expansive conception of liberty, in particular, is perhaps best exemplified by the fact that the American polity and the construction of American nationhood have not been multi-ethnic or multicultural in nature notwithstanding the wide diversity of cultures brought to America's shores by successive waves of immigrants. Will Kymlicka has underscored the contrast between Canada's 'multicultural mosaic' and the United States as a 'melting pot' bent on producing unity out of diversity (Kymlicka 1995: 14). Indeed, in contrast to Canada or Spain where both the polity and constitutional identity are distinctly multi-ethnic, in the United States the nation imagines itself above and beyond ethnic ties and the Constitution is essentially blind to groups and adverse to the recognition of group rights.[13] In other words, though the American nation is multiethnic, it imagines itself as beyond ethnicity and strives to define itself as such (even if at times it bumps against resilient vestiges of ethno-centric identity politics).

To recapitulate: the success of the American 'melting pot' is due to an important extent to the country's constitutional identity and to the latter's expansive conception of liberty. Accordingly, and this is a key feature of the American constitutional model, the constitution provides the mold for the nation to be and makes it possible for people from very diverse cultures to cohere into a single united polity. This is not to say that American integration has been perfect – far from it – or that its brand of liberty has been unmistakably exemplary – after all, American liberty long coexisted with slavery. Nonetheless, American conceptions of integration and liberty steeped in its constitutional culture have been sufficient for purposes of unifying the nation and of empowering a vibrant functioning polity.

In as much as in the American model the constitution prefigures and eventually shapes the nation and the state, it may seem logical to assume that this model would be readily adaptable to transnational settings. A clear glimpse of the American experience does not necessarily validate that assumption, however. Indeed, although the relation between constitutional and national identity seems much more symbiotic in the American case than in the French, American national identity remains distinct from its constitutional counterpart and it retains a significant degree of resilience.

To illustrate this, suffice it to refer back to the case of *Lynch* v. *Donnelly* discussed above in Chapter 2.[14] In *Lynch*, the U.S. Supreme Court's majority interpreted the constitutional requirement of separation between church and state as being consistent with the promotion of mainstream religion. In *Lynch*, that was symbolized by the juxtaposition on state public property of the crèche with the ubiquitous indicia of a commercialized vision of Christmas that had all but lost its links to religion. Neither constitutional commitment to religious diversity, nor the constitutional requirement of separation between church and state, taken jointly or separately, can explain this result. What does explain it, however, is that adherence to some form of mainstream religion figured prominently in the national identity of Americans in the 1980's.[15]

American constitutional identity has never operated in a complete vacuum and never been totally independent from the national identity that it had taken the lead in forging. In the broadest outline, in 1787, the constitutional thrust for religious freedom and religious diversity was launched in the context of a predominantly Protestant population. The nascent nation's identity (or perhaps, more precisely, pre-national identity) was a Protestant one, and the religious toleration prescribed by the Constitution seems most naturally understood as toleration of, and among, various Protestant denominations (Murrin 1990:27–30). As immigration led to much greater religious diversity, constitutionally mandated tolerance had to extend beyond Protestantism. But, as already noted above, the greater the diversity, the greater became the risk of balkanization based on religious affiliation. One way to mitigate this risk is by 'Americanizing' religion through encapsulation of religious diversity within a broader common ideology of liberty and tolerance. And that precisely is what the Court's majority in *Lynch* appears to be endorsing. In short, *Lynch* embodies the tension between a conception of national identity that incorporates mainstream religion and a vindication of a constitutional identity that calls for separation between religion and the state. The four dissenting justices clearly promoted constitutional identity even if it ran counter to the above conception of national identity. The five justices in the majority, on the other hand, tried to reconcile the two identities through metonymic recourse to the contiguity between mainstream religion and the commercialization of traditions, including religious ones.[16]

This brief glimpse into how constitutional and national identity interact in the context of the relation between religion and the state reveals the complex dynamic nature of the relationship between these two identities as they are deployed within the American polity. Even though constitutional identity plays a large role in the creation and shaping of American national identity, the latter becomes a force of its own that in turn affects, and exerts influence on, the former. Because of this, the American constitutional model as it operates within the United States is clearly anchored within the confines of the nation-state. This does not necessarily foreclose, however, that the American model could be adapted for use in transnational settings – an issue that will be further be explored in the course of discussing the European Model below.

5.4 The British Constitutional Model

One may think that Britain does not have a constitution, or at least that it does not have a written one. Indeed, British parliamentary sovereignty means that the laws of Parliament cannot be struck down for being inconsistent with higher constitutional authority as they can in France, Germany or the United States. Moreover, although Britain has had laws that are constitutional in nature going far back as the Magna Carta, these have not been gathered into a single written document (Barendt 1998).

From a functional standpoint, however, Britain does have a full-fledged constitutional system. Though formally unrestrained, pragmatically the British Parliament exercises significant self-restraint. Britain also has a long tradition of adherence to the rule of law and its governmental institutions have consistently afforded substantial protection to fundamental rights, even if these are not guaranteed by a higher law. In other words, the self-restraint associated with strong commitment to the rule of law and to firm adherence to custom and tradition provides a veritable constitutional shield. From a practical standpoint, moreover, that shield affords far greater protection to the rule of law and fundamental rights than would infra-constitutional parliamentary support subject to revocation by simple majority rule.

The British constitutional model is one of immanent constitutionalism that emerges gradually by means of a process of accretion. The British Constitution is in part embodied in laws, but these laws stand for far less than the full constantly evolving story. Thus, for example, as one commentator has noted,

> If someone had knowledge only of the law of the British Constitution, he or she would believe that the governmental system was much the same as it was in 1700 and be totally ignorant of the ceremonial character of the monarchy and of the country's parliamentary form of representative democracy. These immensely important institutions are regulated not by law but by constitutional conventions. . . . Such norms are part of the country's political culture . . . (Gwyn 1994:21)

This gradualism and organic growth is due to many factors peculiar to Britain and to its history. These include the existence of some form of representative government since the end of the thirteenth century, no conquest or domination by a foreign power since 1066, and a cautious common-sense oriented pragmatism that primes adaptation and abhors radical change and rupture (*Id.*:14).

In a constitution that is 'grown,' such as the British one, as opposed to one that is 'made' such as the American, French or German one, it may be difficult to differentiate between constitutional identity, on the one hand, and national and other extra-constitutional identities, on the other. Thus, as noted above when the French gave themselves fundamental rights in the 1789 Declaration, they incorporated the rights of 'man' and of the 'citizen' for use by their countrymen. The British, in contrast, originally cast their fundamental rights as the rights of Englishmen (Hunt 2007:77–78). Within the British model, therefore, constitutionalism springs from within and eventually settles as a barely separable layer of national, cultural and political identity. Nevertheless, though fully integrated in the latter identities, British constitutional identity does remain distinct both within the British context and as set against the constitutional identities linked to the other constitutional models discussed above.

If American constitutional identity frames, and to an important extent informs, American national identity, its British counterpart emerges as an integral by product of British national identity. Fair play, equity and concern with due process may be the cultural and political hallmarks of the English, but they also – particularly, as they find themselves embedded in the common law tradition – cohere into a set of constitutional principles. Moreover, these principles together with gradually evolving firmly rooted political institutions such as Parliament and the Monarchy add up to a constitutional order that presides over British democracy much like the written constitutions of France or the U.S. do over their own country's democracy. It is peculiarly British that institutions that were traditionally incompatible with constitutionalism or democracy such as the Monarchy or the hierarchical and hereditary House of Lords, were gradually adapted to serve the institutional and political needs of a contemporary constitutional democracy. Today, the British Monarch plays a constitutional and institutional role that is largely equivalent to that of a president in a parliamentary democracy. The House of Lords, on the other hand, currently plays role that is akin to that of the second chamber in many parliamentary democracies. And, far from pursuing policies for the privileged by birth, the House of Lords has on several occasions deployed constitution-like obstacles to slow down ill conceived measures resulting from unprincipled surrender to ephemeral majorities by the House of Commons.[17]

British constitutionalism is unique both in that it is progressively grown rather than made and in that it has constitutionally enshrined institutions and practices that differ significantly from their counterparts in other constitutional democracies. Consistent with this, it seems fair to inquire whether there can be much use in carving out a British constitutional model. Is it not preferable to conceive of the British constitutional journey as so *sui generis* as defying any attempt at generalization or at comparison with any other viable constitutional model?

Although British constitutionalism is certainly unique, focusing on a British constitutional model seems justified for at least two important reasons. First, aspects of the British approach to constitutionalism have been at work in several countries, albeit that all of these were once British colonies or under the sway of British common law. For example, the Canadian Constitution's notwithstanding clause whereby the federal or a provincial parliament can override judicial constitutional decisions,[18] not only bears definite traces of British parliamentary sovereignty. It also has proven to work, over the years, to establish a tradition of parliamentary self-restraint, as outside of Quebec, availability of the override combined with its lack of use has bolstered the legitimacy of constitutional adjudication (Hogg 1997:914–917).[19] In other words, in the context of the

Canadian override provision, it is parliamentary self-restraint along the lines of the British model that provides a significant boost to constitutionalism. Similarly, traces of the British model have been at work in other countries such as Australia where in spite of a lack of a bill of rights in the Constitution, certain fundamental rights have been inferred in given circumstances.[20] This arguably, involves 'growing' (in small part to be sure) a constitution in the tradition of the British model rather than 'making' one.

The second reason reference to the British model is useful is that a large extent even polities that 'made' their constitution also 'grow' it. In many cases, as observed by Sartori, there are clear differences between the written constitution and the 'living' one (Sartori 1962:61–62). For example, a thorough reading of the US Constitution would provide no hint of the constitutional jurisprudence generated by *Griswold* and its progeny, which was examined in Chapter 3 above. Moreover, the 'growing' of a living constitution beyond the bounds of the written constitutional text is by no means confined to common law jurisdictions. Indeed, even in countries as deeply steeped in the civil law continental tradition as France, Germany or Poland, the constitutional adjudicator has 'grown' the constitution well beyond the four corners of the established written text. Thus, in France, in the landmark 1971 *Associations* decision, the Constitutional Council extended judicial protection to fundamental rights[21] contrary to the expectations of the makers of the 1958 French Constitution (Stone 2000:41). Similarly, the German Constitutional Court, based on a broad conception of justice, has constitutionalized rights that are by no means directly inferable from the relevant constitutional texts;[22] and, the Polish Constitutional Court, relying upon an expansive conception of rule of law requirements, significantly restricted government policy discretion in an area with substantial budgetary and fiscal implications in the face of stark silence within the written constitution.[23]

The common law system of adjudication is experimental, incremental and marked by broad powers of judicial lawmaking.[24] In contrast, in the civil law system, the judge is supposed to apply the law formally through use of a deductive method of analysis that ought to leave little room for judicial discretion. The civil law judge is called upon to proceed syllogistically with the applicable law of parliament serving as the major premise, the facts of the case as the minor premise, and the decision logically derived from these two premises (Rosenfeld 2004:635). Consistent with this, it may seem that the British model's capacity for 'growing' a constitution is ultimately reducible to the workings of the common law. The latter is certainly distinctly British in origin, but it has been adopted and played a major role in many other constitutional democracies, including the US, that can by no means be subsumed under the British Model. Furthermore, constitutional adjudication has proliferated in civil law jurisdictions in the last half century, such as those mentioned above, thus departing from the deductive model and coming closer to approximating their counterparts in common law jurisdictions.[25]

Upon closer inspection, however, the 'growing' of living constitutions may have become a widespread phenomenon, but the particular way in which such growth figures in the British Model remains distinct from growth within different types of constitutional systems. This is more obvious in the case of civil law jurisdictions than in that of common law ones. Nevertheless, as we shall now see, the British Model is ultimately as clearly distinguishable from those of common law jurisdictions as it is from civil law ones, such as those of France or Germany, where judicial elaboration of the living constitution involves less gradual organic growth than judicial constitution-making or constitution-perfecting. This is plainly true of the French *Associations* decision, which modified the existing constitutional landscape the way a constitutional amendment or revision would have, and which was anti-traditional – at least in that France had no pervious tradition of judicial guarantee of fundamental rights (Stone 1992). Similarly, German decisions based on adherence to the principle of dignity enshrined in the Basic Law or to broad notions of justice can best be understood as broad interpretations and elaborations of the constitutional text or as instances of judicial constitution-making. In any event, these judicial interventions are anti-traditional. They are so either as deployments of values enshrined in repudiation of the legacy of the Third Reich, or as elaborations of the Basic Law, itself 'made' in repudiation of that legacy.[26] In short, what the French and German examples suggest is that in these civil law countries the constitutional adjudicator has taken an active role in constitutional monitoring and engineering.

The differences between the British model and others steeped within a common law tradition, such as the American, are more subtle and less apparent, but nonetheless equally real. Take, for example, the U.S. Constitution, which, as an evolving living constitution propelled by over two centuries of judicial elaboration, has maintained a close and constant nexus to the common law tradition. To a limited extent, American constitutional practice (as distinct from the American constitutional model) has drawn directly from the common law in ways that are essentially identical to those under the British Model. Thus, the US Supreme Court has indicated that the common law right of a person of sound mind to refuse medical treatment even if such refusal might lead to death can be considered to incorporated into constitutional liberty and constitutional privacy rights.[27] This kind of direct constitutionalization of common law norms can be directly subsumed under the British Model.

Such direct constitutionalization of common law rights, however, is the exception rather than the rule in the U.S. Much more prevalent is the use of common law interpretive practices which give judges broad latitude in the construction and elaboration of constitutional doctrine. As we have seen, in *Griswold* various U.S. Supreme Court justices used common law reasoning to infer (or invent depending on one's viewpoint) a constitutional right to privacy. In contrast to substantive uses of common law norms, however, uses of common law interpretive methodology cannot be ordinarily subsumed under the British Model. This is amply demonstrated by *Griswold* and its progeny extensively examined in Chapter 3 above. As stressed there, the 'traditions' purported to be incorporated in the *Griswold* jurisprudence were largely 'counter-traditions', or at least heavily reworked and restructured ones.[28]

More generally, what ultimately sets apart U.S. constitutionalism from the British Model is that in the U.S. the Constitution made in 1787 *transcends* the legal order in which it is deployed whereas under the British Model the constitution remains *immanent* within the corresponding order. In other words, in the U.S., the constitution as made is always in tension with the constitution as grown. This tension has led one critic to draw a line between *the* Constitution and constitutional law – by which he meant the body of US Supreme Court decisions in constitutional cases (Meese 1987) – and to question the authoritativeness of the latter (*Id.*). Some American judges and scholars refuse to accord legitimacy to the 'living' or 'grown' American Constitution or to reliance on precedents *qua* precedents in constitutional adjudication.[29] Moreover, even those American judges and scholars who are partisans of the 'living' constitution and of the 'growing' of evolving norms to suit the needs of each succeeding generation, always do so in reference to the transcendent constitution 'made' in 1787 and amended twenty seven times since then. This is, of course, in sharp contrast to the British Model's reliance an immanent constitutional growth coming from below.

The UK's constitutional picture is changing, primarily due to transnational legal developments that are, at least in part, constitutional in function even of not constitutional in form. Chief among these are the ECHR (incorporated into UK domestic law through the Human Rights Act of 1998) and various treaties relating to the EU, including the pending (as of this writing) 2007 Lisbon Treaty, which to a large extent amounts functionally to a constitution for the EU.[30] Whether these developments will eventually lead the UK to move beyond the British Model, or whether they will lead to an 'internalization' compatible with the functioning of that model, is impossible to predict at this writing. What seems clear though is that the distinct British Model, or at least some of its salient elements, will continue to function and to be emulated for the foreseeable future.

5.5 The Spanish Model

As briefly indicated in Chapter 4, the successful making and implantation of the 1978 Spanish Constitution has given rise to a new constitutional model that differs significantly from the four models discussed thus far. The Spanish Model is distinct in two principal ways. First, it sets a framework for a multi-ethnic polity. And, second, it imports transnational norms, which it incorporated within the ambit of the nation-state.

As discussed in Chapter 4 above, one of the most daunting challenges confronting the making of the 1978 Spanish Constitution was finding a proper balance between national unity and according a meaningful measure of autonomy to ethnic communities, such as the Basque and the Catalans, which had been suppressed ruthlessly during the Franco régime. The Spanish constituents found an ingenious solution that sought to bridge over contentious disputes over national identity – or more precisely, between national and sub-national identities – through masterful use of open-endness and ambiguity. The Spanish Constitution provides for 'autonomous communities' ('*communidades autonomas*') with significant, though by no means fully spelled out, regional self-government powers.[31] These provisions divide the country into several autonomous communities, affords ethnic groups such as the Basques and the Catalans significant, and to an important degree open-ended, autonomy, but do not limit such available regional autonomy to these well-defined and well-organized ethnic groups. Indeed, the Constitution also extends autonomy to other regions, where infra-national self-government aspirations and organization are much less pronounced. (Moreno 2001).

The practical consequences of this nation-wide division into autonomous communities are, on the one hand, a diffusion of the focus from two most problematic ethnic groups from the standpoint of preservation of national unity, namely the Basques and the Catalans. On the other hand, because regions like Andalusia are in fact autonomous in name only, the 1978 Spanish Constitution creates a *de facto* type of asymmetrical federalism where all regions are offered significant local autonomy, but only some want to, can, and do take advantage of it. Moreover, this system has worked

fairly well for three decades, even if there have been certain difficult
moments with potentially momentous constitutional implications, such as
the recent tensions between the national government and Catalunia over
the latter's design to greatly increase the scope of it autonomy.[32]

Although both Spain and the U.S. are multi-ethnic societies, the Spanish
constitutional model is multi-ethnic whereas the American one is not.
That is because through constitutional accommodation of sub-national
ethnic groups, the Spanish Model is suitable for a multi-ethnic *polity*. In
contrast, the American Constitution and the American Model are compatible with a multi-ethnic *society*, but not with a multi-ethnic *polity*. Under
the Spanish Model, constitutional identity is predicated on striking a balance between national identity and unity and a significant though loosely
defined measure of sub-national ethnic identities. American constitutional
identity with its heavy emphasis on individualism and on the country as a
melting pot designed for the equal enjoyment of constitutional blessings,
for its part, leaves little room for ethnic identities within its constitutional
landscape.

The second important respect in which the Spanish Model differs from
the previously examined ones is in its incorporation of transnational (then
European Community now) EU norms as part of its recasting the relationship between the Spanish nation and the Spanish state. In 1977, Spain
requested admission to what is now the EU and membership in that transnational body became an important symbol in the quest to overcome
Francoism. This aspiration to belong to what is now the EU was 'helpful', if
not 'decisive', to the success of the transition to constitutional democracy
(Linz & Stepan 1996:113). Accordingly, with a view to its incorporation
into the larger European polity, Spain imported and internalized European
democratic values. These values though 'external' became easily 'internalized' as they were highly consistent with the economic and cultural position that Spain had come to occupy in the mid 1970's. As indicated in
Chapter 4, to what extent Spain had already internalized European values
and to what extent it embraced them primarily for purposes of eventual
membership in what is now the EU may be difficult to determine. What is
crucial, however, is that the Spanish Model requires importation of transnational norms and redeployment within the confines of the nation-state.

Beyond allowing for internalization of transnational norms, the Spanish
model's opening to Europe also made possible aiming for externalization
of internal conflict for purposes of finding a livable equilibrium within the
boundaries of the Spanish nation-state. Given the difficult and contentious
differences within Spain concerning the proper balance between national
unity and regional autonomy, projection toward the European space could

open new avenues for successful mediation between unity and diversity. Indeed, in theory at least, recourse to the supra-national European space makes possible a number of three way relationships that might defuse the clash of respective visions of the nation as an indivisible entity and of autonomous regions as eventually completely separate entities.

Unlike the Spanish Model, none of the models involving 'made' constitutions discussed above require any comparable process of internalization and externalization. The German Model in its original incarnation requires only internalization (or merely expression assuming internalization as a given) of the nation's ethnos to the exclusion of all alien or external factors.[33] For its part, the French Model requires internalization of the universal values that promote the *demos*, but the process of adaptation that it requires remains clearly confined to the space encompassed by a single nation. In other words, the French Model requires adapting universal norms to the scale of the nation rather than assimilating transnational objectives or projecting domestic concerns onto a supra-national arena. Finally, the American Model is also purely national rather than transnational in scope (regardless of whether it eventually might be susceptible to retooling for purposes of adaptation to constitutionalism on a trans-national scale). Indeed, the American Model calls upon the wave of immigrants destined to form the American nation to shed or downplay their ties to their countries of origin in order to become integrated as citizens within their emergent nation. In short, whatever universal transnational influences may lurk behind American constitutional norms, the latter's constitutional operation has been exclusively focused on building an American nation designed to become inextricably glued to the deployment of American statehood.

Both in its multi-ethnic dimension and in its reliance on incorporation of transnational norms, the Spanish Model has wielded influence beyond the confines of its country of origin. Canada, for example, has embraced multi-ethnic constitutionalism in its 1982 Constitution,[34] and has attempted to institute a workable framework be responsive to demands of Quebec, albeit that such a attempts have thus far been less than successful (Kymlicka 1998:110). On the other hand, many former communist East and Central European polities have completed successful transitions to constitutional democracy in which absorption of European norms have played a major role (Kubicek 2003). Similarly, South Africa's 1996 Constitution has relied on incorporated of international human rights norms and of entrenched constitutional norms prevalent in well-functioning democracies.[35]

5.6 The European Transnational Constitutional Model

As already indicated, the proposed constitution for the EU was approved by the governments of the then 25 EU member-states in 2004, but was not adopted after its rejection in popular referenda held in France and the Netherlands in 2005. The meaning or implications of this rejection are not clear as inter alia, some have claimed that the EU already has a functioning constitution (through not a formal one) prior to the drafting of the 2004 proposed constitution, and as much of the substance contained in that constitution – minus all references to the term 'constitution', and to symbols of constitutionalism or of a constitutionally framed polity – has been approved by all the 27 members of the EU upon the signing of the Treaty of Lisbon in October 2007.[36] Nevertheless, in spite of this, and in spite of the problems surrounding constitution-making in the context of the EU which will be briefly addressed in Chapter 6, the proposed 2004 EU constitution and the substantive provisions of the 2007 Treaty of Lisbon provide sufficient information and elements to allow for construction of a transnational constitutional model tailored to the experience and potential of constitutionalism in the EU.

In terms of erecting a viable constitutional framework and of sustaining a cohesive constitutional identity, the European attempt at transnational constitutionalism appears to suffer from many handicaps that do not affect the constitutional models tailored to the nation-state. All the latter models discussed so far involve similar processes of negation and reincorporation. They all attempt to harmonize *ethnos* and *demos*, and they seek to adapt norms that are originally external to the relevant constitutional locus, or that exceed the latter in their scope (e.g., tailoring universal rights to fit the needs of the French nation-state). The main difference between these models fitted to the nation-state concerns the relative importance that each gives to particular elements, such as *demos* or *ethnos*, and how each model combines or approaches the elements common to all.

In contrast, the EU appears to lack a sufficient common *ethnos* or identity. As Dieter Grimm has emphasized, the various countries that make up the EU do not share a common language, a common political culture or even a commonly shared newspaper of reference (Grimm 1995: 292–297). Moreover, although the failed proposed constitution and the Treaty of Lisbon significantly increase the powers of the European Parliament, intergovernmental institutions may well retain too much power for the development of a workable *demos*. This impression is symbolically reinforced by the shift from the early draft of the failed European Treaty-Constitution (which refers to the peoples of then 25 EU member-states as the constituents) to the final draft (which refers to the EU members' heads of states as the contracting parties[37]) and finally to the 2007 Lisbon Treaty (no longer a *constitutional* treaty, but instead yet one more European treaty *tout court*). As yet one more treaty in a line of European treaties calling for incremental steps, including those of Maastricht (1992), Amsterdam (1997) and Nice (2000), the Lisbon Treaty may well lack the negative force that all new constitutions must have vis-à-vis the status quo ante in order to be successful.

It is of course possible that the EU constitutional project will ultimately fail for the above-mentioned reasons. But this need not be the case. Indeed, as illustrated by the American Model, a constitutional order and identity can be projected, for the most part, into the future. As we have seen, a barely existing American people created a constitution establishing a state for a future nation and thus laid down the bare outlines of a constitutional identity that would become essential not only for the future success of the constitution but also for the self-image of the emerging nation. Why would an adequate, future-oriented constitutional model along comparable lines not work for Europe?

Whereas question concerning the nexus between different means of constitution-making and successful constitutions will be addressed in Chapter 6, suffice it for now to point out that both constitution-making following violent rupture, such as in the case of the French and American revolutions, and constitution-making in the context of peaceful transition to democracy, as in the case of Spain, have led to successful constitutions and constitutional identity building. Consistent with this, there seems to be no reason to preclude *prima facie* the possibility of successful constitution making through the use of treaties.

Finally, the gradualism associated with treaty-based constitution-making does not itself preclude deployment of the kind or degree of negation necessary for purposes of the implantation of a vibrant constitutional identity. This seems particularly likely in the case of Europe where negation need not be deployed against the nature of the prevailing (from an European perspective) pre-constitutional order. Indeed, all the nation-states that are members of the EU are functioning constitutional democracies. Accordingly, the principal target of the requisite negation ought to be the imprisonment of the prevailing constitutional order in Europe within the confines of the nation-state.

It is useful to consider which features of the previously discussed constitutional models might be relevant to the elaboration of an European model, and which must be considered to be completely inapposite. In this respect, both the ethnocentric German Model and the British Model based on gradual internal growth over many centuries seem to offer little that may be relevant to a plausible European model. Indeed, the EU is multi-ethnic and even if one would imagine its transition into a full-fledged constitutional polity to take several centuries, this transition could not be achieved through internal growth. This is because an EU constitution must at the same time both, in part negate and accommodate the constitutional order and identity of the several EU member-states. In contrast, the French Model's emphasis on *demos*, the American Model's projection of a constitutionalized polity into the future and the Spanish Model's accommodation of a multi-ethnic polity and its internalization of externally generated norms all seem to have some relevance to the construction of an European model.

The confluence of factors and forces that might result in an established European model are at best a work in progress. Accordingly, one must imagine plausible ways in which gradual treaty-based negation coupled with a reincorporation that cannot count on a common well of extra-constitutional identities comparable to those of the typical nation-state might result in a working constitutional order. Moreover, assuming that plausible paths of negation and reincorporation can be articulated, one must strive to imagine the kind of constitutional architecture that an European model would engender. Would it be something akin to an over-sized supra-national-state? Or something entirely new and completely *sui generis*?

Cumulative negation over an extended period of time punctuated by a series of treaties forging a trend towards increasing constitutionalization does not seem inherently impossible. Indeed the American process of constitutionalization provides an instructive example of negation over an extended period of time. Not only is the American Model projected into the future thus requiring an ongoing sustained process of negation, but also the core of the present-day American constitutional order and identity took almost a century to entrench. As David Richards has persuasively argued, it took two revolutions, that against the British in 1776 and that brought about by the Civil War in the 1860's, which culminated in the abolition of slavery, to fully carve out the actual constitutional order that currently prevails in the U.S. (Richards 1994). In terms of negation, the American experience comprised at least four crucial moments: the rejection of British rule and of the British system through the Revolution of 1776; the rejection of all the plausible alternatives effectively discarded by the adoption of the Articles of Confederation in 1781; the repudiation of the latter through the making and ratification of the 1787 Constitution; and the suppression of slavery and of its vestiges from the Constitution by mean of the post-Civil War amendments in the later 1860's.

Analogously, assuming the EU constitutional journey culminates eventually in a successful full-fledged constitutional order, its process of negation may well emerge as having proceeded gradually with its origins dating all the ways back to the founding 1957 Treaty of Rome. Under this hypothesis, the principal target of the process of negation is the Europe of nation-states standing against one another that was responsible for triggering two world wars. Moreover, within this perspective, and through a process of retrospective reconstruction, the series of treaties that culminated in the 2007 Treaty of Lisbon (as well as future treaties likely to emerge along the same path) could be regarded as a gradual moving away from the old order while clearing the way for the installment of a new supranational constitutional order. In this protracted process of negation, constitutional patriotism (Habermas 1996) and the institution and consolidation of a common market that transcends all national economic barriers (von Bogdandy 2005) seem poised to play key roles.

In essence, the concept of constitutional patriotism as elaborated by Habermas, refers to adoption and internalization of, and commitment to, the values inherent in constitutionalism and democracy to an extent sufficient to provide a working normative grounding to a well functioning fully sustainable constitutional democracy. Whether constitutional patriotism can play a significant *positive* role in forging and nurturing a viable transnational constitutional identity will be addressed in Chapter 8. From the standpoint of negation, however, it is clear that constitutional patriotism can play a significant role: it can help counter nationalism and promote the negation of patriotism *tout court*. On the other hand, as market-based contractual relations become ever more pervasive and increasingly institutionally backed and propelled, they seem bound substantially to contribute to the negation of the internal bonds that make the nation-state impervious to veritable supranational integration.

Concerning the process of reincorporation that must complement that of negation as part of the implantation of a successful constitutional identity, the American Model's orientation to the future may also be useful to consider in relation to the construction of a European constitutional identity. In this case, however, the analogy seems much more tenuous and speculative. The object of reincorporation is to recombine elements of collective identity in order to forge a workable constitutional identity and to achieve the substantive conditions necessary to reach a viable relationship between *demos* and *ethnos*. As exemplified by the analysis of unenumerated rights under the U.S. Constitution in Chapter 3, reincorporation need not be confined to adaptation of existing traditions: it can also reshape them and even reinvent them. Nevertheless, reincorporation must rely on existing elements or, at least plausible imaginable elements of common identity, and the list of those available for construction of a common European identity seems at first far from impressive.

Europe lacks a common *ethnos*. This by itself is not determinative as attested by the success of various constitutions that come within the ambit of the Spanish Model. However, none of the working multi-ethnic constitutions on the scale of the nation-state involve as extended an area or anything approaching the number of languages or cultures as those found within the confines of the EU.

On the other hand, one can identify several aspects of a common European identity: common origins, common values, common destiny and a common differentiation form American identity (von Bogdandy 2005). Can these, though insufficient for these purposes at present, nevertheless serve to sustain a viable constitutional identity through projection into the future along the lines of the American Model? Whereas this possibility cannot be ruled out, the American Model's capacity to leave certain crucial aspects of identity formation for the future is at best of limited relevance for Europe. This becomes apparent through a comparison of the American motto '*E Pluribus Unum*' with the EU motto 'united in diversity' adopted in connection with the now failed Treaty – Constitution. The American motto projects a dynamic and evolving image. With the Constitution acting as catalyst, the American melting pot will, over time, forge one nation from the multitude of diverse foreign nationals who have landed on American shores in successive waves of immigration. In contrast, the European motto aptly characterized as 'weak' (von Bogdandy 2005:360) is static and flat. Either the European peoples are already united in their diversity, in which case it is difficult to understand why their constitutional project is so problematic; or, the unity in question is a hope for the future, but rings hollow as nothing that has occurred thus far suggests how this abstract aspiration may be transformed into a concrete process of adaptation.

There may be another plausible interpretation of 'unity in diversity' that could prove more productive. In this reading the unity in question would refer not merely to some kind of aggregation of member states. Instead, it could be taken to symbolize, as well, a dynamic process against Balkanization within, and, by extension, among, nation-states. Seen in this light, unity at the European level may serve to defuse tensions within multi-ethnic states and between individual states and their own ethnic minorities. By transferring some powers from the member states to the Union, more room may be made for greater regional autonomy and diversity. Thus, if the constitutional treaty were eventually to lead in that direction, it would prove conducive to the development of future identities. In that case, the identities in question would seem more in keeping with the multiethnic Spanish Model than with its American counterpart.

None of the specific aspects of collective identity referred to above appears suitable for immediate incorporation into a workable European constitutional identity. Nevertheless, Professor von Bogdandy provides insights into what aspects of collective identity eventually may be transformed into appropriate material for a constitutional identity. Thus, a narrative concerning origins is a crucial component of a viable constitutional identity, and the reference to Europe's 'bitter experiences,' introduced into the failed constitutional treaty's preamble, provides a promising starting point. Professor von Bogdandy is right that this reference is 'minimal', but that may be more a virtue than a vice (von Bogdandy 1975:310).[38] The reference itself does not provide a sufficient narrative, but it opens the door to one.

It is clear that Nazism and Soviet communism are both European phenomena and the main culprits behind most of the human-caused misery perpetrated in the twentieth century. Moreover, the European project arose on the ashes of Nazism and, recently, has been extended so as to incorporate within the Union the formerly communist countries of Eastern Europe. Accordingly, a European constitutional identity could easily ground its narrative of origins on a repudiation of Nazism and Soviet communism and on the need to create a political order that would minimize the chances of any return to tyrannical totalitarian rule. Such repudiation serves as a negation of a preconstitutional order that is, 'preconstitutional' from the standpoint of Europe, not from that of the individual member states-that could not ward off totalitarian rule.

From the perspective of constitutional identity, origins depend, in part, on negation. In the French case, it was negation of the absolute monarchy; in the American, negation of colonial rule. Negation alone, however, is insufficient to create a distinct image of origins. In the European case, rejection of the political order that could not ward off Nazism or Soviet communism certainly looms as a propitious starting point. However, it does not of itself suggest why a transnational constitutional order would be needed rather than a series of sound national constitutional regimes.

If Nazism is regarded as involving a pathological and highly disproportionate promotion of *ethnos*, and Soviet communism as fostering excessive suppression of it, a narrative of origins could link the repudiations, mentioned above, to the building of a transnational multiethnic order. An order such as this would promote a proper equilibrium among a multiplicity of diverse ethnicities. It would resemble the Spanish multiethnic model to some extent, but, by remaining transnational, it would avoid the seeming pitfalls of national multiethnic constitutional orders, such as those of Belgium or Canada.[39] In other words, if transnational constitutionalism can create a space that is particularly well suited for the coexistence of a multiplicity of ethnicities while minimizing the potential excesses of *ethnos*, then rejection of the 'bitter experiences,' when coupled with the need for a lasting commonly shared framework that neither unduly magnifies nor unduly represses *ethnos* provides a seemingly viable narrative of origins, and one susceptible of successful incorporation into an emerging European constitutional identity.

The inclusion of German chancellor Gerhard Schroeder and Russian president Vladimir Putin in the 2004 commemoration of the sixtieth anniversary of the D-day invasion of Nazi-occupied Europe, in Normandy,[40] is consistent with the narrative of origins sketched above. The Allies who disembarked in Normandy in 1944 were waging war against Germany. Remarkably, however, Chancellor Schroeder stated that the Allied military success had not been a 'victory over Germany, but a victory for Germany'.[41] Clearly, such a statement would seem most unlikely absent deployment of a narrative of new origins along the lines suggested above.[42]

The other elements of collective identity referred to in the constitutional treaty and discussed by Professor von Bogdandy, namely, Europe as 'a community of destiny,' as 'a special area of human hope,' and as a 'community of values,' could well figure in a European constitutional identity at some point in the future. They sound hollow at this juncture, however, because they remain abstract and largely generic. But this does not mean that in time common threads, found in the history and culture of the various member states, could not be woven together into, for example, a distinct and sufficiently differentiated 'community of destiny.' Or that disparate threads could not be gathered together and aggregated to sketch a 'special area of human hope.'

Constitutional identity like national identity can also be defined, to some degree, by who 'we' are not, as opposed to who we are. Professor von Bogdandy is right to point out that anti-Americanism has a role to perform in circumscribing and thus defining a European identity (von Bogdandy 2005:310–312). Moreover, anti- Americanism can play a significant role in constructing a European *constitutional* identity. American constitutional identity is adamantly fixed on the nation-state and wary of international and transnational norms that are constitutional in substance if not in form. In contrast, the starting point for a new European constitutional identity is the rejection of a constitutional order imprisoned within the nation-state combined with the search for harmonization between national, supranational and international constitutional norms. To be sure, a similar harmonization is sought under the Spanish Model, which is tailored to the nation-state. Nevertheless, if one adds to existing transnational institutional arrangements within the Union its transnational constitutional aspirations, the contours of a plausible European constitutional identity begin to emerge.

In conclusion, it is a quite possible that eventually the EU will create a European constitutional identity and lead to a new transnational European constitutional model. That model, like the American, would be future oriented; like the Spanish, it would be multi-ethnic. Furthermore, for the European Model to foster 'unity in diversity,' most likely it would not do for it to become a supranational version of a nation-state model. Instead, the European Model would have to promote novel vertical and horizontal apportionments of powers allowing supranational, national, and infranational governance to work in harmony without being constrained by traditional forms of federalism or confederalism. The European Model would have to find its own balance between *demos* and *ethnos* a balance that would not be like that of the French or the German. Whether a European constitutional identity and a European constitutional model will emerge depends on the EU's will and capacity to generate a genuine constitutional practice and culture. Whether that will actually happen, however, is still very much an open question.

5.7 The Post-Colonial Constitutional Model

As already noted, unlike all the previously discussed constitutional models, the post-colonial one is not anchored in any single historical experience. It is based, instead, on a number of different historical instances involving decolonization and newly independent former colonies adopting constitutions that are not necessarily similar in content, but that bear a high degree of resemblance in terms of their dynamic relationship to their colonizer and to its constitutional order. Furthermore, it is important to stress from the outset that the postcolonial model by no means extends to all constitutions adopted by former colonies. Indeed, the U.S., Canada, Australia, Mexico and Brazil are all former colonies that enacted post-colonial constitutions yet none of them fits within the Post-Colonial Model. As will be elaborated below, the Post-Colonial Model encompasses above all constitutions adopted by former colonies in Africa and Asia that achieved independence after World War Two, including India, Nigeria and several former French colonies in Africa. Finally, it is important to stress that whereas it was routine for former colonies to adopt a constitution upon achieving independence in the post World War Two period, many of these were purely nominal. In many post-colonial polities, a constitution was enacted but not put to use, leaving government to authoritarian one-man rule (Okoth-Ogendo 1993:65). In the following elaboration of the broad outlines of the post-colonial constitutional model no account will be taken of these nominal constitutions which, while paying lip service to constitutionalism, were in fact cynically paraded by regimes that flouted all the key precepts of constitutional rule (*Id.*).

The most salient feature of the Post-Colonial Model is that both the negation associated with setting the newly formed polity free from its colonizer and the process of incorporation that provides content to the emerging constitutional order of the newly independent state are both shaped as against the colonizer's identity. In other words, the constitutional order and identity of the newly independent former-colony are elaborated in a dialectical process involving an ongoing struggle between absorption and rejection of the former colonizer's most salient relevant identities. At the most abstract level, the former colony adopts a constitutional order fashioned in the image of that of its former colonizer and then seeks to fine tune it to serve its own institutional and identity-based needs. The latter, moreover, will require adjustments to, and departures from, the colonizer's constitutional framework, but the work needed to adapt the inherited constitutional legacy to the needs of the new polity will almost inevitably happen to be defined in terms of the colonizer's political and constitutional framework. Finally, with respect the extra-constitutional material available for use in shaping the new polity's constitutional identity, there is likely to be a significant part deriving from the colonizer (e.g., the colony's elites may have embraced key aspects of the colony's political and general culture) and a significant part from deeply embedded (and likely repressed during colonial times) ethnic, religious, cultural and linguistic, etc., extra-constitutional identities prevalent among the indigenous population in pre-colonial times.

The above abstract construct seems adequate to posit the essential outlines of the Post-Colonial Model. In actual historical cases, however, both the symbiotic relationship between the colonizer and the just emancipated colonized and the dialectic that accompanies them from implantation of the colony to its transformation into a newly independent constitutional democracy are likely to be much more intricate and complex. This is well illustrated by reference to the case of India.

India has had remarkable success in persevering as a constitutional democracy since its independence from Britain in 1947. India's constitutional journey has by no means been at all times smooth. It has come periodically under threat by among other things, abusive invocation of emergency powers such as occurred in the 1970's during the rule of Indira Gandhi (Krishna 1994:167–168), and flare ups of ethnic and religious violence, such as those that have taken place in the states of Punjab and Kashmir (*Id.*:169). Nevertheless, constitutional democracy in India has been resilient and vigorous for over sixty years, and India's constitutional order and culture owes much to that of the UK.

These are certain obvious similarities between constitutional democracy in the UK and in India, most notably centralized power in a national parliament with a vast degree of authority vested in the Prime Minister (*Id.*:164). But there are also salient differences as India's written 1950 constitution establishes a federal republic and entrusts constitutional review to the country's Supreme Court.[43] What is most important though, is much less formal or structural similarities than the similarities in approaches and attitudes that bind the two constitutional cultures together.

India's transition to constitutional democracy started during the colonial period. Primarily with the aim of co-opting and of limiting the push toward independence by the colony's educated elite, the British gave their blessing to the formation of the Indian National Party in 1885, and enacted a series of reforms in 1909 and 1919 allowing Indians limited participation in governance (*Id.*). In addition, in 1935 the British granted Indians limited self-rule at the provincial level (*Id.*). Although these measures failed to stem the drive spearheaded by the Congress Party, which eventually culminated in independence, they definitely left a salient imprint on India's constitutional culture and on its democracy (*Id.*).

Viewed paradigmatically, colonization by a constitutional democracy seems to rest on a contradiction. The colonizing democracy preaches an ideology of constitutionalism, but denies its colony and the colonized people within it most of the constitutional blessings it bestows at home – albeit that the colonizer might seek to explain away this apparent contradiction through some paternalistic rationale such as e.g., the colony's population is not yet culturally or organizationally prepared to assume the burdens of self-government. Consistent with this, at independence the former colony's constitution-makers, for the most part likely to have been educated at the former colonizer's elite institutions, would seem most likely to appropriate the former colonizer's constitutional ideology and culture while repudiating the latter's excertions of power and authority over their homeland. In short, the new constitutionmakers would be negating the former colonial power while affirming its constitutional legacy. Moreover, as pre-colonial identities and those repressed during colonialization reassert themselves, the inherited constitutional legacy will have to be adjusted or redrawn to incorporate the reinstatement of formerly repressed identities.

The case of India generally fits within this overall paradigm, but with many noteworthy nuances. In devolving power and granting India's provinces limited self-rule, the UK produced a change within its own constitutional architecture (as small and peripheral as it may have been). From India's perspective, however, that change looms larger for at least two important reasons. First, it makes the colonial power's constitutional legacy not purely alien, and thus in embracing substantial portions of that legacy India was not merely incorporating the constitutional heritage of the (*its*) 'other'. And, second, the limited self-rule at the provincial level paved the way to the establishment of federalism in India, thus allowing for transformation and adaptation of the colonial institutional legacy to suit the particular constitutional needs of the newly independent former colony. From the British perspective, the grant of limited provincial self-rule may have been for purposes of containment, co-optation and of dividing opposition within India to colonial rule. In contrast, for India besides facilitating the path to independence, provincial self-rule pointed to, and opened the doors towards, federalism which is itself traditionally 'un-English', but which would come to play a central role in India's constitutional order, culture and identity.

India's federalism has been the key to providing the (often-uneasy) requisite balance between the unity of the polity and the diversity of the country's multiple ethnic, religious and linguistic communities. Established to map ethnic and religious communal divides in the 1950 Constitution, Indian federalism was reconfigured starting in 1953 to carve out federated units on a linguistic basis (Muni 1996). This was done to downplay explosive ethnic and religious divisions that threatened to provoke separatism and disintegration (*Id.*).

What is important to retain for our purposes is the dynamic that has bound India's journey to constitutional democracy to British constitutionalism through a process involving successive waves involving opposition, incorporation and transformation. This is perhaps best exemplified by India's highly centralized federalism (Krishna 1994:164). Its seeds were implanted by the British administration; its structure and function adapted to the multi-ethnic needs of India's highly diverse ethnic, religious and linguistic mosaic; and its centralized character with its strong national parliament and dominant prime minister necessary to preserve unity amidst great diversity firmly rooted in the Westminster parliamentary tradition.

In the last analysis, the post-colonial constitutional model is characterized by the predominance of a process involving an ongoing struggle between identification with and differentiation from, the colonizer's constitutional identity, through concurrent negation and affirmation of the latter. This model, as in the case of India, is likely to lead to success where a workable balance between acceptance, rejection and transformation of the colonizer's constitutional culture can be achieved. In other cases, such as that of Nigeria, where constitutionalism has been less successful but nonetheless substantial (Suberu 1994), the model still operates with great vitality. At the other end of the spectrum, adoption of a post-colonial model in a setting in which a workable scheme of identification with and differentiation from, the colonizer's constitutional legacy proves too elusive, is highly likely to result in constitutional failure.

The different constitutional models discussed in this Chapter serve to mold, shape, channel and orient a multiplicity of materials that become incorporated into constitutional identity over time. The contours of different constitutional identities are also significantly determined by discrete momentous events such as making, revising and amending constitutions. As will be detailed in the next chapter, constitution-making can also be fitted into different models, each having a different impact on the shaping of the ensuing constitutional identity.

CHAPTER **6**

Models of Constitution Making

Just as each constitution is unique in the way it produces constitutional identity, the making of each constitution is a singular historical event. Nevertheless, in the same way as it is heuristically profitable to discern diverse constitutional models, it is useful to distinguish among major models of constitution-making. As emphasized throughout, the production of constitutional identity requires a process of negation and incorporation, and as clearly indicated by the Spanish experience with constitution-making examined in Chapter 4 above, *how*, and under what circumstances, a constitution is made seems bound to have a major impact on its modes of negation and incorporation that relate to its building a distinct constitutional identity. There is no necessary correlation between constitutional models and constitution-making models, through it stands to reason that there may be some significant congruences. For example, a constitutional model that depends on a profound and drastic rejection of the pre-constitutional past may be better served by constitutional-making that is particularly suited to the achievement of radical breaks. On the other hand in as much as constitutional identities are built and changed over time, it is quite possible that even in the absence of an optimal 'fit' between constitution – making and constitutional identity building, a polity will eventually evolve into the constitutional order and culture that suits it best.

Although constitutional identity can evolve throughout the entire life of a constitutional regime, the making of a constitution generally plays a crucial role in the determination of that constitution's corresponding constitutional identity. In its paradigmatic form, constitution-making amounts to a 'creation *ex-nihilo*' or what Jon Elster has termed a 'bootstrapping' (Elster 1994:57) which involves a clean break with a pre-constitutional past. For example, if the making of a constitution comes on the heels of a revolution that has overthrown was has become the *ancient régime*, then the new constitutional order cannot look back to that *ancient régime* for normative legitimacy or continuity. The new constitutional order is illegitimate from the standpoint of the pre-revolutionary normative order and thus the constitution makers' claim of normative legitimacy for the new order they have crafted is in an important sense unfounded. Without links to the old legitimacy, that claimed by the new constitution is therefore somehow 'bootstrapped.'

From the standpoint of constitutional identity, constitution-making requires both negation of pre-constitutional identities and creation of a new identity, which calls for reincorporation of material from the pre-constitutional past. In the case of constitution-making in the context of the French Revolution, for instance, there was a conscious act of negation – overthrow and repudiation of the *ancient régime* – followed by imposition of a new constitutional order – the absolute monarchy was replaced by a parliamentary democracy – which reincorporated, at least in part unconsciously, elements and materials from the pre-constitutional past. As already mentioned, the French Revolution's democratic vision was universal in scope but constrained in practice by the French language, civilization and culture; on the other hand, the centralized state erected by the absolute monarchy was reincorporated into the emerging constitutional order to make for the unity and indivisibility of the new parliamentary democracy. Moreover, whereas constitution making generally involves a change of regimes, it does not in most cases result in a total revamping of the self-identity of the people for whom the new constitution is made. There is thus continuity in the national identity of the French people before and after the Revolution, or of the Spanish people during Franco's dictatorship and during the post-Franco era of constitutional democracy. However, even if self-identity is maintained – it is the same people before and after constitution-making – it is very likely that important changes relating to the content of national identity will take place after the implantation of a new constitutional order. Thus, whereas pre-revolutionary France was already a nation (above all due to the achievements in unification and centralization of the absolute monarchy) it was one marked by feudal hierarchy and separate estates. In contrast, post-revolutionary France became a nation of equal citizens.

The creation of a new constitutional identity in relation to constitution-making requires, therefore, a dynamic process of negation and reincorporation that proceeds over time through resolution of tensions and oppositions that may lead to new conflicts and, in turn, to the need for further changes in constitutional identity. The American case provides a good example of a constitutional identity launched by the making of a new constitution evolving over an extended period of time, and requiring resolution of thorny conflicts for its completion. As already noted, one of the essential components of American constitutional identity was encapsulated in the famous dictum that 'all men are created equal' contained in the 1776 Declaration of Independence. This dictum encompasses both a negation of the British colonizing power against which the American Revolution was successfully fought and of the legitimacy of Britain's hierarchical society and concurrently, an affirmation of liberal equality as a foundation of the new constitutional order. This notwithstanding, the 1787 American Constitution acknowledged and condoned slavery as a compromise made to avoid having slave owning states walk away from the constitutional compact.[1] To be sure, accommodation of slavery did not result in a complete negation of liberal equality in the context of the new constitutional order. Thus, for example, the 1787 Constitution eradicates all vestiges of British aristocracy. Nevertheless, so long as slavery remained constitutionally tolerated, it was impossible to construct a coherent American constitutional identity. As already noted, it would take nearly eighty years and a civil war to abolish slavery and to finally make for a coherent American constitutional identity.

To allow a new constitution to become successful, the constitutional identity launched at its making must achieve a delicate balance. On the one hand, such constitutional identity requires a sufficient, though not total, negation of pre-constitutional identities – sufficient to give the new constitutional order a fresh start, but not so radical as to threaten the people's sense of self-identity. On the other hand, the new constitutional identity must transform and reincorporate sufficient pre-constitutional and extra-constitutional material to enable the people to relate to the new constitution as *their* constitution, and to allow its interpreters to endow its key provisions with a content that could command a widespread sense of legitimacy throughout the polity.

As seen in Chapter 5, constitutional identity depends on the constitutional model involved. It also depends on the type of constitution making that led to adaptation of the prevailing constitution. Indeed, it seems logical that if constitution-making is preceded by a violent revolution, the relationship of the new constitutional order to pre-constitutional identity would be different than if there had been a peaceful transition to a new constitution. With that in mind, one can generally distinguish six different models of constitution making which taken together with the seven constitutional models discussed above substantially circumscribe the formation and evolution of the main different types of constitutional identity.

The six models of constitution-making are: 1) constitution-making by revolution or the revolution-based model; 2) constitution-making through subversion of the constituent power or the invisible British model; 3) constitution-making imposed by the victors on the vanquished or the war-based model; 4) peacefully negotiated transition to a new constitution or the pacted transition model; 5) treaty-based transnational constitutional-making or the transnational model; and 6) post-conflict internationally imposed or supervised constitution-making or the internationally grounded model.

6.1 The Revolution-Based Model

In one important sense, the revolution-based constitution-making model seems to be the best suited one for purposes of establishing a new constitution and of forging a distinct constitutional identity. As mentioned in Chapter 4 above, to achieve its fullest power and potential constitution-making should be akin to creation *ex nihilo*. It should be foundational and enduring it should at once 'erase' the past and firmly ground and shape the future. A successful revolution, can presumably free the polity from the shackles of the *ancient régime*, and make room for the triumphant revolutionaries to emerge as the self-proclaimed self-sustaining constituent power without debts or links to the past. Moreover, because of their exalted status as liberators and as victors, the revolutionaries seem best poised to transform their unfettered constitutional power into an authoritative and fully legitimated constituted power through elaboration of a (new) constitution for a recently liberated (from internal or external oppression) polity.

There are, of course, as already indicated in Chapter 4 above, several problems with this idyllic picture. Two major ones already alluded to are: the 'bootstrapping' problem which make the *legal* legitimacy of the newly minted revolutionary constituent power highly problematic; and the problem that too radical a break with the past – such as the wrought by the French reign of terror – may make the new constitutional arrangement unworkable whereas too weak a break may leave too little distance between the *ancient régime* and its newly constitutionalized counterpart to allow the latter to function independently or adequately on its own.

A third major problem, which transcends revolution-based constitution-making, but which is particularly acute in relation to the latter, is that regarding the legitimacy of the link between constituent power and constituted power, or to use a well known shorthand that of 'permanent revolution' (Preuss 2007:220). Successful revolutionaries who emerge triumphant against a reviled and oppressive *ancient régime* seem poised to project sufficient charisma, authority and legitimacy to speak for the relevant 'We the People,' and thus emerge as the rightful bearers of the constituent power. In the French Revolution, the victorious Third Estate stood for the whole and laid claim to the constituent power of the French people.[2] In the aftermath of the American Revolution, those who defeated the British colonists, penned the 1776 Declaration of Independence, and spoke in the name of 'We the People' at the 1787 Philadelphia Convention invoked the constituent power and launched the American polity on its constitutional journey (Wood 1969:306–343).

Once the revolutionary constitution is made and put into operation, however, the constituent power is replaced by the constituted power and the level of legitimacy of the former is unlikely to extend to the latter. In the fervor of the revolution, the newly configured or reconfigured polity may be easily imagined as united in its endeavor to move away from its past and to join hands in the conception and molding of its future. In contrast, once the power is constituted, the constitution in place, and its provisions implemented, the unity of the constituent phase seems bound to dissolve. Indeed, particular constitutions and the legal regime which they legitimate are bound to privilege certain members of the polity at the expense of others, and with the revolutionary heroes having become the leaders and charismatic unifiers of the past, the constituted power may not be convincingly vindicated as a power of the whole. In terms of the permanent revolution, as initially conceived by Marx and Engels and later embraced by Trotszky, so long as the revolution is in full force, there is an unabating struggle against oppression. Once it is over, and the revolutionaries settle down to rule, though, institutionalization takes over, and all instances of it will inevitably give rise to new forms of oppression. Similarly, constitution-making after revolution is poised to wipe out the injustices of the superceded order shattered by the revolutionaries. But after the new constitution comes into effect, there are bound to be new winners and losers. And why should the losers, particularly if they are generations removed from the constitution-making moment, feel bound to maintain allegiances to a constitution in the making of which they had no say, and which puts them at a disadvantage relative to some of their fellow citizens?

Whatever specifics may be needed to address these three problems in any particular case, both a break with the past and a selective and transformative partial repression and partial reincorporation of certain of its key elements are necessary preconditions to successful constitution-making and to the viability of the resulting constitution. The revolution-based model seems best suited to the task to breaking away from the past through negation and of providing for an interim period for settling accounts according to the revolutionaries' conception of political justice.[3] On the other hand, the revolution-based model may seem inherently unsuited for successful reincorporation of the pre-constitutional and extra-constitutional materials originating in the *ancien régime*.

Upon further inquiry, the question of successful reincorporation turns out to be more nuanced and complex. First, the combination of negation and reincorporation necessary to launch a distinct and viable constitutional identity requires an actual substantive break with the *ancien régime*. Otherwise, it would seem difficult to achieve the requisite repression of pre-constitutional materials needed for a new order to emerge above the burdens of the past. And second, the combination of repression and reincorporation in question is likely to be inadequate if the requisite break is too radical. Consistent with this, moreover, the key distinction may be less that between constitution-making as the result of a revolution as opposed to in the absence of any revolutionary break, and more that between a revolutionary break that does not go beyond the minimum necessary to allow for a new constitutional beginning and a more radical revolution that makes it difficult to rethread the indispensable links between past and future.

This last point is well illustrated by the salient difference between the French Revolution and the American Revolution briefly mentioned in Chapter 4. As Hannah Arendt underscores, the French Revolution created such a radical break with the past that the revolutionaries could not muster sufficient legitimacy or continuity successfully to lay down the new law of the land. In sharp contrast, the American revolutionaries – who had just won a war of liberation rather than a revolution in the strict sense of the term – overthrew the colonizer, but not the basic political organization of the newly emancipated colonies. Indeed, the people of the colonies were already organized into self-governing bodies prior to the conflict with England. This, moreover, provided a significant measure of legitimacy and continuity creating propitious conditions for the making of state constitutions, which in turn provided a stepping stone for the making of the 1787 U.S. Constitution (Arendt 1965:165–166).

The radical break unleashed by the French Revolution led to a strong reaction against constituent power among the more moderate revolutionary actors (Jaume 2007:67). As a matter of fact, constituent power became regarded as a dangerous force warranting restriction or suppression (*Id.*) This impression was so strong that after the 1790's France's constitution-making, involving about fifteen constitutions (*Id.*:83), largely avoided reliance on the constituent power as the expression of the sovereignty of the people (*Id.*:68). It would not be till de Gaulle's 1958 Fifth Republic Constitution that open appeal to the constituent power of the people would be restored (*Id.*:79–84).[4]

In the last analysis, the success of revolution based constitution-making depends on striking a proper equilibrium between a sufficiently emancipated constituent power and an adequately legitimated constituted power. This depends, in part, on *how much* and *what* of the past is destroyed. It also depends, in part, on how convincing a narrative of the new constitution's creation and contents can be elaborated on the basis of reworked pre-constitutional and extra-constitutional materials woven together into an emerging and evolving account of constitution-making that can be productively meshed into a vibrant and dynamic working constitutional identity.

6.2 The Invisible British Model

As stressed in 5.4 above, the British constitutional model is an immanent one that emerges through a process of accretion. Accordingly, the British Constitution seems grown not made and British constitutionalism independent from any discrete instances of constitution-making. A closer look at the relevant history reveals, however, that there have been actual constitution-making moments in British history – albeit partial and piecemeal ones – which have remained well camouflaged through subversion or repression of the constitution-making power (Loughlin 2007).

Seventeenth Century England was an era of revolution and of major constitutional change. During the first three decades of that century, there was a 'constitutional' struggle – i.e., one concerning respective institutional powers – between the King and the House of Commons (*Id.*:31). This was followed by a revolution resulting in the execution of the King in 1649; the rule of Cromwell and restoration of the Monarchy in 1660; and the 1689 Revolution (*Id.*:33–42).

Unlike the eighteenth century French Revolution, the English revolutions of the seventeenth century did not result in abolishing the monarchy. Nonetheless, the constitutional conflicts that played out in seventeenth century England resulted in significant, even if not fully-fledged, constitution-making and in concerted efforts at concealment. In the first place, the source of legitimacy of the King's power, which was traditionally conceived as being divinely grounded, became recast as originating in the people (*Id.*:27). This lead to a second major development: the invention of the concept of constituent power and its location in the 'people' (*Id.*:27–28). It was therefore in England that this concept was coined, and where it initially found both practical and theoretical expression. The Levellers pursued this concept in politics to counter certain policies promoted by the Parliament (*Id.*:35–38). Moreover, the most influential articulation of the view that the people was the ultimate sovereign retaining the power to overthrow the government which they entrusted with the pursuit of their common good was in John Locke's *Two Treatises of Government* written before the 1688 Revolution, but first published in 1690 (*Id.*:41).

The third major development, which originated at the time of the restoration of the monarchy in 1660, consisted in the systematic negation of the second above mentioned development. Specifically, the sovereignty of the people as such and their role as actual holders of constituent power was discredited in favor of the view that Parliament was the true representative of the people, thus emerging as the ultimate source of constitutional legitimacy (*Id.*:28). Consistent with this, the role of the constituent power was downplayed and concealed as it became folded into the powers and proceedings of the Parliament.

In the end, the constitutional empowerment of the Parliament and its acquisition of ultimate constitution-making powers at the close of the seventeenth century constitutional conflicts in England is based on more than submersion of the people's sovereignty. After the restoration of the monarchy, it is the King-in-Parliament who obtains his legitimacy from the people as represented in Parliament (as opposed to the King who derived his legitimate power from divine authority and who stood against the Parliament at the beginning of the century) who exercises valid constitutional authority (*Id.*:43). Moreover, if the Commons as mediator between the King and the people and as holder of (largely) concealed constitution-making powers appears above all as the county's supreme legislator, that too does not reveal the full picture, at least at the end of the seventeenth century. Indeed, at that time, England's supreme legislative power was in fact shared by the King, the Lords and the Commons acting as the Crown-in-Parliament (*Id.*).

The suppression of the constituent power as the expression of the people's sovereignty became ever more firmly entrenched in the eighteenth century. It promoted a parliamentary elitism that was used to discredit the French revolutionary experience (*Id.*:45). There is no question as indicated in 5.4 above, that England went through a substantial constitutional transformation from the early seventeenth century to the early twenty first century, with an enormous shift of powers in favor of Parliament. But was that shift the result of constitution-making? Or was it rather the result of a process of constitutional evolution, which went through moments of turmoil and sudden shift but did not live through any veritable constitution-making moment?

As we shall see below, there are no bright lines between constitution-making, constitutional revision or amending the constitution. There are often discrepancies between form and substance as what may be formally constitution-making may in substance amount to constitutional amendment and as extensive amendments to an existing constitution may in substance result in the making of a new constitution.[5] Viewed in this light, there can be no question that England's seventeenth century revolutions triggered *substantive* constitution-making. However, the concealment and displacement of constituent power from the people to the Parliament had two major effects that set a sharp contrast between British and French revolution-based constitution-making. First, whereas French Revolution constitution-making very much approximated creation *ex-nihilo*, its British counterpart, though surrounded by severe traumatic breaks in continuity – the execution of the King, followed by Cromwell's rule, the subsequent restoration and the 1688 Revolution – was nonetheless shrouded in an appearance of continuity. This lessened the bootstrapping problem, but also fostered a partial and ill-defined newly made constitution. Second, by making the Parliament the locus of the people's sovereignty, the British model triggers the collapse of the constituent power into the constituted power, thus abolishing the formal division between constitution-making and merely legislating. Constitution-making can thus become disguised as ordinary legislating, with the inevitable consequence of dissipating constitutional identity. This dissipation, moreover, is twofold: the constitution tends to lose its identity as a constitution; and, the country's constitutional identity, which does have a significant imprint on the polity as indicated above tends to blend seamlessly into other identities at play in the political and institutional life of the country. In other words, the country has a constitutional identity, but that identity is often not perceived as being constitutional in nature.

The collapse of the constituent power into the constituted power can thus have both advantages and drawbacks. Where the constitution can be plausibly depicted as grown rather than made, and as drawing on deep seeded traditions that lend support to the pursuit of the ideals of constitutionalism, the collapse in question may, on the whole, play a positive role. In contrast, where the traditions involved are significantly at odds with constitutionalism, and the blurring between constitutional and ordinary legislation can be easily manipulated to cast expediency as principle, then the absence of an independent constituent power can easily turn into a major liability.

Conflating constituent and constituted power in a way that conceals what amounts to constitution-making is not confined to legislatures. It can also be carried out by the judiciary in the course of engaging in the interpretation of legal texts for purposes of adjudicating cases before them. A striking example of this is provided by the Israeli Supreme Court's landmark decision in the case of *United Mizrahi Bank Ltd.* v. *Migdal Village*.[6] Israel, like the United Kingdom, does not have a written constitution. In the *Migdal* case, however, the Israeli Supreme Court bestowed constitutional status on certain 'Basic Laws' enacted by the Knesset, Israel's parliament, on 'freedom of occupation' and on 'human dignity and freedom.' Whereas it was unclear whether the Knesset intended the basic laws in question to have a constitutional status, the Court concluded they did in the course of interpreting them. Significantly, the Court buttressed its interpretation by reference to the very logic of a constitutional system based on the rule of law and on the 'ideals' of Israeli society (Dorsen, et al. 2003:109).

Both in the British case and in the Israeli one, partial constitution–making was achieved without reliance on a constituent power. In England, the Parliament stood for the people and drew upon the country's evolving constitutional tradition. In Israel, the judiciary appealed to what it regarded as universally applicable constitutional essentials while claiming to be able, through its interpretive powers, to give 'expression to the values of society as they are understood by the culture and tradition of the people as they move forward through history' (*Id.*). In short, in England, Parliament purports to give expression to the constitutional will of the people, whereas in Israel, the judges claim to be in a position to provide an accurate interpretation of the essence of the people's constitutional identity.

6.3 The War-Based Model

The two salient examples of war-based constitution making are those of post-World War Two Germany and Japan. Both in the case of Nazi Germany and of Imperial Japan tyrannical belligerent regimes experienced total defeat and unconditional surrender followed by a transition to constitutional democracy imposed by the victors. The war-based model, just like the revolution-based one involves a radical rupture with the past. Unlike the latter, however, the War-Based Model can only result in successful constitution-making if the citizenry of the defeated polity eventually embraces as its own the resulting constitution launched by the victors. In the context of the war-based model, the negation of the preconstitutional past is first imposed by the victors, and so is the nature of the new constitution, at least in its broad outline. For a constitution made pursuant to this model to succeed, the defeated polity must accept the repudiation of its own (recent) past and embark upon the reconstruction of a constitutional identity initially framed by former foreign enemies to whom it was forced to surrender.

Although the opportunities for negation of the preconstitutional past are similar under the two models, the War-Based Model confronts serious obstacles that are much less likely to challenge the Revolution-Based Model. In the latter case, much of the citizenry is likely to identify with the revolutionaries as did most Frenchmen with those who spoke on behalf of the Third Estate and most Americans with those who led them to their newly gained independence. There was obviously no comparable identification between the defeated Germans and their British, French and American occupiers, or between the vanquished Japanese and their American military rulers led by General MacArthur (Shoichi 1997).

Notwithstanding this serious obstacle, war-based constitution-making has succeeded both in Germany and in Japan, though, as we shall see below, in many key respects, the War-Based Model has proven a greater success in Germany than in Japan. This is in large part due to major differences in the circumstances in each of the two countries after the foreign occupiers eliminated their respective preconstitutional orders and imposed on them the task of crafting a new constitution. West Germany, under the stewardship of the Adenauer government, moved quickly to make the foreign initiated constitution-making project its own. In contrast, the constitution crafted in Japan was much more an imposed one bearing MacArthur's implacable imprint.

Germany did have a constitutional tradition and a working constitutional government during the Weimar Republic which preceded the Third Reich (Möllers 2007:91–93). However, as weaknesses within the Weimar Constitution had facilitated the Nazi's ascent to power, it was not an option for post-war Germany to return to its pre-Nazi constitutional past. Because of this, Germany could not simply take advantage of the *tabula rasa* achieved by the Allied Forces to launch a successful constitutional reconstruction, relying primarily on the revival of its Weimar constitutional tradition.

The military governments of the three occupying powers in West Germany established a Parliamentary Council made up of a number of the state governments of the several West German *Länder*, and charged them with the task to draft a constitution (Germany 1947–1949:277). The occupying powers imposed certain conditions on the constitution-drafters, including the adoption of a federal system, a bicameral parliamentary federal government of limited enumerated powers, strong judicial review and protection of fundamental individual rights (*Id.*:278).

The Parliamentary Council quickly adopted the task of drafting a constitution, within the above constraints as their own, and after consultation with German scholars (Kommers 1997:7–8), came up with a constitution, which they named the 'Basic Law for the Federal Republic of Germany' (Preuss 2007:478). The Basic Law was ratified by all *Länder* except Bavaria, but not submitted to the West German citizenry for plebiscitary approval (*Id.*).

The Basic Law consciously rejected the populist dimensions of the Weimar Constitution, including the plebiscite and the direct election of the president (Möllers 2007:94), which appear the have been used to pave the way for the transition to Nazi rule. Moreover, the new federalism initially imposed by the Allies and then embraced by the German drafters of the Basic Law has had no real purchase on pre-1933 German constitutional consciousness (*Id.*:95). Why would the German people readily accept such new arrangement over which it had not been consulted? And why would the German citizenry fail to raise questions about the extremely powerful German Constitutional Court's legitimacy in spite of its numerous important counter-majoritarian decisions? (*Id.*).

The most obvious answer to these questions is that both the occupying powers and the German citizenry wanted to avoid a return to the conditions that led to war, and were eager to guard as much as possible against the resurgence of a tyranic regime. Whether or not such a coincidence of aims would have emerged without foreign occupation, and whether the West German polity would have, if it had been left completely alone after the war, made a constitution comparable to the Basic Law, remain open questions. What seems incontestable, however, is that after the occupying powers achieved a constitutional *tabula rasa* in vanquished West Germany, the victors and the vanquished came close enough to sharing a common future constitutional vision for Germany to enable them jointly to launch a most successful constitution-making endeavor. Indeed not only has the Basic Law thrived for half a century, but it has done so since 1990 for a reunified Germany.[7]

As indicated above, war-based constitution-making was less successful in Japan than in Germany. Although in the end, constitutional democracy became successfully implanted in Japan, the constitution-making process itself was less instrumental in carving out a new constitutional identity. This was due, above all, to Macarthur's rejection of Japanese proposed constitutional revisions (Shoichi 1997:16) and draft for a new constitution (*Id.*:99), followed by imposition of an American crafted draft as the basis for the new Japanese constitution. (*Id.*:103). Eventually, through Japanese revisions and changes (*Id.*:161,129) and through loose translation and creative interpretation of the imposed constitutional norms, the post-war Japanese constitution became sufficiently adapted to the needs of the Japanese polity to make room for the emergence of a new constitutional identity.

Although Japan's post-war constitutional journey was more convoluted than (West) Germany's, in both cases the war-based model led to ultimate constitution-making success. This is due primarily to the fact that in both cases the victors and (those who came to speak for) the vanquished sought a successful transition from the ashes of total defeat to a reemergence as a stable constitutional democracy. In Germany, success was aided by congruence in the vision of the victors and the vanquished; in Japan, by the space left open for the vanquished to work out their differences with the victors.

6.4 The Pacted Transition Model

The pacted transition model is best exemplified by the making of the 1978 Spanish Constitution discussed in detail in Chapter 4 above. It is therefore sufficient, for present purposes, to recall its principal features summarily and briefly to explore its applicability beyond Spain, most notably in post-communist East/Central Europe and South Africa.

Pacted transition as it occurred in Spain is contrasted to constitution-making stemming from revolution or war in that it occurs in a context in which no clear-cut winners or losers emerge. Negotiation and an eventual pact leading to a new constitution depend on both the leadership of the *ancien régime* (or in Spain their heirs) and the proponents of a new constitutional order being too weak to impose their will or to overtake their opponents by force. Pacted negotiations, moreover, take place without break in legality, thus avoiding the 'bootstrapping' problem that besets revolution or war-based constitution making. As will be remembered, in Spain preservation of legality became possible only because of the certain remarkable and unpredictable events, such as the Franco empowered Cortes voting for free elections, thus knowingly assuring their own political demise.[8]

Furthermore, pacted constitution-making depends on a confluence of internal and external factors. In Spain, the painful memories of the civil war combined with the desire to obtain membership on what would become the EU. The former provided a powerful internal impetus to move away from the past; the latter, inspiration and guidance in relation to the future constitution which needed to be crafted. In other words, memories of the past suggested what had to be negated and visions of a European future contributed elements to be incorporated in Spain's constitution-making undertaking and in the constitutional identity designed to emerge from it.

Pacted constitution-making requires reliance on a symbol of unity which can be perceived differently by the various parties to constitutional negotiation while at the same time projecting an aura of continuity amidst profound, even radical, change. In Spain, that symbolic figure was the king, who meant different things to various political antagonists, and who assumed a courageous leadership role that bolstered the transition to constitutional democracy. A symbolic figure can play a pivotal role, particularly since constitution-making under the pacted-transition model can bring about fundamental changes akin to those triggered by revolution or war-based constitution making. Indeed, the 1978 Spanish Constitution and many of the post-communist constitutions in East and Central Europe resulted in changes that are comparable in magnitude to those instituted by the American Constitution or the German Basic Law.

There were significant differences between pacted constitution-making in East/Central Europe, in South Africa and in Spain. Nevertheless, some of the new post-Soviet constitutions and the new South African 1997 Constitution do fit within the constitution-making model best exemplified in the case of Spain.

Two of the post-Soviet constitution-making experiences that fit within the pacted transition model are those of Hungary and Poland. In both these countries a new conditional order was crafted as a result of round-table negotiations between a politically weakened communist leadership and an ascending and invigorated non-communist opposition that lacked the means to gain power through force. In both countries, moreover, the pacted transition did not lead to the *formal making* of a new constitution, but to a complete *overhaul* of the constitutional order amounting functionality to the making of a new constitution. In Hungary, changes were made through comprehensive amendments to the 1949 communist constitution. Through these 1989 amendments, Hungary was transformed from a socialist state led by a Marxist-Leninist party to a multiparty parliamentary democracy with a market economy. (Ludwikowski 1996:180).

Similarly, in Poland, constitutional change was first instituted through amendments to its 1952 constitution (*Id.*:155). Hungary has still not adopted a new constitution, and Poland had to wait until 1997 for adoption of a full-fledged post-communist constitution (Osiatynski 1997:66).

Both Poland and Hungary went through pacted transitions influenced by internal and external factors as did Spain. Both countries had an eye to integration into the greater European community of nations, and both have since become members of the EU. Also, both countries' constitution-making designs were predicated on eradication of the Soviet legacy, which had largely been external in origin, given the major hands-on role played by the Soviet Union in communist Hungary and communist Poland.

There were, to be sure, important differences between Spain and the two countries under consideration. Spain had a working economy before its transition to constitutional democracy and it did not confront an economic crisis like the countries of East/Central Europe did (Linz & Stepan 1996:88). Moreover, none of the latter countries had a working economic society when they embarked on their transition (*Id.*:252). Furthermore, none of these countries had a unifying figure like the King of Spain – though there are suggestions that the Polish Pope and the Catholic Church played in the Polish pacted transition a role similar to that of the King of Spain in that country's transition (Geremek 1998:1973).

Hungary's and Poland's constitution-making journeys seem to fit easily within the pacted transition model. In other cases in East/Central Europe, pacted transitions were not similarly successful. Most notably, pacted transitions that are purely backward looking – in the sense of being based on a consensus to do away with the existing but much weakened communist regime – are not likely to succeed for lack of a commonly shared vision of the future. This was the case in the former Yugoslavia where emergence from communism led to the triumph of an exclusivist ethnocentric nationalism that proved destructive of the polity (Preuss 2007:224).

More generally, certain of the transitions of East/Central Europe alert us to the two problems that can arise in the context of the pacted transition model. Where transition leads to dissolution of the polity to be replaced by a number of ethnocentric nationalistic states, such as in the case of ex-Yugoslavia, pacted transitions seem bound to fail. Indeed at least substantively, a purely ethnocentric nationalistic political unit bent on repression of pluralism, ethnic cleansing and discrimination of ethnic minorities does not comport with the basic tenets of modern constitutionalism. In such cases, the transition does not open the door for any plausible constitutional identity, but instead collapses all pre-constitutional and extra-constitutional identities into national identity. In the context of an *ancient régime* that operated in a monoethnic polity, a pacted transition may result in a working constitutional order along the lines of the German constitutional model. But even in that case, constitutional success requires moving forward on the basis of more than raw nationalism. Where the transition takes place in a multi-ethnic polity, on the other hand, projection of an identity predominantly based on ethnocentric nationalism seems altogether incompatible with forging a workable constitutional identity. In this respect, moreover, the Spanish transition stands in sharp contrast to the ethnocentric nationalistic transitions of East/Central Europe.

The second problem is that of 'restoration' constitutions (Sajó 1994:335, 341–346). A restoration constitution would reinstate the *status quo ante* before the advent of authoritarianism. In the East/Central European context, this would mean a return to the type of constitutional regime that was in force before the implantation of communist rule. Under these circumstances, the pacted transition would not, strictly speaking, lead to constitution-making. Instead, pacted transition would reinstate an existing constitution with its own distinct institutions and identity after a period of interruption. A restoration constitution is neither good nor bad in and of itself (although such constitutions can be used to return to reactionary or counter-revolutionary political arrangements (*Id.*)). Such constitution, however, should not be viewed and involving any genuine substantive constitution-making.

In both Spain[9] and East/Central Europe, a pure return to the past was impossible (Sajo 1994:342). After several decades of authoritarian rule it was impossible to return to anything resembling the *status quo ante* (assuming there was a working constitutional order before authoritarian rule which was not the case for most of the polities involved). Nevertheless, partial restoration can play a role in pacted post-authoritarian constitution-making, and to the extent that it does reprocess past constitutional identities it may truly contribute to what ought to count as genuine constitution-making.

The pacted constitutional transition in South Africa during the 1990's does fit squarely within the model under discussion. The pact was between a weakened apartheid regime facing both internal and external pressures and the African National Congress (ANC), under the leadership of Nelson Mandela (Dorsen, et al 2003:82). An interim constitution was adopted in 1993, and Mandela elected President of South Africa in 1994 (*Id.*). The negotiations for a permanent constitution were difficult,[10] but agreement was reached conditioned on approval by the South African Constitutional Court in 1996 (*Id.*).

The South African transition did not have a figure that might be considered the exact equivalent of the King of Spain. Nelson Mandela was certainly a widely admired and respected national leader, and he may have well fulfilled, in part, a role akin to that of the King of Spain. Mandela's role was also supplemented by that of the Constitutional Court which was ultimately entrusted with the guaranteeing that the South African Constitution conform with the rule of law and fundamental rights standards comparable to those of other Western democracies. Using these criteria, the Constitutional Court refused to approve the 1996 Constitution.[11] Only after the 1996 Constitution was revised to address the Court's objections, that the latter certified it, and that it entered into force in 1997 (*Id.*:89).

Besides insuring conformity with external norms of constitutionalism, the South African Constitutional Court played a crucial role in the pacted constitution-making process. The impasse was that the white minority apartheid government wanted certain guarantees in the new constitution that would be immune from majoritarian-based rejection or repeal. At the same time, the ANC (and its allies) insisted that only majoritarian elaboration and approval of the constitution would be legitimate.[12] Submission of the constitution to the Court for certification provided a way out of the impasse in question, and offers proof of the Court's stature and crucial role in the constitution-making process.

There are, therefore, several cases of successful constitution-making consistent with the pacted transition model, and although there are significant variations in the respective circumstances of each of these, they are all congruent with respect to the key factors identified above. In the last analysis, the principal virtue of the pacted transition model, besides the avoidance of violence, is that unfolds in an ambit of legal continuity and that it affords far greater opportunities for compromise among a plurality of constitutional interests. The principal drawback of this model, on the other hand, is the twofold one exemplified by the failure of genuine constitution-making in the cases of ethno-nationalism and restoration respectively. In the first of these, there is a break with the past, but no resulting constitutional order; in that of the second, there is simply no break from the standpoint of constitutional tradition or identity.[13]

6.5 The Transnational Model

It is hard to dispute that, at least to some extent, transnational and international relations have become constitutionalized. Some even claim that United Nations Charter amounts to a world constitution (Fassbender

1998). For present purposes however, neither the UN Charter nor transnational documents such as the ECHR – though they may contain certain norms that are functionally equivalent to constitutional ones – can be properly deemed to approximate full-fledged constitutions. In contrast, the EU Treaty-Constitution discussed in section 5.6 above, is a full-fledged constitution that was actually made though never ratified due to rejection in the referenda by the French and Dutch voters. Can something akin to this rejected EU constitution ever be fully ratified – given that the closely approximating version embodied in the form of a treaty rather than a constitution in the 2007 Lisbon Treaty has also not been successfully instituted as of this writing due to its rejection in an Irish referendum? Or, is there no need to because, as some have argued, the EU already has a working constitution?[14] These are difficult and speculative questions that will not be addressed here. Suffice it for now, that the EU constitution-making experience has yielded sufficient material to sketch a plausible transnational constitution-making model and to explore whether, at least in principle, an actual fully working constitutional order fitting within that model could be put in place.

Even before they turned squarely to a treaty in order to resume their constitutional project in 2007, the members of the EU straddled the distinction between constitution and treaty while making the 2004 EU constitution – which they termed 'constitutional treaty' – eventually approved by the governments of the (then) twenty five member states. As already noted, initially the EU constitutional treaty was made in the name of 'We the Peoples of Europe.' Later, the constituents listed in the preamble shifted, and became the heads of state of the EU members, rendering the constitutional treaty, formally at least, more akin to a treaty than to a constitution.

If the constitutional treaty ultimately is a treaty rather than a constitution, two important consequences follow. First, since the EU has been built on a series of successive treaties going back to the 1957 Treaty of Rome, the constitutional treaty provides no real break with the past. Second, and perhaps more importantly, treaties are inherently distinguishable from constitutions as the former regulate external relations among two or more distinct sovereigns whereas the latter regulate internal relations within a unified whole. At least in their respective paradigmatic forms, a constitution establishes, modifies or reestablishes a common unit with an identity of its own, while a treaty, in contrast, carves out a discreet common project among sovereign parties, with each retaining its own distinct identity.[15]

Beneath the surface of this basic distinction, however, matters are more complex. Some contemporary multilateral treaties, such as the ECHR, involve an (external) interstate relationship in relation to a subject matter, fundamental rights, that is typically internal. From the standpoint of fundamental rights, the ECHR looms as a hybrid between a treaty and (part of) a constitution: a treaty in form; part of a constitution in substance. Moreover, the enforcement of the decisions by the ECtHR holding that a state has violated an ECHR right of one of its citizens reflects the hybrid nature of these rights. Unlike the decision of a national supreme or constitutional court, which is binding on, and must be enforced by, all the relevant organs of the national government, ECtHR decisions are not automatically enforceable against member states. Instead, the state held in violation of the ECHR, must decide whether to abide by the ECtHR decision and to redress the violation it has been adjudged to have perpetrated against its own citizen. Nevertheless, when the state, as a matter of policy, regularly acts in conformity with ECtHR decisions, the citizen vindicated by the ECtHR is in much in the same position substantively as the citizen vindicated by her country's supreme or constitutional court.

On the other hand, constitutions cannot be thought of exclusively as the purely internal expression of a polity that coheres as a unified whole. As mentioned, constitution-making requires a break with the past, thus setting the future polity against the past polity, shattering the temporal unity of the whole. Perhaps even more importantly, constitution-making as an act of negation also requires a break with the polity's prevailing conceptions of collective identity. In other words, it is not enough to overthrow the *ancien régime*, it is also necessary to differentiate the constitutional 'we' from the preconstitutional and extraconstitutional 'we.'

Constitutions are often portrayed as social contracts, or as pacts among individuals within a polity. Consistent with this metaphor, constitutions are imagined as contracts among individuals within a state, while treaties are, in fact, contracts among states. Typically, contracts establish external relationships, and commercial contracts external relationships among strangers. As Max Weber stressed, contract is the means whereby strangers from different communities can engage in commercial exchanges at market (Weber 1968:635–639). Thus conceived, a contract stands in contrast to custom and tradition. Similarly, the social contract imagined by the likes of Hobbes, Locke and Rousseau, marks a transition from relations based on prerational customs and traditions (the state of nature) to consensual relations based on reason and rational self-interest (civil society and self-government for Locke and Rousseau and a self-imposed Leviathan for Hobbes).

A commercial contract abstracts – in the etymological sense of 'pulling away' – the individual market trader from his social and cultural milieu.

For example, it does not matter, from the standpoint of a market exchange, if buyer or seller are married or divorced, religious or secular, politically on the right or left, and so forth. Similarly, in relation to the social contract, the citizen is abstracted from his or her mores and cultural, ethnic or religious milieu.[16] In a constitution viewed as a social contract, therefore, settling a structure of governance, apportioning state powers, embracing the rule of law and establishing fundamental rights must be set against an order defined by prevailing preconstitutional mores and traditions. In this sense, constitution-making is clearly an act of negation.

Constitutions, however, cannot function through pure negation any more than contracts can through pure exchange cut off from any desire for that which is subject to being exchanged. The constitutional edifice will remain empty unless it can be filled with a substratum extracted from existing collective identities and reshaped to fit within the new institutional structures. Accordingly, both negation and reincorporation are essential for a constitution to materialize in form and substance.

The constitutional treaty certainly provides a plausible constitutional form. The key question is whether the collective identities of the EU and/or of its member states are likely to provide the requisite substance. In practice, neither negation and reincorporation nor form and substance can be disentangled from one another as they are mutually determining. For example, a constitution's choice of a structure of governance is a matter of form, but the choice between a presidential and a parliamentary system cannot be accounted for without reference to matters of substance. Logically, however, negation precedes reincorporation and form prefigures substance.

The fact that a constitution for the EU may originate in a treaty rather than a constituent act of the peoples of Europe proceeding as one, may not be that significant. This would seem especially true if the eventual European constitution establishes an altogether new constitutional model that is radically different form all the models tailored to the particularities of the nation-state. One can imagine, for example, relations among the peoples involved, among the member states, and among the multiple institutional features deployed by the constitutional treaty to be neither purely vertical nor purely horizontal, neither purely external nor purely internal. In that case, the distinction between contract and treaty would most likely lose much of its importance for the new European order, thus eventually minimizing the relevance of whether or not a constitutional treaty is a treaty or a constitution.

The difference between treaty and constitution seems more significant if the European constitution were to promote a supranational version of any of the models tailored to nation-states, or some hybrid version of these models. Even in that case, however, the difference need not be *that* significant. It could be of virtually no significance, if the constitutional treaty were ratified by referendum in each of the member states. But even without such ratification, it is conceivable that something along the lines of the constitutional treaty would allow for the development of an adequate European *demos*, and, further, that a suitable European constitutional identity could emerge to lead a gradual evolution of originally external treaty-based relations into internal ones sustained by a working European democracy and a sufficient common identity. It is also conceivable, of course that the requisite transition away from predominantly treaty-based relationships would not materialize, in which case the European constitutional project would seem bound to fail. In short, success is certainly possible, but only time will tell.

More generally, the contitutionalization of international norms, as in the UN Charter, and the internationalization of constitutional norms, as in the ECHR, expand the plausible opportunities for, and forms of, transnational constitution-making. As the plurality of legal regimes bearing on the relevant legal actors multiplies and as most of these regimes tend to become internally constitutionalized (Rosenfeld 2008),[17] *how* constitution-making is crafted and brought forth seems less crucial and less determinative. Unlike in the case of all other constitution-making models, where overcoming a pre-constitutional order that is mostly, or at least to a large extent, constitutionally deficient is a necessary prerequisite, that is not the case in the context of an EU Constitution. Indeed, all the EU member-states who approved the now failed Treaty-Constitution have nation-state constitutions that stand in harmony with the fundamental tenets of modern constitutionalism. The challenge confronting the EU constitution-makers was not, therefore, to eliminate some objectionable pre-constitutional order, but to recast the entrenched constitutional way of life within each of the member-states and to redeploy it at the inter-state level carved out by the EU. Under these circumstances, the most important negation does not target unacceptable pre or extra-constitutional norms, but the settled conviction that the horizon for constitutional ordering stops at the boundaries of the nation-state.

Under these conditions, there seems to be no reason why launching an expanded space for commonly shared constitutional norms could not be achieved successfully by means of a treaty. In the last analysis, in a transnational setting such as that of the EU, success of the constitution depends less on who the makers are and on how they make their constitution than on the citizenry of the transnational polity who can accept and internalize the new constitution. Recourse to the referendum is one way to proceed, but by no means the only one. One can imagine a retrospective legitimation of the constitution-making process through gradual internalization of its resulting constitution. That could certainly happen one day within the EU, or it may have already happened if those who claim that the EU already has a *de facto* working constitution are right.

6.6 The Internationally Grounded Model

In the last few decades, the international community has initiated, guided and supervised constitution-making in particularly troubled nation-states (Preuss 2007:493). These initiatives involve 'constitutional intervention' – which unlike 'humanitarian intervention' is thoroughly peaceful in nature – to launch constitution-making in countries mired in political conflict and not otherwise in a position to embark on a successful constitution-making journey (*Id.*). Many of these 'interventions' were launched by the U.N., starting with the U.N. Security Council's Resolution 544 of August 17, 1984. That resolution declared South Africa's new 1983 apartheid constitution 'null and void.' Whereas in the latter case, the intervention was essentially a negative one, the many subsequent cases, such as Cambodia in 1992 (U.N.S.C. Res. 745), East Timor in 2001 (U.N.S.C. Res. 1338), and Afghanistan in 2005 (U.N.S.C. Res. 1589), the U.N. undertook positive interventions. Furthermore, other international actors besides the U.N. have also intervened in various countries raging from Bosnia to Sudan (Dann & Al-Ali 2006:429, 442–445).

Many of the countries in which constitution-making by international intervention was launched were in, or just coming out of, a foreign war, civil war, or a combination of both. Nevertheless, the Internationally-Grounded Model clearly differs from the War-Based Model and from the Pacted Transition Model. In the War-Based Model, total defeat leads to elimination or effective suppression of all political factions other than the ones set up or accepted by the victors. Accordingly, constitution-making can proceed without any unmanageable internal strife. In the Pacted Transition Model, on the other hand, there are antagonistic political forces and the constitution-makers are subject to influence by external factors (e.g. EU membership in Spain), but all relevant players have concluded that their aims were more likely to be achieved through a pacted compromise than through violence.

In contrast, in countries in which international intervention has played an important role, opposing political forces have either been at war with one another or unable on their own to convene and to undertake a genuine pacted constitutional transition. The nature and degree of international intervention has varied greatly from one country to another. East Timor stands at one end of the spectrum as constitution-making began in the context of an U.N. based administration which took a hands on role, imposing a legal framework for the crafting of a new constitution (*Id.*:432). On the other hand, Sudan stands close to the opposite end of the spectrum as the international intervention was mainly confined to achieving peace among the two sides in a long and bitterly fought civil war, largely leaving the constituent power in Sudanese hands (*Id.*:448–449).

International intervention in constitution-making has been brought to bear in many different situations, and its role has varied significantly from one setting to the next. Nevertheless, in terms of an emerging model of constitution-making, three principal factors stand out. First, no genuine constitution-making process could have occurred absent the international intervention. Second, the international intervention leads to incorporation of certain external constitutional norms and standards – be they those adopted in other nation-states, transnational or international ones – into the actual constitution to which it eventually leads. And, third, substantial decision making power over the substantive particulars of the constitution-in-the-making must be left in the hands of relevant political actors within the nation-state affected (*Id.*:430).

Viewed in terms of constitutional identity, these three factors add up to a requirement that the input introduced through international intervention not be regarded as biased or as serving the selfish interests of the intervening countries or organizations; to the acceptance of the legitimacy of incorporating external constitutional norms and standards into one's country's new constitution; and to the need that local actors be in a position to internalize the process coming from abroad and to incorporate substantive norms compatible with plausible legitimate articulations of their country's national and constitutional identity.

With this in mind, reference to certain particular cases can illustrate the scope and versatility of the internationally grounded model.

The negative 1983 U.N. intervention in South Africa played a limited but important role. It constituted an important symbolic part of concerted foreign pressure on the apartheid regime which would eventually lead to the pacted transition that took place a decade later. In East Timor, the U.N. played a major role in the transition from Indonesian occupation to independence, and to prevent certain local political forces from dominating, or stifling the constitution-making process. (*Id.*:431–432). In Sudan, the international intervention was focused primarily on brokering peace between the central government and various rebel groups that had engaged in civil war for two decades. In the course of these peace-making endeavors, the international intervenors played an indispensable role in setting up the procedural and substantial framework for the constitutional-making process without which a viable peace could not endure (*Id*:442–445). In this context, the international intervenors made it possible to fashion conditions, which in substance, set the stage for a foreign supervised pacted constitution-making process.

In the case of Irak, the post conflict constitution-making sequence does not fit squarely within the Internationally Grounded Model. Instead, the constitution-making involved in Irak seems to correspond to a hybrid involving the latter and the War-Based Model. Ideally, the international coalition led by the U.S. that took down Saddam Hussein's regime, would have rid Irak of the *ancient régime* and set the stage for a pacted transition to constitutionalism among the various political actors within the newly liberated Iraki polity. If that had been the case, then the international intervenors would have amounted to liberators that set the stage for pacted constitutionalism, thus falling squarely within the internationally grounded model. What actually happened, instead, is that Irak's constitution-making project began under an American led foreign occupation, and continued after the country officially regained sovereignty in 2005 (*Id*.:435). Irak's post-conflict constitution-making journey was certainly complex and convoluted, but what stands out for present purposes is the extensive meddling by, and lack of neutrality of, (*vis á vis* the various political factions in Irak) of the foreign intervenors, and particularly the U.S. For example, the Americans involved managed to have the constitution-makers include a U.S. styled bill of rights (*Id*.:436). Even after sovereignty was transferred to the Iraqis in 2005, American officials used their leverage to accelerate a final draft of the constitution for U.S. domestic political reasons. As a consequence of this, U.S. pressure resulted in the exclusion of the Sunni community to facilitate prompt agreement among the remaining Iraqi negotiators (*Id*.:439–440).

Whether Irak will succeed in implanting a suitable and legitimate post-conflict constitution is still an open question. What seems obvious from the sketch provided above is that thus far constitution-making in that country cannot count as an example of the internationally grounded model. At this writing, the Iraqi experience may best be captured as a failed example of the War-Based Model. The war against Saddam Hussein was indeed won, and the foreign victors were in a position to help mold the country's constitutional future. They have not, however, overcome thus far the split among the country's three principal political communities, and therefore, it does not seem that the process is destined to lead to a success akin to that achieved by Germany or Japan after World War Two.

6.7 Constitutional Amendment, Revision and Reform

In the last analysis, the exploration of the various constitutional models and constitution-making models discussed above reveals several ways in which constitutional identity can be launched and shaped in relation to, and against, pre-constitutional and extra-constitutional identities. As emphasized throughout, constitutional identities are dynamic and they are bound to evolve after they are initially formed. Constitutions can be amended, revised or reformed. Formally, 'amendments' involve correction or improvements, whereas 'revisions' require some taking apart in order to reconstitute (Murphy 1995:177). 'Reform,' moreover, calls for even greater change, so long as it falls short of revolution.

Whereas the above concepts provide useful points of reference in connection with constitutional change and building or altering constitutional identity, it seems in the end best to rely on substantive rather formal criteria. As we have seen, Hungary substantively made an entirely new constitution through exclusive formal reliance on the amendment process. In contrast, France made around fifteen constitutions, but elements of continuity and congruence among these fairly raise the question of whether some of the new constitutions were essentially vehicles of revision or of reform. Conversely, the U.S. has only amended – and rarely at that – its 1787 Constitution, but, as we have seen, the Civil War Amendments can certainly be regarded as having triggered a constitutional revolution (Richards 1994).

In the last analysis, all construction and development of constitutional identity depends on unique contextual and relational factors. Nevertheless, the various constitutional models and constitution-making models discussed above, which may correlate in diverse ways that seem by no means fixed, make it possible to discern certain patterns and points of congruence. These in turn, circumscribe the necessary dialectic of negation and reincorporation that leads to the emergence of a viable constitutional identity within a constitutionally ordered polity.

CHAPTER 7

The Constitutional Subject and Clashing Visions of Citizenship: Can We Be Beyond What We are Not?

The citizen is the core unit of the constitutional order and of constitutional identity. Both the imagined community that defines the nation and the one that projects an identity on the constitutional order are anchored in the citizen. The citizen is the constituent unit of the constitutional subject in all its multiple identities, chief among them, the *who* that makes the constitution, the *for whom* it is made, and the *to whom* it is addressed. The citizen is at the heart of modern constitutionalism and is the principal actor in its birth, deployment and continuing life. Most dramatically the French Revolution transformed the king's subjects into citizens and equated, in theory if not in fact, being human to being a citizen as attested by the 1789 Declaration of the Rights of Man and the Citizen. Similarly, though less explicitly because of the profound incompatibility between the spirit of the Enlightenment and slavery, the 'We the People' that gave itself the American Constitution in 1787 was made up of 'We the Citizens'.[1]

Besides embodying the constitutional subject in its manifold dimensions, the citizen encapsulates the constitutional identity of his or her polity. Moreover, through his or her defining characteristics, the citizen projects in microcosmic perspective the core elements of the constitutional model prevalent in the polity to which he or she belongs. Thus, citizenship based on *jus sanguinis* enshrined in the German constitutional tradition, which makes citizenship dependent on ancestry, meshes perfectly with the ethno-centric German constitutional model. In contrast, citizenship based on *jus soli*, deeply engrained in the French constitutional tradition, which makes citizenship dependent on place of birth within the confines of the polity, seems in full harmony with the French democentric constitutional model.

The microcosmic standpoint of the citizen affords a privileged vantage point to gauge the nature, scope and potential of the constitutional subject and of constitutional ordering in a rapidly evolving world. This is because citizenship is defined by full active membership in the relevant political community, and in a constitutional democracy, citizenship is both constitutionally delimited and the principal locus of mediation between the constitution's core structure and constitutional identity. Indeed, the constitution decrees who is or can become a citizen and specifies the rights and duties that will circumscribe the citizen's full participation in the political community encompassed within the relevant constitutional polity. Furthermore, the citizen is empowered and constrained by the norms imposed by the constitution. These norms, however, cannot acquire sufficient concrete expression to provide the citizen with sufficient guidance absent linkage to an appropriate, commonly shared, conception of constitutional identity.

The citizen, individually and collectively, is *the* constitutional subject or, more precisely, the focal point through which the constitutional subject in its multiple dimensions[2] must be imagined and constructed. Modern Enlightenment-based citizenship, moreover, is a blend of the universal and the particular – a dynamic blend that remains in tension in function of the ongoing dialectical confrontation between the universal and the particular. Thus, for example, consistent with the French constitutional model's universal conception of the democratic polity encapsuled for practical purposes within the territorial limits of the French state,[3] French citizenship, as envisaged during the Revolution and as enshrined in the 1789 Declaration, is universal in concept, but for practical purposes limited to a particular territory, that of the French nation-state, and a particular common language, French. Indeed, without a common language and a limited contiguous territory, it would have been difficult, if not impossible, for the French citizenry to carve out a common political destiny.

More generally, *who* and *what* is deemed encompassed in the dynamic between universal and the specific forms or limits of the particular seem bound to change in time and depending on circumstances. Thus, the technological limitations that made it inconceivable to build a working polity beyond the bounds of the nation-state in the late eighteenth century no longer seem an insurmountable impediment over two hundred years later. Furthermore, many other aspects of the dynamic between the universal and the particular in relation to citizenship have greatly evolved over the years. Although conceived in the abstract as extending to all human beings, citizenship was once limited to propertied males. Citizenship has also at times been made to coincide with nationality, but today, in many instances, common bonds of citizenship have woven together multinational, multi-ethnic and multicultural polities (Kymlicka 1995). Although originally modern citizenship was tied to the nation-state, today transnational citizenship has become a working reality within the EU.[4] And, concurrent with the recent waves of migration on a global scale, the functional attributes of citizenship have become increasingly decoupled from its identitarian attributes (Fleming 1997).

As we shall discuss below, the dialectic between the universal and the particular plays out through all these shifts and many others in the configuration and understanding of citizenship. Retracing these shifts not only affords another valuable microcosmic perspective on constitutional identity, but also opens up the horizons of the currently farthest conceivable expansion of citizenship, constitutional identity and workable constitutional ordering. In order to obtain a better grasp of the most salient features of the dynamic that has transformed citizenship over the past two centuries, the remainder of this Chapter will proceed as follows. Section One provides a brief account of the theoretical foundations of modern citizenship and of its anchor within the nation-state. Section Two focuses on the extension of citizenship in terms of its functional dimension. Section Three examines the identitarian dimension of citizenship in relation to the evolution from the mono-ethnic polity to the multi-ethnic one. Section Four zeroes in on the decoupling of the functional and identitarian attributes of citizenship in the context of vast migrations due to contemporary social and economic circumstances. Finally, Section Five explores the potential of transnational citizenship and its capacity for recasting the interplay between its functional and its identitarian attributes, and between the universal, the particular and the singular.

7.1 The Theoretical Foundations of Modern Citizenship: Universal Equality within a Particular Nation

Modern citizenship is equal citizenship (Pierson 1996:144) and premised on the universal axiom that all human beings are inherently equal.[5] In contrast, premodern citizenship, be it Greek, Roman or Renaissance, was in no sense equal (Riesenberg 1992). On the other hand, modern citizenship emerged as inextricably linked to the nation-state in the course of the French Revolution (Brubaker 1992:35). This is again contrary to premodern citizenship which lacked any connection to the nation-state. Thus,

214 • The Identity of the Constitutional Subject

for example, in the Roman context the very concept of citizenship loomed as inherently antagonistic to that of the nation (Habermas 1992:20–21).

Equal citizenship within the confines of the nation-state rests on a stark contradiction between universal equality that in principle extends to humanity as a whole and the nation as a particular imagined community to the exclusion of all other nations. A loyal citizen is one who accords undivided allegiance to her nation, an attitude and obligation that was institutionally reinforced until more recent times, by the near universal prevalence of the prohibition against dual nationality. Consistent with this, the modern citizen's identity is constructed on the basis of a combination of two elements that remain in tension with one another: an abstract identification with the universal prescriptions and projected images of an equal citizenship encapsulated in a bundle of civil and political rights fit to extend to humanity as a whole; and a concrete identification that amounts to a full and whole-hearted adhesion to the collectively projected image that endows the nation with its own particular national identity.

Since national identity is a collective construct on behalf of the nation as a whole, the citizen in his individuality assumes an identity that cannot be completely fused into that of his nation. This is well illustrated by the dilemma posed by the foreigner who resides among citizens within the latter's nation state. As an individual and a productive member of society, the foreigner ought to enjoy the same civil and political rights as does the citizen. As one who does not belong to the citizens' nation, however, the foreigner does not partake in the common collective identity and thus lacks sufficient attributes of allegiance to be granted full membership in the relevant political community. Thus, when considered exclusively from the citizen's individual abstract image based on the universal equality of all humans and on the bundle of rights associated with it, the exclusion of the foreigner looms as unwarranted. At the same time, from the standpoint of the concrete particular self-image of the nation, the exclusion of the foreigner seems amply justified. Consistent with this, the more one seeks to instantiate the abstract ideals of citizenship the more one embarks on a collision course with the inevitably exclusionary features inherent in particular expressions of national identity.

To better grasp the dynamic between modern citizenship's universal pole tied to equality and its particular one anchored in nationalism, it is useful to consider briefly modern citizenship's historical and theoretical foundations. Indeed, although the ideal of equal citizenship may appear at times as a purely disembodied abstraction, it has concrete historical roots in the repudiation of feudalism. Moreover, from a theoretical standpoint, the contradictions of modern citizenship imprisoned in the nation-state can be profitably traced back to its derivation from social contract theory.

7.1.1 Historical Nexus Between Equal Citizenship and the Nation-State

The advent of equal citizenship at the time of the French Revolution must be set against the hierarchal stratification of the feudal era and the emergence of the nation-state in the age of absolute monarchy. In the status-driven order mapped out by feudalism, where hierarchal relationships of personal fealty and attachment to the land predominated, citizenship was both exceptional and local inasmuch it was confined to a fraction of the population of certain cities (Garcia 1996:7). On the other hand, as feudalism gave way to the rise of the modern state under the aegis of the absolute monarch, the intricate strata of the feudal order began to dissolve, giving way to implantation of the direct and unmediated authority of the monarch over all those within his realm. Accordingly, former citizens together with all others who owed allegiance to the monarch were treated as mere subjects (Riesenburg 1992:187, 203–05). Furthermore, the unified realm under the consolidated powers of its monarch produced a new identity which would be transformed with the advent of the Revolution into that of the modern nation as the indispensable substratum of the democratic state (Habermas 1992:19ff).

In light of these historical antecedents, equal citizenship promotes above all two different kinds of equality: equality as opposed to feudal status based on an established hierarchy; and equality in terms of the citizen's right to self government, as opposed to the subjects duty to submit to the will of the monarch. These two kinds of equality combine to constitute the minimum standard required by the concept of equal citizenship. Consequently, restricting citizenship to those who own property or even to men (provided differences among the sexes are rationalized along different lines from those of feudal hierarchy or the subordination of subjects to their monarch) is arguably not completely inconsistent with upholding equal citizenship. Be that as it may, projection of the two kinds of equality mentioned above beyond their immediate historical moorings engenders a logic whereby all hierarchy ought to be leveled in order to make room for an entitlement to equal citizenship based on personhood, and for the grant to all persons with the requisite faculties of a right to self-government through equal participation in the political process.

Whereas the link between equal citizenship, personhood and self-determination is logical, that between equal citizenship and the nation-state looms as inherently contingent. Indeed, equal citizenship implies the ascribing of a certain bundle of rights and duties to the citizen, but does not predetermine the institutional setting in which such rights and duties might be best deployed.[6] From a strictly logical standpoint, equal citizenship seems *prima facie* equally compatible with the city-state, or several plausible transnational, regional or global forms of political organization.

Historically, however, equal citizenship has been typically linked over the past two centuries to the nation-state (Pierson 1996:228). This is because the nation-state has proven the optimal locus of social, political and economic organization in the time span between the French Revolution and (at least) the end of World War Two (Habermas 1992:20–21). More particularly, the modern state has proven uniquely suited through its organizational apparatus to coordinate and promote social, political and economic objectives while the nation has supplied the necessary glue to provide a common identity to, and to secure an appropriate level of solidarity and mutual concern among, its various members. Hence, whereas the state and nation remain conceptually distinct, historical developments in the aftermath of the Revolution have made them complementary. Finally, whereas state backing or intervention is primarily responsible for transforming citizenship into equal citizenship – through enforcement of a system of rights and provision of essential welfare benefits – the nation endows citizenship with a concrete identity through concentrated emphasis on the differences – be they ethnic, cultural, historical or linguistic – between nationals and non-nationals.

A closer look at the nexus between modern citizenship, as it originally emerged, and the nation-state reveals that the characteristics of such citizenship tend to vary in significant respects, depending on the historical differences concerning the formation of individual nation-states. For example, in France the state predated the nation (Preuss 1994:150–151) whereas in Germany the nation preceded the establishment of the state (*Id.*). More generally, based on the relevant historical differences, one can construct three different models of the nation-state, each of which corresponding to a constitutional model explored in Chapter 5 and yielding in turn a somewhat different conception of citizenship. These models as the constitutional models to which they correspond can be referred to for the sake of convenience as the 'German Model', the 'French Model' and the 'American Model'.

As will be recalled, the German Model is characterized above all by the predominance of *ethnos* over *demos*, by the existence of a prepolitical nation bound together by a common ethnicity, culture and language (Preuss 1994). Accordingly, in the German Model, the nation is more fundamental and more deeply rooted than the state. Consistent with this, moreover, within the German Model, citizenship is, as already mentioned, determined on the basis of *jus sanguinis*.

In the French Model, on the other hand, *demos* predominates over *ethnos* as the nation supposedly emerges in the very process of democratization launched by the modern state upon its emergence from the ashes of the monarchy (Preuss 1994:151–152). Unlike in the German Model, in the French Model the nation is political rather than prepolitical and it is primarily formed to give embodiment to the democratic spirit. Thus, the French nation is united by a common language, but that language was only spread to all the population in the aftermath of the Revolution in order to generate 'a common sphere of public debate and reasoning' for the newly enfranchised citizenship (*Id*.:152).

On the surface the American Model which relies exclusively on *jus soli*, looks very much like its French counterpart. In both cases, *demos* has priority over *ethnos*, and citizenship emerges in the aftermath of a revolution. However, whereas the French state predated the Revolution (though it was transformed as a consequence of it), the American state only emerged after victory in the War of Independence freed the former colonies from British rule. Both the American state and nation were born at once, and both trace their immediate origins to the American Constitution. Accordingly, in the American Model, the constitution both precedes and frames the state, the nation and citizenship.

At first glance, it would seem that the German Model would be least susceptible to yield post-national citizenship, and that the American, because of being more universal and less steeped in preexisting institutions, would be best suited for purposes of expanding equal citizenship beyond the confines of the nation-state. Before assessing whether further analysis confirms this, however, it is first necessary to examine the theoretical foundations of modern citizenship.

7.1.2 Social Contract Theory and Modern Equal Citizenship

The theoretical roots of modern equal citizenship are found primarily in seventeenth- and eighteenth-century social contract theory, and most particularly in the respective political philosophies of Locke and Rousseau. Underlying such social contract theory is a conception of a prepolitical state of nature populated by individuals who are inherently free and equal (Rosenfeld:1985). The state of nature is very unstable, however, since, by virtue of their very equality, individuals are easily prone to violence. To overcome the dangers of the state of nature, individuals are supposed to agree upon a mutual contract designed to establish a political order capable of securing individual liberty and equality. More precisely, as already noted, the transition from the state of nature to organized society requires either two contracts or one contract dealing with two separate subject-matters. The first of these contracts is between all the individuals in the state of nature and is called the 'contract of association' (Gough 1957:2); the second concerns governance of the political order created by the contract of association and is referred to as the 'contract of government' (*Id.*:3).

The nature and scope of the state in the context of social contract theory depends on the particular conception that one has of the contract of government. Accordingly, as we shall see, Locke and Rousseau embrace different such conceptions, which leads them to articulate different conceptions of equal citizenship.[7] But before pursuing these differences any further, it is necessary to focus briefly on the contract of association.

Although the social contract is to be understood metaphorically rather than literally, it is still important that the metaphor in question have some plausibility, even if only at a very high level of abstraction, for the theory to be useful. In the times of Hobbes, Locke and Rousseau, it was inconceivable that individuals – even when imagined in the state of nature – could communicate on a worldwide basis so as to establish a global contract of association. Instead, an assumption concerning a certain degree of geographic proximity, if not concerning a common language spoken by all would-be contractors, had to be built into the relevant metaphorical picture. A reading of Hobbes, Locke and Rousseau's accounts of passage from the state of nature to a politically ordered society reveals that they, by and large, envisioned individuals within the state of nature as functioning within a space that was, in any event, no larger than that of seventeenth-century kingdoms.[8] Accordingly, though not always explicitly spelled out, Hobbes, Locke and Rousseau's contract of association is the product of a set of individuals who share a contiguous space, and the combination of the contract of association with that of government leads to the establishment of a political order enshrined within the bounds of the nation-state. It follows from this that equal citizenship as derived from eighteenth-century social contract theory must be necessarily linked to the nation-state. Furthermore, this raises as a corollary the question of whether contemporary social contract theory, which may plausibly be grounded on an assumption of the possibility of communication on a global scale, may justify transnational or even universal equal citizenship. Ultimately, the answer turns on whether a plausible contract of association depends on the possibility of communication alone, or whether it also depends on reference to a commonly shared culture or history. Before pursuing this inquiry any further, however, it is necessary to focus on the contrast between the conceptions of the contract of government respectively put forth by Locke and Rousseau and on the models of citizenship which they each promote.

The liberal theory of government and citizenship drawn from Locke contrasts with its republican counterpart originating in Rousseau. According to Locke, social contractors who have joined together so as better to secure their inherent natural rights agree to establish only a limited government (Locke 1690:para. 131). Within this scheme, moreover, the relationship between the contracting citizens and their rulers is in the nature of a trusteeship in which the powers of the rulers are narrowly circumscribed and to be used only for the benefit of the citizens (Rosenfeld 1985:866–867). Hence in the Lockean liberal vision, the citizens retain all rights and impose all the duties on government (Gough 1957:143). This makes for an individualistic and instrumental conception of citizenship, in which citizens are connected to one another through a legal order while remaining external to the state. In the liberal tradition, therefore, the citizen is virtually identical to the private person who seeks to interact with the state for the sole purpose of advancing his or her prepolitical interests (Habermas 1992:25–26).

The republican conception of government and citizenship, on the other hand, establishes a much closer relationship between citizen and state and portrays them as being bound by organic rather than instrumental links. In Rousseau's version of the social contract, the contract of government is subsumed within the contract of association through the ascribing of a dual role to each individual contractor. Thus, for Rousseau, the social contract is between each individual as an individual and society as a whole (of which each individual is a part), with each individual acting as a member of the governed body towards the sovereign as well as a member of the sovereign towards other individuals (Rousseau 1762:II, 2–18). Moreover, within this conception there is an inner split between the privately oriented *bourgeois* and the publicly oriented *citoyen* (*Id.*:II, 1).

To resolve the conflicts within the individual caused by tensions created by his dual role as *bourgeois* and *citoyen*, Rousseau resorts to the general will, which has been described as 'a highly voluntarist formulation of the traditional conception of the common good or the common interest' (Masters 1968:323), and which represents the will by which the people as sovereign must govern and to which each individual as a member of the governed, must yield without reservation.

In contrast to the liberal conception, the republican conception of citizenship emanating from Rousseau is collectivist rather than individualistic, and emphasizes civic duties rather than focusing primarily on rights.

Moreover, whereas the liberal citizen has an instrumental relationship with the state from which she seeks guarantees of negative freedom, the Rousseauian citizen seeks identity and positive freedom through the state. Finally, the liberal citizen pursues fulfillment as a private person with individual interests while the republican citizen's highest aspiration is self-government to advance the collective project for which she is responsible with all other fellow-citizens.

Liberal citizenship is conceivable in the context of a collection of diverse individuals with a broad array of different interests, provided only that they coexist within a territory that is sufficiently contiguous to allow for effective state government. Republican citizenship, on the other hand, requires a much more cohesive collectivity with broadly shared cultural and ethical values. Indeed, although Rousseau's general will is supposed to be highly rational, 'the agreement of all interests' by means of 'opposition to that of each' person (Rousseau 1762:II, 3 n.7) which it prescribes would be hard to imagine unless a common core of values and objectives were already in place.

Based on the preceding brief account of the historical origins and theoretical underpinnings of modern citizenship, one can draw certain salient insights regarding the dynamic that binds universal equality to a particular nationality. First, from a historical standpoint, equal citizenship is set *against* feudal hierarchy when projected into the past, and open to inclusion of all humans on earth when projected into the farthest conceivable future. Furthermore, in its eighteenth century original setting equal citizenship was, of necessity, tied to the nation-state, as a polity made up of politically engaged citizens was inconceivable beyond the contiguous confines of the nation-state. Equal citizenship may have been organically linked to a prepolitical nation awaiting a state as in the German Model; or more contingently associated with an existing nation-state as in the French Model; or even bundled together with an about to emerge nation-state through a constitution as in the American Model.

Second, from the standpoint of social contract theory, the contract of association could conceivably be among all human beings, but the contract of government only seems plausible within the confines of the nation-state. Moreover, the liberal Lockean conception of the social contract stands in sharp contrast to its republican counterpart as elaborated by Rousseau. The latter requires a sufficient degree of communal cohesion to render political self-government meaningful. Indeed, without some commonly shared convictions regarding the public good, it would be impossible to carve out any cogent general will. On the other hand, consistent with the liberal Lockean conception, there seems to be no need for a common identity beyond that conferred by mere spatial contiguity. In theory, even if this be thoroughly implausible in fact, anyone, every individual no matter what his or her individual interests, may become associated with a number of similarly situated individuals within the kind of contiguously configured space that may sustain a working nation-state. In short, in the republican vision, there must be a common political project that depends on some shared sense of collective identity; in the liberal vision, the institutions needed for peaceful association are common, but identities are ultimately individual, tied to self-interest and apolitical. Thus, in the republican vision, the citizen is defined by, and partakes in further elaborating, a common identity whereas in the liberal vision the citizen is but a means to the private person's unimpeded pursuit of self-interest.

7.2 The Functional Dimension of Citizenship

Modern citizenship entails certain rights, including fundamental human rights, as well as certain duties, such as fulfilling military or civilian service requirements. The precise rights and duties involved may vary from one setting to the next and from one period to another, but they are meant to extend to each and every citizen within the relevant polity. Whether considered from a liberal or a republican standpoint, equal citizenship shares a common functional purpose: to allow each citizen to pursue a path to self-realization and to partake in collective self-government with fellow citizens. From a liberal-libertarian standpoint, every individual is conceived as essentially capable of being self-sufficient, placing the emphasis on civil liberties and formal equality (Nozick 1974). From a liberal egalitarian standpoint, on the other hand, it is important to supplement formal equality rights with social welfare rights to guarantee to each citizen a certain minimum of material well being (Rawls 1971). Furthermore, in contrast to liberals, republicans place a greater emphasis on the duty actively to engage in collective self-government, thus enhancing the importance of the citizen's duties as against that of the citizen's rights.

According to Marshall's influential theory, equal citizenship has changed in the course of the last three centuries, becoming ever more inclusive of the various social classes within society. Thus, civil rights were instituted in the eighteenth century; political rights of participation in the nineteenth; and social rights, which may be defined as welfare rights, in the twentieth (Marshall 1987:242). Consistent with this evolution, equal citizenship established in principle in the eighteenth century can be seen as having evolved two centuries later into effective equal citizenship meant to be available to all within the polity. From a functional standpoint, therefore, effective equal citizenship looms as universal in nature and scope as it prescribes the same autonomy, dignity and (minimum) welfare for every individual settled within the same polity. Moreover, from this functional standpoint, equal citizenship is as abstract as it is universal in as much as it allows in principle for any individual whatever his or her particular origins to be or become a citizen of any democratic polity regardless of its history or geography.

From the perspective of the functional dimension of contemporary citizenship, it might seem that globalization should ease the way from nation-state based to global citizenship. On the surface, the worldwide expansion of capital combined with vast movements of labor, liberalism's affinity for universalism, and the spread of social welfare rights ought to pave the way for citizenship based on personhood eventually to replace citizenship based on national origin (Soysal 1994). Upon closer examination, however, even if the identitarian dimension of nation-state citizenship were deemed likely to disappear with globalization, the advent of global citizenship would have to overcome a number of daunting obstacles. For one thing, dependence on social welfare tends to transform citizens into passive 'clients' of the state (Habermas 1996b:776). Furthermore, the evolution towards global capitalism seems inevitably linked with a series of ups and downs. For example, the periodic resurgence of large scale unemployment has both thwarted the full expansion of social rights and fuelled xenophobic attitudes against immigrants and guest workers.

As liberal citizenship which has been historically linked to capitalism (Beiner 1995:1) lived through the evolution from eighteenth century *laissez faire* capitalist to its twentieth century welfare-based counterpart with its massive redistributivist bureaucracy, it increasingly overemphasized rights over duties. This disproportionate focus on rights combined with the passive clientism fostered by the welfare state noted above clearly poses a threat to the functioning of modern citizenship. And this threat exists over and above any other one based on identitarian factors.

Similarly, although the xenophobia associated with the combination of labor migration and periods of vast pockets of unemployment in an economy is typically expressed in identitarian terms, it does also have independent functional roots (*Id.*:3). Indeed, equal citizenship based on a combination of economic opportunity and satisfaction of basic welfare needs is bound to become functionally disrupted when either or both of its mainstays are under serious threat. From a purely functional perspective, therefore, vast migration into the territory of a working democratic polity may well severely strain the material conditions necessary to sustain equal citizenship.

The increasingly passive citizenship associated with the welfare state is certainly at odds with the republican ideal, but does not seem to be similarly antagonistic to the liberal ideal. So long as constitutionalism and the protection of fundamental rights are vigorously upheld, one can imagine an adequate setting for equal liberal citizenship. Government and its administrative bureaucracy would guarantee the rights and welfare needed for the citizen to be in a good position to pursue self-interest while remaining sufficiently accountable through periodic elections. Citizens might basically remain disinterested in the day to day running of their government, but would retain the power to replace it when sufficiently dissatisfied with its functioning.

Upon further consideration, it becomes plain that even within the ambit of liberalism, pursuit of self-interest cannot proceed wholly removed from identitarian issues and concerns. How interests are shaped and which interests are cast as worthy of an individual's special attention seem inevitably culturally conditioned. Thus, religion or other world views, custom, tradition and historically rooted practices and beliefs are bound to play an important role in delimiting the goods and interests that capture the attention of the citizenry within a given polity. Consistent with this, moreover, the functional dimension of citizenship and its universal frame of reference cannot be ultimately separated from citizenship's identitarian underpinning. In the end, the functional dimension of citizenship emerges as one if its two principal poles, and it appears bound to stand in constant dynamic tension against citizenship's identitarian pole, to which I will now briefly turn.

7.3 The Identitarian Dimension of Citizenship and the Evolution from the Mono-Ethnic to the Multi-Ethnic Polity

In the most general terms, the identitarian dimension of modern citizenship is framed, as already suggested, by the interplay between national and constitutional identity. In the political arena, it is the imagined community that endows the nation with its distinct identity, which delimits the common space for self-government and the constitutional contours of the status of citizen which sets the parameters for self-realization and collective self-government within the polity. Viewed more closely, however, the identitarian dimension of citizenship is the product of an ongoing dynamic process that involves negation, reprocessing and reincorporation of constitutional and extra-constitutional materials. Consistent with the preceding analysis of constitutional identity in its many different facets, the identitarian dimension of citizenship must successfully weave together relations of identity with relations that properly account for differences.

The baseline for modern universal equal citizenship is the abstract identity of all individuals within the polity. In other words, *in theory* all persons within the polity are identically situated when it comes to enjoying the benefits and assuming the burdens of citizenship. Historically, however, equal citizenship was denied to certain classes of persons within the polity such as women or non-propertied men. Given the baseline resting on abstract identity, the only way to avoid patent contradiction was to tie inequality to difference. Thus, for example, because of their social role as wives and mothers which largely confined them to the family home, women could be depicted as too removed from the public place to be in a position to act as responsible, active citizens in pursuit of the polity's common good.[9] Accordingly, liberal ideals were coupled with illiberal practices and the struggle for equal citizenship was confronted with a choice between stressing identity beyond difference and pursuing a conception of equality that properly accounts for difference. Returning to the example of women, under the first of these alternatives, in spite of their different social roles, women could be portrayed as identical to men from the standpoint of citizenship as being as caring and as capable as men, in spite of their different social roles, when it comes to the determination and pursuit of the polity's common good. Under the second of these alternatives, on the other hand, equal citizenship between men and women would require taking key differences among the sexes into proper account. Thus, if equal citizenship requires affording every adult full control over his or her own body, then arguably equal citizenship for women would require granting them a constitutional right to have an abortion. Indeed, without that right, women would have less control over their own body than men.[10]

Whether one considers that the historical march of liberalism should concentrate on uprooting the illiberal practices that stand in the way of full realization of the liberal ideal or that liberalism itself is ultimately incompatible with meaningful equal citizenship, it becomes imperative to conceive of equal citizenship as having to incorporate relationships based on difference alongside those based on identity. For some, it is a matter of transcending inequalities based on difference – e.g., treat women, gays, and all others who have been relegated to second class citizenship the same as the men who enjoy first class citizenship rights; for others, to overcome liberalism itself, and, in particular, its conception of citizenship based on the social contract (Pateman 1988).

The pursuit of equal citizenship through gradual and systematic eradication of illiberal prejudices and practices poses little conceptual difficulty. Seeking equal citizenship through increased differentiation, in contrast, does pose serious challenges to the liberal conception of universal equal citizenship. This is because it requires weaving together two seemingly incompatible objectives: universal equal citizenship and differentiated (yet equal) citizenship. Moreover, two distinct types of differentiation come into play: 'lifestyle' based differentiation, such as that advocated by feminist and gay rights proponents; and group-based differentiation in the context of multi-ethnic, multicultural or multi-national polities (Kymlicka 1995: 18–19). To assess how each of these affects the dynamic between universalism and particularism in the context of citizenship, I shall first briefly focus on the feminist case for differentiated citizenship, and then concentrate on the salient issues relating to the claim for differentiated citizenship for national minorities.

7.3.1 The Feminist Case for Differentiated Citizenship

In broadest outline, as indicated above, there are two principal cases for granting and achieving full equality of citizenship for women. The first is based on identity, and fits comfortably within the liberal conception of equal citizenship. Starting from the fact that in many polities women do not enjoy the full equal citizenship rights effectively accorded to men; and, based on the liberal principle that women are entitled to the same rights as those granted to men; it follows for proponents of this case that all barriers to full equal citizenship for women ought to be removed. A similar case can be made, moreover, for all others, be they gay, members of ethnic or religious minorities, etc., who have not yet been granted full equal citizenship. In short, this first case is concentrated on leveling differences in treatment that stand in the way of full, equal citizenship based on the essential bond of identity that unites all the members of the polity.

The second case, in sharp contrast, springs from a rejection of the adequacy of the liberal ideal, and, as noted, from a repudiation of the social contract as the basis of justification for universal equal citizenship. Consistent with Carol Pateman's thesis, for all its apparent neutrality at the highest levels of abstraction, the social contract is sexist, a vehicle for a fraternal bonding against the father that leaves out women (Pateman 1988). The point is not that women were not included in practice, but subject to inclusion in principle at some later time; it is that contract as a mode of association coupled with the process of abstraction necessary to render the social contract theoretically palatable perforce exclude women as potential equal contractors. In other words, because women have needs, attitudes, approaches and objectives that differ from those of men, they could only fit in the role of social contractors if they imagined themselves as men. According to some feminists, 'universal' values and norms are deeply anchored in masculine attitudes and experiences (Young 1995:266). If men's ethics are oriented to rights, equality and justice whereas women profess an 'ethics of care', stressing concern, attachment, interdependence and self-sacrifice (Gilligan 1982:12, 73–74, 164), then it becomes plain why social contract based universal equal citizenship would suppress the feminine, even if it were to fully encompass all women. Furthermore, the changes called for by difference feminists are not only confined to the realm of social citizenship – e.g., instituting a right to maternity leave from the workplace. These changes also extend to the political sphere – e.g., requiring boosting women's representation in government through affirmative action policies (Rodriguez and Rubio-Marin 1998).

To adapt citizenship to meet the demands of difference feminism would require a differentiated citizenship that transcends universal abstract equality to account for the principal different needs and interests of men and women. Similar kinds of considerations calling for differentiated citizenship would apply to gays and other categories of citizens who do not yet enjoy full equal citizenship. In all these cases, all the relevant categories of citizens involved belong to the same overall culture. For example, in the United States, proponents of traditional views on the social and political relations among the sexes, difference feminists and proponents of more radical, distinct gay lifestyles all partake in American culture and the American way of life.

Differentiated citizenship within the same overall culture seems workable even if it gives rise to tensions and conflicts among various segments of the citizenry. Thus, for example, Americans are deeply divided over abortion and same sex marriage rights, the former being currently constitutionally protected whereas the latter are not.[11] Nevertheless, if the embrace of differentiated citizenship required that both these rights be constitutionalized, opposition and tension would seem inevitable, but no insurmountable contradiction or significant threat to American politics, national or constitutional identity, or a overall culture would need to ensue. Accordingly, though many might be upset by the changes necessary for purposes of entrenching differentiated citizenship, no serious threat would be posed to the viability or integrity of the affected constitutional order.

The changes required to entrench differentiated citizenship within the ambit of a common overall culture would have to be constitutionalized. Such constitutionalization, moreover, could be achieved either through constitutional amendment or through appropriate adaptation of judicial

interpretation of citizenship rights. In either case, vindication of differentiated citizenship rights to conform to the ethos of difference feminism and
of other similar movements would require provoking changes in both
national and constitutional identity. These changes may be mutually
reinforcing, or they may exacerbate tensions between national and constitutional identity, depending on whether one of these happens to lag far
behind the other. For example, in the United States judges have been far
ahead of democratic majorities and elected officials in constitutionalizing
a right to same sex marriage.[12] In fact, the judicial thrust to modify constitutional identity regarding this important step in the quest for differentiated citizenship has met with such hostility that many court decisions
extending the right to marry to same sex couples have been overturned by
legislatures and by referenda.[13]

   In the last analysis, the recognition and implementation of differentiated
citizenship rights among a relevant population that adheres to the same
overall culture poses no insurmountable theoretical or practical problems.
This is due, in part, because accommodating the multitude of differences
associated with all the claims to differentiated citizenship within the relevant polity need not lead to contradiction or inconsistencies. It is also due,
in part, to the great potential for interplay between national and constitutional identity. And in this latter respect, it is noteworthy that the number
of Americans who oppose same sex marriage has significantly declined in
recent years.[14] As we shall now see, however, no similar potential for eventual harmony looms on the horizon in cases in which the pursuit of
differentiated citizenship occurs in multinational states.

7.3.2 National Minorities and the Problematization of
Differentiated Citizenship

Unlike difference feminists and similarly situated others, national minorities and the national majority within the same polity frequently appear ill
equipped to coexist adequately within a single overall culture. In the traditional nation-state, there is only one nation, a single imagined community
in which all those who split into self and other in other arenas within the
polity can regroup to form part of the same cohesive (overall) national self.
In the multinational, multi-ethnic, multicultural, multi-linguistic, etc.,
state, in contrast, there are rival imagined communities, and belonging to
any of them is likely to preclude belonging to any other within the same
polity. Moreover, in some cases not only is any unified overall common
imagined community out of the question, but realizing the objectives of
one of the multiple national communities would directly interfere with
achieving those of others. For example, if two antagonistic linguistic

groups seek imposition of their own language as the official one through-out their multilingual polity, then a working unity within the multilingual polity at stake would seem altogether impossible.

Besides being imagined communities, nations are, to use Max Weber's expression, 'communities of sentiment' (Weber 1948). As there are cur-rently many more nations than states (Kymlicka and Norman 2000:19), citizenship in multinational states looms as inherently problematic. In a democratic multinational state, the identitarian dimensions of citizenship will in all likelihood largely reflect the self-image of the national majority. In some cases, such as where the national majority's language is the only official one, and those of the various national minorities are entirely relegated to the private sphere, members of national minorities may feel totally excluded from an identitarian standpoint. Accordingly, even if all share the same civil, political, social and economic rights, the national minority members in question may still regard themselves as second-class citizens.

In other cases, the exclusion may not be total, but the identitarian prob-lem remains, even if in a somewhat attenuated form. Thus, for example, in a multinational state divided along religious lines, there may be ample room for coexistence among the majority and minority religions. There may even be extensive religious tolerance enshrined in the constitution and permeating the social and political ethos. Nevertheless, certain indicia of dominance linked to the majority religion may be inevitable, thus caus-ing members of minority religions to be lacking in significant aspects of differentiated citizenship. For instance, if national holidays, the weekly day of rest, prominent public symbols and dominant, officially promoted standards of public and private morality all derive from the majority religion, then the citizen belonging to a minority religion may well feel somewhat alienated from the self-image projected by the polity as the whole. It would not be surprising, therefore, for that citizen to conclude that she does not enjoy the full citizenship that is endowed upon the members of the majority religion.

There is an important further distinction to be drawn between multi-national polities in which all involved national identities are (or can be made) compatible with the essential precepts of constitutionalism and multi-national polities in which some national identities are inherently incompatible with the tenets in question. In the former case, differentiated equal citizenship may be actually within reach through redeployment of appropriate means of constitutional ordering. In the latter case, however, maintaining the integrity of the national identity of certain particular minorities would seem to preclude sufficient adherence to the ethos of constitutionalism. And, as a consequence of this, achieving differentiated equal citizenship for all would seem altogether impossible.

Canada exemplifies the first of these two cases. In Canada, the principal divide is between the English-speaking and the French-speaking communities, and it has pitted Quebec against the other Canadian provinces. The differences between Quebec and the rest of Canada are certainly profound, and secession has been periodically seriously considered.[15] Nevertheless, Quebec is no less devoted to the ideals of modern constitutionalism than is the rest of the country. Accordingly, even if Quebec were granted the most extensive possible self-government powers within the Canadian federation, it would undoubtedly continue its firm adherence to the ethos of constitutionalism.

In the second case, exemplified by the situation confronted by many indigenous communities including certain Native American tribes, on the other hand, the very survival of a minority community's way of life may well hinge on the preservation of certain norms and practices that are irreconcilable with modern constitutionalism. Thus, in *Santa Clara Pueblo v. Martinez*,[16] the patrilineal mores of the Pueblo tribe deprived a woman who had married someone outside the tribe, but not a man who had done so, of custody over her children upon divorce. As the tribe considered its patrilineal practice essential to its self-identity, this resulted in an unresolvable clash within the Pueblo nation between group identity and women's equality. Under such circumstances, full differentiated equal citizenship is simply impossible, unlike in a case such as that of Canada. Either the Pueblo compromise on their identity or women within their community will be deprived of equal citizenship. In contrast, if Quebec were to secede, both the resulting sovereign Quebec and the reconfigured Canadian federation could easily remain within the normative confines of modern constitutionalism (Mancini 2008).

There are different kinds of minorities with varying identitarian claims and different possible ways in which differentiated equal (group-regarding) citizenship may be pursued without ever becoming fully realized. Distinctions have been drawn between national minorities and *sui generis* groups, such as the Roma (gypsies) (Kymlicka and Norman 2000:18–19). National minorities, such as the Scottish or Catalans, and indigenous peoples, such as Native American tribes, seek to fulfill their yearning for differentiated citizenship through the establishment of broad powers of self-government (*Id.*:20). Immigrant minorities, for their part, are likely, at first at least, to aim for non-differentiated equal citizenship within the polity into which they have immigrated. Thus, Turks who immigrated to Germany as 'guest workers' and their descendants, long denied German citizenship, have yearned to obtain the same citizenship rights as those of German nationals (*Id.*:21). From an identitarian standpoint, the realization of German citizenship depended on a loosening of the national identity of both the Germans and the Turkish immigrants. For the Germans, the requisite adjustment was a departure from strict adherence to *jus sanguinis*, which did occur after a very long period of waiting.[17] For the Turkish immigrants, on the other hand, the necessary adjustment was a willingness to assimilate sufficiently into German culture and mores. In both cases, changes would not have been possible without openness to evolving images of national and constitutional identity.

After having acquired the full citizenship rights fashioned on the self-image of their host nation, which will have required a certain degree of assimilation into that nation's national and constitutional culture, an immigrant minority may seek differentiated citizenship on grounds similar to those pressed by national minorities. Thus, after the descendants of Turkish guest workers in Germany have acquired German citizenship, they may seek parity as Muslims with their Christian fellow citizens. These new citizens may ask for state subsidies for their religion on the same basis as those granted to their Christian fellow citizens, and they may request the same degree of official toleration for their religious practices, such as wearing the Islamic veil in public school, as is granted to Christian practices. These claims for recognition of differentiated citizenship, moreover, are not made from the standpoint of a Turkish immigrant minority, but from that of German Muslims. In short, in the course of their journey over a few generations from immigrant guest workers to German citizens seeking full recognition as Muslims, Germany's population of Turkish origin will have evolved from an immigrant minority to a religious one. In the course of this transformation, the relevant identities of both the immigrants and their hosts will have had to be (in part) negated and (in part) recombined and reconstituted on a national as well as a constitutional plane.

Although the respective identities of national majorities need not be or remain diametrically opposed, they seldom, if ever, seem amenable to full harmonization or reconciliation. Because of this, the most that can be hoped for in multi-national states is the achievement of partially, as opposed to fully, differentiated citizenship. Furthermore, certain types of constitutional ordering seem well suited to stir the multi-national polity to optimize its potential for differentiated citizenship. These types of ordering include: federalization; non-territorial autonomy; multi-cultural integration; and secession (*Id.*:12).

Where national minorities are geographically concentrated, identity-based federalism[18] provides an idoneous means of propagating differentiated equal citizenship. Thus, the nationalist aspirations to self-government and self-determination of the likes of Catalonia or Quebec can be extensively accommodated, without being accorded full satisfaction, through federalization – and in particular through asymmetrical federalism which affords greater self-government powers to autonomy seeking federal units than to other federated units within the same federation (*Id.*:29, n. 25). For such differentiated citizenship through identity-based federalism to succeed, moreover, it is necessary to find appropriate articulations of national and constitutional identity that properly mediate between converging self-images of both the national majority and national minorities, at the level of federation, and diverging, yet not functionally incompatible, self-images at the level of the federated units. In other words, Catalans must be able to view themselves as in some sense Spaniards, and Spaniards outside of Catelonia must be able to imagine their country's unity as compatible with significant local autonomy for the Catalans. Spain's 1978 Constitution is, as we have seen in Chapter 4 above, well adapted for this, but it still remains to be seen if Catalan and Spanish national identity can become sufficiently aligned to allow the (asymmetric) federal solution to work adequately.

Where national minorities are not geographically concentrated, differentiated citizenship can be boosted by non-territorial mechanisms of self-government such as the millet system developed in the Ottoman Empire (Kucukcan 2003) and currently in force in certain constitutional democracies such as Israel. The millet system is designed to grant broad autonomy over communal affairs to majority and minority religious communities. Not only matters concerning religious ritual and practice, but also those relating to the personal relations, among members of the religious community, such as marriage and divorce, are left for each religious community to decide for itself. In Israel, for example, the Jewish religious majority as well as the Christian and Muslim minorities each have control over their own communal affairs. This allows for broad-based differentiated citizenship as Jews, Christians and Muslims are equally enabled to partake in a citizenship status molded by the essential precepts of their respective religions.

Empowerment of diverse religious communities through the millet system often clashes, however, with the minimum requirements for equal citizenship imposed by adherence to modern constitutionalism. The millet system may disenfranchise or accord second-class citizenship to, among others, religious dissidents, atheists or agnostics, and to members of different religions who wish to intermarry. One way to mitigate this problem is to allow for alternatives to regulations by religious communities and for opt-out provisions for religious dissidents and non-believers. When the millet system is tempered by overlapping normative ordering issuing from constitutionalism and by opt-out rights, neither abstract universal equal citizenship nor fully differentiated citizenship based on particularization all the way down can rule the day. Therefore, any attempt to manage the tension between the two can aspire at best to tentative and provisional approximation.

Federalization and the pursuit of non-territorial autonomy are centrifugal trajectories in search of greater differentiations.[19] Multicultural integration, in contrast, proceeds in an opposite, centripetal direction. Its challenge is to pursue integration without sacrificing essential multicultural differences. In this bottom up approach, the search must focus on what may be commonly shared by different conceptions of identity and of citizenship and what may be encompassed within an overlapping consensus. What this requires is a commitment to pluralism rather than to mere liberalism or communitarianism (Rosenfeld 1998:199–234). For example, commitment to multicultural integration requires finding the requisite institutional matrix to accommodate as many of the diverse religions within the polity as possible with as many of their particular differences as may be simultaneously countenanced to flourish without toppling rule in conformity with the basic tenets of constitutionalism.

There may be situations where neither top down nor bottom up approaches may loosen the deadlock between two mutually antagonistic national communities imprisoned within the same polity. In at least some such situations, pacted secession may afford the best road to equal differentiated citizenship (Mancini 2008). This may not always be possible or advisable, as the new majority in an entity formed as the result of secession may find itself locked into irresoluble conflict with a new (or remaining) minority within the newly commonly shared polity. Thus, if Quebec were to secede, the indigenous population, which now counts on the Canadian federal government to protect their collective rights, would most likely feel unduly threatened in terms of their collective identity (*Id.*:570). That may, in turn, call for further secession, but at some point the resulting political units would become too small to be viable or the process of secession for purposes of boosting differentiated citizenship could conceivably have to proceed at infinitum.

None of the above described types of constitutional ordering are apt to fully satisfy the aspiration to thoroughly differentiated equal citizenship or to strike an optimal equilibrium between abstract universal indicia of citizenship and their particular differentiated counterparts. What does emerge from the preceding analysis is that the path to reconciliation between abstract equal citizenship and concrete differentiated citizenship is neither linear nor straightforward. That path requires adjustment and mediation, opened to pluralism, reconsideration and reframing of differences and the willingness to acknowledge, confront and attempt to manage conflict and tension without ever being in a position to eradicate them. In short, any worthy image of equal citizenship is a dynamic and constantly evolving one that springs from the simultaneous pull toward the opposite poles of universalization and particularization, identity and difference. Mediating points along the way is the best that can be hoped for, but they never cohere into a fully formed or lasting imagined picture of citizenship that is equally acceptable throughout the confines of the relevant polity.

7.4 Global Migration and the Decoupling of the Functional and the Identitarian Dimensions of Citizenship

In the nation-state the functional and identitarian dimensions of citizenship tend to complement one another. In the multi-national state, as we have seen, the two dimensions pull in somewhat different directions, but can nevertheless remain sufficiently linked. This is because the functional dimension of citizenship can serve as a basis for unification of all citizens and its identitarian dimension as a means to preserve the key differences among the various nations encompassed within the state. This, in turn, shields the polity from falling into a vexing split pitting first class citizens against second class ones. Moreover, preservation of difference in the multi-national polity without regression toward a multi-tiered citizenship that would be incompatible with fundamental equality is undoubtedly greatly dependent on mutual acceptance and mutual adjustment among the numerous national groups within the polity. Finally, such acceptance and adjustment is often much aided by familiarity and by having lived side by side for centuries.[20]

Globalization has led to great increases in migration as people and capital move ever more quickly from country to country and from continent to continent. Immigrants who settle in a new polity and become integrated into its workforce have a strong claim to the substantive benefits of citizenship, even if they are not yet legally citizens and even if they lack many of the identitarian connections shared by those who are. Arguably, these immigrants are the functional equivalent of those who are already citizens, and as such are entitled to the same civil, social and welfare rights. Moreover, on some views, such immigrants should also be entitled to some, if not all, of the political rights of citizens.[21] And, consistent with these observations, the immigrants should share in the functional attributes of citizenship in their country of adoption, even if they enjoy no identitarian bonds with the existing citizenry within that country.

As people of increasingly diverse national origins interact on a global scale, it would seem that functional citizenship would gradually trump differentiated identity-based citizenship. On the surface, the worldwide expansion of capital, vast movements of labor, liberalism's affinity for universalism and the spread of social welfare rights would appear to lead to global citizenship based on personhood and functional equality rather than national origin (Soysal 1994). Paradoxically, however, whereas globalization does accelerate the decoupling of functional and identitarian citizenship, it often leads to a strengthening rather than a weakening of the latter. Although increased exposure to a vast number of national identities ought to foster greater pluralism and broaden the scope of tolerance toward a wide array of different identities, it actually often results in quite the opposite. Indeed, as immigrants from far afield project an identity that is radically different from that of both the majority and the minorities within the host country, the latter may feel seriously threatened and cling more tenaciously to their own identity. In other words, the foreign immigrant with his unfamiliar and more removed culture and habits looms as a far more threatening 'other' than the 'other' who has long sojourned within the polity and with whom the majority culture has become familiar and fairly well adjusted.

This perceived threat is compounded, moreover, when the ebb and flow of global capitalism leads to periodic surges in unemployment which threaten social welfare and which lead to xenophobic attitudes against immigrants. Under such circumstances, the immigrant may well become perceived as much as posing a material threat as an identitarian one to the citizens of the host state. These combined threats have led to a resurgence of nationalism and even to ethnically grounded regionalism. Multi-national states like Yugoslavia and Czechoslovakia have been broken up (Beiner 1995:7), indicating that the ideal of liberal equal citizenship may be as threatened by a return to localism as it is by globalization. Actually, these two threats are not unrelated as evinced by the simultaneous rise of nationalism in Europe and acceleration towards European integration (*Id.*:3). In the words of one observer:

> Nationalism is typically a reaction to feelings of threatened identity, and nothing is more threatening in this respect than global integration. So the two go together, and although they push in opposite directions, *both* undercut the integrity of the state, and the civic relationship it defines (*Id.*, emphasis in original).

In short, globalization not only decouples functional citizenship from its identitarian counterpart but it also sends them in opposite directions. This exacerbates the tensions and conflicts among these two components of citizenship, propelling functional citizenship towards universality in scope while unleashing a trend towards particularizing and hardening national, ethnic, linguistic, cultural and religious identities. Moreover, these two trends can often often be mutually reinforcing. Take, for example, the case of a large wave of Muslim immigrants coming to a Western European, predominantly Christian country at a time of great demand for labor. Whereas such immigration may provoke certain identitarian tensions, so long as the immigrant labor force contributes to boost the economy and to make the polity as a whole better off, functional citizenship may well become increasingly bestowed on the immigrant population. In a period of economic downturn with a significant upsurge in unemployment, however, resentment of Muslims on economic grounds due to the latter's competition for scarce jobs and benefits is likely to be accompanied by sharper tensions over the differences between the country's predominant Christian mores and the immigrants' Muslim ways of life.

The concurrent globalization of the economy, accompanied by a trend towards universalization of functional citizenship, and the fragmentation due to balkanization of national, ethnic and cultural identities poses a serious threat to the continuing viability of the nation-state. Functionally, from an economic standpoint, and even to some extent from a political one, the state is ceding much of its prior control to supra-national agents such as the EU or the WTO. From an identitarian standpoint, on the other hand, the various national, religious, ethnic and cultural groups within the polity become increasingly prone to focusing on their differences at the expense of concentrating on what may serve to unite them. With the resulting threat to citizenship within the confines of the nation-state, there seems to be an urge to explore the potential of supra-national citizenship beyond the bounds of the nation-state.

7.5 Transnational Citizenship and Recasting the Dynamic between Function and Identity

Globalization and the decoupling between functional and identitarian citizenship that it unleashes underscore the inadequacy of the nation-state paradigm for the contemporary polity (Baubock 2007:454). The nation-state may provide an adequate framework for citizenship in cases in which all citizens concerned belong to the same nation. If we add together all national groups, immigrant groups, cultural, religious and linguistic groups that populate the typical present day nation-state, however, it becomes clear that the horizontal space the latter provides for citizenship is seriously lacking in terms of potential for accommodating an adequate measure of differentiation. The most promising avenue toward overcoming this limitation seems to call for complementing horizontal citizenship relationships with vertical ones through the establishment of supra-national citizenship. Supra-national citizenship may be global or regional and it may interact with national and even sub-national citizenship, such as a federated unit, province or canton.

It is easy to see that the combination of horizontal citizenship with many layers of vertical citizenship would make room for greater differentiation, and hence enhance the possibilities for greater satisfaction of identitarian claims. What is not so clear is how the vast number of national identities that coexist within a supra-national polity may be integrated and sufficiently harmonized. Moreover, it is also not obvious how the functional dimension of citizenship would fare in a supra-national setting. Prior to globalization, the nation-state seemed apt to guarantee both democracy and universally conceived but locally adapted and implemented fundamental rights. With globalization, the grip of the nation-state loosens, but can the supra-national polity complement or replace it?

Supra-national citizenship has actually been put into place within the EU pursuant to the 1992 Maastricht Treaty (*Id.*). Thus far, this kind of citizenship has been confined to Europe (*Id.*), though there seems to be no logical reason why it could not become established in other parts of the world. To better assess the potential of supra-national citizenship for reconciling functional and identitarian concerns, I shall first focus on the principal features of EU citizenship; then examine how EU citizenship interfaces with EU member-states' citizenship; and, finally, attempt to determine certain broader implications stemming from the EU example.

7.5.1 The Case of EU Citizenship

All citizens of countries that are member-states of the EU, and only those citizens, are citizens of the EU, thus making EU citizenship contingent on member-state citizenship (Rostek and Davies 2006:6). EU citizenship bestows political rights both at the level of the Union as EU citizens are entitled to vote in elections to the EU Parliament (*Id.*), and at that of member-state as citizens of one member-state who reside in another such state are eligible to vote in the latter's local elections (*Id.*). In addition, EU citizens enjoy freedom of movement throughout the EU and, with a few exceptions, the right to employment in all EU member-states (Baubock 2007:459). As of this writing, EU citizenship does not entail any duties though it is quite possible that it will in the future as a consequence of further expansion of EU competences (Rostek and Davies 2006:7).

To a significant degree, EU citizenship resembles citizenship in federal republics. Thus, in the U.S, every citizen is a citizen both of the federal entity and of the federated entity in which she resides.[22] Unlike in the EU, however, in the U.S federal citizenship is paramount and not dependent on federated state citizenship. Although that represents an important difference, EU citizenship arguably complies with the essential requirements of functional citizenship within a well-working constitutional democracy on the scale of the nation-state.

EU citizenship, however, is much more problematic from an identitarian standpoint. The EU level provides one more arena of differentiation in a federalized scheme that joins together the supra-national, the national and the sub-national. To the extent that it can succeed in federalizing difference, the EU can certainly play a positive identitarian role. Furthermore, the addition of an EU dimension allows for mediation and for defusing tensions that remain difficult to manage within the framework of the nation-state. For example, federalization within Spain may not be sufficient for a lasting mutual accommodation between the Catalans and the Spanish-speaking national majority. The addition of an EU polity and EU citizenship, however, can provide a valuable safety valve. First, matters placed within the competence of the EU provide relief in so far as they obviate or mitigate certain conflicts between Spain and Catalonia. And, second, the Catalan minority can escape in part from unwanted Spanish control by joining together with other sub-national entities in EU fora devoted to regional affairs. The Scots and Catalans could avail themselves of such fora and help fashion EU policy while at the same time opening some space between themselves and the United Kingdom and Spain respectively. Conversely, the availability of working EU fora for interaction among sub-national units may also play an important role from the standpoint of the member-states involved. If Catalonia and Scotland can channel some of their drive towards greater autonomy into EU-sponsored venues for interaction among units, then Spain and the United Kingdom may have less to fear regarding escalating divergences that may raise the specter of secession.

In spite of creating these new avenues for greater differentiation, EU citizenship has been viewed as a serious threat to national citizenship and to the national identities of the EU's member-states (*Id.*). Fear of loss of national identity and of absorption into an EU identity led to Denmark's rejection of the Maastricht Treaty and to a subsequent declaration by the European Council that the grant of EU citizenship in no way

'displaces' national citizenship (*Id.*:8). But notwithstanding this declaration, some remain convinced that EU citizenship contradicts the preservation of the integrity of the nation-state involved and leads inexorably to
nation-building on an EU scale (Weiler 1999). If these fears were to prove
warranted, then, far from providing a path toward greater differentiation,
EU citizenship would minimize difference and frustrate the aims of
identitarian citizenship.

As evinced by the trajectory of the (now failed) proposed Treaty-
Constitution for the EU – first in the name of the '*peoples* of Europe', not
'We the People of the EU', and then in the name of the heads of state of the
twenty-five nation-state signatories[23] – the actual relationship between EU
citizenship and its member-state counterparts remains problematic.

Three alternative approaches have been suggested for purposes of overcoming the problems that stem from the interface between EU and nation-
state citizenship. These are: the 'statist', the 'unionist' and the 'pluralist'
(Baubock 2007:466). The statist approach would provide the EU with the
citizenship model prevalent in federal democracies (*Id.*:467). Whether the
sui generis EU could or should be transformed into a federation is an open
question, but more importantly, for present purposes, it is unclear that
making the EU into a transnational federation would ameliorate the prevalent identitarian difficulties. Indeed, as we have seen in Chapter 5 above,
the identity of the EU remains problematic. In contrast, the identity of the
United States or Germany is not only well-formed and firmly entrenched
but it is also accorded greater importance than that of the American states
of the German *Länder*.

The second, unionist, approach seeks to strengthen EU citizenship and
make it more independent from nation-state citizenship (*Id.*). This goes
beyond the arrangement found in federations by seeking to emancipate
EU citizenship from its nation-state counterparts (*Id.*). This approach
seems undesirable from an identitarian standpoint for at least two reasons.
First, making EU citizenship dominant would most likely result in a very
significant loss of differentiation; and, second, given the difficulties regarding arriving at viable common EU identity, it is difficult to imagine how
the latter would become sufficiently dense and coherent to dominate the
entire EU landscape.

The third, pluralist, approach, on the other hand, seems more promising. This approach calls for a looser form of mutual accommodation
between EU and nation-state citizenship (*Id.*). The vertical relation between
the two is not meant to be hierarchical as congruence, compliance with the
standards of democratic legitimacy and balancing are primed to determine
the parameters of mutual coexistence. This approach appears to make

much more room for differentiation than do its rivals and to be therefore better suited to the identitarian cause. Before exploring the pluralist approach any further, however, it is necessary to take a closer look at how the current interplay between EU citizenship and the various relevant nation-state ones actually impact and transform them.

7.5.2 The Changing Dynamic between EU and Member-State Citizenship

The principle is very simple: whoever is a citizen of a member-state is a citizen of the EU and correlatively no one who is not a citizen of a member-state can be an EU citizen. Consistent with this principle, reinforced as a result of the member-state concerns alluded to in §7.5.1 above, moreover, EU citizenship may have an impact on the functional dimension of member-state citizenship, but is supposed to have none on its identitarian one. However, as we shall now see, precisely *because* of significant identitarian differences concerning the nature and scope of citizenship among the various member-states within the EU, the implantation of EU citizenship has proven far from neutral when it comes to the identitarian dimension of citizenship *within* member-states.

The identitarian differences among member-states that impact on EU citizenship and that have led to pressure for changes in the criteria for citizenship within the member-states include: the dichotomy between *jus sanguinis* and *jus soli*; the status of long-term non-EU immigrants; amnesty policies regarding waves of illegal immigrants; recognition or rejection of dual nationality; and treatment by a member-state of citizenship accorded to natives of that member-state's past or present overseas territories (Rostek and Davies 2006).

In this context, Spain and Germany stand at opposite ends of the spectrum. Spain has long had accords with Latin American countries, allowing for dual nationality based on a shared common language and culture (*Id.*:15). Taking advantage of this, many Latin American nationals have used Spain as a springboard for immigration to other EU member-states (*Id.*). Furthermore, Spain's liberal amnesty policy toward illegal immigrants, coupled with its grant of citizenship after two years to legal residents from a number of countries, has meant that illegal immigrants that fled from another EU member-state and entered Spain illegally could eventually return to the EU country they originally fled from as full-fledged EU citizens. This has led to strong protest from France against Spain's amnesty policy (*Id.*). Moreover, because of pressure by other EU member-states within the Schengen zone[24] Spain tightened its entry requirements for citizens from the Maghreb and certain Latin American countries (*Id.*:14).

Germany's tight adherence to ethnocentric citizenship based on *jus san-guinis* foreclosed a large segment of its population, including two or three generations of residents who had immigrated from Turkey, from becoming EU citizens (*Id.*:22). This created a wide discrepancy between permanent non-EU immigrants in Germany and those in Spain and most other EU countries concerning the opportunity to acquire EU citizenship. This led to EU pressure for Germany to loosen its citizenship requirements. A new German immigration law entered in force in 2000, allowing for the first time residents of Turkish origin to acquire German citizenship. But in spite of this, Germany remains relatively closed to immigrants (*Id.*:24–25). Set against this, a 2003 EU Directive[25] seeks to achieve parity for non-EU long-term immigrants with those coming from a member-state, and to grant those persons originary from outside the EU uniform rights that approximate as much as possible those enjoyed by EU citizens.

Concerning citizenship tied to overseas territories, the UK and France have different policies which impact on EU citizenship. A British overseas citizen does not have the right to reside in the UK, and hence has no right to EU citizenship (*Id.*:11). In contrast, natives of Martinique or Reunion, among others, are full-fledged French citizens and are hence also entitled to EU citizenship (*Id.*:13).

What all these examples point to is that there is an ongoing dynamic that inevitably shapes and alters the contours of both EU and member-state citizenship. Not only is the identitarian dimension of EU citizenship affected by the different identities associated with the respective member-states' citizenship, but also by the differences among the latter. In other words, differences among the UK and France determine in part who is and who is not an EU citizen, but *the* difference between Spain and Germany affects the very nature of EU citizenship. And conversely, the nature of EU citizenship influences the evolving identitarian attributes of Spanish and German citizenship. What this implies is that the nation-state no longer furnishes an adequate model for citizenship (Soysal 1994:167). Further-more, these observations also enhance the attractiveness of a pluralist approach in as much as neither a hierarchy of identities nor a full recon-ciliation among vertically and horizontally aligned identities encompassed within the space delimited by the EU seems realistically plausible. Before exploring this pluralist alternative in greater depth, and placing it in the greater context of constitutional identity and the constitutional subject in the next chapter, this chapter will close with a brief examination of the prospects of transnational citizenship beyond the EU.

7.5.3 Transnational Citizenship Beyond the EU?

Two important questions arise as a consequence of the preceding examination of EU citizenship and the suggestion that a pluralist approach may be best to deal with citizenship that extends beyond the bounds of the nation-state. The first of these is whether other regions besides the EU might be suited for transnational citizenship; the second, whether global citizenship is altogether plausible. These questions, moreover, are not only important in their own right, but also because they underscore the vexing problem concerning reconciliation of the universal and the particular in its irreducible singularity beyond the confines of the nation-state – or, more precisely, of the mono-national, mono-ethnic and mono-cultural state.

Although EU citizenship remains problematic from an identitarian perspective, Europe does possess a sufficiently distinct common history, culture and shared values to form a common identity, particularly as against the identities of non-Europeans, such as, for example, Americans.[26] Whether European identity will prove sturdy or enduring enough to sustain a thriving EU citizenship in the long run cannot yet be determined, but it is apparent that there is sufficient congruity among Europeans to make the success of EU citizenship plausible.

There also seems to be little question that other regions of the world could muster a common identity comparable to that of the Europeans, and thus also sustain transnational citizenship within their own region. Thus, for example, the countries of Latin America share much closer linguistic and cultural bonds than do European countries. Accordingly, at least from an identitarian perspective, Latin American would seem to be in at least as good a position as Europe to sustain a viable common citizenship throughout the region.

The prospects for global citizenship, on the other hand, seem much more uncertain. A region can garner distinct clusters of identity commonly shared among all the national communities within it and at the same time set its self-image as against those of other regions. On the global level, in contrast, there is no external 'other' against whom one could construct an identity, and one would have either to construct an identity above all differences or one that fully accounts for all existing differences. In the former case, the resulting global identity would be a purely abstract universal one that could hardly command the kind of attachment and allegiance necessary for the successful implantation of citizenship relationships. In the latter case, the commitment to account for all differences or all identitarian nuances would make it impossible to come up with any shared sense of identity or common conception of citizenship. In short, unless the pluralist approach can lead us out of this impasse, global citizenship seems doomed to failure on identitarian grounds.

Matters are altogether different, however, when viewed from a functional standpoint. Indeed, universal equal citizenship is not only conceivable on a global scale, but its ultimate achievement would seem to depend on the establishment of global citizenship. As all human beings are entitled to the same citizenship rights, and as nation-states and supra-national polities have failed to extend equal citizenship rights to all, the establishment of global citizenship would seem to afford the best means for remedying that failure.

For all its promise, global citizenship may not be ultimately desirable if it proved dependent on global government. Arguably, however, global citizenship could be sustained by global *governance* without global *government*. Furthermore, if international human rights are regarded as providing partial global citizenship rights on all human beings, then we already have in place elements of global governance that are linked to certain of the attributes of global citizenship. Whether or not full global citizenship will eventually materialize, it is clear that the deployment of global governance will require recourse to a pluralist approach.

This last observation will be explored further in the next chapter. Suffice it for now to underscore that the dynamics and contradictions of citizenship, and in particular those that pit functional citizenship against identitarian citizenship, track on a microcosmic scale the same dialectical predicaments of the constitutional subject and of constitutional identity that have emerged throughout the various facets of the preceding analysis.

CHAPTER **8**

Can the Constitutional Subject Go Global? Imagining a Convergence of the Universal, the Particular and the Singular

There cannot be a full accounting of the constitutional subject at present without confronting the question of whether it would be plausible for it to function properly as a transnational or global one. The preceding analysis revealed a split between the American approach and its European counterpart, with much remaining unsettled. American exceptionalism has been challenged by those who are prepared to look elsewhere to enrich the U.S.'s constitutional jurisprudence, thus opening the door to a (at least partially) transnational constitutional identity even if the American constitutional subject itself remains firmly ensconced within the confines of the nation-state. The Europeans, on the other hand, have certainly worked assiduously to implant a transnational constitutional subject with a distinct European constitutional identity, but have thus far fallen short of their intended goal.

As detailed in the preceding chapter, constitutional identity as it emerges through the prism of citizenship also projects an unresolved tension-filled state of affairs. Citizenship seems caught between its functional pole oriented toward the universal and its identitarian pole deeply entrenched in the particular. The constitutional subject as embodied in the citizen appears therefore split between an inclusionary self aspiring to the universal and an exclusionary self clinging to a singular communal identity as against all others.

Before investigating whether these difficulties may be managed or overcome, it is useful to remember that, even in the context of the traditional

243

nation-state, constitutional identity and the constitutional subject first emerge as a lack, as an empty place holder, to be filled through a process of negation, deconstruction, reconstruction, reincorporation and recombination. As closely detailed in Chapter 3, in the context of unenumerated American constitutional rights, constitutional identity is produced rather than given. It is erected against existing traditions, yet at the same time built up out of reprocessed and recombined elements deeply embedded in the socio-political fabric of the relevant polity.

Whether the above noted tensions and contradictions can be overcome or redirected, and whether, with the aid of creative constitutional identity building, a veritably transnational or even global constitutional subject can be turned into a key player in an increasingly unified and differentiated constitutional domain, cannot be determined with any reasonable degree of certainty under currently prevailing conditions. What can be done profitably at this juncture, however, is to assess whether the emergence of a transnational or global constitutional subject is plausible rather than merely Utopian. Moreover, if such a constitutional subject can be envisaged as plausible, this must be so without recourse to the premise of a full-fledged all-purpose world government, or in other words, of a world government that would roughly replicate the model of a nation-state with the whole globe as its national territory. And this last premise must be rejected both because world government seems highly implausible within the foreseeable future and because it would in any event, be undesirable as many, going back to Kant, have argued (Kant 1970). Indeed, it is not hard to imagine the parade of horribles that would besiege humanity were it confronted with a central global government.

Global *governance*, as distinguished from global *government*, on the other hand, is already, in part, a working reality, and it has important implications for the conception and construction of a transnational constitutional subject. More generally, the recent trend towards globalization and the concurrent trend towards privatization have led to significant changes in constitutional ordering (Rosenfeld 2008). These will be briefly examined in 8.1 below. Furthermore, to the extent that the nature and interpretation of constitutional rights both influences, and is influenced by, constitutional identity, the question of a transnational or global constitutional subject can be profitably elucidated through focus on the relationship between human rights and constitutional rights, which will be undertaken in 8.2 below. In the end, the constitutional subject, whether national or global, requires a corresponding constitutional identity. As we have seen, in relation to the construction of an European constitutional identity, Habermas suggested the concept of constitutional patriotism as a plausible means of transcending the strictures of national identity.[1] The limited analysis of this concept provided thus far has been inconclusive. But after an assessment of constitutional reordering and of the nexus between human and constitutional rights, a more systematic critique of constitutional patriotism will be possible and it should allow for a better grasp of the potential for a working transnational of global constitutional identity. This critique will be provided in 8.3 below. Finally, in the concluding section, 8.4 below, I will argue that a transnational constitutional subject, and even a global one, is indeed plausible, provided it is conceived as being plural and yet, in its own dialectical way, as being able to maintain its singularity while managing the gap between the universal and the particular.

8.1 Constitutional Reordering in an Era of Globalization and Privatization

As already made manifest through the numerous references made above to the EU, legal actors today are subject to a plurality of legal regimes, including supernational ones. This is most evident in the context of the twenty seven EU member-states in which legal actors subjected to their own nation-state's legal regime, to that of the EU, and to the human rights regime of the ECHR. Unlike the legal obligations that derive from traditional treaties among independent nation-states, EU regulations have direct effect within member-states without prior action by the latter.[2] Moreover, decisions of the ECtHR are binding on the nation-state parties before it (Janis, Kay & Bradley 1995:82–87). Unlike in a federal scheme within a nation-state, where the unity and harmony of the legal system is constitutionally guaranteed – e.g., through a supreme or constitutional court that authoritatively settles conflicts between federal and federated entity law[3] – legal actors within the EU are not protected from conflicting obligations arising under the different regimes to which they are subjected. Indeed, several member-state constitutional courts have declared their country's constitution to be superior to conflicting EU regulation, thus denying supremacy to the latter.[4] Furthermore, it is certainly possible for obligations imposed by the EU on member-states to conflict with obligations that latter have under the ECHR, thus setting the ECJ, the ECtHR and national constitutional courts on a collision course (Garlicki 2008).

Some legal regimes purport to be global in scope. Arguably, the UN Charter functions as a world constitution (Fassbender 1998). Similarly, the legal regime framed by the World Trade Organization (WTO) is meant to be global in scope, though it remains segmentary as it singles out trade from all other human activity that can be made subject to law.[5] Another segmentary global legal regime is the one deriving from the 1948 Universal Declaration of Human Rights and resulting in the 1966 ICCPR and the 1966 ICESCR, which as of 2008 have been ratified respectively by 161 nations and 158 nations (Rosenfeld 2008:420, n. 26).

The intersection between global segmentary legal regimes, supra-national and national regimes is prone to multiply conflicts without providing any authoritative means for resolving them. Thus, for example, full EU implementation of free trade regulation imposed by the WTO seems bound to produce 'reverse discrimination' within EU member-states as certain tariffs would have to be lifted for imported goods but not for domestic ones (von Bogdandy 2008). There are many other even more complex, cases which have led one commentator to conclude that 'it makes no sense to try to identify the proper law through resort to some two-dimensional notion of mutually exclusive or unilaterally dominant jurisdiction' (Walker 2008:383).

Not only does the trend towards globalization expand the plurality of operating legal regimes bearing on the same legal actors, but so does the concurrent trend towards privatization. For example, recourse to the *lex mercatoria* (Carbonneau 1998) allows multinational corporations to avoid, at least in part, regulation by nation-states, supra-national and international legal regimes. A contract between two multi-national corporations can thus be made subject to the *lex mercatoria*, and any dispute arising from such contract can be confined to private arbitration.

The concurrent trends toward globalization and privatization and the plurality of legal regimes that they generate pose a serious challenge to the constitutional order of the nation-state. As these trends progress, less and less of what was traditionally subsumed under the nation-state's constitution and the order it imposed on the legal system as a whole remains in place. Thus, WTO regulation of trade and the supremacy it claims over that area supersede or diminish the nation-state's corresponding powers. Similarly, ECHR free speech rights as interpreted by the ECtHR may contradict an ECHR signatory state's constitutional court's interpretation of similarly phrased free speech rights under that state's constitution, effectively taking ultimate control over free speech protection away from the state's own constitution and constitutionally empowered institutions.

Consistent with these observations, globalization and privatization shift the nature and locus of constitutional ordering. As constitutional law is internationalized and international law constitutionalized (Rosenfeld 2008:425), the determination of both the material content and application of constitutional norms[6] increasingly shifts to supra-national and international levels of governance. At the same time, and at least to some extent, privatization seems to altogether de-constitutionalize certain segmentary legal regimes. Thus, if *lex mercatoria* and the private arbitration mechanisms associated with it allow certain legal actors to escape all other legal regimes when interacting with one another, then all transactions involved would seem to remain beyond otherwise applicable constitutional norms and the legal order over which these norms preside.

These developments pose a clear challenge to the constitutional subject and to the constitutional identity constructed for, and nurtured in, the traditional nation-state. One possible and, in many ways tempting, reaction for the constitutional subject would be to retrench and to look exclusively inwards, treating the supra-national, international and non-governmental segmentary private legal regimes that impinge upon the nation-state's legal order as being purely external. And in this context, 'purely external' norms would be synonymous to norms that are not constitutional in nature, being instead more akin to norms deriving from traditional bilateral treaties among two sovereign states. This inward looking approach approximates the position of the German Constitutional Court in its *Solange I* decision[7] where it declared that EU regulation that contravened the German Basic Law's protection of fundamental rights would be unenforceable in Germany.

The temptation to resist forging a supra-national constitutional subject and constitutional identity is very strong. This becomes plain in reference to the above discussion of the European constitutional model and the European constitution-making model. Indeed, first, the EU tried to give itself a constitution through a treaty-constitution that failed, and then through a treaty *tout court*, the 2007 Lisbon Treaty, which incorporates much of the content of the discarded treaty-constitution, but assiduously avoid labeling itself a constitution. Moreover, even under these conditions, the Lisbon Treaty has not yet, as of this writing, come into effect, having been at least temporarily derailed by rejection in an Irish referendum.[8]

Notwithstanding such strong resistance, the changing constitutional order and the current dynamic between human rights and constitutional rights are bound to bring changes both to the constitutional subject and to constitutional identity. Such changes need not necessarily foretell the demise of the nation-state molded constitutional subject, but they do call for adjustments, supplementation and diversification. To be in a better position to grasp the new directions that lie ahead for the constitutional subject, the rest of this Section will focus on the particulars of the current constitutional reordering, and the next section will concentrate on the nexus between human and constitutional rights.

There are two crucial distinctions between the constitutional order that inheres in a traditional nation-state and any constitutional order that may emerge in a supra-national or global setting. Although there are divergent interests in the (even mono-ethnic) nation-state, two major factors are always present regardless of the particular constitutional identity involved: First, there is a cohesive, unified, hierarchically ordered constitutional/legal system that maximizes formal convergence among all diverse elements and interests; and, second, there is a sufficient degree of perceived commonality or overlap among competing interests to secure sufficient material convergence to avoid unduly disruptive challenges to the constitution's or the law's legitimacy. In other words, in the context of nation-state constitutions, there is a formal institutional mechanism to resolve disputes about the meaning of the constitution – e.g., a constitutional court, the parliament – recognized by the polity as a whole as authoritative even if large numbers within it disagree with numerous substantive results. At the same time, material divergences are kept within manageable bounds through adherence to *inter alia*, a commonly shared national and constitutional identity.

In the transnational setting, in contrast, there is no comparable hierarchy or unity within which the plurality of operative legal regimes can be neatly inserted. Moreover, material divergences are likely to be much greater at the transnational level than at the level of the nation-state – e.g., there is much more religious divergence in the world as a whole than in any given nation-state – and the basis for commonly shared values seems much weaker. Indeed, there seems to be nothing akin to the bonds of the national identity on a transnational scale and the possibility of a transnational constitutional identity, which will be further investigated below, remains very much in question.

The plurality of legal regimes linked to the concurrent trends towards globalization and privatization seem bound to involve multiple sets of norms that intersect, overlap, divide the field, or that relate to one another horizontally rather than vertically. As exemplified by the case of the EU, a number of different legal regimes interact significantly,[9] and combine to structure the legal universe into an aggregated multilevel edifice comprising both global, supranational, regional and national norms and a expanding array of largely separate and self-contained, segmented limited purpose fields, such as *lex mercatoria*. This results in a multi-level layered and segmented combination of legal regimes that converge at times – e.g., in spite of the potential for conflict between EU law and member-state constitutions, all sides have thus far worked hard to avoid any actual direct clash (Rosenfeld 2008:419) – diverge or conflict, at other times, and frequently overlap and intersect.

Whether constitutional order can prevail in a world in which legal actors are constantly subjected to a plurality of different regimes depends on the possibility of tempering centrifugal tendencies with centripetal ones, and of striking a proper balance between poles of convergence and poles of divergence. Moreover, any appropriate constitutional order in this context must be comprised of a combination of formal/structural elements and of material elements. Thus, for example, the EU is not structurally a federation in the same sense as is the U.S., and its vertical ordering must therefore be distinguished from that of a unified and fully integrated federalized nation-state. The German constitutional polity cannot be as seamlessly integrated into the EU as California is into the U.S. In the context of the EU, there is a layering along the vertical axis, with the various layers being partially, but not fully, structurally and formally connected to one another. Indeed, alongside the reservation of constitutional supremacy at the level of the nation state – with particular emphasis on certain key areas, such as fundamental rights,[10] democracy and (for a federal republic such as Germany) federalism[11] – member-states, including Germany, do accept EU regulatory supremacy as well as the direct effect of EU regulations. Moreover, this partially federalized vertical relationship is structurally and formally secured by the ECJ, which functions, in part, like a constitutional court (Rosenfeld 2006).

The structure and formal convergence produced by the above described vertical relationships would not suffice for purposes of assuring the viability of an EU constitutional order. They need to be supplemented by a significant degree of material convergence, and that precisely is what the ECJ undertook to achieve after Germany's *Solange I* decision. Specifically, the ECJ stressed its adherence to the 'rule of law' and to 'fundamental principles' as well as to the 'common constitutional traditions of the EU's member-states' (Rosenfeld 2006:623–624). The ECJ's approach met with great success as twelve years after *Solange I*, the German Constitutional Court declared in its *Solange II* decision[12] that incompatibility between EU law and German constitutionally protected fundamental rights no longer raised serious concerns due to the incorporation of constitutional norms in ECJ interpretations of EU law.

The combination of layering and segmentation coupled with the concurrent trends toward internationalization of constitutional law and internationalization of constitutional law does lay the ground work for a new constitutional order of transnational, international and even potentially global dimensions. This new order is not based on unity, but layering can accommodate a fair amount of diversity. This order cannot avoid conflict, but segmentation can help keep that conflict within manageable bounds. For example, WTO regulation purports to enjoy supremacy over conflicting signatory state domestic regulation. This may, of course, produce conflict or inconsistency from the internal constitutional standpoint of an affected nation-state. But even if it does, it ought to be confined and contained in as much as it would only relate to the area of trade.

Layering and segmentation are also apt to minimize the above mentioned disparity in the scope of divergence between the nation-state and the world at large. Indeed, whereas there may be wide divergences *among* layers or segments, there are often likely to be great convergence *within* them. Thus, for example, the commonality of interests among the multinational corporations that interact in the segmented realm of *lex mercatoria* is likely to be far greater than that at work in even the most homogeneous and harmonious of nation-states. Finally, whereas layering and segmenting may make for greater divergences and discrepancies among layers and segments, that centrifugal tendency is mitigated by the centripetal tendency to constitutionalize all legal regimes, including segmentary ones, be they public or private. Indeed, in addition to the national, supranational and international constitutionalization already alluded to, private and non-governmental legal networks, that have carved out distinct spheres of segmented self-regulation have generated their own internal constitutional framework (Hamann and Ruiz-Fabri 2008). This leads to increases in convergence within layers and segments, to dispersion of divergences among layers and segments, and to establishment of parallel processes of constitutionalization throughout the plurality of existing legal regimes.

In such a reordered constitutional universe, the constitutional subject must itself adjust to encompass layering and segmentation. The constitutional subject must learn to live with greater dissonance and to develop an identity that is plural without losing all traces of singularity. Integrating a plurality of poles of identity is a challenge that confronts every contemporary person and citizen living in any developed society. For example, a German Catholic feminist woman is likely to identify as a German as opposed to an American or an Italian, as a Catholic as opposed to a Protestant, and as a feminist as opposed to those who advocate preservation of traditional roles for women. At an international feminist conference, the person in question's nationality may be of little importance, but it would spring to the foreground in a discussion concerning disagreements over U.S. foreign policy. Moreover, several of the plural elements of identity that combine to constitute the self-identity of the person under consideration may be in tension, or even come into conflict, with one another. That person's feminism may thus conceivably be at times in tension or even in conflict with her Catholicism to the extent that the latter may not be always consistent with full equality between the sexes. Our Catholic feminist may accept to live with these conflicts and inconsistencies, or she may seek to reform the Church's ways from within, by, say, advocating for opening the priesthood to women. What seems clear, however, is that dissonances and conflicts can only be accommodated up to a certain point. Thus, if Catholicism and feminism were radically incompatible, it would seem impossible to integrate them both within a single person's self-identity. But conversely, so long as they are not (or may foreseably become not) squarely incompatible, then they may both combine to forge (part of) the same self-identity.

One can imagine some plausible analogous handling of plural elements of identity at the level of the transnational constitutional subject. For example, in the context of a dispute between Germany and the EU, a German citizen may focus primarily on her national identity. But, at the same time, when focusing on a policy disagreement between the EU and the U.S., that same German citizen may quite readily regard herself as a proud citizen of the EU. Similarly, in a moment such as that surrounding *Solange I*, German constitutional identity would quite logically predominate through the country. But at other times, one can certainly imagine a weaving together of German constitutional identity, EU constitutional identity (were such an identity to become sufficiently distinct) and a partial constitutional-like identity deriving from the ECHR. In short, a plural transnational constitutional subject and identity seem possible, but, for the moment, the particulars remain unclear. Accordingly, and for purposes of further elucidation, I now turn to an analysis of the nexus between human rights and constitutional rights.

8.2 The Nexus between Human Rights and Constitutional Rights

As previously discussed, similarly phrased constitutional rights may be interpreted quite differently, depending on the respective constitutional identities involved.[13] Given that international and supra-national human rights and fundamental rights contained in constitutions are expressed in very similar terms, an analysis of the nexus between them may shed useful light on the possible nature and identity of the supra-national constitutional subject. Moreover, the supra-national human rights regime is a segmented one, and the interplay between human and constitutional rights takes place across different layers. Because of this, not only is a distinct image of the transnational constitutional subject likely emerge, but also an idea of its deployment and operation in a setting defined by a dynamic interplay among a plurality of legal regimes.

In light of the striking similarities in enunciation involved, on first impression the principal distinction between human and constitutional rights is one of scope. Human rights extend to all human beings; constitutional rights to the citizens of the polity ruled by the relevant constitution or to all persons within that polity.[14] Another important difference between human and constitutional rights stems from what they respectively stand against. Concepts are to an important extent determined by what they are meant to negate or oppose, and contemporary human rights and modern constitutional rights stem respectively from two different declarations standing one hundred and fifty years apart. The 1948 UN Universal Declaration of Human Rights was clearly set against the Holocaust whereas the 1789 French Declaration of the Rights of Man and the Citizen was set against the hierarchy and privileges stemming from the feudal order. The 1948 Declaration was therefore set against the unspeakable debasement and dehumanization of entire classes of human beings. Its main response to the utter barbarity perpetrated by the Nazi regime was the assertion that all human beings *qua* human beings possess inherent dignity, and that accordingly they are all entitled to a set fundamental rights conditioned exclusively on their being human. In contrast, the 1789 Declaration was set against the hierarchy based on birth or on the cloth and against the conditions of serfdom typical of the feudal order. Consistent with this, the main thrust of the 1789 Declaration was the stipulation that all individuals are free and equal to one another.

Although the 1789 Declaration is in some sense universal for, as we have seen, it speaks of the rights of 'man' and 'citizen' and not of the rights of 'Frenchmen',[15] it is not universal in the same sense as the 1948 Declaration. Indeed, the 1789 Declaration is universal in concept, but fitted to the nation-state, in scope. The 1948 Declaration, on the other hand, is universal in both concept and scope. This is, by no means a trivial difference from the standpoint of identity. Because of their limitation in scope, universally conceived constitutional rights can be interpreted differently from one polity to the next. The French interpretation of constitutional freedom and equality is thus likely to differ from its American counterpart, and each of these will be influenced by its own constitutional identity. In the human rights context, however, at least in principle, all human beings everywhere are entitled to exactly the same human rights which ought to foreclose diverging interpretations from one polity to the next. Thus, for instance, the human right against torture should not have one meaning in China and another in Sweden.

Another key difference between the two declarations is that whereas the 1948 Declaration is primarily moral, the 1789 Declaration is above all political. From the standpoint of 1948 Declaration, regardless of political divisions, and of apportionment of the planet among a multiplicity of political sovereigns, there is a Kantian-like universal moral imperative to treat every human being as the possessor of an inherent dignity that transcends all politics. From the standpoint of the 1789 Declaration, in contrast, the main thrust is to signal a shift in the conduct of the life of the polity. The *ancient régime's* entrusting of politics to the monarch and those entitled to feudal privileges is to be replaced by a political order ruled by and for free and equal citizens (Rousseau 1762).

This last difference has several important implications. First, as morally-based human rights acquire legal dimension, they quite naturally transcend the bounds of the nation-state whereas when constitutional rights become legally enforceable they do not. One important consequence that follows from this is that human rights is everybody's business whereas constitutional rights only concern those within the relevant polity. Human rights protection and redress of violations may therefore justify transnational, international or global level intervention, and even humanitarian intervention by one sovereign-state against another in cases of genocide or of large-scale crimes against humanity. For their part, and strictly speaking, violations of constitutional rights or variations in their interpretation or enforcement from one sovereign to the next should not give rise to any legitimate legal or political right of intervention by anyone beyond the boundaries of the polity involved.[16]

Second, the human rights subject (*who* generates them and *for whom* they are deployed) is universal in both nature and scope whereas the constitutional subject, thus far at least, is tied to the nation-state or to a particularly tightly knitted supra-national political entity, such as the EU. Moreover, the human rights subject is a special-purpose one that operates in a segmented sphere that cuts across all layers of legal ordering from the global to the most local. In contrast, the constitutional subject is an all-purpose subject one as all areas of law and all legal ordering, be they national or transnational (e.g., foreign treaties, EU regulations) come within its sweep. In order words, not all matters of legal ordering come within the purview of the human rights regime (e.g., most issues pertaining to the apportionment of powers among the legislative and the executive branches of government), but they are all within the scope of the prevailing constitution. And it is precisely because the constitutional subject has emerged as an all-purpose one, anchored within the confines of the nation-state, that it may be so difficult to construct a transnational constitutional subject or to imagine its identity in any great detail.

Although universal in nature and scope, the identity of the human rights subject is historically situated, and from its very origins fairly precisely defined in terms of what it does, and ought to, stand against. Unfortunately, in the sixty years following the 1948 Declaration, there have been numerous genocides, mass killings, systematic torture and other large scale assaults against basic human dignity. Accordingly, the 1948 Declaration's original stance against the Holocaust does not merely provide a backward-looking basis for identity, but also an ongoing, forward-looking one. From the UN, other international and transnational organizations to constitutional democracies and human rights NGOs, the struggle against the most horrendous acts perpetrated on an organized large scale basis by humans against other humans is an ongoing imperative unifying banner of universal human rights.

If what they were, and continue being, against gives human rights a fairly concrete *negative* identity, their *positive* identity seems highly abstract, making a unified conception or application hard to imagine. Indeed, human rights norms as they emerge from of the two 1966 UN covenants[17] and other international and supranational instruments go far beyond what the 1948 Declaration was set against. The 1966 ICCPR has a full catalogue of civil and political rights and much resembles, in terms of the nature of the rights it enshrines, the bill of rights contained in numerous nation-state constitutions. Similarly, the 1966 ICESCR contains a panoply of rights similar to those found in several of the post World War Two nation-state constitutions. As we have seen, at the level of the nation-state, such rights acquire concrete embodiment through the mediation of the relevant nation's constitutional identity. But what about the universal human rights level? Can anything beyond a purely abstract identity without any practical purchase be achieved? Or, in other words, from a positive standpoint, can universal human rights ever rise above amounting to mere platitudes?

Concepts evolve over time and may expand or shift direction from their original setting. Sixty years after the 1948 Declaration and more than two hundred years after the 1789 Declaration, both human and constitutional rights have evolved to the point that they bear but a partial and diffused relation to what they were originally set against. Thus, for example, as already noted, and quite understandably, the German Basic Law sets human dignity as it paramount constitutional value rather than individual liberty or equality. On the other hand, for all their aspiration to remain universal in nature as well as in scope, divisions have developed over the positive meaning of human rights and over the fundamental precepts of a working human rights regime. One notorious example is the controversy over 'Asian values'. Proponents of Asian values have accused Western powers of using human rights to impose their liberal ideology and free market orientation (Bauer and Bell 1999).

Human rights and constitutional rights do carve out distinct legal regimes. But, as the examples relating to the German constitutional order and to Asian values reveal the relationship among these two legal regimes are more intricate and complex then may appear at first. Most notably, there are convergences cutting across the two regimes involved as well as divergences within the same regime. Although human rights ought to be universal, there are disagreements concerning at least part of their positive content. On the other hand, though constitutional rights remain tied to a particular constitutional identity, they may well converge in content. What this suggests, moreover, is two distinct subjects with interlocking, intersecting and partially overlapping identities. Does that mean that human rights will ultimately prove to be relative to political ideology and legal culture? Or can they remain at once universal and plural?

Ideally, the regimes of human and constitutional rights ought to be fully integrated. Although it is segmented, the human rights regime is meant to cut across all layers, including that framed by the (nation-state fitted) constitutional subject. Moreover, within that latter layer, human rights ought to interlock most closely with fundamental constitutional rights. To the extent that constitutional rights are deficient from the standpoint of the human rights subject – e.g., constitutional group rights benefiting certain groups within the polity at the expense of the human rights of other persons subject to the same constitutional regime – human rights would be called upon to trump incompatible constitutional rights. Otherwise, the two regimes may complement one another, or overlap. Furthermore, if the human rights regime were elastic enough to tolerate a certain degree of internal divergence, there may be room for a dynamic interaction between the universal and the plural, and better means of adaptation to a wider range of constitutional orders and constitutional identities.

Practically speaking, the system of human rights and that of constitutional rights is far from being systematically integrated. In many parts of the world, international human rights lack a significant legal dimension or are greatly underenforced. There is one region of the world, however, where both human and constitutional rights have been systematically enforced and become highly integrated. That region is the Europe made-up of the forty seven countries that are members of the Council of Europe and subject to the ECHR and to its interpretation by the ECtHR. The human rights enshrined in the ECHR are not strictly universal in scope, being instead European and confined in their application to that continent. Nevertheless, the Europe of the Council of Europe is widely diverse as it brings together countries such as the UK, France, Russia, Poland and Turkey. Accordingly, because of its combined high degree of integration, and significantly diverse array of national and constitutional cultures, the Europe under the ECHR regime seems to offer particularly fertile grounds to further explore the nexus between human and constitutional rights and their possible interaction in a setting that is simultaneously oriented towards the universal and the plural.

The ECHR creates among its member states a transnational community that can be conceived as a special or limited-purpose self. Some of the provisions of the ECHR, such as the prohibition against the death penalty,[18] require strict uniformity. Others, however, seem best handled through a proper balancing of convergences and divergences. To preserve cohesion within the entire ECHR community and to avoid a degree of divergences that might tear it apart from within, there is a need to rally around common objectives without undue sacrifices regarding each state's core all-purpose identity.

The ECtHR has developed a judicial instrument, the 'margin of appreciation' standard, which is designed to strike the requisite equilibrium between convergence and divergence in the application of ECHR. Although the ECtHR's use of this standard has been attacked as being too 'toothless' and too 'political' (Mahoney 1998), even if such criticism proved fully warranted, proper application of the margin of appreciation standard seems well suited for purposes of forging a workable path to a newly minted common identity without unduly eradicating or repressing crucial differences. From a practical standpoint, the margin of appreciation standard is designed to safeguard adequate convergence at the transnational level – all states subject to the ECHR must be treated as equally bound by its provisions – while, at the same time, allowing each nation to diverge from its neighbors so long as the margin of deviation involved does not threaten the maintenance of the requisite convergence at the transnational level.

The ECtHR's decision in the *Handyside* case[19] well illustrates the potential of the margin of appreciation standard. In this case, the UK was alleged to have violated the complainant's ECHR freedom of speech rights by banning as indecent a book that had been adjudged to be protected speech in the Scandinavian countries. The ECtHR upheld the UK ban as being within the margin of appreciation. Consistent with the above conception of the standard, the ECtHR's conclusion would be justified if the following two conditions had been satisfied. First, the book ban at stake was not incompatible with a plausible European conception of the scope of free speech. And, second, taking all the relevant cultural differences (i.e., those compatible with the just mentioned plausible European conception) into proper account, freedom of speech as delimited in the UK could be regarded as the equivalent to freedom of speech as delimited in the Scandinavian countries. In the context of *Handyside*, therefore, if the UK and Scandinavia agreed on the essential value of free speech and both drew the line at indecent expression, but disagreed – on the basis of adherence to different cultural criteria closely linked to national and constitutional identity – on where that line ought to be drawn, then granting the margin of appreciation to the UK would have been fully justified.

More generally, accommodation of the differences, dissonances and even inconsistencies falling short of incompatibility that a proper application of the margin of appreciation standard would allow seems clearly preferable to insisting on unity to the exclusion of differences. If no incompatibilities are involved, it seems best to allow for differences in the interpretation of the same human right so long as its core integrity remains intact. Moreover, greater acceptance of differences in this context is desirable on both normative and pragmatic grounds. From the normative standpoint, in pluralist settings, in which a number of distinct communities with different identities interact preserving as much as possible as is important for the identity of each of the communities involved without compromising either human or constitutional rights seems clearly more normatively attractive than demanding a leveling uniformity (Rosenfeld 1998:199–223). From a pragmatist standpoint, on the other hand, it seems fair to assume that there would be greater commitment to human and constitutional rights if these did not require suppression of certain of the most valued attributes of one's core collective self-identity.

If we add together that there is room for divergences within the realm of human rights and for convergence between that realm and its constitutional counterpart (Garlicki 2008), then it becomes manifest that transnational human rights need not be conceived as being singlehandedly imposed from above. Whereas human rights as they emerge through the implementation of the ECHR have a definite transnational identity, that identity is as much built with elements found within the precincts of the nation- states involved as with elements standing against the national and constitutional identities in play. Human rights may aspire to be universal and the ECHR has certainly projected a transnational identity (whether it could also count as universal depends on whether the kind of human rights regime at work in Europe could be successfully deployed on a global scale), but the identity in question does not preclude the singular or the plural. What is involved in the legal universe within the sweep of the ECHR is an amalgamation of distinct layers, with communication and exchanges among then, and with significant room for plurality within each layer. In this layered legal universe, the respective identities of the human rights subject and of the adapting constitutional identities of the nation-states involved can neither be imposed in a top-down fashion nor assembled in a bottom-up one. Instead, what is at play is a complex process of construction that resembles the one that operates in the context of the elaboration of a nation-state's constitutional identity. The interpretive tools are the same, but the identity is distinct. And it is distinct because the subject is different: In spite of all possible convergences, the human rights subject is not the constitutional subject, though it may form part of the global or transnational constitutional subject. Indeed, in a global constitution, universal human rights may correspond to the bill of rights in a nation-state constitution. And so may the ECHR in the context of a putative European (i.e., Council of Europe as opposed to EU) constitution. This still leaves open the question of the content of a plausible transnational or global constitutional identity. With this in mind, it is now time to take a closer look at the concept of 'constitutional patriotism', which, as previously mentioned,[20] Habermas has suggested could potentially supply the requisite substantive glue to a working transnational constitutional order.

8.3 Constitutional Patriotism as Transnational Constitutional Identity?

As indicated in Chapter 5, constitutional patriotism can play a significant *negative* role in any evolution towards transnational constitutionalism, by countering nationalistic patriotism.[21] Indeed, some extreme expressions of nationalistic, ethnocentric patriotism, such as that prevalent in Nazi Germany, are pernicious and must be fought with all available means. But even in less extreme, settings, nationalistic patriotism may foster xenophobia, intolerance and anti-democratic tendencies, and may thus prove hostile to the core values of constitutionalism. By shifting loyalty away from illiberal forms of nationalism (at least to the extent that these set one nation against another, albeit in the context of peaceful competition), may conceivably pave the way to transnational constitutionalism.

But can this shift in loyalty, which might plausibly work as a tool of negation, have a positive context? And, what might that context be? At first, one might be quite skeptical, for the very expression 'constitutional patriotism' seems an oxymoron. Nationalistic patriotism in its most undesirable forms evokes images of blind and oft fanatical loyalty based on ties of blood, ethnicity, religion, language, etc. Should not loyalty to constitutionalism, in contrast, be regarded as an antidote to patriotism and as a means to combat excessive nationalistic patriotism? But if that is the case, how could loyalty (commitment) to abstract ideals ever loosen or uproot the unquestioning passionate loyalty that the fanatical nationalist patriot nurtures? And, perhaps even more basically, in light of the insights regarding the formation of constitutional identity in the context of the nation-state that have emerged throughout the preceding analysis, how could a transnational constitutional identity be elaborated in the absence of established instances of transnational identity that may be reprocessed through negation, metaphor, metonymy, reincorporation, etc.?

8.3.1 Constitutional Patriotism in Historical Perspective

An inquiry into whether the concept of constitutional patriotism may be ascribed a plausible positive content and that would allow it to play a significant positive role in the elaboration of a transnational constitutional identity can draw valuable insights from a brief consideration of the concept's historical origins. Constitutional patriotism is a thoroughly German concept in origin (Sternberger 1979) which was adopted and later given a transnational dimension by Habermas (Habermas 1996:491–515, 566–567). Viewed from a nation-state perspective, in post World War Two West Germany the concept of the nation had become problematic (Müller and Scheppele 2008:68) for two important reasons: first, because of the nation's Nazi past; and second, because of the nation's split into two separate polities, East and West Germany. Under these circumstances, recourse to constitutional patriotism was overdetermined and became unquestionably endowed with positive content. Adoption of constitutional patriotism signified a clear negation of the Nazi past while at the same time setting West Germany apart from communist East Germany. In addition, by embracing constitutional patriotism, West Germany became *the* nation (after all, it was still a nation-state no matter how problematic its national identity may have been) that puts the constitution and the nomos of constitutionalism first.[22] Moreover, even if the first two of these three roles played by constitutional patriotism were deemed to be primarily negative, the third one is unquestionably positive. West Germany reprocessed its national (and for that matter also its constitutional) identity, determined to overcome the darkest legacies from the past. It did so by passionately embracing the ethos of constitutionalism and by giving it the place of pride in its endeavors to rebuild a viable national identity. Accordingly, West German patriotism was genuinely above all constitutional patriotism.

Constitutional patriotism thus played an important positive role in West Germany, but that involved an unique situation that is highly unlikely to repeat itself. Significantly, even in Germany, constitutional patriotism has become largely superfluous in the 1990's, after reunification (*Id.*). More than sixty years after the demise of the Nazi regime, contemporary reunited Germany a well entrenched constitutional democracy and leading member-state of the EU, does indeed seem to have transcended the conditions that made West Germany such fertile soil for constitutional patriotism.

It is instructive to assess Habermas's adaptation of constitutional patriotism for purposes of use in the EU, in particular, and in trans-national settings, in general, in terms of the German experience. From the standpoint of a negative role, there are striking analogies. First, as noted in Chapter 5, to the extent that there is an emerging EU constitutional identity it is set against the horrors perpetrated by Nazism and Soviet communism.[23] And, second, just as the concept of the German nation was problematic when Germany was divided into two separate polities, the concept of an EU 'nation' is likely to remain vexing so long as the EU member-states continue to regard themselves as sovereign nations entitled to accord primacy to their own nation-state constitution.

When constitutional patriotism is considered in terms of its positive role, however, there appear to be no significant analogies between the German situation and that of the EU. First, even if Nazism or Soviet communism had caused for many European polities the same kind of crisis regarding national identity as was produced in Germany, the plausible positive uses of constitutional patriotism would have logically been confined to the context of the nation-state constitution. Accordingly, as the EU member-states have working democratic constitutions, there seems no impetus for them to embrace constitutional patriotism at the EU level. Indeed, as evinced by *Solange I* discussed above, (West) Germany itself asserted its nation-state anchored constitutional patriotism *against* the EU, albeit an EU that was then less constitutionalized than it is today.

Second, West German constitutional patriotism did not have as its object an abstract constitutionalism comprised of universal rights and generic limitations on governmental powers. As discussed above, the German Basic Law is anchored in the German constitutional model and it has emerged through a reworking of the German constitutional tradition – readapting certain particulars originating in the Weimar Constitution and discarding others – and by redirecting the country's constitutional orientation – e.g., by adopting dignity as a paramount constitutional value. In this process, constitutional patriotism was *oriented to* making the constitution invulnerable to anti-constitutional and anti-democratic threats and to stirring up the citizenry's loyalty to their nation's project of deploying an exemplary commitment to the constitutionalist ethos. There are, of course, no analogous circumstances or similar concerns in the case of the EU. From the standpoint of *content*, it is hard to see any need for the EU to rework the constitutions of the EU member-states. And from the standpoint of a project, the EU's objective is to institute the constitutional order that would optimize its functioning as a supra-national polity, not to promote constitutionalism for purposes of restoring an impaired sense of nationhood. Consistent with this, moreover, it is not surprising that Habermas's call for constitutional patriotism for the EU and beyond sounds rather hollow as it seems to boil down to a call for abstract rights and for reapportionment of powers among national and transnational governing entities. Indeed, passionate feelings of loyalty for such abstract rights and such structural changes seem highly unlikely.

Third, although establishing an EU constitution and building a more solid EU identity have been important subjects in recent years, these are, in the last analysis, subordinated to the paramount concern confronting the EU citizenry. That concern is the one that divides the Union into Europhiles who want 'more Europe' and Euroskepticks who want 'less Europe' and even the reversion of some EU powers to the member-states (Kumm 2008:134). Under these circumstances, Europhiles who seek the adoption of an EU constitution do it, strictly speaking, for political reasons – a stronger, more integrated and more unified EU would be in the public good – and not predominantly out of devotion to constitutional rule at the transnational level as such. In short, Europhiles are much more likely to be EU patriots than constitutional patriots.

8.3.2 Constitutional Patriotism in a Layered and a Segmented Transnational Legal Order?

Leaving aside whether constitutional patriotism continues to be relevant for certain nation-states beyond Germany, notwithstanding the above critique, there may be room for adapting the concept for use in a layered and segmented plural transnational legal order. More precisely, within such a legal order one can conceive of something that bears some affinity to constitutional patriotism playing an important positive role. That 'something,' however should more accurately be broken down, as will be argued below, into 'human rights patriotism' coupled with 'constitutional necessity.'

There is an analogous kind of fervor and passion concerning human rights as there was regarding constitutionalism in post World War Two

West Germany. Both of these passions share the same origins, being propelled as reactions against the Holocaust. West Germany reacted at the level of the nation-state and what can be called the 'universal human rights movement' spearheaded by the 1948 Declaration, at the level of humanity as a whole, transcending all political regimes and all national boundaries. The Holocaust was perpetrated by some humans again other humans while yet other humans – e.g., the U.S. and the UK – refrained from intervening directly to put a prompt end to the systematic annihilation (Wyman 2007). The human rights movement has mounted an intense and passionate worldwide initiative fueled by a fervent commitment, reminiscent of profound religious devotion, to the promotion and protection of human dignity. The human rights movement is diverse in its multiple institutional, social and political arenas, but its passion for human dignity and for the extension of human rights protection to every human creature who inhabits the earth is certainly reminiscent in its intensity of the passions characteristic of a loyal patriot who closely identifies with the destiny of his nation.

The human rights movement is indeed diverse and it does share a common passion, but with varying degrees of intensity. Some human rights activists make the fight for human rights their paramount life project, enduring many sacrifices, and some are even willing to assume martyrdom for the cause. Human rights NGOs also make the spread and protection of human rights their *raison d'être*, even if the intensity of commitment of an institutional actor is of a different kind than that of an individual champion of the cause. Those who institutionalize human rights, through international conventions, those who monitor them, or those who interpret them and apply them, such as judges on human rights courts, may all experience and act on their loyalty for the human rights movement differently. Nevertheless, whatever their differences, they all partake in the same essential loyalty and committed engagement that makes them 'human rights patriots.'

These last observations are by no means diminished by the politicization of human rights or by divisions over their true meaning or correct interpretation. The fact that human rights have been politicized, and even at times politicized cynically for pure political advantage, seems no different than the deliberate exploitation of genuine patriotic sentiments for purely partisan political power purposes. Indeed, properly focused and channeled, patriotic sentiments serve to consolidate and to motivate the collective self framed by national identity toward worthwhile purposes, such as the peaceful advance of the collective project of a community that shares a common history, culture, etc. The fact that manipulation of loyalties can be used to subvert a potentially enriching common project is a genuine danger that one must endeavor to fight against, but it does not discredit patriotism or loyalty to one's community as such (Soltan 2008). This is particularly true since, as stressed throughout the present analysis, particular identities cannot be simply supplanted by more abstract and more universal ones. Similarly, the fact that the emotions surrounding human rights can be exploited to pernicious ends does not diminish the need to continue the fight for human rights or to be able to draw on the positive passions that give such fight a crucial impulse.

Divisions over the true nature and meaning of human rights, such as that over Asian values discussed above,[24] also do not weaken the case for human rights patriotism. Leaving aside any cynical use of such divisions, they seem much more about particulars than about passion or loyalty regarding the fight for human rights. Indeed, one can advance an argument based on Asian values for greater emphasis on communal rights than on certain individual rights without being any less militant in the fight to establish and protect human dignity for everyone. People can disagree on whether human dignity requires greater protection of communal rights or liberal individual rights, or, for that matter, whether it requires greater emphasis on economic or social rights or on civil and political rights. Similarly, patriotism to the same nation is compatible with plural and even conflicting convictions in regard to certain particulars. Some may feel it patriotic to support their country going to war while other may deem it patriotic, under the same circumstances, to resist the impulse to go to war. What makes proponents of these two conflicting courses of action all patriots is their equal commitment to working for their nation's public good. A similar interplay of convergences and divergences may operate with respect to international human rights. Neither proponents of Asian values nor their liberal Western counterparts are likely to diverge concerning preventing or fighting against genocide or torture all while they diverge concerning the contours of the precise rights regime needed to boost human dignity.

If the human rights movement is plural in its conception, so too it is in its deployment, and that is because it must operate in a legally pluralistic universe. As described in 8.1 above, the contemporary era is a legally pluralistic one, and as indicated in 8.2 above, working human rights legal regimes, such as that of ECHR, are segmented ones giving rise to a special purpose legal self. Accordingly, putting human rights into operation differs significantly from doing the same with respect to a constitution in the context of a nation-state. And this is particularly true in relation to building of an appropriate identity. In other words, the human rights subject encounters different opportunities and obstacles in its quest to develop an identity in a legally pluralistic universe than does the constitutional subject aiming for the same in the unified and consolidated legal universe of the nation-state.

The segmentation and layering of the contemporary plural legal universe place the human rights subject and its movement in a highly compartmentalized arena. That arena combines areas of great concentration where the human rights subject is dominant, even all-encompassing, and remote areas where the human rights subject has at best a diffuse, indirect effect. The human rights movement in its capacity as a legal actor carves out an area in which the human rights subject is all-encompassing, but in which its capacity to build a positive identity is limited. Such capacity is largely confined to drawing the positive content of human rights in its most general, abstract outlines and to fill in certain details at the most particular level, depending on the actual legal battles of the moment. For example, while engaged in having a certain specific form of treatment of prisoners adjudged to amount to torture, the human rights movement elaborates a handful of details concerning the particulars entailed by the protection of human dignity. What remains indeterminate, in this context, is the filling of most particulars and the articulation of links between the most abstract and the most concrete levels of human rights identity. Moreover, given internal segmentation within the human rights movement itself – e.g., regional conventions and charters, special subject international conventions, such as CEDAW dealing with the rights of women – there is great fragmentation in the construction of an human rights agenda even in the legal space where the human rights subject is all-encompassing. (This is not to imply that the different legal orders, segments and layers are closed to one another. Quite to the contrary, as demonstrated in 8.2 above in relation to the ECHR, there is significant openness and communication among the different legal orders at play. The point is rather to underscore that although borrowing, adjusting and reconfiguring among legal orders can be, and is, done, the actual content of the positive identity produced depends *both* on the input *within* each order involved and on the reprocessing of that input *among* all these orders).

Regional human rights charters and conventions and their implementation allow for further elaboration of the human rights subject's identity at levels of abstraction below those associated with the legal actors who approach the subject from a worldwide perspective. Indeed, as exemplified by the implementation of the ECHR, the ECtHR must carve out an European human rights identity by securing an adequate degree of convergence among all the nation-states involved without unduly suppressing differences. There is, moreover, in Europe a convergence between (European) human rights, and that convergence is one that encompasses similarities as well as differences across the European legal-constitutional landscape. The judges on the ECtHR can endeavor to promote such overall convergence through proper use of the margin of appreciation standards. In addition, these judges are bound to draw upon their country's own constitutional tradition and identity to resolve concrete cases under the ECHR,[25] and constitutional judges in ECHR member states have every incentive to look to and, where possible, conform to ECtHR decisions when deciding under their own country's constitution.[26]

Not only is there mutual influence between human and constitutional rights in Europe with significant areas of convergence and overlap between them, but also European human rights can be further specified and evaluated by references to other sources of identity, both vertical and horizontal. Thus, European standards should be assessed in terms of the international standards described above, under a margin of appreciation criterion equivalent to the one in force under the ECHR. Similarly, European standards should be evaluated in comparison with other regional human rights regimes, such as the inter-American or the African.[27]

Combining vertical and horizontal analysis and comparison can be very valuable in determining the legitimate content and boundaries of human rights. The Arab Charter of Human Rights, for example, enshrines women's equality rights that must remain consistent with the prescriptions of Shariah law.[28] Many of these prescriptions are clearly inconsistent with Western liberal standards of equality between the sexes. Does that mean that the Arab Charter, in spite of its *bona fides* as a human rights instrument fails, in part, because it falls outside the permissible bounds of human rights identity? Or do the Arab Charter's provisions on the equality of women fall within an acceptable margin of appreciation? Whatever the answer to these questions, they must be determined in relation to a complex dynamic construction of human rights identity based on an interplay between multiple vertical and horizontal relationships.

So far we have focused on the segment of the contemporary and legal universe in which the human rights subject and the determination of human rights identity are paramount. We have found this segment to be internally pluralistic and fragmented. We have also found, through the example of the interpenetration between the ECHR and the constitutions of the countries coming within the ECHR's sweep that a segmentary legal regime such as that carved out by the human rights movement interacts with other layered and segmented legal regimes with which it intersects.

Moreover, these intersections have identitarian consequences flowing in both directions.

By shifting the focus to the legal regimes on which the human rights regime impacts, we can shed further light on yet many more facets and phases of the identity building process unleashed by the juridification of human rights. First, as revealed in the case of the ECHR, human rights law has both direct and indirect effects with significant identitarian consequences, on the legal regime framed by the nation-state's constitution. Human rights both impact, and are impacted by, that latter regime, with an effect on the constitutional identity linked to that regime. As a result of this mutual impact, the nation-state regime can contribute to greater differentiation within human rights identity. And, at the same time the influence of human rights law can lead to greater convergence among the respective constitutional identities operating in the various countries affected. Moreover, this two way shaping can extend beyond the constitutional realm. For example, a country's labor law may be indirectly affected by the human rights legal regime. Thus, such a labor law may be drafted so as to avoid vulnerability under human rights standards regarding child labor. Also, if the precise contours of such standards have not yet been drawn, the national labor law in question may seek to, and even succeed in, contributing to the establishment of boundaries and in the setting of acceptable limits to the relevant margin of appreciation.

Second, human rights law has a similar impact across many other layered and segmented legal regimes going beyond the nation-state. Thus, the ECHR has an impact on the EU (though the EU is not a signatory to the ECHR) which can create convergences and divergences among the ECHR legal regime, the EU one and the nation-state constitutions (Garlicki 2008). Furthermore, human rights law can have a direct or indirect impact on both private and public, layered and segmented, legal regimes ranging from international law to *lex mercatoria* or private regulation of the internet. In the case of a private segmented legal regime, the relation to human rights law may not be obligatory, but may well be embraced voluntarily to pre-empt public interference with that segmented regime's autonomy in order to secure minimum compliance with human rights standards. To be sure, the more a segment or layer is remote from the central concerns of the human rights regime, the less likely will significant interaction be, and the more indirect and dispersed its impact. Nevertheless, even in such remote cases, it is quite possible for there to be two way interaction with perceptible identitarian consequences.

In sum, construction of the positive identity of human rights as law is a cumulative ongoing process that progresses piecemeal from a number of

different sources, including constitutional rights and constitutional identity, and that, in turn, influences the further development and elaboration
of the latter. As human and constitutional rights converge, the seeds of
transnational constitutionalism emerge concurrently with the particularization and pluralization of human rights. As noted, in neither case is
the process of identity formation purely a top down or bottom up one,
though they both contain elements of each. Overall, human rights and
transnational constitutional rights identity formation in a layered and
segmented legally pluralistic universe involves complex intertwinings of
vertical and horizontal determinants. All this is propelled to a large extent
by human rights patriotism and, in as much as human and constitutional
rights converge and overlap, arguably a limited and interstitial form of
constitutional patriotism is also derivatively at play.

How far and for how long will human rights patriotism extend its
current surge is hard to predict. But if the analogy to West Germany's
reliance on constitutional patriotism is on target, then human rights patriotism's run will not end before human rights become fully consolidated
and integrated throughout the world. And that, at the present writing,
seems unfortunately in some far off future. Also, to what degree human
rights patriotism will serve to integrate and reconcile the human rights and
constitutional rights regimes ranging from the most local to the most
global levels of legal regulation, remains largely a matter of conjecture.
What seems clear, though, is that human rights patriotism still has great
potential in both national and transnational arenas.

What complements human rights patriotism in the ordering of a multilayered and segmented legally pluralistic universe is the universalization
of 'constitutional necessity.' For a legally pluralistic order to function
adequately, each unit within that order must have a sustainable and stable
internal mode of organization. Moreover, to the extent that different units
interact on a regular basis, they require a legal framework that provides
regular procedures and that makes for the stabilization of expectations. For
both pragmatic and ideological reasons, the fundamental elements of a
structural constitution provide the requisite framework. The structural
constitution does so pragmatically for at least two important reasons: first,
it is a proven means to institute a working hierarchy of legal norms and
unity to the entire legal system of a legal unit; and, second, legal units not
otherwise connected who must nevertheless occasionally interact seem
more likely to do so successfully, if they are both internally regulated by
a working structural constitution. On the other hand, the structural
constitution's ideological appeal stems from the pervasive legitimation of
constitutional rule throughout the contemporary world. In other words, as

constitutional rule is nearly universally acknowledged as the only legitimate means of government in nation-states, it stands to reason that it should be widely regarded as being similarly valid and desirable beyond the confines of the nation-state.

A structural constitution can thus be regarded as a necessity at all levels, and for all layers and segments, of the contemporary legally pluralistic universe. Structural constitutions are actually operative within all types of existing legal units, including private legal networks (Hamann and Ruiz-Fabri 2008). Moreover, structural constitutions must be, and can be, elaborated and perfected for a multilayered legal order to function adequately. Thus, even though there is no constitutional hierarchy or unity in the EU comparable to those prevalent in constitutionally ruled nation-states, a combination of EU treaty provisions, EU laws, regulations, and ECJ decisions do provide the EU with a working structural constitution (Rosenfeld 2006). That structural constitution apportions powers between the EU and the member states, and functions fairly well notwithstanding the lack of a comprehensive multilayered hierarchy or unity as made manifest by the *Solange I* decision.

The structural constitution which has emerged at all levels, and among levels, of the contemporary legally pluralistic universe does allow for convergence and congruity, but it by no means resolves all conflicts. This is made plain by the previously mentioned example of the inconsistencies and conflicts caused within the EU by operation of WTO regulation.[29] Moreover, the identity of the structural constitution as a necessity in a legally pluralistic universe is both thin and shallow. The structural constitution within a nation-state or a particular segment or layer can be thick and deep and it is likely to fit part and parcel within the overall constitutional identity of the corresponding all-purpose or limited-purpose constitutional subject. Whether a constitution embraces a parliamentary form or government or a presidential one, and what kind of parliamentary or presidential regime is involved, are issues that are inextricably tied to the kind of constitutional identity that is prevalent in the relevant polity. In contrast, constitutional necessity and the structural constitution that it *requires* (as opposed to the structural constitutions that it is *compatible* with) is any plausible one that may guarantee the requisite hierarchy and unity within the relevant legal unit. Constitutional necessity *itself*, therefore, only requires a confluence and convergence of structural constitutions at the highest levels of generality – each unit must have a structural constitution to function properly and to be able to interact in a coherent manner with others – leaving the particulars to each unit to develop for itself. Moreover, congruence at the highest levels of abstraction opens the door to harmonization, but does not itself produce it. In other words, the identity that issues from the recognition of constitutional necessity is too thin and shallow to suggest or favor actual paths of harmonization among existing and available models of the structural constitution. Needless to say, under these conditions there are no grounds for the emergence of any kind of 'constitutional necessity patriotism.'

Constitutional necessity and human rights patriotism do create opportunities for convergence that may provide a workable foundation for a viable transnational constitutional subject with a potentially coherent corresponding constitutional identity. What is lacking thus far, however, is an account of how the structural elements yielded by constitutional necessity may be combined with the content-based elements thus far generated by human rights patriotism to yield a viable and coherent supra national constitutional subject with a full-fledged working corresponding constitutional identity. Because the structural requirements flowing from constitutional necessity are so thin and shallow, they provide neither sufficient incentives for harmonization nor sufficient directives for how to undertake it successfully. On the other hand, human rights patriotism does produce content-based norms that are both thick and deeply rooted. These norms, however, are at once meant to be congruent and convergent as deriving from universal principles and actually plural and diverse in their concrete incarnations. What seems to be lacking with respect to these norms, therefore, is a cogent way to reconcile the universal and the particular, the singular and the plural. In the following concluding section, I will address how this may be done based on the insights garnered throughout the analysis of the traditional nation-state based constitutional subject.

8.4 Concluding Remarks: Reaching for the Transnational Constitutional Subject by Reconciling the Universal and the Singular Through the Plural

What clearly emerges from the preceding inquiry is that transnational and global legal regimes share with constitutional ones fitted to the nation-state commitment to the three essential components of constitutionalism: limitation of powers; adherence to the rule of law; and protection of fundamental rights. In the multilayered and segmented legally pluralistic universe, it is, as we have seen, in the interest of each legal unit to adopt a structural constitution for both internal (self-organization) and external (interaction with other units) reasons. Furthermore, any legal unit that bears any relation to, or has any effect on, fundamental (human) rights – and it is very difficult to think of legal units that bear strictly no relationship to such rights – must either internally afford protection to, or conform to externally imposed protection of, such rights. Finally, there seems to be a global convergence towards embracing the rule of law or, at least, rule through law. Indeed, even if certain active participants on the global scene, such as multinational corporations, may prefer to avoid all governmental and international public organizations' regulation, they are nevertheless firmly committed to submission of all interactions in their own segmented areas of interest to a legal regime. Otherwise, businesses dealing with other businesses would lack protection and stabilization of expectations, which only a system of legal rules with enforcement mechanisms, such as institutionalized private arbitration, can provide.

Both the transnational constitutional subject and the national one must construct an identity in a pluralistic environment, and do so under conditions that are overall similar. In both cases, identity is not given but must be built, and the tools of construction are the same: negation and reworking of available materials. On the other hand, the principal difference noted above between the two subjects is that the transnational one seems bound to confront a much greater plurality and diversity than the national one. This makes the transnational subject's task of harmonizing convergences and divergences a much more daunting one. Specifically, the national constitutional subject has a palpable national identity to work *with* and *against* whereas global and transnational identities, such as they are, appear completely schematic and pallid in comparison. Moreover, the traditional national constitutional subject has a solid basis for unity in spite of having to confront plurality and diversity because it is inextricably linked to a distinct nation within a unified state. In contrast, the transnational constitutional subject is neither symbiotically attached to any particular single nation nor embedded within any unified state or statelike structure. Far from it, merely to exist or survive, the transnational constitutional self must not lose its sense of selfhood due to fragmentation into the multitude of legally and constitutionally bounded segments and layers in which it must simultaneously dwell. Accordingly, as already stressed, transnational constitutional identity cannot essentially amount to a kind of national constitutional identity drawn on a larger scale.

Whereas the just evoked differences between the national and the transnational constitutional subject remain considerable, the gap between them is in the process of shrinking at a fairly rapid pace. As evinced by the analysis of contemporary citizenship in Chapter 7, and of human rights and legal pluralism in this chapter, the contemporary nation-state is becoming increasingly pluralistic and prone to greater internal divergences. At the same time, a trend toward greater convergences is manifestly afoot in the transnational and global spheres regulated by law. Whether it be global trade under WTO regulation or transnational legally segmented or layered units coming under the sway of the human rights movement, points of convergence among transnational legal actors are on the increase.

From an identitarian standpoint, these combined trends that narrow the gap between the national and the transnational legal-constitutional arenas pose opposite problems for each of the aforementioned arenas. On the national level, the unity of the traditional constitutional subject and unified vision projected by its prevailing constitutional identity tend to stand as obstacles to the acceptance of greater diversity and of a higher degree of internal divergence, therefore thwarting pluralism of its full potential consistent with constitutionalism. On the transnational level, in contrast, the lack of a unified constitutional identity make it difficult to tap increasing convergences for purposes of achieving greater harmonization among the plurality of operative legal spheres.

Consistent with these last remarks, to optimize the potential of the constitutional subject and to enable it to craft the most suitable constitutional identity would require priming paths of convergence at the transnational level while at the same time making room for greater divergence (without compromising the unity of the whole) at the national level. Systematic use of certain legal tools, such as the margin of appreciation standard, can help promote this objective. Indeed, as exemplified in *Handyside*, by allowing the UK and Scandinavian countries to diverge in their conception of indecency, the margin of appreciation makes it easier for all the countries involved to rally around the ECHR freedom of expression provision and to internalize its core normative thrust. Other existing constitutional tools, both structural ones, such as federalism, and legislative and judicial standards, such as the principle of subsidiarity,[30] allow, in turn, for greater internal diversification. Thus, in a multi-ethnic state in which the different ethnic groups are all geographically concentrated, federalism permits greater divergences at the federated units level without sacrificing essential unity at the federal level. Furthermore, certain constitutional standards, such as the widely judicially used proportionality standard, can serve to foster at once greater intercommunal convergence and intracommunal divergence. By submitting all legal regulation to a test of 'fit' between means and ends and to a balancing of the conflicting interests at stake, the proportionality standard at once promotes a uniform measure of constitutionality among all constitutionally framed legal systems (Beatty 2004:159–188) and allows for differences to be granted substantial constitutional accommodation. Such accommodation is achieved by taking each relevant difference into account for purposes of balancing the conflicting interests at play, and by granting each such difference its proportionate weight in the actual balancing. Thus, for example, concerning the constitutionality of abortion, Ireland's deep religious objections to abortion firmly engraved on the nation's conscience would factor quite differently than Japan's apparent lack of major normative concern on the issue (*Id.*:168).

Whereas deployment of the above discussed legal tools can certainly play a constructive role, it is by no means sufficient to generate a workable constitutional identity for a legally pluralistic universe that is becoming at the same time more interrelated and more fragmented. Two major challenges must be addressed before being in a position to determine whether the kind of workable constitutional identity in question is possible and, if possible, what its main features might be.

The first challenge is to determine what kind of convergence might be suitable for an increasingly interrelated and fragmented universe. The second challenge is to ascertain whether there may be a satisfactory workable criterion for purposes of establishing legitimate bounds in relation to the interplay between convergences and divergences. For example, can principled limits be set regarding the legitimate scope of the margin of appreciation?

A suitable kind of convergence would be one tailored to the constitutional subject likely to emerge in the new transnational order. That subject is a complex one that plays different roles in a large number of legal and sociopolitical communities. Thus, the transnational constitutional subject can be analogized to a contemporary person who is a citizen in her polity and who partakes in many of the spheres of action comprised within that polity, such as the German Catholic feminist woman referred to above. The obvious difference between the transnational constitutional subject and a contemporary citizen with various intersecting interests and commitments is that whereas the latter is likely to become involved in a limited number of different spheres, the former is bound to remain active in a very large number of spheres. This difference, moreover, makes it a much more daunting challenge for a transnational constitutional subject to successfully negotiate and integrate all the intracommunal and intercommunal dealings with which it is confronted.

One way to deal with all this complexity is through use of the distinction already alluded to between an all-purpose self and a limited or special-purpose self. What constitutes an all-purpose as opposed to a limited-purpose self is above all a relational issue involving the self-perception, self-understanding and notion of selfhood of the subject involved. In the case of an individual, it is highly likely that individual personhood is constructed as the locus of the all-purpose self. On the other hand, spheres of interaction such as the Catholic or feminist communities to which an individual may belong would most likely be perceived as providing a basis for a limited-purpose intracommunal self-identity.[31] In other words, an individual person's sense of selfhood is given unity by reference to the individual 'me', but also derives its identity in part from belonging to the Catholic community, the feminist community, etc. Moreover, since the distinction is a relational one, a Catholic feminist's feminism may figure as limited-purpose self within her Catholic community and her Catholicism as a limited-purpose self in her feminist community.

In the traditional constitutionally ruled nation-state the nation emerges as an all-purpose subject and so does, in its domain, the constitutional subject as reflected in its constitutional identity.[32] Even in a Federal republic, where different identities may obtain at the Federal and Federated entities levels, there is an overall constitutional subject and identity that provides the requisite unity and hierarchy to the entire Federal edifice, and that projects itself as an all-purpose self.[33] In contrast, no all-purpose constitutional self *akin to* that prevalent in nation-states appears at present possible on a transnational scale. Even what is now the EU, which originated as a limited-purpose coal and steel supra-national project and which now may from within seek to project the image of an all-purpose constitutional subject, cannot consistently sustain such an image. Indeed, so long as EU member-states can resist EU constitutional unity and hierarchy, and so long as the EU cannot impose its constitutional order on recalcitrant member-states, the EU cannot successfully live up to its aspirations as an all-purpose constitutional subject.

The more compartmentalized the life of the self becomes, be it that of an individual person living in a complex pluralistic society, that of a nation-state ever more entangled with supra and extranational spheres and actors, or that of a supranational legal order, the more difficult it becomes to integrate coherently all facets of that self's search for self-realization and self-fulfillment. Under such circumstances, two types of convergence play a major role: intracommunal convergences and intercommunal ones. Although all relevant actors, whether operating on a small or large scene, are affected by both, at the transnational constitutional level, finding appropriate intercommunal paths of convergence proves much more problematic. This inevitably leads to conflicts that can ordinarily be handled within the context of the traditional nation-state constitutional order, but which cannot be similarly authoritatively be dealt with at the transnational level.

There are two principal ways to cope with such conflicts when one cannot resolve or avoid them: either to relativize them or to learn to live with a fair, yet tolerable, degree of dissonance. Relativization goes hand-in-hand with segmentation, and segmentation facilitates reduction, diversion and diffusion of conflict. Thus, for example, a French citizen may feel alienated from the EU concerning a dispute between the latter and France, and yet, at the same time identify with the EU concerning economic competition between the latter and the U.S. In this example, conflict is minimized and contradiction avoided by making each of the identifications involved context specific. In some cases, however, contradictions cannot be avoided. As already mentioned, if Catholicism and feminism are to some significant extent mutually contradictory, then a Catholic feminist must live with the contradiction and be able to tolerate dissonance. But that would only be possible up to the point where living the contradiction becomes unbearable as it threatens to tear one's sense of selfhood apart. In short, in a complex compartmentalized setting, a self may adequately cope with unavoidable conflicts and contradictions provided the latter can either be relativized or experienced as inconsistent or dissonant, but not as downright incompatible.

From the standpoint of constitutional ordering, the kinds of convergence that would best suit relativization and living with inconsistency that falls short of incompatibility are twofold. First, relativization can be boosted through deployment of thin and shallow bonds of convergence which are best suited for linking constitutional domains with a limited-purpose constitutional subject. Thus, for example, as we have seen, the structural constitution provides a functionally essential highly abstract point of intercommunal convergence that could plausibly operate across all segments and layers of a legal pluralist order that would extend throughout the globe. Second, accommodation of dissonance and inconsistency short of incompatibility is particularly important in constitutional domains with an all-purpose constitutional subject or, like in the case of the EU, with a limited-purpose subject that approximates an all-purpose one. The kind of bonds of convergence that would be most suitable in this context would be thick and deep ones. Indeed, paradoxically, communities that are bound together by thick and deeply rooted commonly shared norms are often best equipped to cope with dissonances and inconsistencies.

This second kind of convergence, which relies on thicker and deeper bonds, must be ultimately grounded on shared substantive norms. Moreover, the norms that are best suited to promote at once greater room for divergence within the nation-state and increased points of convergence in the transnational areas are those that derive from the ethos of pluralism.

In a legally and ideologically pluralistic world, a pluralist ethics prescribes the greatest possible accommodation of difference and divergence consistent with maintenance of the necessary conditions for pluralism to remain functional and viable (Rosenfeld 1998:199–233). Unlike relativism, normative pluralism does not hold to the view that the ethos of a particular community cannot be legitimately or systematically normatively assessed or condemned by those who are outside that community and who do not share its ethos. Indeed, normative pluralism promotes a bounded plurality of divergent ideologies and ways of life which must not impede the realization of the pluralist ethos. In other words, pluralism depends on legitimation of non-pluralist ideologies for its survival for if everyone were a pluralist, there would be no need for a pluralist ethics as it would be useless to make room for divergence where none existed. But, on the other hand, if pluralism indiscriminately legitimated all non-pluralist ideologies, it would jeopardize its own survival. This gives rise to a 'paradox of pluralism' that is analogous to what Karl Popper called the 'paradox of tolerance' (Popper 1965:265, n.4). According to Popper, tolerance of the intolerant can lead to a takeover by the latter with a consequent abolition of tolerance. Similarly, accommodation of those ideologies that actively promote the destruction of pluralism may eventually foster conditions that render the survival of pluralism impossible.

To overcome the threat posed by the paradox of pluralism, normative pluralism must set limits to plurality as such. It is obvious that a political ideology prescribing the destruction of all those who do not share its views cannot be given room to operate freely within a polity that seeks to live up to the ideals of normative pluralism. Accordingly, the pluralist ethos must depend on a dialectic between, on the one hand, a fixed non-negotiable set of norms designed to safeguard the essential foundations necessary to sustain a pluralist way of life, and, on the other hand, openness and acceptance of a large range of different ideologies, including – and this is crucial as suggested above – non-pluralist and anti-pluralist ones.

Which ideologies ought to be accommodated and to what extent under the pluralist ethos is ultimately a contextual issue. Thus, in a polity in which the entire population is divided among Catholics and Protestants, it would be senseless to worry about devising institutions suited to the particular needs of Jews and Muslims. But regardless of the particular context involved, the pluralist ethos requires extending inclusion to all ideologies within a relevant polity that are *inconsistent* but *not incompatible* with normative pluralism's fixed non-negotiable set of norms.

Placing normative pluralism within the ambit of constitutionalism, human liberty and equality originating in the 1789 Declaration and human dignity enshrined in the 1948 Declaration emerge as the backbone of the fixed non-negotiable norms against which compatibility must be assessed. As we have seen, there are, to use Dworkin's characterization, different conceptions of these key concepts, but the range of permissible legitimate interpretations of the concepts in question is clearly bounded. Human dignity may be given a more individualistic or more communal gloss, for example, but it cannot be stretched to encompass a status of quasi-servitude. In other words, the permissible conceptions of the key pluralist normative concepts are confined, but within the proper bounds, there is room for diversity and some measure of divergence. This allows human rights and fundamental constitutional rights to become thickly and deeply embedded in particular constitutional cultures while at the same time providing for thicker and deeper bonds at the transnational level as exemplified by the worldwide deployment of the human rights movement.

Furthermore, because of the dialectical relationship between pluralism' fixed norms and the great variety of norms associated with the various ideologies at play in the relevant legal universe, the pluralist ethos is particularly well suited to promote greater convergence at the transnational level while encouraging increased diversity at the level of the nation-state. The concepts, such as dignity, liberty and equality, which are embedded in pluralism's fixed norms, provide nodes of convergence at the transnational level. Moreover, consistent with the above discussion of the margin of appreciation, the plural conceptions of the concepts in question that are consistent with the pluralist ethos allow for putting flesh and bones on abstract concepts. And that, in turn, makes it possible for these concepts and for the pluralist ethos to which they are tied to generate thicker and deeper bonds among persons who do not share the same national identity and the same nation-state based constitutional identity. On the other hand, integrating the pluralist ethos into the constitutional order carved out by the nation-state will facilitate acceptance of greater diversity, by providing effective tools to challenge the constitutional status quo and the settled limitations built in the prevailing nation-state's constitutional identity. Thus, if current exclusions of certain ways of life or of self-realization or self-fulfillment can be shown to contravene a conception of dignity consistent with the pluralist ethos, then these exclusions ought to be declared unconstitutional. Accordingly, a pluralist constitution within a nation-state would pave the way for as much diversity and divergence as would be consistent with maintenance of the pluralist ethos.

The pluralist ethos also provides the means to meet the second challenge referred to above, finding a satisfactory, workable criterion for purposes of setting the legitimate bounds regarding the interplay between convergences and divergences. Either insisting on conformity with, or granting official acceptance to, divergent practices that would contravene any legitimate conception of liberty, equality or dignity would thus be incompatible with constitutionalism as framed by the pluralist ethos. Again, though, issues of compatibility with the latter kind of constitutionalism would be open to debate, and all those involved should be entitled to voice their position, in the end, there would always be cogently defensible bounds to demarcate the constitutionally permissible from the impermissible. For example, whether the Arab Charter of Human Right's conception of equality for women as having to be in conformity with the prescriptions of the Sharia would be compatible with the pluralist ethos would depend on several factors. These would include the particular interpretation given to the Sharia and the self-understanding and projects of self-realization and self-fulfillment of women in the relevant polity. But it would be beyond question in certain cases and under certain interpretations of the Sharia, such as those that prevail in Saudi Arabia where women are subjected to lifelong male guardianship, that the link between the Sharia and women's equality rights would be plainly incompatible with the pluralist ethos.

Imagining the transnational constitutional subject and its identity from a pluralist vantage point suggests the ways in which that subject might weave together the universal, the particular, the singular and the plural. This work is done by piecemeal construction through use of the same tools that figure in the construction of a traditional nation-state constitutional identity. For what is imagined as universal (whether it is or not, which is a metaphysical question) to have an impact on constitutional ordering, it must be particularized, and particulars differ from one constitutional setting to the next. What pluralism makes room for is a range of possible universalizations of the particular and of particularizations of the universal. This allows for greater diversity and increased opportunities for constitutional convergence as evinced by the discussion concerning the margin of appreciation.

On the other hand, pluralism fosters an inextricable dialectic between the singular and the plural. That dialectic operates at many levels and cobbles together a complex network of relationships between intracommunal and intercommunal settings. As we have seen, in the contemporary arena, the individual person, the increasingly diverse nation-state and transnational orders all construct a self and develop a sense of selfhood based on a plurality of interests, pursuits and commitments. Accordingly, the contemporary self's singularity is truly plural: it represents a singular way in which to handle inevitable plurality. At the same time, the proliferation of pluralities allows for ever more complex and finely tuned determinations of singularity as the self encounters more opportunities and more nuanced alternatives for self-definition, self-realization and self-fulfillment. Moreover, segmentations and layering of the legally plural-istic order potentially affords a wider and more encompassing array of opportunities for the mutual enrichment of the singular and the plural.

In conclusion, there are plausible paths to transnational constitutional-ism and means for the construction of a transnational constitutional identity. But will transnational constitutions actually come into being and thrive? And what will they be like? So far, nothing suggests anything like the American constitutional identity firmly grounded in freedom, or the German, on dignity, or the Canadian, on multicultural accommodation. As already indicated, it is unlikely that transnational constitutionalism will replicate its traditional nation-state counterparts. What is actually more likely, if current trends continue, is that the constitutional subject and constitutional identity will evolve into yet undiscovered combinations at both the national and the transnational levels.

Will there ever be the kind of unity – be it imagined and under constant construction – at the transnational level as has been achieved at the national one? The most that can be said at this moment is that unity with respect to certain particular areas is certainly foreseeable, and may even already be in play. Is international consensus over human rights, in spite of differences in conception, akin to consensus over the bill of rights in a nation-state? Arguably, yes, as national constitutional identities tend to be elastic enough to encompass certain variations in the conception of fundamental constitutional rights as made clear by the discussion in Chapter 3 of the dispute between exceptionalists and universalists working within the bounds of American constitutional identity. Be that as it may, even clearer cases seem entirely plausible. For example, if the threat to the earth's environment becomes so severe that human survival becomes imminently at stake, the global community would face a stark choice between strict worldwide regulation or warfare over scarce and dwindling environmental resources. Under these circumstances, it seems quite plaus-ible, and much preferable, that there would be global constitutionalization of environmental regulation with little room for margins of appreciation.

On the other hand, unification of all areas at all levels seems both unlikely and, based on current insights, undesirable. Thus, for example, segmented regulation of global trade seems highly preferable. This is both because of the likelihood of much greater convergence on this subject than on any much broader number of subjects and because compartmentaliza-tion allows for greater relativization and diffusion of conflicts. Indeed, diverging religious ideologies may either be relatively indifferent to issues relating to trade – as contrasted to issues relating to personal relations such as marriage or divorce – or may face limited and confined conflicts stemming from global trade regulation. Such regulation may thus cause either minor religious conflict, or even if it did cause a major conflict for a particular religion, it could well only affect but a limited number of that religion's essential prescriptions.

Modern constitutionalism is over two hundred years old, and it has spread immensely since the second half of the last century. At the same time, a constitutionalism that fully conforms to the pluralist ethos remains an ideal that may be further approximated but appears impossible to ever fully achieve. The traditional nation-state constitutional subject and its constitutional identity may rest on firm grounds, but confront major challenges due to the need for greater transnational coordination and cooperation and to the call for greater diversity within the traditionally delimited democratic polity. Transnational or global constitutionalism and a transnational constitutional subject with its own plural yet, at the same time, singular identity are possible but by no means certain. In the face of all this, constitutionalism and the legacy of the Enlightenment, to which it is inextricably tied, confront several serious threats. Globalization may yield to rule based on military and economic might rather than to a worldwide spread of constitutionalism. Balkanization can degenerate into blind ethnic conflict and to a clash of intransigent anti-pluralist ideologies. To this, must be added the threat of global terrorism with increasingly sophisticated and lethal weapons at its disposal which has led some of the most firmly established constitutional democracies to react by pulling back on some of the most basic constitutional guarantees. And, last, but by no means least, is the expanding politicization of fundamentalist religion with its often virulent anti-pluralist and, at least indirectly, anti-constitutionalist agenda.

The constitutional subject and its identity may be more fragile than would initially appear. Their trajectory and future potential confront manifold obstacles and complexities and require painstaking and belabored deployment on many distinct fronts. They remain, however, the best hope for the legacy of the Enlightenment to endure. And to live up to that hope, the constitutional subject must seek to reconcile self and other in accordance with the precepts of the pluralist ethos. In short, the constitutional subject can and, at best, will combine what we share in common and what separates us to make room for us to coexist peacefully in our plural ways in an atmosphere of equal dignity and mutual respect.

Notes

Introduction

1 *See* Elaine Sciolino, *French Voters Soundly Reject European Pact*, N.Y. Times, May 30, 2005, at A1.; Marlise Simons, *Dutch Voters Solidly Reject European Pact*, N.Y. Times June 2, 2005, at A10.

2 *See* Henry Giniger, *Quebec Tries to Override Part of Constitution*, N.Y. Times, May 8, 1982, at 17.

3 *See, e.g.*, Neela Banerjee, *Families Challenging Religious Influence in Delaware Schools*, New York Times, July 29, 2006 (describing an overwhelmingly Christian community's refusal to desist praying and referring to Jesus Christ in public schools in defiance of constitutional ban and of objections by parents of non-Christian students).

4 *Classroom Crucifix Case*, 93 BVerFGE 1 (1995); *Bavaria Schools to Keep Crucifixes Despite Ruling*, N.Y. Times, Sept. 8 1995, at 10.

5 Strictly speaking, a 'religious fundamentalist' is one who interprets religious texts and precepts *literally*. For present purposes, however, I will use the term 'fundamentalist' in a political rather than religious sense. Accordingly, I will deem fundamentalist anyone who maintains that the state and its policies must conform to religious dictates or precepts (whether those are taken literally or not) as opposed to what an Enlightenment-based constitution or democratic decision-making process calls for.

6 See, e.g., Andy Newman, *Couple Plead Guilty to Aiding Man Who Killed Abortion Provider*, N.Y. Times, April 16, 2003, at D8; John Kifner, *Finding a Common Foe, Fringe Groups Join Forces*, N.Y. Times, Dec. 6, 1998, at 43.

7 *Cf. Dandridge* v. *Williams*, 397 U.S.471 (1970) (U.S. Constitution does not guarantee minimum subsistence or welfare rights).

8 'Theocracy' as used here should be understood broadly as denoting not only a polity ruled exclusively pursuant to the precepts of an organized religion, but also one subject to the dictates of sects, cults or non-theistic intransigent and non-negotiable ideologies, such as those based on beliefs of racial or ethnic supremacy, which from a political and constitutional standpoint would loom as the functional equivalent to an organized fundamentalist religion.

9 Although the universalist justification in question may seem to amount to a natural law-type justification, it need not be. Indeed, constitutionalism and constitutions may not be normatively imperative for all times or all circumstances even if they are equally compelling for everyone at this time. Accordingly, if natural law is meant to be valid for all places at all times, 'universalist' (in the sense used here) justifications of modern constitutionalism may well be cogently distinguished from natural law ones.

10 *See Holocaust Denial Case*, 90 BVerfGE 214 (2994).

11 *Compare* German Basic Law, Art. 5 (1) *to* U.S. Const. Am. I.

12 *See* German Basic Law, Art. 1.

13 *See Roper* v. *Simmons*, 543 U.S. 551 (2005); *Atkins* v. *Virginia*, 536 U.S. 304 (2002).

14 See *Lawrence v. Texas*, 539 U.S. 558 (2003); *Bowers* v. *Hardwick*, 478 U.S. 186 (1986).

15 *See Washington* v. *Glucksberg*, 521 U.S. 702 (1997).

16 See *Printz* v. *United States*, 521 U.S. 898 (1997).

17 *See Id.*, at 921, n. 11.

18 *See Lawrence, supra* (Justice Scalia rejects relevance of Western European recognition of right to intimacy among consenting homosexual adults); and *Roper, supra* (Justice Scalia refuses to be influenced by near worldwide rejection of the death penalty for juveniles).

19 *See Roper, supra.*

20 There are of course, many different possible ways of interpreting reliance on the Western European example. One interpretation is that it expresses an universalist position that has yet to be adopted by others. Another interpretation is that the Western European experience, which differs not only from that of the United States but also from that of many other parts of the world, such as Latin America and Asia, is in essence a particularistic one even if not one tailored to the particularism of a nation-state. This latter interpretation, moreover, raises the further question of whether a transnational particularism is more universalistic than a national one, or whether it is merely a different expression of particularism that is just as singular. Further discussion of these questions will be postponed pending closer exploration of the dynamic between universalism and particularism in the context of constitutionalism.

21 *Compare, e.g.*, the Constitution of Hungary, Art. 13 and the U.S. Constitution's Contract Clause, Art. I 910) Takings Clause (Am. V) and Due Process Clauses

(Amendments V and XIV), which would not collectively prevent nationalization of the U.S. economy providing fair market compensation for
expropriations.

22 *Cf.* note 4, *supra*.

1 The Constitutional Subject: Singular, Plural or Universal?

1 Lacan 1966: 517 ('I think where I am not, therefore I am where I do not
think') (my translation).

2 Although in theory Enlightenment egalitarian solidarity was meant to
include all human beings, in practice women were to a large extent left out.
See Pateman 1988.

3 For example, modern dictatorships, such as Franco's Spain, shared all the
essential attributes of a nation-state without living in conformity with the
fundamental precepts of modern constitutionalism or with the strictures of
modern constitutional rule. *See* Chapter 4, below.

4 As used here, a 'counterfactual' serves to demarcate a gap between a model
or 'reconstructed picture' and actual institutional arrangements or sets of
practices. That gap in turn, provides a space for either a critique or a vindication of the status quo. For example, the image of a pristine market economy
with evenly matched competitors, perfect information, and no transaction
costs is a counterfactual, which can either be used to critique existing markets
as supposedly self-legitimating mechanisms or to support such real life
markets because they better approximate the relevant counterfactual than any
plausible alternative. (Rosenfeld 1995: 1166).

5 For an extended comparison of social contract and legal contract, *see*
Rosenfeld 1985.

6 This characterization of the constitutional pact is consistent with Kant's
conception of the social contract as based on universal acceptance within
the polity of the dictates of reason as opposed to an actual agreement entered
after bargaining among all those who count as members of the polity. *See*
supra, at 19.

7 For example, the French Revolution involved a clash among the country's
various estates, and the ensuing constitution reflected the vision of the Third
Estate (Sieyès 1789)). But even within that latter estate, there were competing
viewpoints and interests (*Id.*).

8 'Individualistic pluralism' refers to differences in the respective interests,
'plans of life' (Rawls 1971: 92–94), or goals of various individuals. 'Communal
Pluralism,' in contrast requires a multiplicity of competing group-based
conceptions of the good. *See* Rosenfeld 1998: 201–03.

9 The terms of the contract of government differ among the various social
contract theorists. For Hobbes, the social contractors essentially trade in their
liberty for a guarantee of security from the Leviathan (Hobbes 1651:Ch. XIII).
For Locke, in contrast, the contract of government establishes a trusteeship,
and the governors can be dismissed, if necessary by means of a violent

revolution, if they abuse their powers as trustees (Locke 1690: Para. 220). For his part, Rousseau conceives the social contract as establishing the contractors at once as the governors and the governed, thus collapsing the contract of government into the contract of association – i.e., upon entering into the social contract, each individual agrees to obey the government of the newly agreed to polity as well to assume the obligation to partake in governing and implementing the general will (Rousseau 1762: I,7) For a more extended comparison of these contrasting visions, *see* Rosenfeld 1985.

10 *See infra*, at 46ff.

11 Such joint interest would be both deeper and of longer duration in the context of a contract of employment or of an exclusive continuous supply of a product needed for an ongoing manufacturing operation. In other words, there is a more substantial and more enduring joint interest in a relational contract. *See* MacNeil 1980.

12 Germany is perhaps today's most constitutionalized polity as its constitution reaches farther and deeper into its legal and political order. Contemporary Germany has evolved from its pre-Hitlerian roots as a *Rechtsstaat* (state rule through law) to a *Verfassungstaat* (state rule through the constitution), *see* Karpen 1988: 173. For a critique of Germany's 'over-constitutionalization', *see* Schlink 1994.

13 *See supra*, at 19.

14 *See, e.g.*, Elaine Sciolino, *European Charter Architect Faults Chirac for its Rejection*, N.Y. Times, June 15, 2005, at A3.

15 There is, of course, something troubling about the notion that a person who has actually refused to agree to a proposed constitution ought to have agreed to it on the basis of reason, unless one assumes that the original refusal was irrational or contrary to reason – an assumption that is both unlikely and unattractive. Rawls seemingly circumvents this problem by placing his contractors behind a veil of ignorance. Consistent with this, it may be perfectly reasonable to reject a constitution based on one's own individual interests and, at the same time, find acceptance of that same constitution to be compelled by reason once one is cut off from one's own interests and one does not know what interests he or she will have once the constitution in question becomes implemented. But Rawls's solution comes at a high price for the less a contractor knows about his situation, needs and interests, the less incentive he would have for contracting, and the more it would seem logical for him to simply follow the rule of reason. In that case the contractarian counterfactual would seem merely derivative if not highly superfluous (see Rosenfeld 1985: 858–863 drawing a distinction between 'pure' and 'derivative' social contractarian theory). For present purposes, however, this difficulty need not be discussed further as the constitutional subject cannot ultimately choose between fact and terms of agreement. Indeed, we shall see below, the constitutional subject must tackle both at the same time.

16 It is conceivable that a myth of agreement could be adapted so as to allow for

an inference that each generation could be deemed to have actually accepted for its time the constitution devised by its ancestors. But such a myth would either have to incorporate, at least implicitly, the social contractarian counter-factual in its narrative or present the myth of actual agreement as purely contingent. In the latter case, it would seem impossible to mount a persuasive argument for why future generations would or should accept the legitimacy of a constitution that was imposed on them. In other words, tradition alone or inertia do not appear sufficient to provide positive legitimation to an existing constitution. Thus, for example, mere reliance on the fact that a constitution was ratified two hundred years ago seems insufficient to generate broad based genuine commitment to it. However, if to the latter reliance is added the argument that the constitution-makers crafted a wise, useful, and fair constitution which has proven adaptable to the needs of all succeeding generations up to the present one, then that might well foster widespread support.

17 See U.S. Const. Art. I sec. 2, cl. 2 (slaves referred to as 'other Persons' to count each as 3/5 of a person for purposes of drawing population based districts for the U.S. House of Representatives); art I, sec 9 cl. 1 (slave trade referred to as 'The Migration of Importation of such Persons as any of the States now existing shall think proper to admit' could not be prohibited by the U.S. Congress prior to 1808).

18 See Gibbons v. Ogden, 22 U.S. 1 (1824).

19 See Wickard v. Filburn, 317 U.S. 111 (1942).

20 See United States v. Lopez 514 U.S. 549 (1995) (Thomas, J. concurring) (for an interpretation of the Commerce Clause that is based on this latter alternative).

21 South Africa's apartheid laws also drew distinctions between various classes of 'non-whites' (White 2002) which allows for further classifications in terms of identification and negation.

22 See infra, at 46ff.

23 For example, the text of the fourteenth Amendment's Equal Protection Clause of the U.S. Constitution has remained unchanged since its adoption in 1868, yet as a consequence of its judicial elaboration it was understood as condoning racial segregation from 1896 to 1954, and as prohibiting it thereafter. Compare Plessy v. Ferguson, 163 U.S. 537 (1896) (equal protection consistent with 'separate but equal' treatment of the races) with Brown v. Board of Education, 347 U.S. 483 (1954) (racially segregated public schools are inherently unequal).

24 See e.g., German Basic Law, Art. 79.

25 See e.g., U.S. Const. Art. I Sec. 9, cl. 1 expired in 1808. See note 17 supra.

26 Compare U.S. Const. Art. V (In the absence of convening a constitutional Convention, proposed amendments must be approved by a two thirds votes in each of the two Houses of Congress and ratified by three quarter of state legislatures) with Hungarian Constitution ch. I § 24 (3) (amendments can be adopted by a two thirds vote in the unicameral parliament).

27 This does not necessarily mean, however, that the amendment in question

could not potentially trigger important shifts in *political* identity in case, for example, the eighteen to twenty one years old cohort voted as a block thus upsetting settled equilibria among theretofore clearly formed political polarities.

28 Hungarian Const. Ch. XIV, § 74 (3).

29 If one considers the first ten amendments to the U.S. Constitution, which are collectively referred to as the 'Bill of Rights', as material part of the original constitution, then the U.S. Constitution has for practical purposes only been amended seventeen times in more than two hundred years, and some of these amendments, such as the twenty sixth discussed above, seem hardly likely to impact the continuity of the prevailing constitutional identity. Moreover, there is a strong argument for lumping together the 1791 Bill of Rights and the original 1787 Constitution in the context of constitutional identity. First, that the original constitution would be supplemented by a bill of rights was basically agreed upon prior to setting on the final text of the former (Finkelman 1990). And, second, the two went into operation virtually contemporaneously, the 1787 Constitution in 1789 and the Bill of Rights barely two years thereafter.

30 *See Lochner* v. *New York*, 198 U.S. 45 (1905). (State law designed to improve working conditions of employees held to violate constitutionally protected properly and freedom of contract rights).

31 *See, e.g., West Coast Hotel* v. *Parrish*, 300 U.S. 379 (1937) (overruling *Lochner* era precedent and holding minimum wage constitutional as Constitution does not mandate freedom of contract); *NLRB* v. *Jones & Laughlin Steel Corp*, 301 U.S. 1 (1937) (federal administrative finding regarding ten of ten thousand workers employed by a corporation organized on a nationwide basis held to be within federal power to regulate interstate commerce).

32 'The glue that binds Rousseau's individual to civil society is the general will. Indeed, the general will is that by which the people united as sovereign must govern, and that to which each individual, as a member of the governed, must yield without reservation.' (Rosenfeld: 1985: 868); *see also* Rousseau 1762 I,7.

33 *Cf.* Habermas 1996:409 (advocating a proceduralist paradigm of law, according to which law's legitimacy is predicated on establishing an identity between the law's authors and those made subject to its prescriptions).

34 *See* Bureau of the Census, U.S. Dep't of Com., Historical Statistics of the United States: Colonial Times to 1970, at 22 (1975) (at the time of the adoption of the Constitution, approximately 50% of the population was female and approximately 24% was African American).

35 For an enlightening historical and theoretical discussion of these issues, *see* Richards 1994.

36 *See* U.S. Const. art. I,§§ 2, 9.

37 That African Americans had to suffer from constitutional prescriptions of which they could in no way be considered the authors is vividly illustrated by the infamous decision of *Dred Scott* v. *Sanford, 60 U.S. (19 How.) 393 (1857)*

(emancipation of slave pursuant to federal law held unconstitutional as it violated the former slave owner's property rights under the Fifth Amendment's Due Process Clause).

38 *See infra*, at 158–163.

39 One such change was the nationalization of the Bill of Rights which occurred over time after adoption of the Fourteenth Amendment. Originally, the Bill of Rights was interpreted as only affording protections as against the Federal government. By the mid-twentieth century, virtually the entire Bill of Rights, had become 'incorporated' through the Fourteenth Amendment making it applicable to the several states. *See Duncan* v. *Louisiana*, 391 U.S. 145 (1968).

2 The Constitutional Subject and the Clash of Self and Other: On the Uses of Negation, Metaphor and Metonymy

1 This is not meant to imply that the premodern world did not experience its fair share of dissent and internal conflict, but rather that it was more bent on suppressing or subordinating dissenters than on tolerating or accommodating those who did not subscribe to the officially endorsed normative value system.

2 For further discussion of the relationship between internal and external other, *see infra* at 150.

3 *See, e.g.*, U.S. Const. art I, 9, cl. 1 (slave trade practices established prior to the Constitution not subject to Congressional abolition for more than twenty years); U.S. Const. amend. VII (right to a jury trial in certain types of cases established prior to the Constitution given continued protection by the Constitution).

4 *Cf.* Hegel 1989:115, 122–29 (all negation is determination).

5 *See* U.S. Const. arts. I, II, III (enumerating respectively the legislative, executive, and judiciary power of the United States government), and Amendment X (powers not delegated to federal government belong to the states).

6 *See, e.g.*, The Federalist No. 57 (James Madison).

7 This effort at mediation does not always lead to smooth or stable results. Compare, e.g., *National League of Cities v. Usery, 426 U.S. 833 (1976)* (federalism prohibits imposing certain federal labor standards on employees of a state) with *Garcia v. San Antonio Metro. Transit Auth., 469 U.S. 528 (1985)* (federalism permits imposing the same labor standards on employees of a state).

8 *See* Const. (1793) art. I (Fr.).

9 *See* Rosenfeld 1985:869–70 (Rousseau locates conflict between private and common interest within the individual and links bourgeois and citizen through internalization of the public interest.).

10 The constitutional text in question may, but does not have to, be a written constitution. Indeed, an unwritten constitution or one made up of written provisions that are not assembled into a single document, such as that of the United Kingdom (Barendt 1998:26–34) can function just as a written one inasmuch as they can both be regarded as texts which depend for meaning on context.

11 For an excellent discussion of counterfactual imagination in the context of Habermas's work, *see* Power 1998.

12 410 U.S. 113 (1973).

13 *See* Tribe 1992 6–7, 139; Lawrence Van Gelder, *Cardinals Shocked – Reaction Mixed*, N.Y. Times, Jan. 23, 1973, at A1; Tamar Lewin, *Legal Abortion Under Fierce Attack* 15 Years After *Roe* v. *Wade Ruling*, N.Y. Times, May 10, 1988, at A20; *Statements By 2 Cardinals*, N.Y. Times, Jan. 23, 1973, at A20.

14 *See, e.g.*, Tribe 1992 161–70; Linda Greenhouse, *Reagan Administration Renews Assault on 1973 Abortion Ruling*, N.Y. Times, Nov. 11, 1988, at A20; Leslie H. Gelb, *U.S. Will Ask Court to Reverse Abortions Ruling*, N.Y. Times, July 15, 1985, at A1; *Transcript of Oral Arguments Before Court on Abortion Case*, N.Y. Times, Apr. 27, 1989, at B12.

15 *See* Rosenfeld 1994 (national, regional, linguistic, religious, ethnic, political, and ideological identities are likely to figure in the determination of constitutional identity).

16 As Hegel states: 'To transcend (*Aufheben*) has this double meaning, that it signifies to keep or to preserve and also to make to cease, to finish . . . Thus, what is transcended is also preserved; it has only lost its immediacy and is not on that account annihilated.' 2 Hegel 1966:119–20.

17 This is hardly surprising given that constitutionalism depends on pluralism and can ultimately be regarded as providing the means to institutionalize pluralism.

18 For a more extensive discussion of pluralism as a substantive conception of the good, *see* Rosenfeld 1998.

19 *Cf.* Marx 1967:216–48 (arguing that religious emancipation can only be obtained at the cost of relegating religion to the private sphere).

20 *60 U.S. (19 How.) 393 (1857).*

21 The slave owner's asserted property right was based upon the Due Process Clause of the Fifth Amendment, which provides that 'no person shall be . . . deprived of life, liberty, or property, without due process of law. . . .' U.S. Const. amend V. Arguably, Due Process rights are purely procedural, but for the first time in *Dred Scott*, the Supreme Court interpreted the Due Process Clause as protective of substantive property rights.

22 In his opinion, Chief Justice Taney stated that at the time of the Declaration of Independence and the adoption of the 1787 Constitution, African Americans had 'been regarded as beings of an inferior order, and altogether unfit to associate with the white race . . . and so far inferior, that they had no rights which the white man was bound to respect.' *Dred Scott*, 60 U.S. (19 How.) at 407.

23 The metonymic function and metonymy are discussed below. *See 2.3.3 infra.*

24 *See* Jakobson 1968:70 (the relation of substitution or 'between elements of one and the same series of alternations is called associative, or, following the more exact term of Hjelmslev, paradigmatic').

25 For a more extended discussion of the postulate of equality and its relation to American constitutionalism, see Rosenfeld 1991:135–36.

26 *Plessy v. Ferguson, 163 U.S. 537, 559 (1896)* (Harlan, J., dissenting).

27 This dictum also evinces a strong imprint of negation. In a society so constantly attuned to racial differences, colorblindness stands in direct contradiction to prevailing social mores. Therefore, for colorblindness to become incorporated into constitutional identity would require the negation of a defining aspect of the country's national identity. *Cf.* Smith 1997 (conceiving U.S. Citizenship as based on tension between race-based identity and universal equality based identity).

28 *Cf. Swann v. Charlotte-Mecklenberg Bd. of Educ., 402 U.S. 1 (1971)* (busing to integrate *de jure* segregated public schools permissible under the Equal Protection Clause of the Fourteenth Amendment). Although the idea of a colorblind constitution is often mentioned in the United States, it has thus far not been adopted by the Supreme Court. *See, e.g., City of Richmond v. J.A. Croson Co., 488 U.S. 469 (1989)* (all justices deem color-conscious remedies constitutionally permissible under certain circumstances).

29 Through an infinite series of objects which do not bring it satisfaction, desire, in the last analysis, aims at itself.

30 Indeed, desire can only maintain a relation to itself through the mediation of not-yet-incorporated objects.

31 *See* Rosenfeld 1989:*1761–62* (contrasting acontextual 'atomistic mode of interpretation' with contextual 'ecological mode of interpretation').

32 It is interesting, in this connection, to note that one of the frequent arguments against race-conscious policies designed to improve the plights of traditionally disadvantaged racial minorities is that once the colorblind barrier is lifted, even for a worthwhile purpose, there is no principled way to insure that racists will not take advantage of this development to better perpetuate their reprehensible aims. *See, e.g., City of Richmond v. J.A. Croson Co., 488 U.S. 469 (1989).* Underlying this line of argument may be a fear that left to their own devices people will be unable to properly contextualize issues regarding race.

33 But *see Braunfeld v. Brown, 366 U.S. 599 (1961)* (Sunday-closing law held not to violate Orthodox Jew's First Amendment right to freely exercise his religion).

34 *See, e.g., Department of Human Resources v. Smith, 494 U.S. 872 (1990)* (sacramental use of peyote not exempted from criminal prohibition); *Reynolds v. United States, 98 U.S. 145 (1878)* (criminalization of bigamy upheld notwithstanding Mormon claim that polygamy was a religious duty). In contrast, ritual use of wine by Catholics and Jews was exempted from prohibition mandated by the Eighteenth Amendment. *See Board of Educ. v. Grumet, 114 S. Ct. 2481 (1994)* (Kennedy, J., concurring) (referring to Prohibition exemption for use of alcoholic beverages for sacramental purposes). For a more systematic argument that abstraction beyond differences is not neutral, *see* Rosenfeld 1991:234–38.

35 The First Amendment provides in relevant part that 'Congress shall make no law respecting an establishment of religion, or prohibiting the free exercise thereof.' U.S. Const. amend. I. These two clauses are referred to respectively as the 'Establishment Clause' and the 'Free Exercise Clause.'

36 Although the Religion Clauses of the First Amendment were originally only applicable to the federal government, see *Barron v. Mayor and City Council of Baltimore, 32 U.S. 243 (1833),* they have now been made applicable to the states by incorporation through the Fourteenth Amendment, *see Everson v. Board of Educ., 330 U.S. 1 (1947)* (Establishment Clause applicable to states); *Cantwell v. Connecticut, 310 U.S. 296 (1940)* (Free Exercise Clause applicable to states).

37 *See Lynch v. Donnelly, 465 U.S. 668, 674 (1984)* (stressing historical role of religion in the United States); *Zorach v. Clauson, 343 U.S. 306, 313 (1952)* (Americans are a religious people); Note, *Developments in the Law – Religion and the State, 100 Harv. L. Rev. 1606, 1612–13 (1987)* (95% of Americans believe in God and 60% belong to some religious organization).

38 *See Reynolds v. United States,* 98 U.S. 145, 164 (1879) (citing Thomas Jefferson).

39 *Marsh v. Chambers,* 463 U.S. 783 (1983).

40 *Zorach v. Clauson,* 343 U.S. 306, 313 (1952).

41 *United States v. Seeger,* 380 U.S. 163, 165 (1965) (upholding § 6(j) of the Universal Military Training and Service Act, 50 U.S.C. App. § 456(j) (1958), though broadly interpreted). Statutory reference to a 'belief in a relation to a Supreme Being' was deleted in a 1967 amendment to 6(j). Nonetheless, the statute still precludes exempting an avowed atheist claiming an exemption on purely moral grounds. *But see* Justice Black's plurality opinion in *Welsh v. United States,* 398 U.S. 333 (1970), reading the relevant statutory language so broadly as to blur the distinction between religious and nonreligious ethical views.

42 *See Reynolds v. United States,* 98 U.S. 145 (1879).

43 *See Department of Human Resources v. Smith,* 494 U.S. 872 (1990).

44 465 U.S. 668 (1984).

45 *Id.* at 679. In *Lemon v. Kurtzman,* 403 U.S. 602, 612–13 (1971), the Supreme Court adopted a three-pronged test applicable in Establishment Clause cases: first, the law must have a secular legislative purpose; second, its principal or primary effect must be one that neither advances nor inhibits religion; and, third, it must not foster 'an excessive government entanglement with religion.' The Court in *Lynch,* however, was unwilling to be confined to any single test. Subsequent to *Lynch,* the Court has not consistently followed the Lemon test, but it has not repudiated it. *See Lee v. Weisman,* 112 S. Ct. 2649 (1992); Teitel 1993:769 & n.76.

46 *See Lynch,* 465 U.S. at 676.

47 In the words of Justice O'Connor, the 'crèche is a traditional symbol of the holiday that is very commonly displayed along with purely secular symbols . . .' *Id.* at 692 (O'Connor, J., concurring).

48 An adherent to a non-Christian religion could either side with the separationist if he or she most fears state favoritism towards Christianity, or with the profoundly committed Christian if his or her greatest concern is surrender to secularism and trivialization of religion.

49 By including both the singular and the plural, I mean to emphasize the dual possibility of strict separation between church and state – which can inure to the benefit of both secularists and adherents to religion – and the state's equally active promotion of all religions – which may be to the equal benefit of mainstream and nonmainstream religions, but which is to the detriment of atheists and agnostics.

50 *See Lynch*, 465 U.S. at 668.

51 465 U.S. at 676–77, 683.

52 465 U.S. at 671, 685.

53 As noted by Jakobson, in aphasia leading to destruction of the capacity to establish relations along the paradigmatic axis, words tend to become perceived exclusively in terms of their syntagmatic relations, thus making it impossible to name things (Jakobson 1973:54).

54 Jakobson points out that when children are given a name and asked for a verbal reaction, they invariably react in one of two ways: they either utter a verbal expression linked to the name in question by a relation of similarity, or else, by a relation of contiguity (Jakobson 1973:61). Thus, for example, confronted with the term 'ice cream,' a child may be more drawn towards metaphoric processes and answer 'cake,' or be inclined towards metonymic processes and respond 'summer.'

55 For example, the colorblind principle can be regarded as premised on the belief that racial differences are irrelevant for purposes of constitutional equality, or on the belief that beyond racial differences, there is an identity shared by all human beings that is relevant for purposes of constitutional equality.

56 Compare the majority opinion in *Plessy v. Ferguson* (racial apartheid held consistent with Equal Protection Clause of the Fourteenth Amendment) with Justice Harlan's dissenting opinion (consistent with the color-blind principle, racial apartheid should be deemed unconstitutional).

57 Thus, if all government business must be conducted in the majority language, equal opportunity to compete for government employment may in fact result in a disadvantage for speakers of the minority language.

58 *See, e.g., Bradwell v. Illinois*, 83 U.S. 130 (1873) (state denial of right to practice law to women held constitutional and justified in terms of woman's role as wife and mother).

59 Good examples in the American case include the treatment of African American slaves in the context of formal adherence to the proposition that 'all men are created equal,' and the treatment of women even after adoption of the Fourteenth Amendment as illustrated by the *Bradwell* case.

60 *See supra*, at 288, n. 16.

61 For example, if contextualization of the plight of women confronting unwanted pregnancies is pushed to the point that the basic identity between men and women slips beyond the horizon, differences – and particularly those that relate to the presence and the potential life of the fetus – may well lead to a denial of abortion rights, and hence of full equality rights to women.

62 Even if one agrees with Rousseau that each member of a democratic polity is at once an integral part of the sovereign who enacts laws conforming to the general will, and an individual who is obligated to obey such laws (Rousseau 1762:II, 1,2), there still seems to be an insurmountable split between these two roles which makes the obligation to obey the law both constraining and alienating, *see* Rosenfeld, 1985:868. Indeed, in Rousseau's own famous words, 'whoever refuses to obey the general will shall be compelled to it by the whole body: this in fact only forces him to be free' (Rousseau, 1762:II,4). Needless to say, legislative minorities subjected to laws which they have opposed are even more clearly subjected to onerous external impositions.

63 The most obvious example of the emancipatory potential of constitutional law is furnished by the protection of fundamental rights. Thus, freedom of expression protects against submission to majority views.

64 It is true that today's American people is not the same as the 1787 (embryo of an) American people in contrast to today's German people which is not altogether but pretty much the same – in its 'peoplehood' even if not in its self-perception as a nation-state, the latter being arguably profoundly affected by the post – 1989 reunification of East and West Germany – as the late 1940's German people that adopted the current German Constitution (known as the 'Basic Law'). Accordingly, though there is no question that the German people adopted the German Basic Law, it is an imagined American people (only imaginable through backward looking projections issuing from its current self-perceptions) that adopted its 1787 Constitution. In the American case unlike in the German one, therefore, had peoplehood not cemented *after* adoption of the 1787 Constitution, the 'We The People' of 1787 would have lost all claims to meaningful singularity.

65 See Canada Const. Sec. 23 (Anglophone and francophone linguistic minority education rights) and Sec. 35 (aboriginal rights).

66 *See* U.S. Const. Amend. V (1791) (prohibiting government expropriation of private property except for a public purpose and subject to just compensation).

67 *See supra*, at 19.

68 *See supra*, at 23.

69 This construct is neither settled nor stable as it has been, and continues to be, in tension with an inconsistent construct of Americans as a superior race. *See* Smith 1997:3–5 (construing American citizenship as an uneasy amalgam between an universalist and a racist conception of the citizen).

70 French was not only one among many languages within Europe at the time of the Revolution, but one among many in France itself. Indeed, only about half the population in France spoke French in 1789, and the Revolution endeavored to impose French, often by means of brutal force, throughout the national territory. *See* Preuss 1994:151–152.

3 Reinventing Tradition Through Constitutional Interpretation: The Case of Unenumerated Rights in the United States

1 *See supra*, at 18.

2 For example, in contrast to the American Constitution, which plays a prominent role in shaping national identity, the Indian Constitution looms as being quite removed from that country's identity (Tushnet 1999: 1270–71).

3 *See, e.g., R.A.V. v. City of Saint Paul*, 505 U.S. 377 (1992).

4 While it is unquestionable that many different ethnic, racial and religious groups have been the victims of intolerance in the course of American history, African-Americans can be singled out for having confronted greater sustained intolerance than any other group, thus suggesting a gap between self perception and historical experiences.

5 The protection of unenumerated rights found in the Ninth Amendment must be understood in terms of a Lockean conception of rights as innate and inalienable negative rights that the individual holds against the state. Consistent with this conception, the 1787 American Constitution did not include a bill of rights because in prescribing a limited national government, it was thought obvious that such government would not be authorized to trample on pre-existing fundamental individual rights, *see* Section 3.4.2 *infra*. The adoption four years later of the Bill of Rights was prompted, at least in part, by fears that the national government might otherwise exceed Lockean constraints (*Id.*). Viewed in this light, the enumeration of particular rights is a precaution to insure government respect, and the Ninth Amendment an explicit reminder that the listing of certain fundamental Lockean rights should not be read as implying any exclusion of other equally fundamental Lockean rights.

6 Whereas the Fourteenth Amendment protects persons against state infringements, the Due Process Clause of Fifth Amendment (1791) does the same with respect to federal infringements.

7 *See supra*, at 29ff.

8 *See infra*, at 190.

9 For example, constitutional democracy depends on protection of freedom of expression rights, because uninhibited expression of minority views plays an important role in the legitimation of majority rule. How far such rights should extend, however, is problematic as it is unclear whether unlimited protection of extremist speech ultimately promotes or inhibits constitutional democracy. (Rosenfeld, 2003).

10 For example, arguably, constitutionalism is compatible both with a constitutionalized liberty that encompasses flag-burning and with one that does not. Accordingly, the determination of whether constitutional liberty should include a right to burn one's country's flag in political protest would ultimately depend on the relevant sociocultural heritage (Rosenfeld and Sajo 2006).

11 *See, e.g., Nebbia v. New York*, 291 U.S. 502 (1934).

12 *See, e.g., Lochner v. New York*, 198 U.S. 45 (1905).

13 See, e.g., *Moore v. City of East Cleveland, 431 U.S. 494 (1977); Roe v. Wade, 410 U.S. 113 (1973); Eisenstadt v. Baird, 401 U.S. 934 (1972);* and *Griswold v. Connecticut, 381 U.S. 479 (1965).*

14 Rarely, if ever, is a constitutional provision stated with such precision as to preclude further determination through reconstructive interpretation. Nevertheless, the range and scope of interpretive possibilities left by the Due Process Clause is singularly vast.

15 381 U.S. at 486.

16 491 U.S. 110 (1989).

17 *Id.* at 128 n.6.

18 *Id.* at 127.

19 See *Id., at 140–41* (Brennan, J., dissenting).

20 *Id.* at 141–42.

21 *Id.* at 141.

22 This argument was advanced in support of constitutionalizing the genetic father's visitation rights in *Michael H, 491 U.S. 110 (1989).*

23 401 U.S. 934 (1972).

24 413 U.S. 113 (1973).

25 478 U.S. 186 (1986).

26 839 U.S. 558 (2003).

27 318 U.S., at 485–86.

28 *Id.*

29 There were state constitutions in the newly independent United States prior to the framing of the 1787 federal Constitution and therefore it would have been possible for the privacy right under consideration to originate in these state constitutions. Nevertheless the rhetoric in *Griswold* strongly suggests that the long standing tradition of martial privacy relied upon by the Court was anchored both in an ancient pre-constitutional past and in extra-constitutional (Judeo-Christian) values.

30 381 U.S., at 484.

31 *Id.*, at 487–495.

32 *Id.*, at 487.

33 *Id.*

34 *See supra*, at 73.

35 *See supra*, at 78.

36 413 U.S., at 120.

37 *See supra*, at 84.

38 410 U.S., at 172.

39 478 U.S. 186 (1986).

40 539 U.S. 558 (2003).

41 In his dissenting opinion, Justice Scalia intimates as much, arguing that the reasoning of the Court's majority leaves no room for a principled rejection of a constitutional right to same-sex marriage. 539 U.S., at 601–602.

42 In her concurring opinion, Justice O'Connor does hint at the possible link

between the right to homosexual sex and that to same-sex marriage, but only to dismiss any implication that there may be any constitutional dimension to that latter right. 539 U.S., at 585.

43 381 U.S, at 500.

44 *Poe* v. *Ullman*, 367 U.S. 497, 523 (1961) (Harlan, J. dissenting). Justice Harlan relied on his dissent in *Poe* to elaborate his position in *Griswold*.

45 367 U.S., at 552.

46 *Id.*, at 552–53.

47 *See supra*, at 77.

48 *See supra*, at 83.

49 *See* 367 U.S., at 552.

50 *See Id.* at 552–53.

51 U.S. Const. Art. I Sec. 8 after listing the powers of Congress, states that Congress, is also empowered '[to] make all laws which shall be necessary and proper for carrying into execution the foregoing power . . .' granted it for purposes of carrying out its constitutionally circumscribed legislative mandate (*Id.*:808–809).

52 *See* U.S. Const. Amend. I.

53 See U.S. Const. Amend V. This latter right was not absolute as government can appropriate private property 'for public use and subject to 'just compensation'. Accordingly the right to private property may not be inviolate, but the right to it or to its fair price is.

54 See U.S. Const. Amends. VI and VII.

55 In his dissent in *Griswold*, Justice Black advanced a completely different interpretation of the Ninth Amendment, arguing that it was enacted to protect state powers against federal intrusion, thus casting this amendment as a guarantee of federalism rather than as a preserver and protector of individual rights.

56 *See* U.S Const. Amend. XIII.

57 Locke does subject this right to the following proviso: 'at least where there is enough and as good left in common for others' (*Id.*). But that proviso need not concern us here.

58 These premises are consistent with the logic of Locke's theory, not with all the particulars of his actual views, which seem at times to contradict his theory. For example, in spite of his labor theory of property, Locke asserts that 'the turfs my *servant* has cut . . . become my property' (*Id.*:Para. 28, emphasis added); and in spite of his general repudiation of slavery, he condones it under certain circumstances (*Id.*: Paras, 22–24).

59 *See Slaughter House Cases*, 83 U.S.26 (1873).

60 Besides the Due Process Clauses which impose on the states the same constitutional obligation as its Fifth Amendment counterpart does on the federal government, the Fourteenth Amendment provides, among other things, that no state 'shall abridge the privileges or immunities of citizens of the United States' nor 'deny to any person within its jurisdiction the equal protection of the laws'.

61 198 U.S. 45 (1905).

62 To date only two minor requirements issued from the Fifth and Eighth Amendment respectively, the requirements that indictments be made by grand jury and the prohibition against excessive bail – neither of which is a natural right in the Lockean sense. *See* Sullivan and Gunther 2007:360.

63 *See* 3.4.1 *supra.*

64 *See supra*, at 82–83.

65 *See supra*, at 83–84.

66 Locke also clearly regarded sodomy and incest as against the law of nature. *See* Locke 1690:*First Treatise*, Para 59.

67 *See Nebbia* v. *New York* 291 U.S.502 (1934); *West Coast Hotel v. Parrish*, 300 U.S. 379 (1937).

68 Locke considered sodomy a sin principally because it was contrary to the 'main intention of nature, which willeth the increase of mankind, and the continu- ation of the species in the highest perfection … with the security of the marriage bed, as necessary thereunto'. Locke 1690:*First treatise*, Para. 59.

69 *See* note 67 *supra.*

70 405 U.S., at 440–442.

71 *Id.*, at 446–448.

72 *Id.*, at 448.

73 *Id.*

74 405 U.S., at 453.

75 *See supra*, at 86–87.

76 *Id.*

77 *See supra*, at 43–44.

78 505 U.S. 833.

79 One of the important factors leading to the U.S. Senate's rejection of the nomination of Robert Bork to the U.S. Supreme Court was his view that the unenumerated right to privacy had no proper constitutional foundation. *See Bork Confirmation Battle*, CQ Press, Online Editions 717–720 (1987).

80 *Griswold* itself did not arise in a vacuum as it relates back to many precedents, such as *Pierce* v. *Society of Sisters* 268 U.S.510 (1925) (parents' right to choose religious education for their children) and *Meyer* v. *Nebraska* 262 U.S. 390 (1923) (freedom to teach and learn German in post-World War One America) and even arguably to *Lockner* with which *Griswold* shares common Lockean roots. Nevertheless, *Griswold* does mark a turning point, both in terms of the particular cluster of rights which it constitiutionaizes and of the particular way in which it reinvents tradition.

81 410 U.S. 129–152.

82 410 U.S. 139–141.

83 *Id.* at 131.

84 *Id.* at 140–141.

85 *Id.*, at 159.

86 *Id.*, at 162.

87 *Id.*, at 163–164.

88 *Id.*, at 163.

89 The constitutional right to abortion recognized in *Roe* is virtually unlimited during the first trimester of pregnancy, subject to regulation for the protection of the health of the mother during the second trimester and subject to prohibition (except where inconsistent with protection of the life or health of the mother) in order to protect the potential life of the viable fetus during the third trimester of the pregnancy. The trimester structure established by *Roe* was abandoned in *Casey*, but a woman's broad right to an abortion prior to the fetus' viability was substantially preserved.

90 *Id.*, at 154.

91 *Id.*, at 163.

92 39 BVerfGE 1 (1975).

93 *See supra*, at 87.

94 478 U.S., at 188.

95 478 U.S., at 188 n. 2.

96 478 U.S., at 196–197.

97 478 U.S., at 203 (dissenting opinion citing *amici* briefs of American Psychological Association and American Public Health Association).

98 478 U.S., at 218–219.

99 *Id.*, at 217.

100 *Id.*, at 213.

101 *Id.*, at 209, n.4

102 Only five of the six justices in the majority adopted the position expressed by the dissenting justices in *Bowers*. The sixth Justice O'Connor (who had been in the *Bowers* majority), relying on the fact that the challenged Texas law in *Lawrence* only criminalized homosexual sodomy unlike the Georgia law in *Bowers* which criminalized all sodomy, concluded that because it distinguished between heterosexual and homosexual sodomy the Texas law violated the Equal Protection Clause.

103 539 U.S., at 567. Viewed narrowly, the move from sexual intimacy to the enduring bonds of which it is a part occurs within a metonymic path. The predominant interpretive move, however, is metaphorical as the object is to reach the level of abstraction at which homosexuals and heterosexuals become indistinguishable as beings whose well being and self fulfillment depend on achieving enduring bonds with a partner of their choice.

104 *Id.*

105 *Id.*, at 568.

106 *Id.*

107 See *supra*, at 107.

108 539 U.S., at 572–573.

109 *Id.*, at 577.

110 *Id.*, at 576.

111 *See* Senate Resolution 92, 109th Cong. (2005).

112 *See Goodridge v. Dept of Public Health*, 798 N.E. 2nd 941 (Mass. 2003).
113 *See* Pew Research Center Report 'Religions Beliefs Underpin Opposition to Homosexuality' Nov. 18, 2003.
114 539 U.S., at 604–605.
115 *Id.*, at 578.
116 *Id.*, at 590.
117 *Id.*, at 598.
118 *Id.*
119 *See Roper* v. *Simmons* 543 U.S. 551 (2005) holding for the first time the death penalty for juveniles unconstitutional over Justice Scalia's dissent.
120 *See supra*, at 295, n. 58.
121 *See* BBC News, *France and allies rally against War*, March 5, 2003, http://news.bbc.co.uk/go/fr/-/z/hi/middle_east/2821145.stm
122 One way to exclude present day foreign influences systematically is by adhering, as Justice Scalia does, to originalism (*Id.*).
123 *See supra*, at 115.
124 A less sweeping though consistent variant would be that Europe best exemplifies Western culture and tradition of which the U.S. is a part.
125 *See supra*, at 115.

4 Recasting and Reorienting Identity Through Constitution-Making: The Pivotal Case of Spain's 1978 Constitution

1 (Quoting Duke of Clermont-Tonnerre).
2 Abortion I Case, (1975) 39 BVerfGE, 1 (quoting GG art. 2(2)[I]), translated in. Kommers, (1997:336, 337).
3 *Cf.* Elster 1994:63–64 (arguing that America's eighteenth century Constitution was more successful than its French counterpart as a consequence of America's political break with its colonial past as opposed to the French Revolution's much more radical break with the *ancien régime*).
4 For a succinct account of Spain's transition to constitutional democracy, *see* Rubio Llorente 1998:239.
5 'There is growing consensus that the Spanish transition is in many ways the paradigmatic case for the study of pacted democratic transition and rapid democratic consolidation. . . .' Linz & Stepan 1996:87.
6 Both Spain's nearly 40 years of authoritarian dictatorship, and East Europe's equally long experience with totalitarian regimes could not be seriously thought to have been susceptible of mere erasure. *See generally* Linz & Stepan 1996:110–12. Moreover, South Africa's abandonment of apartheid opened an entirely new chapter in that nation's history. *See* 1 Department of Public Information, United Nations, The United Nations and Apartheid 1948–1994, at 3 (1994).
7 For a discussion of these historical events, *see* van Caenegem, 1995:209–17.
8 As indicated above, *see supra*, at 31–32, France has had 15 constitutions since the Revolution (Bell 1992:1), but that does mean that the French have a

completely fragmentary constitutional identity. For example, France's current 1958 constitution incorporates part of its immediate predecessor, the 1946 Constitution, and has been interpreted as incorporating the 1789 Declaration of the Rights of Man. (*Id.*:66–67).

9 As David Richards points out, the implantation of American constitutionalism required not one but two revolutions, with the Civil War being viewed as the second American Revolution (Richards 1994:85).

10 The paradigmatic example is, of course, that of the French Revolution and of its Reign of Terror. *See generally* van Caenegem 1995.

11 For example, injustices under the old regime, such as torture or the killing of a loved one, may lead to claims for retribution or revenge. If the acts complained of were legal when committed, or illegal but not prosecuted in a timely manner for political reasons, then the new regime would face a dilemma: it can either prosecute, thus promoting political justice at the expense of respect for the rule of law; or it can strictly abide by the rule of law but allow glaring injustices to remain unpunished, thus undermining its claim to legitimacy. (Rosenfeld, 1996:309).

12 Although the United Kingdom does not have a written constitution, it does have a number of written texts going back to the *Magna Carta* generated throughout its history which together with a set of institutionalized practices and traditions that from a functional standpoint endow it with a working constitution. It is fair to say that it generally adheres to the fundamental tenets of constitutionalism and that it hence provides an example of gradual, largely peaceful, evolution towards constitutional democracy. As will be explored in Chapters 5 and 6 below, a more complete typology of constitutional models must account for the British experience, but given the time frame involved and the lack of a written constitution, the case of Britain does not seem directly relevant to that of Spain or to those of more recent transitions in Eastern Europe, Latin America, or South Africa.

13 Political society is 'that arena in which the polity specifically arranges itself to contest the legitimate right to exercise control over public power and the state apparatus.' (Linz & Stepan 1996:8).

14 An 'economic society' mediates between state and market as 'there has never been and there cannot be a non-wartime consolidated democracy in a command economy. Second, there has never been and almost certainly there never will be a modern consolidated democracy in a pure market economy.' (*Id.*:11).

15 The following account is not intended to be in any way comprehensive or to provide a full sketch of the relevant historical events. For fuller accounts of the transition, *see Peaceful Transitions to Constitutional Democracy: Transcript of the Proceedings, 19 Cardozo L. Rev. 1953, 1954–67 (1998)* (comments of Jose Pedro Perez Llorca); López Guerra 1998, as well as the vast literature available on this subject. *See generally* Linz & Stepan, 1996:87–115 and works cited therein. For a thorough discussion of the making of the Spanish constitution, *see* Bonime-Blanc, 1987.

16 Juan Carlos's father Juan of Borbon, who was then living in exile, was the legitimate heir to the Spanish throne (Rubio Llorente 1988:248).

17 In Poland, the pacted transition resulted from 1989 roundtable agreements between the communist regime of General Jaruzelski and the Solidarity Movement headed by Lech Walesa. *See* Linz & Stepan 1996:265–69. In Hungary, the transition resulted from the roundtable negotiations held between the Communist Party 'increasingly led by reformists' and 'organized democratic party opposition.' *Id.*:295.

18 *See* Spanish Constitution arts. 1, 2, 6, 143.

19 The period in question spans at most 11 years, 1975–1986, if one accepts that Spain's entry into the European Community (now the EU) signals the enduring success of its transition.

20 *See supra*, at 134.

21 During World War II Franco issued 'fundamental laws' that provided a legal framework to his regime (Rubio Llorente 1988:241–42).

22 Rubio Llorente, for example, argues that the tensions that arose at the end of Franco's regime were largely due to 'a continuous process of economic development into which Spain was dragged rather than led by European prosperity' (Rubio Llorente, 1988:242).

23 *See supra*, at 137.

24 Because its hierarchy was conservative and because of its collaboration with Franco's regime, the Spanish Catholic Church did not play a significant role in the Spanish transition to democracy in stark contrast to the major roles played by the Polish Church and the Brazilian Church in their respective polity's transition (Casanova, 1994:85–89).

25 *See supra*, at 136.

26 *See supra*, at 135.

27 *See supra*, at 139.

28 This lack was presumably as much of a problem for traditionalists who considered legitimate tradition to require reinstitution of the Monarchy abolished in 1931 – for whom Juan Carlos was not the legitimate heir to the throne – as for Francoist traditionalists who sensed that Juan Carlos was not a true believer in their cause.

29 Aldofo Suarez requested Spain's admission to the EC in 1977 and although the degree of influence of the (now) EU example on the Spanish transition may be a matter of disagreement, there is little question that the (now) EU became an important symbol in the quest to overcome Francoism, and that it was 'helpful' if not 'decisive' to the success of the transition. *See* Linz & Stepan 1996:113.

30 The 1978 Spanish Constitution was itself the product of a consensus among the various political parties that participated in its elaboration. *See* Rubio Llorente 1988:257.

5 Constitutional Models: Shaping, Nurturing and Guiding the Constitutional Subject

1 This is, of course with the proviso that those who seek constitutional recognition on the basis of their ethnic identity will be cast as an (internal) 'other' on that very account.

2 *See* 5.2 *infra.*

3 *See supra*, at 2.

4 *See* Spanish Const., Art 141–158 (recognizing and conferring powers on '*comunidades autonomas*' – i.e., 'autonomous communities').

5 To the extent that Canada's recent constitutional experience points to a hybrid between the Spanish and British models, this raises the question of whether it would be warranted to add to the existing list a Canadian model which would be in great part a hybrid between the former two models. More generally, all constitutional models are constructs and by no means the only ones, or even the only plausible ones, that may be fairly derived from mediation between abstract constitutionalism and actual historical constitutional experience. In view of this, the best defense I can offer for settling on the seven constitutional models discussed in this chapter and for excluding addition of others such as a Canadian model is a heuristic one. My claim is that the seven models on which I have settled offer a better and more economic account of prevalent constitutional orderings than do other conceivable alternatives. My claim is of course contestable, and I myself consider it subject to revision upon significant departures from the prevalent array of constitutional orderings.

6 German Basic Law, Art. 1.

7 German Basic Law, Arts. 18 and 20.

8 Cited in Birnbaum 1988:44–45 (my translation).

9 This conception continues to dominate the contemporary French constitutional landscape. Thus, Corsica's recent aspirations for greater -self-rule were held to be unconstitutional. *See* decision 2001-454 DC of Jan. 17, 2002 of the French Constitutional Council (Devolution of limited legislative powers to Corsican Parliament held unconstitutional for breaching principle of national unity).

10 I leave aside, for present purposes native Americans, the indigenous peoples who have been largely cast aside from the standpoint of the American constitutional subject. They have been formally treated as 'sovereign peoples' and linked to the American polity through a series of treaties (Holm 2005:2), thus making them, in certain ways relevant here, into 'outsiders'. The actual treatment of native-Americans throughout history has been troubling and at times shameful (Barkan 2001:ch.8). Moreover, native-Americans figure in the elaboration of American national and constitutional identity. Nevertheless, their perceived place in the construction of the American people and of the American nation is at best peripheral.

11 *See supra*, at 73.

12 Whereas this application has proved time and again a powerful tool of

(negative) identification and national bonding, its use (or overuse) has by no means been an unmitigated success as evinced by disenchantment and repudiation of President Bush's war in Iraq in spite of his unflinching defense of it as indispensable to the defense and preservation of freedom *see* April 16, 2007 ABC News/Washington Post Poll (two thirds of Americans said Iraq War was not worth fighting).

13 *See, e.g., Shelley* v. *Kramer* 334 U.S. 1 (1948) (constitutional equality held to be an individual not a collective right).

14 *See supra*, at 57–59.

15 This predominance of mainstream religion has become challenged since then, by the proliferation of more radical or more fundamentalist strands of religion in more recent times. Whether this has changed American national identity or will do so in the future is not important for the point stressed here. That point is that in spite of the priority of constitutional identity in the American model, in present-day America constitutional and national identity are engaged in a two-way dynamic process of interaction.

16 *See* the discussion *supra*, at 57–59.

17 For example, on October 13, 2008, the House of Lords refused to extend the period of detention under the UK Counter-Terrorism Bill which had been approved by the House of Commons. *The Public Whip Online.*

18 1982 Const. of Canada, Sec. 33.

19 Quebec's contrary position is the manifest consequence of that province's refusal to accept the 1982 Canadian Constitution (Hogg 1997: 67–71). To that, one may add, that as a civil law jurisdiction, Quebec lacks the traditions of British constitutionalism and hence displays no congruity with the British Model.

20 *See Australian Capital Television Pty Ltd* v. *Commonwealth*, 177 CLR 106 [1992] HCA 45 (High Court of Australia).

21 71-41 DC of July 16, 1971 (French Constitutional Council).

22 *See, e.g.,* the *Princess Soraya Case* 34 BverfGE 269 (1973) (German Constitutional Court) (civil defamation right of action constitutionalized in spite of statute making criminal defamation exclusive).

23 *See Pensions* Case K. 14/g1, Feb. 11, 1992 (Constitutional Court of Poland) (ruling that pensions cannot be reduced in times of severe economic downturn due to rule of law guaranteed expectations).

24 In a 'pure' common law setting with no statutory law, the judge's decision sets the law, either outright, if there are no precedents or in harmony with prior judicial decisions, thus requiring the judge to harmonize her law-making decision with prior judicial decisions that count as relevant precedents. *See* Rosenfeld 2001:1337–1338.

25 This is particularly startling in the area of fundamental rights. *See* Rosenfeld 2004: 663.

26 More precisely, as noted in the discussion of the German Model in 5.1 above, contemporary German constitutionalism is an amalgam of the traditional German Model and of elements that cannot be subsumed under that model.

Contemporary German constitutionalism, therefore, is at least in part anti-traditional.

27 *See Cruzan* v. *Director, Missouri Dept. of Health*, 497 U.S. 224 (1990); *Washington* v. *Glucksberg*, 521 U.S. 702 (1997).

28 *See* 3.4.1 *supra.*

29 This is a position taken by strict originalists (Dorsen et. al 2003: 189.

30 Precisely because of its constitutional import, the UK has become a party to the Lisbon Treaty only after becoming a beneficiary (with Poland) of a Special Protocol exempting it of certain obligations under the Charter of Rights which is part of the Treaty. *See* House of Lords European Union Committee, *The Treaty of Lisbon: and impact assessment*, 10th report of session 2007–08, pp. 100–103.

31 *See* 1978 Spanish Const., arts 143–158.

32 *See* Renwick McLean, *New Power Granted to Catalonia: Opponents See Threat to Integrity of Spain*, International Herald Tribune, March 31, 2006.

33 As noted above, this is not entirely true of the current German Basic Law which requires filtering the expression of ethnic identity through certain fundamental constraints, such as respect for human dignity *see* German Basic Law, art. 1, § 1.

34 *See* e.g., Canadian 1982 Const. Sec. 23 granting linguistic rights to Anglophone and Francophone minorities.

35 *See* South Africa Cons., Art 39.

36 The Lisbon Treaty was rejected by Irish voters in a June 12, 2008 referendum, and cannot enter into force if any of the EU twenty seven member states fails to ratify it. A second Irish referendum is scheduled for November 2009. BBC News Online, Jan. 14, 2009.

37 *Compare* Preamble, art. I Draft Constitutional Treaty, July 18, 2003 *to* Preamble Constitutional Treaty, July 18, 2004.

38 Indeed remembering that the experiences were 'bitter' is undoubtedly a potent incentive for cooperation and unity. Dwelling on who was ultimately responsible and on what led to that bitter experience in contrast, is still likely to be quite divisive.

39 The increasing tensions between French-speaking and Flemish-speaking population had led to an increasing fragmentation of the constitutional order Belgium. In Canada, Quebec has yet to officially accept the 1982 Canadian Constitution, and periodically considers secession from Canada. *See Reference re Secession of Quebec* [1998] 2-S.C.R. 217.

40 *See Leaders and Veterans Mark D-Day*, BBC News UK Edition, June 6, 2004.

41 *Id.*

42 The new origins at stake in the construction of a European constitutional identity require reinterpretation of the 'bitter experiences' of the twentieth century, but not of the many European wars that preceded them. For example, it seems highly implausible that a French President would characterize the decisive 1815 victory over Napoleon in Waterloo as a 'victory for France.'

43 *See* Cons. of India, Arts. 131–132.

6 Models of Constitution Making

1 US CONST. art I §§2 (three fifths of slaves counted for legislative apportion-ment); U.S. CONST. art I § 9 (barring any prohibition of international slave trade prior to 1880); US CONST. art IV § 2 (extradition of fugitive slaves).
2 See *supra,* at 68–69.
3 *See supra,* at 132–133.
4 It seems significant in relation to de Gaulle's appeal to the people in 1958, that the Fifth Republic Constitution was made in a period of crisis brought about by the Algerian war, in which France was confronting the danger of a military coup (Dorsen et al. 2003:89). Although, formally France's 1958 Constitution involved constitution-making in a time of crisis, functionally and taken in context that constitution amounted more to a constitutional revision than to constitution-making. Indeed, though the 1958 Constitution changed the French from a parliamentary to a semi-presidential democracy, it also retained many features of its 1946 predecessor and of many earlier French constitutions (*Id.*). *See* 6.7 *infra,* for further discussion of constitutional revision.
5 This was the case of the Hungarian Constitution after 1989 discussed *supra,* at 31.
6 C.A. 6821/93,49(4) P.D. 221 (Supr. Ct. of Israel 1995).
7 During the reunification process, there was discussion concerning the need for a new German constitution, but that option was rejected (Möellers 2007:99–100).
8 *See supra,* at 139.
9 *See supra, at* 130.
10 *See Certification of the Constitution of the Republic of South Africa,* 1996(v) SALR 744(cc) Parc. 11 (Constitutional Court of South Africa).
11 *Id.*
12 *Id.,* at para. Iz
13 In this latter case, the result is not automatically a 'drawback.' If a vibrant constitutional order is briefly interrupted by an authoritarian usurpation, and then peacefully restored, the pacted transition should be regarded as a great success, even if it does not, strictly speaking, involve constitution-making. In a large number of instances where the authoritarian regime has lasted for decades, as was the case in communist East/Central Europe, however, restoration is likely, as is already mentioned, to favor some interests over others thus failing to command any legitimate consensus.
14 *See supra,* at 172.
15 For example, a treaty between countries A and B to guarantee the security of country C creates a joint project not a merger.
16 *Cf.* for example, Rawls' hypothetical contract behind a 'veil of ignorance.' *See* Rawls, 1971:136–42.

17 Some regimes, such as that carved out by the ECHR, operate on partial constitutions superimposed on the nation state constitution of the states that are party to the ECHR. For example, a French citizen enjoys speech rights under the French Constitution and under the ECHR, and these rights may diverge somewhat. Furthermore, even some non-governmental segmentary legal regimes, such as that concerned with the regulation of the internet, have generated their own internally applicable constitutional norms (Hamann & Ruiz-Fabry 2008).

7 The Constitutional Subject and Clashing Visions of Citizenship: Can We Be Beyond What We are Not?

1 To the extent that the United States was a confederation before ratification of the 1787 Constitution, it is unclear whether 'We the People' was made up of citizens of the various American states or whether in the very act of constitution-making, 'We the People' transformed itself into 'We the Citizens' of the newly constitutionally minted American Federation. In any event, the constitutional dimension of American citizenship could not be settled until the abolition of slavery after the Civil War. *See* U.S. Const Amend. XIII (1865) (abolishing slavery) and XIV (1868) (defining U.S. citizenship).

2 *See* ch.1 *supra.*

3 *See* 5.2 *supra.*

4 See 2007 Treaty of Lisbon, Art. 8 ('Every national of a member state shall be a citizen of the Union').

5 At the highest levels of abstraction, the famous phrase 'all men are created equal' that figures prominently in the American Declaration of Independence should be understood inclusively as referring to all *human beings.*

6 Although equal citizenship may be interpreted as requiring certain correlative rights and duties among citizens, the latter would still need the mediation of an appropriate functioning institutional framework before they could be harnessed for purposes of political self-determination. For further elaboration of this point, *see* 7.1.2.*infra.*

7 For Hobbes, the contract of government is actually a contract of submission whereby individuals leaving the state of nature voluntarily submit to the authority of the sovereign (Rosenfeld 1985: 864–65). Because of this, Hobbesian social contractors end up being much more like subjects rather than citizens.

8 For a more detailed comparison of the conceptions of the state of nature espoused respectively by Hobbes, Locke and Rousseau, *see* Rosenfeld 1985: 851 ff.

9 *Cf. Bradwell* v. *Illinois,* 83 U.S. 130 (1873) (State prohibition of the practice of law by qualified women held constitutional on account of social differences among the sexes).

10 *Cf.* Ginsburg 1985:375 (arguing for grounding the right to abortion on constitutional equality).

11 As of this writing, however, same sex marriage is protected under some state constitutions, *see* Robert D. McFadden, *Gay Marriage is Ruled Legal in Connecticut*, NY Times, October 10, 2008 (Both Connecticut and Massachusetts state constitutions legitimate same-sex marriage).

12 See *Baehr* v. *Lewin*, 852 P. 2d 44 (1993) (Supreme Ct. of Hawaii), *and Goodridge v. Dept of Public Health*, 798 N.E. 2d 941 (2003) (Supreme Judicial Court, Massachusetts).

13 California Proposition 8, adopted by referendum on November 4, 2008, amended the California Constitution to prohibit same-sex marriages, *see Ban in 3 States on gay marriage*, the New York Times, Nov. 5, 2008.

14 A March 22, 2006 PEW Research Center poll showed that 51% of Americans opposed same-sex marriage in 2006 as opposed to 63% in 2004.

15 *See Reference re Secession of Quebec*, 161 D.L.R. (4th) 385 (1998) (Canadian Supreme Court).

16 436 U.S. 49 (1978).

17 See 7.5.1 *infra*.

18 'Identity-based federalism' is distinguished from 'distributive-based federalism' which carves out federated units within a federation on the basis of distributive rather than identitarian criteria. The United States provides an example of distributive-based federalism whereas Belgium's federalism is clearly identity-based as it is predicated on maximizing the relative autonomy of the Flemish and Walloon communities (Dorsen, et al. 2003: 351–352).

19 It is obvious that not all federalization is centrifugal as attested by American federalism which bound together a number of loosely confederated states into a veritable union. Nevertheless, identitarian-based federalizations such as those launched in Belgium and Spain tend, for the most part, to evolve towards increasing differentiation.

20 It is, of course, possible to treat a national minority within one's polity as a pure 'other,' thus perpetuating lack of understanding and unwillingness to adjust. This, however, does not preclude there being opportunities to learn more about national minorities, to come to understand them more fully and to adjust so as to better accommodate them.

21 Within the European Union, for example, a citizen of one member-state who resides and works in another member-state is entitled to vote in the local but not the national elections of the state of immigration. *See* 7.5.1. *infra*.

22 *See* U.S. Const. Amend. XIV.

23 *See supra*, at 172.

24 Countries who are parties to the 1985 Schengen Agreement have abandoned border controls among themselves (Baubock 2007:459).

25 Council Directive 2003/103/EC of 25 Nov. 2003 concerning the status of third-country nationals who are long-term residents.

26 *See supra*, at 176–179.

8 Can the Constitutional Subject Go Global? Imagining a Convergence of the Universal, the Particular and the Singular

1 *See supra*, at 175.
2 See, Case 26/62 *Van Gend en Loos* v. *Netherlands Inland Revenue Admin.*, 1963 E.C.R.1 (European Court of Justice) (ECJ).
3 *Cf.* U.S. Const. art. VI (establishing supremacy of federal law).
4 *See e.g.*, *Solange I*; 37 BVerfGE 271 (1974) (Germany); *Frontini* v. *Ministerio delle Finanze*, 1974 C.M.L.R. 372 11 21 (Italy).
5 *See* WTO Agreement of April 15, 1994, 1867 U.N.T.S. 154.
6 Technically speaking, some of the norms in question, such as those instituted in the ECHR, are conventional norms rather than constitutional ones. Nevertheless, these conventional norms are the functional equivalents of constitutional norms. Thus, a citizen of an ECHR signatory state cam sue her own state for a violation of one of her ECHR rights, and have a judgment in her favor by the ECtHR enforced against her own state.
7 *See supra*, note 4.
8 *See supra*, at 303, n. 36.
9 In contrast, in the world of the traditional nation-state, each of them has its own legal regime that interacts only peripherally and interstitially with those of other nation-states.
10 *See Solange* I, *supra*, note 4.
11 *See Maastricht Treaty Case*, 89 BVerfGE 155 (1993) (German Constitutional Court).
12 73 BVerfGE 339 para. 35–36 (1986).
13 *See supra*, at 3–4, 74–75.
14 *Cf. Rasul* v. *Bush*, 542 U.S. 466 (2004) (U.S. constitutional rights do not apply to non-citizens outside U.S. and outside territory not within complete control of U.S.).
15 *See supra*, at 156.
16 'Strictly speaking' is used here to distinguish a pure constitutional rights regime such as those of eighteenth century France and the U.S., from contemporary regimes where human and constitutional rights are somewhat conflated. Today, systematic violations of constitutional rights are also likely to trigger serious violations of human rights making calls for international reaction justified, but, strictly speaking, only on human rights grounds.
17 *See supra*, at 1.
18 *See* ECHR, Protocol No. 13 concerning 'the abolition of the death penalty in all circumstances' (2002).
19 *Handyside* v. *United Kingdom*, 24 Eur. Ct. H.R. (ser. A) (1976).
20 *See supra*, at 175.
21 *Id.*
22 Although in the U.S., the constitution preceded the nation and the state and constitutional identity figures prominently in the national psyche, contemporary America does not privilege its commitment to constitutionalism the

way West Germany did. Indeed, the kind of unabashed patriotism that is commonly found in the U.S. was unthinkable in West Germany.

23 *See supra*, at 177.

24 *See supra*, at 255.

25 Some judges on the ECtHR have been constitutional judges in their own country before their appointment on the European Court. Thus, for example, Judge Lech Garlicki served as a judge on Poland's Constitutional Court 1993–2001 before being appointed as the Polish judge on the ECtHR in 2002. *See* ECtHR Website

26 This is due, in part, to the trend towards increased borrowing from one jurisdiction to another, prompted by increased dialogue among judges across the globe (Slaughter 1994), and in part, to the extent that if a country's constitutional standard deviates from an analogous ECHR standard, then that country is subject to being adjudged by the ECtHR as being in violation of the ECHR.

27 *See* American Convention on Human Rights (1969) and African Charter on Human and Peoples' Rights (1981).

28 *See* Arab Charter on Human Rights (2004), Art. 3.3.

29 *See supra*, at 246.

30 This principle holds that 'regulation of a matter ought to be entrusted to the most local level of government at which it might be regulated effectively.' (Rosenfeld 2008:446).

31 It is, of course, possible for an individual person to make a 'sphere of interaction' the locus of her all-purpose self. Thus, if a person considers herself to be above all a Catholic and to process all other commitments and self-perceptions, including her self-perception as an individual person and citizen, through her Catholicism, then for that person Catholicism provides the locus for the construction of her all-purpose self.

32 Whereas our entire focus is on the constitutional subject and its identity, it is important to stress for present definitional purposes, that outside of its own domain, even within its own nation-state, the constitutional subject may be construed as a limited-purpose one. Thus, a religious monk devoting his entire life to his God and his religion could well acknowledge his citizenship in a constitutional democracy, but consider such citizenship but a small peripheral factor in the definition of his image of selfhood and self-identity.

33 *See, e.g., Television I Case*, 12 BVerFGE 205 (1961) (German Constitutional Court specifying that German federalism is three tiered, including the perspectives of the *Länder* or federated entities, that of the federal entity and that of the whole conceived as the unity of the federal and federated spheres).

Bibliography

Ackerman, Bruce. 1991. *We the people.* Vol. 1. Cambridge, Mass.: Belknap Press.

Albert, Richard. 2006. Religion in the New Republic. *Louisiana Law Review* 67:1.

Amann, Diane Marie. 2000. Harmonic convergence? Constitutional criminal procedure in an international context. *Indiana Law Journal* 75:809.

Anderson, Benedict. 1991. *Imagined communities: Reflections on the origin and spread of nationalism.* New York: Verso.

Arendt, Hannah. 1965. *On revolution.* New York: Viking Press.

Barkan, Elazar. 2001. *The guilt of nations: Restitution and negotiating historical injustices.* Baltimore: Johns Hopkins University Press.

Baubock, Rainer. 2007. Why European Citizenship? Normative Approaches to Supranational Union. *Theoretical Inquiries in Law* 8:452.

Bauer, Joanne R. and Daniel A. Bell. 1999. *The East Asian challenge for human rights.* Cambridge: Cambridge University Press.

Barendt, Eric. 1998. *An introduction to constitutional law.* Oxford: Oxford University Press.

Beatty, David. 1995. *Constitutional law in theory and practice.* Toronto: University of Toronto Press.

———. 2004. *The ultimate rule of law.* New York: Oxford University Press.

Beard, Charles A. 1935. *An economic interpretation of the constitution of the United States.* Toronto: Collier-Macmillan Canada, Ltd.

Beiner, Ronald. 1995. *Theorizing citizenship.* Albany: State University of New York Press.

Bell, John. 1992. *French constitutional law.* New York: Oxford University Press.

Berkowitz, Daniel, Katharina Pistor & Jean-Francois Richard. 2003. The transplant effect. *The American Journal of Comparative Law* 51:163.

Birnbaum, Pierre. 1988. *Un mythe politique : 'la République juive' : de Léon Blum à Pierre Mendès France.* Paris: Fayard.

Bollinger, Lee. 1986. *The tolerant society: Freedom of speech and extremist speech in America.* New York: Oxford University Press.

Bonime-Blanc, Andrea. 1987. *Spain's transition to democracy: the politics of constitution-making.* Boulder: Westview Press.

Bork, Robert. 1990. *The tempting of America: the political seduction of the law.* New York: Free Press.

Brubaker, Rogers. 1992. *Citizenship and nationhood in France and Germany.* Cambridge: Harvard University Press.

Cain, Patricia A. 1991. Feminist legal scholarship. In *Iowa Law Review.* 77:19.

Carbonneau, Thomas. 1998. *Lex mercatoria and arbitration: a discussion of the new law merchant.* Cambridge, Mass.: Kluwer Law International.

Casanova, Jose. 1994. *Public religions in the modern world.* Chicago: University of Chicago Press.

Cogan, Neil. 1999. *Contexts of the constitution: A documentary collection on principles of American constitutional law.* New York: Foundation Press.

Comfort, Allen. 1972. *The joy of sex.* New York: Crown.

Dann, Philipp and Zaid Al-Ali. 2006. The internationalized pouvoir constituant constitution-making under external influence in Iraq, Sudan and East Timor. *Max Planck Yearbook of United Nations Law* 10:423.

Diggins, John P. 1984. *The lost soul of American politics : Virtue, self-interest, and the foundations of liberalism.* New York: Basic Books.

Dorf, Michael C. 1997. Integrating normative and descriptive constitutional theory: The case of original meaning. *Georgetown Law Journal* 85:1765.

Dorsen, Norman, Michel Rosenfeld, András Sajó and Susanne Baer. 2003. *Comparative constitutionalism: Cases and materials.* St. Paul: Thomson/West.

Drobnig, Ulrich and Sjef van Erp, eds. 1999. *The use of comparative law by the courts.* Boston : Kluwer Law International.

Dworkin, Ronald. 1986. *Law's empire.* Cambridge, Mass.: Belknap Press.

Elster, Jon. 1994. Constitutional bootstrapping in Philadelphia and Paris. In *Constitutionalism, identity, difference and legitimacy: Theoretical perspectives,* ed. Michel Rosenfeld. Durham: Duke University Press.

Encarnación, Erik. 2005. Desuetude-Based Severability: A New Approach To Old Morals Legislation. *Columbia Journal of Law and Social Problems.* 39:149.

Fassbender, Bardo. 1998. The United Nations Charter as a constitution of the international community. *Columbia Journal of Transnational Law* 36:529.

Farber, Daniel and Suzanna Sherry. 1990. *A history of the American constitution.* St. Paul: West Publishing Company.

—— . 2005. *A history of the American constitution.* 2d ed., St. Paul: Thomson/West.

Finkelman, Paul. 1990. James Madison and the Bill of Rights: A reluctant paternity. *Supreme Court Review* 1990:301.

Felsen, David. 1989. Developments in approaches to establishment clause analysis: consistency for the future. *American University Law Review* 395:38.

Fleming, Mark C. 1997. The functionality of citizenship. In *Harvard Law Review*. 110:1814.

Freud, Sigmund. 1961. *Civilization and its discontents*. New York: W.W. Norton.

—— 1965. *The interpretation of dreams*, ed. and trans. James Strachey. New York: Avon.

—— 1970. Repression. In *General psychological theory: papers on metapsychology*, ed. Philip Reif. Trans. C.M. Baines. New York: Collier Books.

Fort, Timothy L. 1993. The free exercise rights of Native Americans and the prospects for a conservative jurisprudence protecting the rights of minorities. *New Mexico Law Review* 187:23.

Garcia, Soledad. 1996. Cities and citizenship. *International Journal of Urban and Regional Research* 20:7.

Garlicki, Lech. 2008. Cooperation of courts: the role of supranational jurisdictions in Europe. *International Journal of Constitutional Law (I. CON)* 6:509.

Gerard, Gene C. 2005. Conservatives, Judicial Impeachment and Supreme Court Justice William O. Douglas. *Dissident Voice*. www.dissidentvoice.org.

Geremek, Bronislaw. 1998. Peaceful transitions to constitutional democracy: Transcript of the proceedings. *Cardozo Law Review* 19:1953.

Germany 1947–1949: The story in documents. 1950. Washington, D.C.: United States Government Printing Office.

Gilligan, Carol. 1982. *In a different voice: Psychological theory and women's development*. Cambridge, Mass.: Harvard University Press.

Glendon, Mary Ann. 1992. Rights in twentieth-century constitutions. *University of Chicago Law Review* 59:519.

Gough, J.W. 1957. *The social contract: A critical study of its development*. Oxford: Clarendon Press.

Grey, Thomas. 1975. Do we have an unwritten constitution? *Stanford Law Review* 27:703.

Grimm, Dieter. 1995. Does Europe need a constitution? *European Law Journal* 1:282.

Gwyn, William B. 1994. Political Culture and Constitutionalism in Britain. In *Political culture and constitutionalism: A comparative approach*, ed. Daniel Franklin and Michael J Baun. Armonk, N.Y.: M.E. Sharpe.

Habermas, Jürgen. 1992. Citoyenneté et identité nationale. In *L'Europe au soir du siècle: Identité et démocratie*, ed. Jacques Lenoble & Nicole Dewandre. Paris: Editions Esprit.

—— . 1996. *Between facts and norms: Contributions to a discourse theory of law and democracy*. Trans. William Rehg. Cambridge, Mass.: MIT Press.

—— . 2006. Why Europe needs a constitution. In *The shape of the new Europe*, ed. Ralf Rogowski and Charles Turner. New York : Cambridge University Press.

Hamann, Andrea and Hélène Ruiz Fabri. 2008. Transnational networks and constitutionalism. *International Journal of Constitutional Law (I. CON)* 6:481.

Hegel, G. W. F. 1966. *Hegel's Science of Logic*. London: Allen & Unwin.

—— 1979. *Phenomenology of spirit*. Trans. A.V. Miller. Oxford: Oxford University Press.

Hirschl, Ran. 2004. The political origins of the new constitutionalism. *Indiana Journal of Global Legal Studies* 11:71.

Hobbes, Thomas. 1962. *Leviathan*. New York: Collier-Macmillan.

Hogg, Peter. 1997. *Constitutional law of Canada*, 4th ed. Scarborough, Ont.: Carswell.

Holm, Tom. 2005. *The great confusion in Indian affairs: Native Americans and whites in the progressive era*. Austin: University of Texas Press.

Holmes, Stephen. 1988. Gag rules or the politics of omission. In *Constitutionalism and democracy*, ed. Jon Elster and Rune Slagstad. Cambridge: Cambridge University Press.

Hunt, Lynn. 2007. *Inventing human rights: A history*. New York: W.W. Norton & Company.

Inside out: A report on the experience of lesbians, gays, and bisexuals in America and the public's views related to sexual orientation. 2000. *The Henry J. Kaiser Family Foundation*. Publication Number 3193.

Jacobsohn, Gary. 1993. *Apple of gold: Constitutionalism in Israel and the United States*. Princeton: Princeton University Press.

Jakobson, Roman. 1968. *Child language aphasia and phonological universals*. Trans. Allan Keiler. The Hague: Mouton.

—— . 1973. *Essais de linguistique générale*. Paris : Les Éditions de minuit.

Janis, Mark, Richard Kay and A.W. Bradley. 1995. *European human rights law: Text and materials*. New York: Oxford University Press.

Jaume, Lucien. 2007. Constituent power in France: The revolution and its consequences. In *The paradox of constitutionalism: Constituent power and constitutional form*, ed. Martin Loughlin & Neil Walker. Oxford: Oxford University Press.

Johansen, Robert C. 1993. Toward a new code of international conduct: War, peacekeeping, and global constitutionalism. In *The constitutional foundations of world peace*, eds. Richard A. Falk et al. Albany, N.Y.: State University of New York Press.

Johnson, Brandon R. 2006. 'Emerging awareness' after the emergence of Roberts: Reasonable societal reliance in substantive due process inquiry. *Brooklyn Law Review* 71:1587.

Kant, Immanuel. 1970. *Kant's political writings*, ed. Hans Reiss. Cambridge: Cambridge University Press.

Karpen, Ulrich. 1988. *The Constitution of the Federal Republic of Germany : Essays on the basic rights and principles of the Basic Law with a translation of the Basic Law*. New York: P. Lang.

Kegley Jr., Charles W. et al. 1998. The rise and fall of the nonintervention norm: Some correlates and potential consequences. *The Fletcher Forum of World Affairs* 22-SPG:81.

Kim, Samuel S. 1993. In Search of Global Constitutionalism. In *The constitutional foundations of world peace*, eds. Richard A. Falk et al. Albany, N.Y.: State University of New York Press.

Kommers, Donald. 1997. *The constitutional jurisprudence of the Federal Republic of Germany.* Durham: Duke University Press.

Krishna, Sankaran. 1994. Constitutionalism, Democracy and Political Culture in India. In *Political Culture and Constitutionalism: A Comparative Approach*, eds Daniel P. Franklin and Michael J. Baun, Armonk, NY: ME Sharpe.

Kubicek, Paul. 2003. *The European Union and democratization.* New York: Routledge.

Kucukcan, Talip. 2003. State, Islam, and Religious Liberty In Modern Turkey: Reconfiguration of Religion in the Public Sphere. *Brigham Young University Law Review* 2003:475.

Kymlicka, Will. 1995. *Multicultural citizenship: A liberal theory of minority rights.* New York: Oxford University Press.

——— . 1998. Is federalism a viable alternative to secession? In *Theories of Secession*, ed. Perry B. Lehning. New York: Routledge.

Kymlicka, Will and W.J. Norman. 2000. *Citizenship in diverse societies.* New York: Oxford University Press.

Lacan, Jacques. 1966. *Écrits.* Paris: Éditions du Seuil.

Le Bon, Gustave. 1913. *The psychology of revolution.* New York: G.P. Putnam.

Linz, Juan and Alfred Stepan. 1996. *Problems of democratic transition and consolidation: southern Europe, South America, and post-communist Europe.* Baltimore: Johns Hopkins University Press.

Locke, John. 1960. The second treatise of government. In *Two treatises of government*, ed. P. Laslett. New York: Mentor Books.

Loughlin, Martin. 2007. Constituent power subverted: From English constitutional argument to British constitutional practice. In *The paradox of constitutionalism: Constituent power and constitutional form*, ed. Martin Loughlin & Neil Walker. Oxford: Oxford University Press.

Ludwikowski, Rett. 1996. *Constitution-making in the region of former Soviet dominance.* Durham: Duke University Press.

Macneil, Ian. 1980. *The new social contract.* New Haven: Yale University Press.

Madison, James. 1961. Federalist #10. In *The Federalist Papers*, ed. Clinton Rossiter. New York: New American Library, 1961.

Mahoney, Paul. 1998. Marvelous Richness of Diversity or Invidious Cultural Relativism? *Human Rights Law Journal* 19:1.

Mancini, Susanna. 2008. Rethinking the boundaries of democratic secession: Liberalism, nationalism, and the right of minorities to self-determination. *International Journal of Constitutional Law (I. CON)* 6:553.

Marshall, Thurgood. 1987. Justice Marshall's views: Constitution 'defective from the start.' *Legal Times* 15.

Marx, Karl. 1967. On the Jewish question. In *Writings of the young Marx on philosophy and society*, ed. and trans. Lloyd D. Easton and Kurt H. Guddat. Garden City, N.Y.: Anchor Books.

Macpherson, C.B. 1975. *The political theory of possessive individualism*. London: Oxford University Press.

Masters, Roger. 1968. *The political philosophy of Rousseau*. Princeton: Princeton University Press.

Meese III, Edwin. 1987. The law of the Constitution. *Tulane Law Review* 61:979.

Möllers, Cristoph. 2007. 'We are (afraid of) the people': Constituent power in German constitutionalism. In *The paradox of constitutionalism: Constituent power and constitutional form*, ed. Martin Loughlin & Neil Walker. Oxford: Oxford University Press.

Montesquieu, Charles de Secondat. 1949. *The spirit of the laws*. New York: Hafner Publishing Company.

Moravcsik, Andrew. 2006. Why Europe should dare to be dull. *Europeanvoice.com* 12/22.

Moreno, Luis. 2001. *The federalization of Spain*. New York: Routledge 2001.

Müller, Jan-Werner and Kim Lane Scheppele. 2008. Constitutional patriotism: An introduction. *International Journal of Constitutional Law (I. CON)* 6:67.

Muni, S.D. 1996. Ethnic conflict, federalism and democracy in India. *Ethnicity and power in the contemporary world*, ed. Kumar Rupesinghe & Valery A. Tishkov. New York: United Nations University Press

Murrin, John M. 1990. Religion and politics in America from the first settlements to the Civil War. In *Religion and American politics*, ed. Mark A. Noll. New York: Oxford University Press.

Murphy, Walter. 1995. Merlin's memory: the past and future imperfect of the once and future polity. In *Responding to imperfection: The theory and practice of constitutional amendment*, ed. Sanford Levinson. Princeton, N.J.: Princeton University Press.

Nelson, Caleb. 2003. Originalism and interpretive conventions, *University of Chicago Law Review* 70:519.

Nolette, Paul. 2003. Lessons learned from the South African Constitutional Court: Toward a third way of judicial enforcement of socio-economic rights. *Michigan State University College of Law Journal of International Law* 12:91.

Nozick, Robert. 1974. *Anarchy, state, and utopia*. New York: Basic Books.

Okoth-Ogendo, H.W.O. 1993. Constitutions without constitutionalism: reflections on an African Political Paradox. In *Constitutionalism and democracy: Transitions in the contemporary world*, eds. Douglas Greenberg et. al.

Osiatynski, Wiktor. 1997. A brief history of the constitution. *Eastern European Constitution Review* 6(2–3):66.

Pateman, Carole. 1988. *The sexual contract*. Stanford: Stanford University Press.

Pierson, Christopher. 1996. *The Modern State*. London: Routledge.

Popper, Karl. 1965. *The open society and its enemies. Volume II, The high tide of prophecy: Hegel, Marx and the aftermath*. London: Routledge.

Power, Michael K. 1998. Habermas and the counterfactual imagination. In *Habermas on law and democracy: Critical exchanges*, ed. Michel Rosenfeld and Andrew Arato. Berkeley and Los Angeles: University of California Press.

Preuss, Ulrich K. 1994. Constitutional powermaking of the new polity: Some deliberations on the relations between constituent power and the constitution. In *Constitutionalism, identity, difference and legitimacy: Theoretical perspectives*, ed. Michel Rosenfeld. Durham: Duke University Press.

——. 2007. Perspectives on post-conflict constitutionalism: reflections on regime change through external constitutionalization. *New York Law School Law Review* 51:467.

Rawls, John. 1971. *A theory of justice*. Cambridge, Mass.: Belknap Press.

——. 1993. *Political Liberalism*. New York: Columbia University Press.

Reid, John Phillip. 1988. *The Concept of Liberty in the Age of the American Revolution*. Chicago : University of Chicago Press.

The relevance of foreign legal materials in U.S. constitutional cases: A conversation between Justice Antonin Scalia and Justice Stephen Breyer. 2005. *The International Journal of Constitutional Law (I. CON)* 3:519.

Richards, David A. J. 1994. Revolution and constitutionalism in America. In *Constitutionalism, identity, difference and legitimacy: Theoretical perspectives*, ed. Michel Rosenfeld. Durham: Duke University Press.

Ricoeur, Paul. 1990. *Soi-même comme un autre*. Paris: Éditions du Seuil.

Riesenberg, Peter N. 1992. *Citizenship in the Western tradition: Plato to Rousseau*. Chapel Hill: University of North Carolina Press.

Rodríguez, Ruiz Blanca and Ruth Rubio-Marín. 2008. The gender of representation: On democracy, equality, and parity. *International Journal of Constitutional Law (I. CON)* 6:287.

Rosenfeld, Michel. 1985. Contract and justice: the relation between classical contract law and social contract theory. *Iowa Law Review* 70:769.

——. 1989. Decoding Richmond: Affirmative action and the elusive meaning of constitutional equality. *Michigan Law Review* 87:1729.

—— 1991. *Affirmative action and justice: A philosophical and constitutional inquiry*. New Haven: Yale University Press.

—— 1994. *Constitutionalism, identity, difference and legitimacy: Theoretical perspectives*. Durham: Duke University Press.

——. 1995. Law as discourse: Bridging the gap between democracy and rights. *Harvard Law Review* 108:1163.

——. 1996. Restitution, Retribution, Political Justice and the Rule of Law. *Constellations* 2:309.

——. 1998. *Just interpretations*. Berkeley: University of California Press.

——. 1998a. Constitution making, identity building and peaceful transition to democracy: Theoretical reflections inspired by the Spanish example. *Cardozo Law Review* 19:1891.

——. 2000. Bilingualism, National Identity and Diversity in the United States. *Revista de Llengua I Dret* 34:129.

——. 2001. The rule of law and the legitimacy of constitutional democracy. *Southern California Law Review* 74:1307.

———. 2003. Hate speech in constitutional jurisprudence: A comparative analysis. *Cardozo Law Review* 24:1523.

———. 2004. Constitutional adjudication in Europe and the United States: Paradoxes and contrasts. *International Journal of Constitutional Law (I. CON)* 2:633.

———. 2006. Comparing constitutional review by the European Court of Justice and the U.S. Supreme Court. *International Journal of Constitutional Law (I. CON)* 4:618.

———. 2008. Rethinking constitutional ordering in an era of legal and ideological pluralism. *International Journal of Constitutional Law (I. CON)* 6:415.

Rosenfeld, Michel and András Sajó. 2006. Spreading liberal constitutionalism: An inquiry into the fate of free speech rights in new democracies. In *The Migration of Constitutional Ideas*, ed. Sujit Choudry. Cambridge: Cambridge University Press.

Rostek, Karolina and Gareth Davies. 2006. The impact of Union citizenship on national citizenship policies. *European Integration online Papers* 10/5. http://eiop.or.at/eiop/texte/2006–005a.htm.

Rubio, Llorente Francisco. 1988. The Writing of the Constitution of Spain. In *Constitution makers on constitution making*, ed. Robert A. Goldwin & Art Kaufman. Washington, D.C.: American Enterprise Institute for Public Policy Research.

Rousseau, Jean-Jacques. 1947. *The social contract*, ed. C. Frankel. Riverside, N.J.: Hafner Press.

Sartori, Giovanni. 1962. *Democratic theory. Based on the author's translation of Democrazia e definizone.* Detriot: Wayne State University Press.

Sajó, András. 1994. Preferred generations: A paradox of restoration constitutions. In *Constitutionalism, identity, difference and legitimacy: Theoretical perspectives*, ed. Michel Rosenfeld. Durham: Duke University Press.

Schauer, Frederick. 1994. Free speech and the cultural contingency of constitutional categories. In *Constitutionalism, identity, difference and legitimacy: Theoretical perspectives*, ed. Michel Rosenfeld. Durham: Duke University Press.

Schlink, Bernhard. 1994. German constitutional culture in transition. In *Constitutionalism, identity, difference and legitimacy: Theoretical perspectives*, ed. Michel Rosenfeld. Durham: Duke University Press.

———. 1996. Why Carl Schmitt? *Constellations* 2:429.

Schmitt, Carl. 1928. *Verfassungslehre.* München & Leipzig: Duncker & Humblot.

——— 1996. *The concept of the political.* Chicago: University of Chicago Press.

Shoichi, Koseki and Ray Moore. 1997. *The birth of Japan's postwar constitution.* Boulder: Westview Press.

Sieyès, Emmanuel Joseph. 1963. *What is the third estate?*, ed. S. E. Finer, trans. M. Blondel. New York: Praeger.

Simon, Larry G. 1985. The authority of the framers of the constitution: Can originalist interpretation be justified? *California Law Review* 73:1482.

Smith, Rogers. 1997. *Civic ideals: Conflicting visions of citizenship in U.S. history.* New Haven: Yale University Press.

Soltan, Karol Edward. 2008. Constitutional patriotism and militant moderation. *International Journal of Constitutional Law (I. CON)* 6:96.

Soysal, Yasemin. 1994. *Limits of citizenship: Migrants and postnational membership in Europe.* Chicago: University of Chicago Press.

Stephanson, Anders. 1995. *Manifest destiny: American expansion and the empire of right.* New York: Hill and Wang.

Sternberger, Dolf. 1979. Verfassungspatriotismus [Constitutional Patriotism]. *Frankfurt am Main : Insel Verlag.*

Sunstein, Cass R. 1994. On property and constitutionalism. In *Constitutionalism, identity, difference and legitimacy: Theoretical perspectives,* ed. Michel Rosenfeld. Durham: Duke University Press.

Stone, Alec Sweet. 1992. *The birth of judicial politics in France: the constitutional council in comparative perspective.* New York: Oxford University Press.

——. 2000. *Governing with judges: Constitutional politics in Europe.* New York: Oxford University Press.

Suberu, Rotini T. 1994. Institutions, Political Culture and Constitutionalism in Nigeria. In *Political Culture and Constitutionalism: A Comparative Approach,* ed. Daniel P. Franklin and Michael J. Baum, Armonk, NY: ME Sharpe.

Sullivan, Kathleen M. and Gerald Gunther. 2004. *Constitutional Law.* 15th ed., New York: Foundation Press.

——. 2007. *Constitutional Law.* 16th ed., New York: Foundation Press.

Teitel, R. 1993. Critique of Religion as Politics in the Public Sphere. *Cornell Law Review* 78:747.

ten Broeck, Jacobus. 1939. Use by the United States Supreme Court of extrinsic aids in constitutional construction. *California Law Review* 27:399.

Tribe, Laurence H. 1988. *American constitutional law.* Mineola, N.Y.: Foundation Press.

——. 1992. *Abortion: The clash of absolutes.* 2d ed. New York: Norton.

Tushnet, Mark. 1999. The possibilities of comparative constitutional law. *Yale Law Journal* 108:1225.

——. 2006. Referring to foreign law in constitutional interpretation: An episode in the culture wars. *University of Baltimore Law Review* 35:299.

Van Alstyne, William W. 2002. *The American first amendment in the twenty-first century.* 3d ed., New York: Foundation Press.

Van Caenegem, Raoul. 1995. *An historical introduction to western constitutional law.* Cambridge: Cambridge University Press.

von Bogdandy, Armin. 2005. The European constitution and European identity: text and subtext of the Treaty establishing a Constitution for Europe. *International Journal of Constitutional Law (I. CON)* 3:295.

——. 2008. Pluralism, direct effect, and the ultimate say: On the relationship between international and domestic constitutional law. *International Journal of Constitutional Law (I.CON)* 6: 397.

Walker, Neil. 2008. Beyond boundary disputes and basic grids: Mapping the global disorder of normative orders. *International Journal of Constitutional Law (I. CON)* 6:373.

Weber, Max. 1948. *Max Weber: Essays in Sociology*, trans H. Gerth & C. Wright-Mills. London, Routledge & Kegan Paul.

———. 1968. *Economy and society*, ed. Guenther Roth and Claus Wittich. Berkeley: University of California Press.

Weiler, Joseph. 1999. *The constitution of Europe: 'Do the new clothes have an emperor?' and other essays on European integration.'* New York: Cambridge University Press.

White, Kevin. 2002. Assessing the world's response to apartheid: A historical account of international law and its part in the South African transformation. *University of Miami International & Comparative Law Review* 10:241.

Wilden, Anthony. 1968. Lacan and the discourse of the other. In *The language of the self; the function of language in psychoanalysis.* Baltimore: Johns Hopkins Press.

Wood, Gordon. 1969. *The creation of the American republic: 1776–1787.* Chapel Hill: University of North Carolina Press.

Wyman. David. 2007. *The abandonment of the Jews: America and the Holocaust, 1941–1945*, New ed. New York: Pantheon Books.

Young, Iris M. 1995. Polity and group difference: A critique of the ideal of universal citizenship. In *Theorising citizenship*, ed. Ronald Beiner. Albany: State University of New York Press.

Young, Peter. 1980. *World War II.* New York: Crowell.

Index

Abortion: judicial construction, 43–44; and stages of equality rights, 62; as deriving metonymically from contraception, 85; and the challenge of fitting within the reinvented tradition, 99–104; as deriving metonymically from contraception, 85–87

Abstraction: defined, 3; and confronting negation against identification, 33; and dialectic between metaphoric and metonymic processes, 61; and the metaphoric and metonymic dimensions of tradition, 78–81; and metaphorical reasoning in *Griswold*, 83, 89; and the Lockean gloss on *Griswold*, 93; and metaphorical reasoning in *Bowers*, 106, 109–110; and metaphorical reasoning in *Lawrence*, 110–111, 113; and grounding reinvented traditions, 124–125; and constitutional models, 151; and modern citizenship's historical and theoretical foundations, 214; and social contract theory, 218; and the feminist case for differentiated citizenship, 225; and regional human rights charters and conventions, 264

Ackerman, Bruce, 32
Albert, Richard, 84
Amann, Diane Marie, 17
American Constitutional Model, 158–163
Anderson, Benedict, 12, 18

Arendt, Hannah, 190
Atkins v. Virginia, 282 n. 13
Australian Capital Television Pty Ltd v. Commonwealth, 302 n. 20

Baehr v. Lewin, 306 n. 12
Barkan, Elazar, 301 n. 10
Barron v. Mayor and City Council of Baltimore, 290 n. 36
Barendt, Eric, 163, 287 n. 10
Bauböck, Rainer, & 235, 236, 238, 306 n. 24
Beatty, David, 5, 271
Beard, Charles A., 34
Beiner, Ronald, 222, 234
Bell, John, 31, 32, 298 n. 8
Berkowitz, Daniel, 68
Bill of Rights, 66, 75, 82–93, 98, 166, 208, 254, 258, 278, 286 n. 29, 287 n. 39, 293 n. 5
Birnbaum, Pierre, 301 n. 8
Bollinger, Lee, 73
Bonime-Blanc, Andrea, 141, 299 n. 15
Board of Educ. v. Grumet, 289 n. 34
Bork, Robert, 4, 296 n. 79
Bowers v. Hardwick: reinventing tradition through overdetermination from the sanctity of marriage to the dignity of homosexual sex, 81; and stretching the tradition in *Griswold* beyond marriage or procreation, 86; and drawing the line at homosexual sodomy, 105–110; and

Bowers v. Hardwick – continued
  Lawrence's overruling by taking the
  metaphoric link at a higher level of
  abstraction, 110–115; and reliance on
  foreign legal authorities, 119–122
Bradwell v. Illinois, 305 n. 9
Bradwell v. State, 291 n. 58 & 59
Braunfield v. Brown, 289 n. 33
British Constitutional Model, 163–169
Brown v. Board of Education, 32, 285 n. 23
Brubaker, Rogers, 154, 213

Cain, Patricia A., 61
Cantwell v. Connecticut, 290 n. 36
Carbonneau, Thomas, 246
Casanova, Jose, 300 n. 24
Citizenship: theoretical foundations of
  modern citizenship, 213–215; and
  historical nexus between equal citizenship
  and the nation-state, 215–217; and social
  contract theory, 217–221; and the
  functional dimension, 221–223; the
  identitarian dimension and evolution from
  the mono-ethnic to the multi-ethnic
  polity, 223–227; the feminist case for
  differentiated citizenship, 225–227;
  national minorities and the
  problematization of differentiated
  citizenship, 227–233; global migration and
  the decoupling of the functional and
  identitarian dimensions of citizenship,
  233–235; transnational citizenship and
  recasting the dynamic between function
  and identity, 235–240. *See also* European
  Union; citizenship.
City of Richmond v. J.A. Croson Co., 289 n. 28
Cogan, Neil, 91
Comfort, Allen, 106
Common law: defined, 302 n. 24; and
  adjudication based on precedent, 52; and
  metonymy, 55; and *Bowers*, 106; and the
  French Constitutional Model, 157; and the
  British Constitutional Model, 164–168.
Communitarianism, contrasted to liberalism,
  232. *See also* Liberalism; Republicanism;
  Pluralism.
Constituent Power (*pouvoir constituant*),
  contrast between amending the
  constitution and constitution making, 30;
  and constitution-making through
  subversion and the Invisible British Model,

188, 191–194; and the Revolution-Based
  Model of Constitution Making, 188–191;
  and the Internationally Grounded Model of
  Constitution Making, 207; and Preuss, 38,
  130
Constitution making: in the context of Spain's
  1978 Constitution, 128–132; and the place
  of violence, 132–134; Constitutional
  Discourse: as interplay between negation,
  metaphor and metonymy, 58–65
Constitutional Identity: defined, 10; as
  distinguished from national identity,
  11–12; and historical origins, 12;
  as opposed to pre-, extra-, and
  infra-constitutional identities, 23, 63, 85,
  174, 180, 187, 199, 203; and manifestation
  as a lack, 27, 36–41, 43, 46, 48, 54, 64, 244;
  and relationship between the singular and
  the plural, 23, 26; and dynamic between
  sameness and selfhood, 27–36; and
  construction, deconstruction, and
  reconstruction, 41–45; and negation,
  46–51; and metaphor, 51–53; and
  metonymy, 53–58; and interplay between
  negation, metaphor, and metonymy,
  58–65; building and differentiating, 73–75;
  and models of constitution making,
  185–186
Constitutional Interpretation, and the
  dynamic between sameness and selfhood,
  27–28, 30; and original intent, 33; and
  reconstructive theory, 43; and
  unenumerated rights, 73–127
Constitutional Patriotism: defined, 5, 175;
  negative function, 175–176, 258–259;
  positive function, 258–259; as
  distinguished from human rights
  patriotism, 261, 263, 267–269; as
  distinguished from nationalistic
  patriotism, 258–259; as a means of
  transcending the strictures of national
  identity, 244–245, 258–; in a historical
  perspective, 259–261; in a layered and
  segmented transnational legal order,
  261–269. *See also* Habermas, Jürgen.
Constitutional Subject: defined, 17; who is
  the constitutional subject, 18–27; and
  constitutional identity, 29, 34–36; and the
  clash of self and other, 38–41; and
  construction, deconstruction, and
  reconstruction of constitutional identity,

41–45; and constitutional discourse in general, 45–46; and negation, 46–51; and metaphor, 51–53; and metonymy, 53–58; and interplay between negation, metaphor, and metonymy, 58–65; and the potential reconciliation of the singular, the plural and the universal, 65–69; and building and differentiating constitutional identity, 73; and tradition in the U.S. Constitution, 77; and constitutional models in general, 150; and the German Constitutional Model, 155–156; and visions of citizenship, 211–212; and globalism, 243–244; and problems posed by globalization and privatization, 247, 250–251; and the interplay between human rights and constitutional rights, 251–252; as opposed to the human rights subject, 253–255, 258, 264; and constitutional patriotism, 268–269; transnational and national constitutional subject compared, 270–272, 277, 279

Constitutionalism, defined, 3, 5–7; and the constitutional subject, 19, 38, 66–67; and the citizen, 211, 223, 228, 231–232; and social contract, 19, 25; as an ideal; 19, 151, 193–194; and pluralism, 21, 39–40; as a counterfactual, 25; in tension with constitutional history, 25–26, 42; normative restraints, 44–45; and negation, 49–50; and metaphor, 52–53; and metonymy, 56; as not having been sufficiently realized in the U.S. until the Civil War, 50–51; and structural constrains, 77; and *Griswold*, 89; transnational constitutionalism, 119–120, 171, 172, 178, 258–259, 267; and reliance on foreign legal authorities, 122–123; and an ethnocentric model, 154–156, 229; and Habermas, 175; and colonizing democracy, 181–182

Construction, Deconstruction, and Reconstruction: defined, 36; constitutional subject as a lack, 36; and constitutional identity, 41–45; and negation, 49–50; and interplay between negation, metaphor, and metonymy, 59–60, 63; and the U.S. Constitution and tradition, 76–77, 84; and Spain's 1978 Constitution, 134, 136, 138; and the German Constitutional Model, 154; and the American Constitutional Model, 161; the British Constitutional Model, 168; the European Transnational Constitutional Model, 172, 174–176; and the War-Based Constitution-Making Model, 195; and constitutional amendment, reform, and revision, 209; and globalism, 244; and human rights, 258, 264–266;

Cruzan v. Director, Missouri Dept. of Health, 303 n. 27

Dandridge v. Williams, 282 n. 7

Dann, Philipp, 206

Department of Human Resources v. Smith, 289 n. 34, 290 n. 43

Diggins, John P., 91

Dorf, Michael C., 24

Dorsen, Norman, 33, 42, 67, 100, 154, 194, 200, 303 n. 29, 304 n. 4, 306 n. 18

Dred Scott v. Sanford, 286–287 n. 37

Drobnig, Ulrich, 8

Duncan v. Louisiana, 287 n. 39

Dworkin, Ronald, 43, 276; *Eisenstadt v. Baird*, 81, 86–87, 96–101, 104, 106, 108, 116, 294 n. 13 & 23; and molding the tradition to encompass non-marital heterosexual sex, 96–99

Elster, Jon, 128, 129, 186

Encarnación, Erik, 100

European Convention of Human Rights (ECHR), 67, 168, 202–205, 245, 256–258, 263–266, 271, 305 n. 17, 307 n. 6, 308 n. 26

European Transnational Constitutional Model, 172–179

European Union: The Euroepan Transnational Constitutional Model, 1–2, 172–179; and U.S. reliance on foreign legal materials, 8–9, 112, 115, 121–122; and legitimacy based on actual agreement, 24; and pacted constitution making, 198–200; and the Transnational Constitution-Making Model, 202, 204–206; and EU citizenship, 236–239; and the changing dynamic between EU and member-state citizenship, 139–140; and transnational citizenship, 240; and globalism, 243–244; and legal actors subject to a plurality of legal regimes, 245–249, 251; and the human rights subject, 253–254; and constitutional patriotism, 260–261

Everson v. Board of Educ., 290 n. 36

Fassbender, Bardo, 201, 245–246, 251
Farber, Daniel, 90, 91, 128
Finkelman, Paul, 286 n. 29
Felsen, David, 56
Feminism: the case for differentiated
  citizenship, 225–227
Foreign Legal Authorities: and the reinvented
  tradition, 119–123.
Fort, Timothy L., 56
French Constitutional Model, 156–158
Freud, Sigmund, 36, 37, 38, 51–54, 64–65,
  123
Frontini v. Ministerio delle Finanze, 307 n. 4

Garcia v. San Antonio Metro. Transit Auth.,
  287 n. 7
Garcia, Soledad, 215
Garlicki, Lech, 245, 257, 266, 308 n. 25
Gerard, Gene C., 112
German Constitutional Model, 152–156
Geremek, Bronislaw, 199
Gibbons v. Ogden, 285 n. 18
Gilligan, Carol, 226
Glendon, Mary Ann, 5
Globalization: defined, 1; functional
  dimension of citizenship, 221–222; and the
  decoupling of the functional and
  identitarian dimensions of citizenship,
  233–235; and recasting the dynamic
  between function and identity, 235–236;
  and constitutional reordering in an era of
  globalization and privatization, 245–251;
  and impact on nation-states' constitutions,
  222, 223, 235–237, 244–250, 279; and
  transnational citizenship, 235–242; and the
  European Union, 243, 245–251; and
  fundamental rights, 236, 247, 249; and
  Balkanization, 162, 176, 235, 279
Goodridge v. Dept of Public Health, 298 n. 112,
  306 n. 12
Gough, J.W., 218–19
Grey, Thomas, 33
Grimm, Dieter, 172
Griswold v. Connecticut, unenumerated
  rights, 77–78, 81, 83–85, 87–88, 94, 100,
  102, 122–125; and the metonymic path
  from marriage to contraception, 82–90;
  and the Lockean gloss, 90–96; and the
  Ninth Amendment, 83–85, 87, 91–92, 94,
  96; 295 n. 55; and negation, 81–82, 84,
  88–89, 92–93, 96
Gwyn, William B., 164

Habermas, Jürgen, 5–6, 43, 151, 175,
  214–216, 219, 244, 258–261, 286 n. 33, 288
  n. 11
Hamann, Andrea & Hélène Ruiz Fabri,
  268
Handyside v. United Kingdom, 307 n. 19
Hegel, G.W.F., 36, 37, 47, 62, 287 n. 4,
  288 n. 16
Hirschl, Ran, 119
Hobbes, Thomas, 21, 43, 203, 218, 283 n. 9,
  305 n. 7 & 8
Hogg, Peter, 165, 302 n. 19
Holm, Tom, 301 n. 10
Holmes, Stephen, 48
Holocaust Denial Case, 282 n. 10
Homosexuality: reliance on foreign legal
  authorities, 8–9, 122–124; reinventing
  tradition through overdetermination from
  the sanctity of marriage to the dignity of
  homosexual sex, 81–115; and
  unenumerated rights, 81, 86–87, 89, 94,
  122, 124; and traditional privacy rights,
  87–89, 94, 105–106, 109, 111; and sanctity,
  108, 111, 113–114, 124; and metaphor,
  105–106, 108–110
Human rights: clash between universalism
  and particularism, 7; European
  Convention of Human Rights, 67, 168,
  202–205, 245, 256–258, 263–266, 271, 305
  n. 17, 307 n. 6, 308 n. 26; and the functional
  dimension of citizenship, 221; and nexus
  between human rights and constitutional
  rights, 251–258; and constitutional
  patriotism, 261–269; and historical
  origins, 66–67; and human rights
  movement, 262–265, 271, 276; and
  the Holocaust., 4, 7, 252, 254.
  See also European Convention of Human
  Rights (ECHR)
Hunt, Lynn, 164

Illiberalism, defined, 116–117; and relation to
  liberalism, 117–118; and the reinvented
  tradition's contradictory approaches to
  homosexual sex, 104–105, 110.
  See also Reinvented Tradition, clash
  between liberalism and illiberalism

Jacobsohn, Gary, 2, 74, 76
Jakobson, Roman, 52–54, 61, 288 n. 24, 291 n. 53 & 54
Janis, Mark, 245
Jaume, Lucien, 191
Johansen, Robert C., 130
Johnson, Brandon R., 78

Kant, Immanuel, 6, 19, 23–25, 67
Karpen, Ulrich, 284 n. 12
Kegley Jr., Charles W., 68
Kim, Samuel S., 130
Kommers, Donald, 152, 196, 298 n. 2
Krishna, Sankaran, 181–182
Kubicek, Paul, 171
Kucukcan, Talip, 231
Kymlicka, Will, 161, 171, 213, 225, 228–229

Lacan, Jacques, 36, 38, 52–54, 63, 283 n. 1
Lawrence v. Texas: stretching the tradition of *Griswold* beyond marriage or procreation, 81, 86–87; and contrasted with *Bowers*, 105, 108, 110; and encompassing homosexual sex within the reinvented tradition, 110–116; and reliance on foreign legal authority, 114–115, 119–121; and same sex marriage, 86, 112–114; and tradition, 114–115, 123; and metaphor, 110; and struggle between liberalism and illiberalism, 118–119
Le Bon, Gustave, 39
Lee v. Weisman, 290 n. 45
Lemon v. Kurtzman, 290 n. 45
Liberalism, defined, 116–117; and relation to illiberalism, 117–118; contrasted with communitarianism, 232; contrasted with pluralism, 232, 234; and Lockean gloss on *Griswold*, 93; and the reinvented tradition's contradictory approaches to homosexual sex, 104–105, 110; and the identitarian dimension of citizenship, 222–224, 233–234. *See also* Reinvented Tradition, clash between liberalism and illiberalism; Communitarianism; Republicanism; Pluralism
Linz, Juan, 21, 134–135, 137–140, 144, 170, 199, 298 n. 5, 299 n. 15, 300 n. 29
Lochner v. New York, 286 n. 30
Locke, John, 89–97, 99–105, 108, 110, 114, 116, 192, 203, 217–220, 232, 283–284 n. 9,

293 n. 5, 295 n. 57 & 58, 296 n. 62, 66, 68 & 80, 305 n. 8
Loughlin, Martin, 191
Lynch v. Donnely, and metonymy, 57–58; and the interplay between negation, metaphor, and metonymy, 59; and American national identity as distinct from its constitutional identity, 162–163; American adherence to mainstream religion, 162–163
Ludwikowski, Rett, 119, 198

Maastricht Treaty Case, 307 n. 11
Macneil, Ian, 284 n. 11
Madison, James, 91, 287 n. 5
Mahoney, Paul, 256
Mancini, Susanna, 229, 232
Mandela, Nelson, 200, 201
Marsh v. Chambers, 290 n. 39
Marshall, Thurgood, 31, 221
Marx, Karl, 137, 189, 208, 288 n. 19
Macpherson, C.B., 90
Masters, Roger, 219
Meese III, Edwin, 6, 168
Metaphor: defined, 45–46; and condensation 45, 51–52, 80; and Freud, 45, 51–52; and levels of abstraction, 61, 78–80; as a constructive tool of constitutional discourse, 45–46, 51–53; and interplay with negation and metonymy, 58–65; and dimensions of tradition, 78–81; and reinventing tradition through overdetermination from the sanctity of marriage to the dignity of homosexual sex, 81–83, 86, 88–89, 92–93, 96, 98–99, 101
Metonymy: defined, 53–54; and Freud, 53–54; and Lacan, 53–54, 63; and levels of abstraction, 61, 78–80; as a constructive tool of constitutional discourse, 45–46, 53–58; and interplay with negation and metaphor, 58–65; and dimensions of tradition, 78–81; *Griswold* and the metonymic path from marriage to contraception, 82–90; and reinventing tradition through overdetermination from the sanctity of marriage to the dignity of homosexual sex, 93, 96, 108
Meyer v. Nebraska, 296 n. 80
Michael H. v. Gerald D., 78–81. *See also* Abstraction; metaphoric and metonymic dimensions of tradition

Models of Constitution Making: in general, 185–188; and violence, 201, 206; and negation, 185–187, 190, 192, 195, 203–205; and incorporation, 185–187, 190, 204, 207, 209; and transnational constitutions, 188, 201–202, 205–207; and the revolution-based model, 188–191; and the invisible British model, 191–194; and the war- based model, 194–197; and the pacted transition model, 197–201; and the internationally grounded model, 206–209; and constitutional amendment, revision and reform, 209. *See also* Constitutional Identity; models of constitution making
Möllers, Cristoph, 195–196
Montesquieu, Charles de Secondat, 5
Moore v. City of East Cleveland, 294 n. 13
Moravcsik, Andrew, 151
Moreno, Luis, 169
Müller, Jan-Werner, 259
Muni, S.D., 182
Murrin, John M., 162
Murphy, Walter, 209

NLRB v. Jones & Langlin Steel Corp., 286 n. 31
National League of Cities v. Usery, 287 n. 7
Nebbia v. New York, 293 n. 11, 296 n. 67
Negation: defined, 27; in relation to sameness and selfhood in constructing constitutional identity, 28–33; as a constructive tool of constitutional discourse, 46–51; interplay with metaphor and metonymy, 58–65; and the potential reconciliation of the singular, the plural and the universal, 65–68; interplay with incorporation, 73–74; and setting American unenumerated rights against tradition, 75–78; and reinventing tradition through overdetermination from the sanctity of marriage to the dignity of homosexual sex, 81–82, 84, 88–89, 92–93, 96; and the German Constitutional Model, 154; and the European Transnational Constitutional Model, 172–179; and the Post-Colonial Constitutional Model, 183; and models of constitution making, 185–187; and the Revolution-Based Model, 190; and the Invisible British Model, 192; and the War-Based Model, 195; and the Transnational Model, 203–205; and constitutional amendment, revision, and reform, 209; and the

identitarian dimension of citizenship and the evolution from the mono-ethnic to the multi-ethnic polity, 223; and constitutional patriotism, 258–259. *See also* Hegel, G.W.F.
Nelson, Caleb, 6
Nolette, Paul, 3
Nozick, Robert, 221

Okoth-Ogendo, H.W.O., 180
Osiatynski, Wiktor, 199

Pateman, Carole, 224–225, 283 n. 2
Pensions Case, 302 n. 23
Pierce v. Society of Society, 296 n. 80
Pierson, Christopher, 213, 216
Plessy v. Ferguson, 285 n. 23
Pluralism, defined, 21, 26; and confrontation between self and other, 38–39; as conception of the good, 47; and negation, 49; and metonymy, 56; and Preuss, 153; internal, 150, 153, 155; and multicultural integration, 232–233; contrasted with liberalism, 232, 234; contrasted with communitarianism, 232; and identitarianism, 271; and accommodation of difference and divergence, 274–277. *See also* Communitarianism; Liberalism; Republicanism
Poe v. Ullman, 295 n. 44–46
Post-Colonial Constitutional Model, 179–183
Popper, Karl, 275
Power, Michael K., 288 n. 11
Preuss, Ulrich K., 38, 130, 152–153, 157, 189, 196, 199, 206, 216–217, 292 n. 70
Princess Soraya Case, 302 n. 22
Printz v. United States, 282 n. 16 & 17

R.A.V. v. City of Saint Paul, 293 n. 3
Rasul v. Bush, 307 n. 14
Rawls, John, 6, 23–25, 67, 90, 221, 283 n. 8, 284 n. 15, 304 n. 16
Reid, John Phillip, 128
Reinvented Tradition: as distinguished from tradition, 75; and the sanctity of marriage, 81; and abortion, 99–101; and homosexual sex, 106–115; and the Lockean gloss on *Griswold*, 89, 94; and reinventing through constitutional interpretation, 71–125; and contradictory approaches to homosexual

sex, 104–110; and the clash between liberalism and illiberalism, 116–119; and reliance on foreign legal authorities, 112–113, 119–123; blending tradition and counter- tradition, 123–125

Republicanism, Rousseauian republicanism, 158. *See also* Communitarianism; Liberalism; Pluralism

Reynolds v. United States, 289 n. 34, 290 n. 38 & 42

Richards, David A. , 25, 31, 174, 209, 286 n. 35, 299 n. 9

Ricoeur, Paul, 27

Riesenberg, Peter N., 213

Rodríguez Ruiz, Blanca & Ruth Rubio-Marín, 250

Roe v. Wade: judicial construction, 43–44 ; and privacy, 99–100, 102–104; and self-regarding conduct, 100; and division within the polity, 100; and unenumerated rights, 100, 102; and marital and non-marital sex, 101; and freedom in sexual relations, 103–104; and when life begins, 101–103; and paternalism, 103–104; and reinventing tradition, 81, 99–104; as deriving metonymically from *Griswold* and *Eisenstadt*, 86–87, 101

Roper v. Simons, 282 n. 13, 298 n. 119

Rostek, Karolina, 236, 239

Rousseau, Jean-Jacques, 6, 20, 34, 40, 41, 68, 156–158, 203, 217–220, 253, 283–284 n. 9, 286 n. 32, 287 n. 9, 292 n. 62, 305 n. 8

Rubio Llorente, Francisco, 135–136, 138–142, 298 n. 4, 300 n. 16, 21, 22 & 30

Sartori, Giovanni, 166

Sajó, András, 74, 116, 130, 200, 293 n. 10

Santa Clara Pueblo v. Martinez, 229

Schauer, Frederick, 4

Schlink, Bernhard, 152, 284 n. 12

Shelley v. Kramer, 302 n. 13

Shoichi, Koseki, 195, 197

Sieyès, Emmanuel Joseph, 131, 157, 283 n. 7

Simon, Larry G., 34, 281 n. 1, 282 n. 13

Smith, Rogers, 5, 68, 122, 289 n. 27, 292 n. 69

Social contract theory: modern constitutions as a product, 18–20; compared to legal contracts, 20–26; and the reconciliation of the singular, plural, and the universal, 66–67; and the Lockean gloss on *Griswold*,

90, 93; and the French Constitutional Model, 156; and the Transnational Model, 203–204; and modern equal citizenship, 217–221; and the feminist case for differentiated citizenship, 225–226; and Hobbes, 21, 203, 218; and Rousseau, 20, 156, 203, 217–220. *See also* Citizenship; and social contract theory; the identitarian dimension and evolution from the mono-ethnic to the multi-ethnic polity

Solange I, 247, 249, 251, 260, 268, 307 n. 4 & 10

Solange II, 249

Soltan, Karol Edward, 263

Soysal, Yaesmin, 222, 234, 240

Spain's 1978 Constitution, 127–146

Spanish Constitutional Model, 169–171

Stephanson, Anders, 123

Stenberger, Dolf, 259

Suberu, Rotimi T., 183

Sunstein, Cass R., 11, 133

Stone, Alec Sweet, 166–167

Sullivan, Kathleen M., 119, 296 n. 62

Swann v. Charlotte-Mecklenberg Bd. Of Educ., 289 n. 28

Teitel, R., 290 n. 45

Television I Case, 308 n. 33

ten Broeck, Jacobus, 24

Textualism, and evolving trends in constitutional interpretation, 28; and *Griswold*, 82

Tribe, Laurence H., 57, 288 n. 13 & 14

Tushnet, Mark, 120, 292 n. 2

Unenumerated rights: defined, 75; and the Ninth Amendment, 75–76, 83–87, 91–92, 94; and the Due Process Clause of the Fourteenth Amendment, 75–78, 87–89, 91–92; and setting American unenumerated rights against tradition, 75–78; and reinventing tradition through overdetermination from the sanctity of marriage to the dignity of homosexual sex, 81–88; and the Lockean gloss on *Griswold*, 91, 94; and *Roe* and the challenge of fitting abortion within the reinvented tradition, 100, 102; and reliance on foreign legal authorities, 119–122; and blending tradition and counter-tradition, 123–125.

Unenumerated rights – *continued*.
  See also Griswold v. Connecticut;
  Homosexuality; Negation
United Mizrahi Bank Ltd. v. Migdal Village,
  194
United States v. Lopez, 285 n. 20
United States v. Seeger, 290 n. 41

Van Alstyne, William W., 84
Van Caenegem, Raoul, 129, 298 n. 7,
  299 n. 10
*Van Gend en Loos v. Netherlands Inland
  Revenue Admin.*, 307 n. 2
von Bogdandy, Armin, 175–178, 246

Walker, Neil, 246
Washington v. Glucksberg, 282 n. 15, 303 n. 27
'We The People', disanalogy between social
  contract and ordinary legal contract, 20;
  and Rousseau, 20; and the constitutional
  subject, 34–35; and negation, 49–50; and
  the potential reconciliation of the singular,
  the plural, and the universal, 65–66; and
  the American Constitutional Model,
  158–159; and the Revolution-Based Model
  of Constitution Making, 189; and the
  Transnational Model of Constitution
  Making, 202; and EU citizenship, 238.
  See also Ackerman, Bruce.
Weber, Max, 203, 228
Weiler, Joseph, 238
Welsh v. United States, 290 n. 41
West Coast Hotel v. Parrish, 286 n. 31,
  296 n. 67
White, Kevin, 285 n. 21
Wickard v. Filburn, 285 n. 19
Wilden, Anthony, 52–54
Wood, Gordon, 189
Wyman, David, 262

Young, Iris M., 225
Young, Peter, 128

Zorach v. Clauson, 290 n. 37 & 40